OUT OF EXILE

Additional Interviews
Rebecca Hansen

Transcribers
Teresa Cotsirilos, Kristen Fergot, Lara Fox, Sam Cate-Gumpert, Teresa
Iacobelli, Amy Jacobowitz, Jennifer King, Adam Krefman, Rachel
Meresman, Thomas Neely, Gwendolyn Roberts, Maddy Russell-Shapiro,
Selena Simons-Dufin, Alyssa Varner, Graham Weatherly, Wyatt Williams

Interpreters
Mohammed Salah Ali, Reham Hussain, Akram Osman

Proofreaders
Sandra Allen, Zack Alcerro, Théophile Sersiron

Copyeditors
Carol Reed, Oriana Leckert

Research
Christopher Benz, Megan Borsuk, Alexandra Brown, Mary Dain, John
Farley, Darren Franich, Drew Gilmour, Erica King, Adam Krefman,
Greg Larson, Sharareh Lotfi, Susie Pitzen, Zoe Quittner, Peter Rednour,
Jacob Rothing, Selena Simons-Dufin, Graham Weatherly, Matthew
Werner, Jay Whiteside, Michael Zelenko

Additional Assistance
Brian McMullen, Jordan Bass, Eli Horowitz, Eliana Stein

Research Editor
Alex Carp

Managing Editor
Chris Ying

OUT OF EXILE

The Abducted and Displaced People of Sudan

EDITED BY CRAIG WALZER

WITH ADDITIONAL INTERVIEWS AND A FOREWORD BY
VALENTINO ACHAK DENG AND DAVE EGGERS

AFTERWORD BY EMMANUEL JAL

Haymarket Books
Chicago, Illinois

© 2022 Voice of Witness

Originally published in 2008 by Voice of Witness.

Published in 2022 by
Haymarket Books
P.O. Box 180165
Chicago, IL 60618
773-583-7884
www.haymarketbooks.org
info@haymarketbooks.org

ISBN: 978-1-64259-542-0

Distributed to the trade in the US through Consortium Book Sales and Distribution
(www.cbsd.com) and internationally through Ingram Publisher Services International
(www.ingramcontent.com).

Special discounts are available for bulk purchases by organizations and institutions.
Please call 773-583-7884 or email info@haymarketbooks.org for more information.

Cover design by Jamie Kerry. Cover photo by Ron Haviv.
Illustrations by Lart C. Berliner.

Printed in Canada by union labor.

Library of Congress Cataloging-in-Publication data is available.

10 9 8 7 6 5 4 3 2 1

CONTENTS

FOREWORD: *The Amplification of Seldom-Heard Voices* 1

INTRODUCTION: *We Shall See with Our Own Eyes* 5

BENJAMIN BOL MANYOK 17
ABUK BAK MACHAM 37
TARIG OMER 59
MUBTAGA MOHAMMED ALI MOHAMMED 91
MATHOK AGUEK 117
NADIA EL-KAREEM 133
MOTUZ SALAH AL-DEEN 149
ALWEEL KOL 163
BOB (AHMED ISHAG) 197
MARCY NAREM AND ROSE KOI 237
JOHN MAYIK 251
MARGARET IBADYO BAGET YON 275
APOBO KALIFA 289
PANTHER ALIER 307
ACHOL MAYUOL 345
GAZAFI ABDALLA 357

AFTERWORD 377

APPENDIX A: *Sudan—History, Land, War, and Peace* 381

APPENDIX B: *Displacement and Refugeeism* 409

Foreword

THE AMPLIFICATION
OF SELDOM-HEARD VOICES

by Dave Eggers and Valentino Achak Deng

This is the fourth book in the Voice of Witness series, but it is the first book that the series contemplated. Giving voice to the victims of the civil wars in Sudan was the very reason that the Voice of Witness was conceived.

It started in 2003, when we traveled together to. Valentino's hometown of Marial Bai. It was the first time Valentino had been back home since he fled, as a young boy, almost seventeen years earlier. The town had survived many attacks by militias and the Government of Sudan both before Valentino fled, and in the years of war that remained. When we arrived in Marial Bai, there had been a year or so of ceasefire in place, and the town was beginning to recover.

During our time in the region, we sat down with three women who had been abducted by *murahaleen* raiders during the war, and had been brought to the North, where they were made to be slaves, serving as household servants and concubines. Save the Children and other agencies had recently helped rescue these women—and thousands like them—and had begun returning all such abductees (women, men, children) to their homes in Marial Bai and throughout South Sudan.

For the women we interviewed, the return was extremely difficult. The women spoke little or no Dinka—the language of Marial Bai and much of the South—because they had been abducted at a very young age and were made to speak Arabic. They knew little of the beliefs, lifestyle, or customs of the South. And most significantly, two of the three women we spoke to had left children in the North, with the men who had enslaved and impregnated them.[1] When they spoke of their struggles since coming back, they wept, and thus the interviews were fraught and relatively brief.

After we spoke to these women, we were determined that their voices should be heard. Though we were both aware of the practice of slavery during the war between the SPLA and the Government of Sudan, we had not read extensive reports or narratives of such women's lives. So while we worked on telling Valentino's story—in what became *What Is the What*—we also made plans for a book of oral histories of the lives of Sudanese women during the war. The Voice of Witness series was conceived as a forum where victims of gross human rights abuses could tell their stories not in brief sound bites, but from beginning to end, encompassing the full scope of their humanity. We wanted to make sure that a reader knew the narrators not just as victims or statistics, but as fully human. In this way a reader has a far better chance at empathy, and is more likely to be outraged when the narrators' basic rights are trampled upon. When it comes to the lives of the Sudanese women we met and you'll meet in this book, a bit more outrage is surely warranted.

A few years after our trip to Marial Bai, *What Is the What* was published, and we embarked on many months of touring through-

---

[1] One of our narrators, Achol Mayuol, provides a different outcome to this injustice.

out the United States, speaking to audiences about the book and the continuing struggles of the people of South Sudan. When we were invited by Samantha Power to speak at the Carr Center for Human Rights Policy in Cambridge, we met a man named Craig Walzer. He was studying for degrees at Harvard Law School and the Kennedy School of Government, and had spent the previous summer in Khartoum and the surrounding areas, using much of that time talking to the refugees who were living in the camps near the city. We were very interested in the stories that Craig told, and when he told us that he would be returning to Khartoum the following summer, the plan for *Out of Exile* took shape. Craig would conduct interviews with refugees in Khartoum, Cairo, Nairobi, and Kakuma, and we would interview women in Marial Bai the next time we traveled there. In this way, our original plan to record the voices of women who had suffered silently during the war gave way to a broader plan, to give voice to women, men, and children who had unwillingly become victims of war—displaced, endangered, exploited, enslaved, tortured.

The result is this book, *Out of Exile*. We had no idea that this chance meeting with Craig would produce a book of such scope and depth. He was able to foster such a warm and open atmosphere with the men and women he interviewed that the resulting narratives are stunning; each has novelistic scope and unparalleled candor. We feel that the narratives in *Out of Exile* are essential reading for anyone interested in contemporary issues in Sudan, and in the lives of refugees throughout Africa and indeed the world. When you read these stories, you will be moved, you will be enraged, and, we hope, you will never read a headline about Darfur or South Sudan, or indeed any member of the Sudanese diaspora, the same way again. There are as many stories, indelible and startling and tragic and inspiring, as there are Sudanese. As there are people. Let us keep our ears open to them.

— *Valentino Achak Deng, Marial Bai, June 2008*
— *Dave Eggers, San Francisco, June 2008*

Introduction

WE SHALL SEE WITH OUR OWN EYES

by Craig Walzer

In the course of compiling this book, only one person chose to cut off her interview before we had finished. A woman named Mary welcomed us into her corrugated-iron hut in the slums of Kawangware, on the outskirts of Nairobi, Kenya, in the summer of 2007. She made space for us to sit on her bed, her only piece of furniture. She swept away the muddy water streaming across the floor. She introduced us to her son, maybe six or seven years old, wearing a faded Green Bay Packers jersey.

The interview started normally. After fifteen minutes or so, we arrived at this point:

So who is the man that you married?

My husband is called Majok.

How did you meet him?

He came to my village and spoke with my parents. He said, "I want this woman to be my wife. I saw her and she looks beautiful." And my parents agreed.

What did you think about this? Were you happy?

I love him, so that's why we went together.

Did you have a conversation with him before you were married?

We talked.

Did you think he was handsome?

Yes, he was handsome.

Where was he from?

He was from a Dinka tribe.

From which city—do you know?

He is from Aweil.

And you were eighteen?

Yeah. I'm tired, I don't want to do this anymore. You can continue for five minutes, then I'm finished.

Okay. If you had to describe the story of your life, what is the five-minute story of your life?

Even if I tell you my life, what will you do about it?

What we are doing with this is making a book. The idea is to educate people about the situation of the people of Sudan.

I have been asked these questions before and nobody has come to our help. We have never been helped. They say money will go to building schools and hospitals. We have been told about this all the time, and nothing ever happens.

I guess I can't give you evidence, but I can tell you that I am coming from a faraway place, and there are many of us who think this is very important and are trying to help. I understand why you are skeptical, because it's very difficult here, and nobody has been helping you, but we're trying to change that. We're trying to help.

I have been living this bad life, and many people come and say they will do everything, and nobody has been doing it. And not only are many people in Sudan living in these conditions, but all these people come here, and nothing has been happening for all this time.

Well, I will not lie to you. I can't promise you everything, because the situation is very bad, and there is so much to do. We will not do everything, and we cannot fix everything, but we are just trying to do something small, because it's a start.

We will not believe now. Until we can see with our own eyes in Sudan, maybe that's when we shall believe that you people are helping us in Sudan.

What would you like to see? What would make you believe?

We would like to see that Sudan is in peace, and that Sudan is more like other countries. That's when we will believe that changes have come to Sudan.

How long do you think that will take?

I don't know. I don't want to live in Kenya any longer. It's very bad here. I want to live in Sudan.

But you realize it will take a lot. It's a huge project, and it will take a very long time to do something like this.

How shall we know when change comes? How shall we know that? How will I know when changes have come to Sudan?

There's no easy answer. I suppose that it's when one person goes to Sudan and sees and returns and tells family here.

When these things come, then we shall see with our own eyes.

May I ask one more question? Have you ever told your life story to anyone before?

I have been telling many people about my life, and their lives are just like this one.

How many years have you been in this house now?

Fifteen years. All of my children were born here.

Do you think they will ever go back to Sudan?

If Sudan is in peace, then we'll go back to Sudan. I was trying to settle in America, but it was not so easy, so that's why I am living here. Americans come and say they will help, but those who have lost their families, those who have lost their parents know they are not helping. What you are doing now, if it is good, then will you be able to help me?

I think, indirectly, yes. I think these stories will be read by people in America and people in Europe, who will become more aware. And not just five-minute stories, but the story of a whole person, so they will feel more of a connection with the people. Very often, people in America or Europe see Sudanese people as victims, but not as people, and there's a difference, because when they're victims you can push them away. But when they're people, then they become closer; they become more real.

{After a long pause} I'm sorry, I don't know what to say. I wish that it was working better for you, and this is what we are trying to do to help. I hope that I have not offended you at all.

I will go and rest.

* * *

In the year since, I've listened to this exchange time and again. I wonder what would have been a better answer than, "I'm sorry, I don't know what to say." I wish I had had a better answer.

* * *

After more than a century of colonial rule, the country of Sudan declared independence on January 1, 1956. Sudan is geographically the largest country in Africa, and nearly twice the size of Alaska. The north of Sudan is the Sahara desert and the Nile valley. The west is in the heart of the Sahel savanna. The east runs from semiarid land over mountains to the coast of the Red Sea. In the center are fertile clay plains that stretch from the Nuba Mountains to the Ethiopian highlands. The south braces the Nile and covers jungles, plains, and a swamp the size of Belgium before meeting the Kenyan desert not far from the ridge of the Great Rift Valley.

The peoples of Sudan speak 134 different languages—or more than 400 if one counts distinct dialects. The population is divided into 19 ethnic groups, with 597 subgroups. While Islam dominates the North and Christianity the South, indigenous religions and their legacies still pervade and shade the ritual practices of nearly every ethnic subgroup.

The country of forty million shares no single common language, religion, skin color, economic agenda, cultural history, or political consensus. A light-skinned Arabic-speaking Muslim from the northern railroad hub of Atbara is in most ways a stranger (or worse, a media caricature) to a Christian Dinka from a pastoral village whose skin tone is the deepest black. Within Sudan's borders, the diversity is at once mesmerizing and terrifying.

Here is why it is terrifying:

Sudan's first civil war, between the North and South, lasted seventeen years, from 1955 to 1972. Open war between North and South reignited in 1983 and lasted until 2005. The people and culture of the Nuba Mountains were nearly eradicated in the crossfire of a military campaign by the North's Army that, in the words of scholar Alex de Waal, "was genocidal in intent and at one point appeared to be on the brink of success." It is estimated that thousands were abducted into slavery during the height of the fighting, and even more were systematically raped as a tactic of war. In 1998 a combination of drought, war, and obstruction of humanitarian aid led to a famine in South Sudan that killed more than seventy thousand people. Low-level conflict in East Sudan began in the 1990s as the Beja Congress fought for a share in governmental power; a 2006 peace agreement between Khartoum and the Eastern Front currently stands on shaky ground. From approximately 1992 to 1996, Osama bin Laden and al-Qaeda posted their headquarters in Sudan at the invitation of the Islamist political leader Hassan al-Turabi. The current Darfur conflict has raged since 2003, and there's no end in sight. In 2004, the United Nations labeled Darfur the world's "worst humanitarian crisis."

The death toll from these conflicts is over three million. Perhaps eight million Sudanese have been forced to flee their homes at one time or another because of war. Malnourishment, sexual violence, political oppression, and disease pervade more quietly. All told, it's been enough to keep Sudan at the top of *Foreign Policy*'s Failed States Index, as the country narrowly edged out Iraq, Somalia, and Zimbabwe in 2007 to retain its spot.

One could argue that during the brief life of the modern Sudanese state, the thread shared by the country's myriad peoples is a living memory of violence.

This book is based on that tragic common thread. The unifying characteristic of the narrators in this book is forced displacement. Each person has been forced, by violence or the threat of violence, by ideological oppression, or by extreme economic injustice to leave his or her home. These displaced persons are at once the living testimony to their young country's sorry bond of violence and a critical human resource for rebuilding and reconciliation when that day comes.

The world doesn't really know what to make of Sudan. We hear news reports of rebels fighting central commands, of warring factions breaking and turning, of starving children with flies in their eyes. We have Google Earth's satellite photos of Darfur's scorched earth. We have legal definitions of genocide and crimes against humanity. We have formal condemnations by the United Nations. We have a multibillion dollar humanitarian aid industry slowing the burn. We have prosecutors seeking justice, if not peace, through indictments by the International Criminal Court. But we do not take forceful action to change the existing order of Sudan.

Perhaps it is wise not to intervene. Perhaps it is an excuse and the reason why so many feel free to condemn with such volume: the knowledge that the world will never go so far as to actually put ourselves on the line for this cause. Nor do we have to. Who will hold us accountable? We hear the sheer numbers, the thousands, the hundreds of thousands, the millions, and after wincing, we can safely categorize these stories under the rubrics of *tribal conflict* or *African suffering*.

Or, like thousands are doing right now, we can plunge in head first and scratch and claw against the currents of bureaucratic inertia, scarce available resources, and tepid political will.

Or, resigned, we can back away and call ourselves prudent, reciting the catalog of interventions that have resulted in more harm than good. Harvard professor Samantha Power has often recounted that at the height of the debates over Darfur at the United Nations Security Council, Sudanese diplomats wandered the halls whispering warnings to their colleagues on the council: "If you like Iraq, you'll love Darfur."

* * *

The modern law pertaining to refugees was conceived in the wake of World War I and was truly born in 1951, with the ratification of the UN Convention Relating to the Status of Refugees. Currently 147 countries are signatories to the convention or its ancillary document, the 1967 Protocol Relating to the Status of Refugees. A refugee is, by the convention's definition:

> A person who owing to a well-founded fear of being persecuted for reasons of race, religion, nationality, membership of a particular social group or political opinion, is outside the country of his nationality and is unable, or owing to such fear, is unwilling to avail himself of the protection of that country; or who, not having a nationality and being outside the country of his former habitual residence as a result of such events, is unable or, owing to such fear, is unwilling to return to it.

Millions of lives have been protected under the current international regime of refugee protection. There have been successes brought about through the grace and tenacity of so many who have worked so hard. Yet a glance at global context shows another harsh truth: There are thirty-two million recognized refugees in the world according to the official count of the United Nations, and though we have no official tally of the number of people forcibly displaced within their own countries' borders, there is no question that that number is in the tens of millions and maybe higher still. It is a truth that the stories in this book will confirm: For all our incantations of the "inherent dignity and of the equal and inalienable rights of all members of the human family," the world does not adequately care for those without a country.

More than half a century ago, the scholar and World War II refugee Hannah Arendt charged that "the concept of the Rights of man,

INTRODUCTION

based on the supposed existence of a human being as such, collapsed in ruins as soon as those who professed it found themselves for the first time before men who had truly lost every other specific quality and connection except for the mere fact of being humans." Today, we still have yet to reach robust consensus on this, the purest of cases, those who ask for our consideration not as a citizen of a great country or as an owner of property, not with a paper trail or resources to barter, but merely as humans.

The ongoing stalemate strikes at a central question of the New World Order. Two traditionally sacred values clash. One is the fundamental diplomatic principle of a nation's sovereignty. The other is the mere human's right—as stated in the United Nations Declaration—to "life, liberty, and the security of person."

* * *

In this book, you will meet Marcy and Rose, young women who have lived their whole lives in a massive refugee camp in the desert of northwest Kenya. You will meet Alweel, who survived attempts on her life, rape, and gross, sick negligence at the hands of her own government. Alweel fled Sudan only to arrive in Cairo and be denied refugee protection, left to her own devices in a cruel, strange city that abused her further until she fought back in an act of epic courage. You will meet Tarig, whose political dissent against his government cost him a comfortable life in Khartoum and sentenced him to a self-described "purgatory" roaming the streets of Cairo. You will meet Abuk, a human spoil of war who escaped from a decade of slavery and now keeps a lovely home for her young family in a suburb of Boston, a world away from both her traumas and her people. You will meet Bob, who sought protection by smuggling himself into Israel, only to find that the Israelis did not know what to make of this dark-skinned Muslim from an enemy state. You will meet Nadia, who fled from war in Darfur as a child. She became a young mother in Cairo

13

and after three years in exile has decided to return to Sudan no matter the peril, since, as she says, "It's just better to die in my country, in my home." As you meet these people and others, remember that this this is only a sliver, a section of a cross-section. There are hundreds of thousands of displaced Nubians you will not meet. Hundreds of thousands of marginalized people in East Sudan you will not meet. And those from Kordofan. And from the far north of the country. And those still silently enslaved in the caravans and the back rooms of nomadic traders and urban elites. We could not get to them all.

It has been a privilege helping to build this book—meeting kind, gracious, strong people and conveying their stories. But like so much when it comes to Sudan—to what end comes this project undertaken with the best of intentions?

The answer still eludes me.

EDITOR'S NOTE

The narratives compiled in this book have been edited from interviews that took place during the summer of 2007, at the locations noted at the beginning of each chapter. The interviews ranged in length from two hours to ten hours. In some cases, interviews were conducted through an interpreter.

Once the recordings of these conversations were transcribed, they were then edited into narratives. In no cases were any changes made to the content or meaning of the interviewees' words. Editing was done to make the narratives concise, as linear as possible, and grammatically correct. Whenever possible, the edited versions were then sent to the interviewees for their review and approval. In cases where it would be impossible to reconnect with the interviewees after the initial encounter—such as the interviews done in refugee and IDP camps—the interviewees gave their prior approval to the editors' discretion in producing the final narrative.

Changes were made when passages or details were incorrect or unclear, though the editors sought to maintain each person's distinct voice. In the interest of safety, some of the interviewees use pseudonyms in the book. Each narrative was checked against news reports and research documents to ensure factual soundness. The editors of Voice of Witness are dedicated to presenting these stories as accurately as possible.

BENJAMIN BOL MANYOK

AGE: *45*
TRIBE: *Dinka Rek*
BIRTHPLACE: *Gogrial, South Sudan*
INTERVIEWED IN: *Jebel Aulia camp, Sudan*

WE DON'T PLANT TREES

The Jebel Aulia camp is home to forty-five thousand Sudanese. The vast majority were displaced by war from their homes in South Sudan and Darfur. The camp is located in the desert southwest of Khartoum. Homes there are made of mud and straw. There is no electricity or running water. Everything is coated in the desert dust of the Sahara.

Benjamin Bol Manyok has lived in Jebel Aulia for fifteen years. He is well over six feet tall and built solidly. He wears long dress shirts with brightly colored prints.

Benjamin spoke about his life while sitting in the Kodra schoolhouse, a single long, empty room made of corrugated iron. Benjamin is the principal of Kodra. He told his story in Arabic. The interview ended when Sudanese police entered the school and dismissed everyone present.

In 1962, I was born and was named Benjamin Bol Manyok. I am of the Dinka Rek. Like many born in the south of Sudan, I do not know my birthday, as we do not have birth certificates.

I was born in a small village called Gogrial, in Warab state, the north-central part of South Sudan. It is the same village where Salva Kiir comes from, the current Vice President of Sudan. It's a place where they farm and herd goats. My village was one of the biggest in Warab state, a real town with neighborhoods and centers. Right now it's one of the worst-damaged areas in the South. It was one of the last places where they fought before the peace came. There was no electricity in the village even before the war. Now it's worse.

My father was the area's police officer; he held the job from 1922 until he retired as an old man. It's not like many places you probably know of, where policing is a twenty-four-hour job. He had time to have another job on the side, working as a farmer on his land and herding goats. My father was an orphan as a child, no father or mother, no brothers or sisters, so that really drove him to take care of us. Even when he grew old and retired as a police officer, he always stayed devoted to raising his children.

And there were many children! You could say he was a ladies' man—he had eleven wives. Myself, now, I have four wives. So you could say I learned from him pretty well. That's why he married eleven women, so he could have a big family. I have wanted the same. Yes, yes, I've been a ladies' man for some time. When I was seventeen I had my first child; my oldest is a son in his late twenties. I have twenty-one children total, and, well, some of them are out of wed-lock. But I know them all, and nine of them are with me right now in Khartoum. The others are with my family in South Sudan. I let them stay there, because in the North the lessons are in Arabic, but in the South they learn English.

My mother was the seventh of my father's eleven wives. She passed away in October, 2006. I hadn't seen her for fifteen years before her death. My mother was a very smart woman and a leader, and she became the head women's representative in our county. She was our local leader until the day she died. No other woman had ever held such a position.

By the time she passed away last October, she'd become a very well-known and respected woman. Many government officials from the South came to my brother's house in Khartoum where we were mourning.

My mother was rooted in the land and insisted that we have the same roots. Even during the war, when my children reached the age of three or four, my wives would take the children to my mother's house in the south of Sudan. My mother didn't like the idea of the children being raised in the environment of Khartoum. She wanted our children to be raised as southerners in our southern land, no matter what.

I have five brothers and two sisters from my mother. With all of my father's wives, there were fifty-one children total. My father would split up the wives—in one neighborhood he'd have three of his women living together, in another district there would be five. So whenever my father would spend time at a house, it would be a special event, and we'd all eat with him, all the children of different mothers.

I entered school at a young age and studied well. I was growing up between the civil wars, after the Addis Ababa agreement ended the first war, so in my youth there was peace. We were free, and I could be educated. I went to secondary school in my state, to a place called the Toch Institute, and graduated in 1977. I slept in the dormitories, made friends, was a good student. You could say that high school was like university at that time, because once you entered high school you could choose classes to prepare you for the job you would like. I chose education and teaching.

At first, the people close to me scorned my decision to become a teacher. My father wanted me to be a police officer, like him. I had many brothers that went to university; my father saw my older brothers going off to study, and I think he saw me as the last opportunity for someone to follow his path as a police officer. He would ask me, "Why are you doing this?" But I would not be deterred from my path of teaching. I am a natural teacher; I was born for this job. After my father retired from the police, he was appointed a member of the teachers' council in our area, which would advise the local schools. Through his work with the school, he started to appreciate my choice.

When I graduated from school I was qualified as a teacher and I was given a job at the local school immediately. At the time, students and teachers were pretty relaxed. The school building was a nicely sized mud hut with a zinc roof. We had some books, we were able to teach, and we taught well. There was respect for teachers—each teacher was given one cow, so we'd always have milk to drink and we were never hungry. We had farms and fruits, we could fish in the river—we never heard a story of somebody going really hungry. We received a small salary, but we didn't have to spend it. We might buy a radio, or some new shoes; we could be comfortable and save. We needed nothing. It's not like now, where a family depends on a salary for food. There and then our salary wasn't important, because we had cows, we had land to farm, we had nature.

It was different being a teacher back then. At the time the rules said you could beat or whip a child for misbehaving, but I really didn't follow that rule myself. Sure, sometimes you'd have to resort to whipping a child, I guess, to put him on the right path. But back then it was done too often. It's good that these days it's more frowned upon to do such things.

SIMPLY A MATTER OF EQUALITY

I remember when the war started in the early 1980s. I was about twenty years old. Our village was a population center, an important area with police and government offices, so of course the SPLA—the Sudan People's Liberation Army, the resistance—grew there. The leaders were mostly former government officials who had turned away. I told my family I hoped to join the SPLA, but my father absolutely refused. His main goal was to keep his children close to him.

I supported the war. There were problems for us, for our people, and they had to be solved. It was simply a matter of equality. We would ask the government to do simple things for us, a bit of development, and they would refuse. It was just filled with corruption. And of course, we weren't free. The best example is when the *sharia* laws came, and we suddenly had to follow Islamic laws. They told me that if I break an Islamic law, I could go to jail for it. But I am a Christian!

In *sharia* law, if I steal something, they can cut off my hand just for stealing. The alcohol issue was big.[1] At wedding parties, if you did not bring the local brew—*merissa,* we called it—what was the point of going to the wedding? Say you love a girl and you want to marry her, but your father doesn't want you to, because she will cost a dowry of many cows. You might agree with the girl to run away—it's pure love, it's no harm, but *sharia* law would say it's not a marriage, and therefore it deserves a real punishment.

DEAD GOATS AND DONKEYS EVERYWHERE

It was 1986, and I was a teacher, a husband, and a father, when the bombing started. Before we were bombed, the SPLA leaders had information of what was coming—remember, they had histories in the government, they had connections. The SPLA would try to calm us down, saying, "They're not coming here to bomb you, they're coming here to bomb us."

Before the bombing came, the SPLA units crossed the nearby river. When the first strikes came, I was in a classroom hosting an examination. It was an important testing session for students from grade six through junior high school. The blasts came and came, and we hid in the corners.

That first day, we fled the area to a village nearby, but we came back the second day to collect our things. It was chaos when we re-

---

[1] Under Sudanese *sharia* law, production and consumption of alcohol are criminal offenses.

turned. You'd see dead bodies on the roads. We dug through the houses and you could lift up a piece of rubble and see a dead man, or dead animals—there were dead goats and donkeys everywhere. It seemed everything was killed. In truth, I guess about twenty people died.

We could tell the SPLA were scared. The next day the government chased them, bombing the place to which they had fled, and the government took control of our village. After that day, we just left.

My parents stayed in a village close to our own. I decided to go farther. My mother agreed with my decision to leave. Really, I think she was scared that if I stayed in the village area I would join the SPLA, like most of my brothers already had. But I decided I wouldn't—it wasn't necessary for me to join to prove my manhood. Instead I needed to take care of what we had left. My father took many of his cows and some savings, and gave them to me. I left and I am still gone, to this day, twenty years later.

YOU'RE FROM GOGRIAL AND YOU'RE STILL ALIVE?

After the bombing I walked to Wau, the closest city to home. The journey was two days of walking, following the river straight south. The SPLA used to bother me a lot along the way, stopping me on the road and asking me questions: "Where are you going, why are you going?" You see, there was a government checkpoint coming before I could enter Wau. The SPLA was worried that I was going to give information away to the government in Wau. They asked many questions, and I would answer until it was clear I had become annoyed, and then they would let me pass.

The SPLA was right, though. When I came to the checkpoint outside of Wau, the government soldiers interrogated me: "Where is the SPLA? How many guns do they have?" These soldiers could also look at me and see I was educated; I couldn't simply act dumb. So when they asked me simple obvious questions like, "Is the SPLA in your village?"

I would say yes, because we all knew that. But I could lie when it came to the details and secrets, and tell them I knew nothing.

In Wau, I used my father's money and cows to try to become a businessman, buying wheat and selling it for profit. It did not go so well. It was difficult to make money in general, and if you got really rich, then soldiers would steal from you or kill you. The government had hired a special militia to deal with the Dinka. These men would come to me as a businessman and demand my allegiance to the Northern government. They would come in and demand prices— they'd come in and say, "Sell that radio for seventy-five, for a hundred pounds." That radio wasn't even for sale; I was selling wheat! But they'd make their prices and I had to accept. If I said anything wrong to them, they could kill me, and I knew it.

In Wau, we would hear news of the war, through radio and from mouth to ear. I would get messages from my parents sometimes— every day there were new refugees coming from the villages to the city, and they would bring news. After several months, I sent for my first wife to come to the city. In addition to my business, I had been hired by a primary school, and I was pretty interested in sports, so I was not only a teacher at the school but a basketball coach, too. I had earned some respect among the people.

I stayed in Wau for a few years, but I could never feel relaxed there, and I couldn't feel safe. There weren't many bombings around us, but for me, it wasn't bombs, but people that were my trouble. I remember the moment I decided to leave. Government army officers came to my home and told me they wanted my old Land Rover truck. It was the rainy season, and they wanted to use it to pull other cars out of the mud; they wanted it for their missions. I said no. I told them, "If you want my truck, you can rent it or buy it from me." One of the head officers was there, a notorious man in town. He kept staring at me as I was saying this. I remember him staring. He asked, "Who is this person?" I told him where I was from, and he said "You're from Gogrial, and you're still alive?" He continued to stare. After that, I sold my stuff, sent the animals to my mother, and I moved.

WHAT IS HE GOING TO STEAL?

At that point I had a choice between returning to my village or going to Khartoum. I decided to go to Khartoum, because the route from Wau back to my village was loaded with checkpoints, mines, ambushes, and more. You know what's funny? I actually paid the government to take me with their own plane to Khartoum. I went to the airport in Wau and found some sympathetic soldiers there who got me a seat on a flight to Khartoum. So I took a plane and left my woman in Wau. I was nervous that if we both had gone together, the authorities would get suspicious and would know that I would not be coming back—I was scared they wouldn't allow me to leave. By myself, I could tell them that I was just going to Khartoum on business and I would be back. I did not come back.

I arrived in Khartoum in 1992, I think. My brother and cousin were in the military, living right by the airport, and I stayed with them at first. It might seem strange that they were Southerners and in the government, but there were many Southerners, many Dinka, in the Khartoum forces. The army paid money, gave jobs. It was just work in the city, not fighting in the South. There was no passion in the job. It was just a job. As for the war going on, people would switch sides all the time. I could put it like this—if I'm a soldier and you're an officer, and if I have problems with you, I could just quit and switch sides. It would happen all the time, even at the highest levels. Loyalty was always changing. Factions would split off from Dr. John Garang[2] and would sit down and try to have an agreement

[2] John Garang founded the Sudan People's Liberation Movement/Army (SPLM/A) and was a leader of the rebel movement. For a timeline of independent Sudan, see page 382.

with the North. And then the North would lie to them, and they would reconcile with Dr. John. It wasn't about switching sides or loyalties by that time. People were just tired of the war, and they would do anything to make it go away.

I went first to live with my brother. I quickly got two jobs, one as a referee for the football association, and one as a coach for a small swimming team. I became part of the council of a school in Jebel Aulia camp, a small school named Kodra. Soon I started working in this school as a teacher and a coach. After four or five months, my wife and children came to join me in Khartoum. My family continued to grow. It was weird—I have married two women here in Khartoum, and the dowry of goats was exchanged between our families in South Sudan. The third time, the dowry of goats was paid there, and then the woman was sent up here to be with me.

About a year after coming to Khartoum, I finally had all my family with me and we needed our own place; my brother's place was far too small. Jebel Aulia was a camp for internally displaced people, for people from the South like me. Plus, I already had work at the school in Jebel Aulia; it had been taking three hours to come to work every day, and that was too much. So I was willing to go. In the camps you could just build a house out of mud, without paying rent. I wouldn't have to pay for waterworks; I could just go to the local pump and pump water. So it was the smartest move.

I am still here, almost fifteen years later. I'm now the principal of the school here. The land I live on is not really mine, but not many people want to live here, so for a long time I wasn't so worried about losing the place. Now, though, I hear lots of stories of people being pushed off their land. It's all up to the planning ministers in Khartoum. Most of the current residents of Jebel Aulia have been "transferred" here from Khartoum. What that means is this: they were displaced people living in other open areas of Khartoum until the government saw an opportunity for developing that land and sold it off to private investors. People were just bulldozed off the land—police would come, sometimes at midnight, and push them away. So these people come to places like Jebel Aulia. I'd say there are about eleven or twelve thousand people living here now. Millions more like us are all across the corners of this city.

How can I describe this place to people who have never been here? It's a simple place. We are mostly from the South. Some are from the Nuba Mountains, and others here have come recently from Darfur. We all get along—even the Northerners that have come to live here. Once we're here, we're all in the same situation with the same status. So we get along. There are some small troubles, certainly. Even here, we sit and talk, a Sudanese and a foreigner, and a drunken Arab man has come in and told me I should be ashamed of myself for talking to a white man like this. But these are only small troubles. Besides, how could we have crime? I mean, even if someone wanted to commit robbery here, what is he going to steal?

The ground is dry and the air is hot. There's no chance to grow food. We do have water, because we have hand-pumps donated by organizations. There's no electricity. We build our houses from mud. Right now, it is the summer rainy season, and two days ago a flood came and my house collapsed, because it has no concrete foundation. Now I will live with my neighbors until the end of the rainy season and then I'll build another house. This doesn't happen every year, but it happens when there's a lot of rain. To rebuild, the people in the village come together—for a day or two, all the men in the village come together and make a start on the house, usually building one room and one *rakuba,* a tent out of plastic sheets. It is a camp of mud and plastic. And later on I can finish the house and build a wall around the perimeter; that's pretty easy. Just bake some bricks and stack them and stick them together with more mud and sticks. It will take about seven days to be ready.

A woman here will find work cleaning for a wealthy Arab family, and they'll give her a few pounds and some leftover food, never enough. If the men find work, they can bake clay bricks, or work as diggers, or clean the streets near the markets. Some people go out of the city to work as farmers. People here are below the poverty line, and they receive no care from the government. There are no hospitals here for us, and children can die easily. There are hospitals close by—just out the school window we can see a shiny new hospital, only a year old. It's a military hospital, though. It does not belong to us. It's for the retired military veterans, and for other rich people who buy care, but it is not meant for the public. If one of our children is sick, we would have to pay money to get in. And if we don't have money, the child dies.

Right now, there are no government schools in Jebel Aulia. My salary does not come from the government, and it cannot come from the students—the classes are free, because nobody could afford them otherwise. For my work as the principal of the school, I receive one hundred pounds—fifty American dollars—for the month from Save the Children UK. In the language of the humanitarian workers, that's not even enough money to call it a salary—they call it an incentive. But one hundred pounds a month is still better than many schools. Sometimes there's no money at all, so we have to cut school for almost two months, find some other way for the teachers to make money, and then start classes again.

WE ARE OUTSIDE OF TIME

In the years since I've come to Jebel Aulia, hardly anything has changed in this place. It is as if we are outside of time. You could say that people get poorer and poorer. Years ago, organizations would come and give us food. We had four medical centers, a tailoring center for women to sew clothes, and sometimes the organizations would come to the schools to bring food. But now there's nothing!

They've all gone to Darfur, and since the peace agreement, some have gone to the South to rebuild. But they've forgotten us. I have no opinion about the organizations leaving. Maybe Darfur is a better place for them to be than here. Organizations cannot stay with us for our entire lives.

Recently, with nobody looking at us here, the government took the opportunity to pass a new law. Now everyone from outside must have permits to get into camps like this one. It makes it even harder for people to come and help. Basically, these were once camps that were run by aid organizations, but now they are government camps. It has become really hard for organizations to enter.

I do realize that relief has a time and a place—it should not go on forever. When the aid organizations were here, they cared for us much more than the government. They cared for us for years, but then they stopped—and the problem was that we got used to them; we started to depend on them instead of depending on ourselves. I remember they were feeding us for about two years at one point in the 1990s, and then in the third year, when the food didn't come, we went hungry because we failed to care for ourselves. Once that food does stop, and you're in need, you need to find work as a carpenter, as a driver, or something. The organizations would come and give us food but they wouldn't train us in basic skills, so people didn't learn ways to get money.

Now, when the organizations can come, they've learned that when they give us something, they should teach us, too. Now the food has really stopped. We don't get food for free anymore. Classes and waterpumps, yes. But no food. And the government treats us with talk. They have nothing for us. Even the SPLM people here— the Southern representatives in the government—do not do much either. They come to the camp sometimes and see that we are impoverished. They tell us to live a good life, to be good men, and they tell us that if we feel we cannot survive here any longer, they will provide services for us in South Sudan. I don't know about that. I do know we are still here.

THE PROBLEM SEEMS TO BE FAR AWAY

I really want to return to the South.

Since the Comprehensive Peace Agreement was signed between the North and the South, I feel less tension among the people—the problem now seems to be far away, among the politicians. If you ask the nation's people, they just want to go around normally—but once you put politics in their heads, it's a different story. You go to the universities in Khartoum, you can see a Southerner and a Northerner eating together, studying together, with no problem. The government used to tell Northerners that if you die for us, you'll be dying for *jihad*. That's a key to heaven right there, and so people were convinced by this propaganda. They'd say that if you killed a Southerner, you'd automatically go to heaven. Now those voices are quiet, and the people are quiet, too.

I really think that Dr. John Garang—may he rest in peace—did so much for us. But still very little changes! Everything we can touch is still run by the Arabs—the water, the electricity, the housing, and most of the money belongs to the Arabs. That was the whole point of the peace, that we Southerners would get some control. I believed it was possible when the peace first came.

I remember when Dr. Garang came to Khartoum in July 2005, after the peace was signed. I went out to greet him, and so many others went, too. It felt like six million singing in the streets to greet him! People always think of us as violent people, but on that day, with millions joined together, there were no problems. Transport was moving as usual. If you couldn't fit in transport, you would walk or share a ride. That day opened people's minds, when we saw that we could have movement and still be okay.

I went to the city center to greet Dr. Garang. When he arrived he didn't say anything—how can you express words before millions of people? And on a more basic level, I should say that there weren't nearly enough amplifiers to let us hear him anyhow. So Dr. Garang could only wave, there was no way to say anything more. We could see he was so happy that he could not stand still. We saw that his people had to calm him down. We sang and shouted. The men danced. We were millions, and we all had so much hope!

When Dr. Garang died, those millions were turned upside down. I was in school on that day. Six hours after he died, I first heard about it. Everything was just a mess. People didn't know anything because the government information minister was sending out false reports, saying that everything was okay, trying to calm things down. Soon the truth came. I told everyone in school to stay inside. We didn't know what would happen. I divided the school up, and I sent a teacher to take each group of children home. I couldn't control my feelings. After the children went home, many older men gathered in the school, and we could not control our feelings; we were all upset, and we did not know what to do. I stayed in my house, and I saw very little. I hear there was violence, but I saw nothing. Everyone felt a great loss that I cannot explain. I tell it to you now, two years later. I am a large man, a leader, a father. And I still cry.

We Southerners have a new leader now. Salva Kiir is Salva Kiir, and Garang was Garang. They are different men with different ideas. Right now Kiir is working, and in some ways he has the heart of Garang. But I tell you this—Kiir is not a quarter of the man that Dr. Garang was.

SLEEPING IN THE SOUTH

Many people are returning to South Sudan. We wish them well and they leave. Right now when you go to the South, we cannot give them anything. Many of us have family there, ready to welcome us. I did go back in late 2006. I wanted to return to my own village of Gogrial. Everyone around was thinking about building and developing, but I just wanted to go home. Yet I could not go because I had even more pressing business. My parents are dead, but I wanted to visit one of my brothers, whom I had not seen in twenty-three years. He had been fighting as a soldier in the SPLA for over twenty years. Now he lives in Yei, deep in the South, close to Congo. I decided I would visit him instead of my village.

I took my savings and I left Khartoum on a Friday at nine o'clock in the morning, on a flight to Juba, the capital of the South. It was a big event for me. I remember thinking, I woke up in Khartoum and I will be sleeping in Yei, in the South. In the airport in Juba, I called my brother, told him I had arrived, and asked, "Where are you?" He told me, "Wait, I'll be there in a minute to pick you up." In Sudan you never know how long that really means. But as I was waiting for my luggage, I saw my brother through the glass. We made so much commotion! There was screaming and laughing—I tell you, he was laughing and yelling even more than me. Then I took a step back and saw he was walking with a cane. He had been injured during the war. Suddenly we looked like old men.

I arrived at eight o'clock that evening in the town of Yei. The road from Juba to Yei was a clean route, and I could see the changes. On the way from Juba to Yei, that whole drive, my brother would just tell me stories. I knew the basic story of the war, as not much had passed by me while I had my ear to the ground in Khartoum. My brother showed me the places I had heard of. He drove me by the place where he'd been shot. He would show me sites of little battles. Once he stopped the car and told me to walk with him, told me he wanted to show me something. Fifteen meters from the road, he showed me a circle of mud, and a boot in the middle. "See that boot? That's where a man is buried." He said if we walk for a mile, we would see six thousand more boots along the way. I asked my brother, "How did you gather all these bodies?" "We were fighting here for seventeen days," he said, "and after that both sides fell back. Dr. Garang told us to come collect bodies and put them in this one place."

WE WILL COME TO MEET AND
KNOW EACH OTHER AGAIN

There is a difference between those who stayed in the South and those who left. There are four different kinds of Southerners, really. First there are Southerners who lived in America, and in Europe; they're all in a culture of their own now. There are people who lived in other African countries as refugees. There are people who stayed in the South, and there are those who went to the North. Sure, each group has had a different experience and different lessons. As we rebuild, of course, there will be division, with each group and each person coming from a different place. But I have a feeling that after a while we will come to meet and to know each other again. Again, it all comes back to politics—we must think of something, a common cause, to bring all people together.

Some people say there will be separation in 2011 when the referendum comes.[3] But it won't happen, I tell you. We have to have responsible SPLM members, and we do not have them yet. Say we do separate—there might be war inside South Sudan! There are many veterans of SPLA in the South, and they have not fully decided on our future path. I do know that right now, there's a lot of freedom in the South, unlike here. The thing is, though, we must have our foundation first—schools, hospitals. I believe that if the Northern government would simply help provide that for the Southern people,

---

[3] As a condition of the 2005 Comprehensive Peace Agreement, there will be a referendum in 2011 to determine whether the South will become an independent state.

if they gave us basic services and respect, there would be no need for separation.

Being away from my land for these many years just makes me very sad. That is the only way I can describe it. I am told of so many changes that are happening in the South, and I am sad I'm not a part of it. Soon I will go, once I have a plan for my new life. I look forward to going back and finding the things that I have missed here. I feel it's not my place to be here, and it's time for me to go home. I do find myself with a feeling of big hope. There's money and a future in the south of Sudan.

And here in Khartoum, after fifteen years, I just feel that I do not belong. The land I'm on right now—it does not belong to me. I cannot build something that belongs to me. The people of Jebel Aulia don't grow trees, because these are not our homes! It would be so much work to grow trees in this soil, and then we say, "This is not our land anyhow." That's the smallest thing I can do once I have my own house: just grow a tree. I come from a family of farmers and goatherds—the least I could do, if this was my own land, would be to have a couple of goats, to give some milk for my children—but there is no grazing land for that here. It is these little things. If you ask my young son, "This milk you drink, where does it come from?" He would say, "It's donkey milk!"

Of course, the donkey doesn't make it, but it comes from barrels carted around on the sides of donkeys, and the donkeys come to our houses, and we pay to buy some milk. Who knows how pure this milk is? It could come from anything, it could come from powder. My child knows nothing of milk. But in the south of Sudan, I could bring the children out to the farm, and we could milk cows. I could tell them, "That's my cow." I could give them a cow of their own to care for. I know that when we return to the South, my children will quickly come to love the animals. The south of Sudan—in the end, that place is ours.

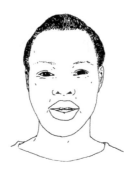

ABUK BAK MACHAM

AGE: *33*
TRIBE: *Dinka*
BIRTHPLACE: *Achor, South Sudan*
INTERVIEWED IN: *Boston, Massachusetts*

THE ONLY WORD I HEARD WAS "ABEEDA." THAT MEANS SLAVE

Abuk told her story of abduction, enslavement, liberation, and resettlement while drinking tea in her den in suburban Boston. It was clear that she is well-practiced at this: she often speaks at churches and community centers on behalf of anti-slavery campaigns. During the interview and throughout the editing process, she remained insistent that her involvement not be limited to her storytelling alone. She needed to know that we would use her narrative as a platform to launch concrete action for rebuilding South Sudan.

I am from Sudan. I was born in 1975 in South Sudan, in a small town called Achor, in the region of Bahr al-Ghazal. My family was wealthy, but not wealthy with money. In our lives, we didn't have money. Our cows and goats were our wealth. My grandfather and my father all lived in the same area in Achor. I had two brothers and three sisters. We were close. We laughed and played, you know? We were still young. I was the oldest. I lived with my cousins around, and my grandfather and grandmother, aunts and uncles. We didn't have a lot, but we had a normal life. We were happy.

My father was a farmer. The children did not work, but we helped around the house. We just stayed home, took care of the animals and checked on the cows, brought the water from the river, washed the dishes, and cleaned the floor. We didn't have flour so we needed to mill it so we could cook. Most women and girls did that. I would do that. I would take care of the baby cows, and I helped take care of the children too.

In the village, we had a garden to grow something to eat, and there were mango trees. We had a small lake nearby, and the kids would go swimming and fishing. We went into the jungle and looked at animals like monkeys, giraffes, and elephants. When you were sleeping, you heard the sound of a lion. Most boys went to the jungle with the animals, and the girls were usually at home.

At night we danced, sang, and played games. I had a favorite game where you put small beans on the floor to play and took, like, five in your hand, and you had to jump them.

We didn't have school over there, and we didn't know how to read. It was hard because when you're a kid and you need to go to school, you need to go to the city, like up in Khartoum in the North. It's hard to go and live up there. Most people in the North were Arabs. You couldn't go to the city because you didn't know if something would happen there, and when you go there you need to know Arabic; we just spoke Dinka. We had heard some Arabic words, but nobody usually speaks Arabic when you go to the South, just Dinka.

I HEARD THE FIRE

The Second Sudanese Civil War began in 1983. The Sudan People's Liberation Army SPLA was formed when John Garang encouraged a series of mutinies in South Sudan. Approximately two million people were killed and four million southerners were displaced from their homes during the twenty-three-year war. Abuk's village was among those affected.

I was twelve. We were playing in my yard outside the house. It was in the morning, around noontime. We were playing and we heard gunfire. Suddenly we heard people running and guns being shot. They set fire to the houses and we all ran in different directions. We didn't know where to go. The children were screaming, and the people were being shot and killed. Mostly they killed the men; when they saw men, they shot them right away. My father was running; he hid and I didn't see him, but I thought at that time that he had been killed. I didn't have any idea because they shot a lot of people, all men. The militiamen wore a *jallabiya,* a long robe, and something on their head. They spoke Arabic. Some had light skin, but some had dark. Some of them looked like us. They came with horses, all running with horses. They came by groups, like, a hundred or two hundred, village to village.

People said the Arabs were taking control in the South. We had heard that they had come to other towns to take cows and other valuable things. The people were fighting; we were all Christian, and they are Muslim. When the British came to Sudan, they brought Christianity everywhere, but the Arabs didn't want us to be Christian.[1] We heard there was fighting, and we didn't know if they would come to the village. We heard about the SPLA and John Garang, but we thought it was just for politics, for the capital city, you know? In my village, we didn't have a lot of people go off to the SPLA, and I never met any of them. We didn't know they could come in the village and kill people. The Arabs that came to the village to do business didn't look like soldiers.

Sometimes my grandfather would say, "Maybe the Arabs are here. We should go into hiding." My grandfather would take us to the jungle to hide, and we would be scared. We hid in the jungle, so many people. Sometimes we hid for a month, because we didn't know

---

[1] For a timeline of independent Sudan, see page 382.

if the militia would come to the town. We didn't know. We hid by the trees and the children could not cry there. We had to be quiet, because maybe an animal could come and eat you, you know?

We thought that people from the North came to the South for business. In my village, we didn't have sugar, or tea. People used to come for business, to bring sugar, tea, and such things to South Sudan. We didn't have money but we paid them by trade, with things we grew. We knew the people that came for business. Even my grandfather said those people just came to do business, you know? I thought they were there to trade and that's it. Then they came back to kill us, to set fire to the houses and kill the men and take the cows.

The day the Arabs came to the village, my grandfather came to where we were playing and he ran with us. We were crying, me and my cousin and my brother, and we didn't know what we were doing. We were just running. Then they shot my grandfather. I was running and I heard the fire. When they shot him, he never got up. They shot him, even though they knew him, because he was the chief. They killed him right away. I ran back to him and I was screaming. I tried to take him but he never got up. That's how I knew he had been killed. At that time I saw my aunt, the sister of my father, and we started running. I didn't find my mom at that time, or my brother or anybody.

They took us. The Arab militia took the women and children. They killed many people and the city was quiet. They grabbed us and tied us all together by the neck, with a rope. We walked. We didn't know where they were taking us. We walked all day. It was so far. They gave us no food or water, nothing. It was very hot. My aunt talked to me as we walked, trying to calm me down, telling me things would be okay. I thought we would die.

We walked north. I didn't know where we were going, but when we arrived there we heard that they called it Ad-Da'ein. When we got there, they put us in a big place that looked like a market. They sold horses there, food and spices, anything a market sells. It was a small town, and we weren't in the jungle anymore. We were in the desert. It looked different than in the South. All the people there were Arab, and all wearing *jallabiyas*.

YOUNG BABY, GET UP!

We were so scared. We didn't know where they would take us. They could kill us. The men that captured us went to talk to the people who were in the market. They came and called us one by one: "You need to go with this person. You need to go with this one." At that time I knew they were selling us. You sat down and they came up and said, "Oh, I need this one," and they called you, "Young lady, come up."

When someone came and called you, you couldn't say no, because they could kill you. We were afraid, and we didn't know Arabic. I don't speak Arabic; how could I even say something I needed to tell them? The men said to me, "Young baby, get up!" I was crying so much because I saw my aunt nearby with the baby; some women and some children from my village were all tied together with me. I was screaming for my aunt because that's the person I knew. They told me, "You need to go with this man. You need to go with us." As they grabbed me, my aunt told me to be calm.

A man named Mohammed Adam put me on a camel and tied up my hands. I didn't see him pay for me, but he was talking with the people who brought us. I don't know what happened to the other people. Maybe the same thing that happened to me.

Mohammed Adam took me to his house. When I got to that place they made me a slave. Mohammed Adam had a wife, Fatima, and two children, and his house was different than the houses in my village; it was like a big tent, something they could move, but they

OUT OF EXILE

never moved when I was there. In the day, Mohammed Adam went into town. I didn't know what he was doing. Maybe he had work to do. Maybe they had to do business, to go and kill people; I don't know. I didn't see any job or office, nothing. Fatima didn't work or go anywhere. Usually she was just at home and doing things in the house. She was always quiet, but she was happy. The children were quiet, normal children. They just went walking around and came back. They were just a normal family. I didn't see anyone really angry or fighting.

I worked from morning until night. I didn't speak Arabic, only Dinka, so Mohammed Adam pointed and showed me how to do things. I cleaned the floors and took care of the cows all day. I carried water on my head from the well. It took twenty minutes to get to the well, and they would tell me to come right back. I couldn't run away. I couldn't. I didn't know how. They were all Arab in the city, and maybe if I ran, they could kill me. I didn't have a choice. I was twelve years old. When he called me, the only word I heard was *"abeeda, abeeda."* That means slave. They would call *"abeeda,"* and I would go over. I have a name, you know? Sometimes they would call my name, but usually they just pointed to me.

When I wasn't working I would just sit. I would sit in one spot and the family would sit in another. When the father talked to me, he looked angry, and the other people in the family didn't talk to me at all. They gave me leftovers when they finished eating. They just threw some flatbread down or left a bowl of soup. Sometimes I ate. Sometimes I was sad and angry, so I didn't really feel hunger. Some days I didn't eat anything. Sometimes when I was very hungry, I would steal some food when nobody was looking. They never caught me, but I had such fear. If I had been caught, I know they would have beaten me.

I slept in the kitchen, in a small place on the floor. They just put some dirty clothes down and I slept on them. I didn't have any clothes of my own, really. Sometimes I just wore something small. I didn't really care. I didn't think about clothes; I thought about my family. I was thinking about how I could get to my mom and my father. I didn't know anything about them. I wished I had friends to sit with, and to play with, and to talk with. Sometimes I cried all day and all night, until the next morning. Maybe I wouldn't find my family again.

I was with Mohammed Adam for ten years, and I didn't meet anyone else from South Sudan during that time. I didn't speak at all. I didn't learn Arabic, because I didn't play with the children. Nobody played with me. The children were a few years younger than me, but they never tried to talk to me. I was someone to come work with them, to do some housework and everything; they didn't think I could be a friend. Maybe the father told the children, "Don't be close to her, she's *abeeda.*" They could beat me and they would; maybe their father told them to. If I ever said, "I'm tired; I can't do it," they would beat me. They'd bring a stick like the one you hit a horse with, and they'd beat me and beat me, calling me *"abeeda, abeeda."*

They were religious people. They taught the children the Koran, and I saw them call the children to sit down together and pray. They tried to teach me the Koran too, but I didn't speak Arabic. They taught me to wash my hands and feet in the Islamic way. They have some special water when they pray. They would open the Koran and say, "Wash your hands," because you don't touch the book when your hands are dirty. But I didn't know the words. They said, "Sit down," and tried one time to make me pray with them. I was so confused. I had never seen it before and I didn't know what it meant. I learned *"Allah hu Akbar,"* because they said that all the time. They prayed and they screamed loud, made a loud sound. I wanted to know what that meant but I didn't understand. They tried to get me to pray and bow like them but I couldn't. Sometimes they were angry because I didn't know what I was doing.

MAYBE GOD IS WITH ME AND I CAN RUN

When I was twenty and I was grown up, Mohammed Adam tried to rape me. One night he came and grabbed me. When I said no and pushed him off, he stabbed me with a knife in my right leg. I started crying, and he left. He was worried about his wife. He was a religious man, and she would have been angry about it if she had found out. I thought maybe the next time he would kill me. I said to myself, No more. I started running. I said, Maybe God is with me and I can run. It was the middle of the night, and they were all sleeping. My leg was bleeding, but I ran, and ran, and ran.

In the morning I came to a town, and I saw a big truck taking animals to market. I snuck in and hid on the back of the truck. The drivers were Arab, and if they found me, they would have brought me back to Mohammed Adam. The driver didn't see me, though, and they drove the car to another town.

When the truck got to town, I saw a lot of people walking and selling everything. Most were Muslim, but some people looked like Dinka. They called the city Babanoussa. It looked like a marketplace town. I saw one Dinka man from South Sudan. He was sitting down and he looked so honest, I trusted him before I even spoke to him. I went over there and I said, "I speak Dinka," and he said, "Oh! Why did you come here? Who has brought you here?"

I said, "I walked by myself. I was with the militia." The people in that town knew what was happening in South Sudan.

The man said, "Oh, you come from a master." He asked, "What's your father's name?" And I told him my father's name and my grandfather's name. He said, "Oh! I know this man! I know your grandfather's name. It's good now that you found me."

This man's name was Majak, and he was older than me, maybe thirty-something or forty. He bought me a train ticket to join his family on the way to Khartoum. The trip took two days. There were other Dinka on the train, and when we would stop at a station, the guys would say, "Okay, I'm going to bring water," and they would get off to run and buy something to eat and drink. I didn't go down because I was worried someone would take me away again, so the guys would get things for me. Majak's wife helped me clean my wounded leg, using salt water and wrapping it in clean clothes. We had no medicine, and it took such a long time to heal.

I spoke with the people on the train about my mom, my family, everything. They said they had heard a lot of children were taken. They said a lot of South Sudanese people lived over there in Jabrona, where Majak lived. It was a place for the people who were running from the fighting back in South Sudan; when they set fire to the villages, nobody needed to see that, so they all came from the South to the North, to Khartoum, and they lived in this special place. There were a lot of tribes there and a lot of Dinka people. They said, maybe you can find your mother or your brother, you know, because a lot of people ran from the South to the North.

So we came to Khartoum, and Majak put me in his house in Jabrona camp. He opened his house to me and said, "You can do anything you want." He had a wife and five children, and they took care of me. They were good people and I was happy there. Happy because I found some people that looked like me and spoke my language. I said to myself, Oh, this will be okay now; I found some people who know my family and my language. Majak can help me a lot and he can find my dad. I thought I could find my mom and everything.

In the morning I would get up and go to the market where Majak worked. At the market, people searched for their families. People were missing their children. I kept looking and I didn't find my mom or my father. Nobody. I kept asking and telling people my mom's name. I was there for three months, just talking to people and asking and asking and asking.

Sometimes the police came into the market when people were

fighting. I would get so scared that they would take me again. I didn't talk to the police; I was worried. I had been enslaved, and maybe the police could take me back. I didn't trust the police.

Majak was worried too. Maybe the people would hear, "Oh, Majak, he helped this lady that the Arab militia took a long time ago." Maybe the people would talk. Maybe the Arabs could hear it. They didn't need to know. People couldn't know about that, that there was a slave in the city.

MAYBE HIS BROTHER WOULD BE A GOOD GUY, TOO

After I was there for about three months, Majak said, "You've been here awhile now. I will keep looking to find your father and your mom, but you need a place to go in case there is trouble. I'd like you to marry my younger brother, Atak." His brother was in Egypt, in Cairo. And the good thing was, he was originally from Marial Bai, close to my home of Achor. His family had known my grandfather a long time ago. And I trusted Majak; I saw that he was a nice guy. Maybe his brother would be a good guy, too.

Majak said we could go to the big Catholic church in Amarat to help me get passport documentation.[2] When the people got in trouble they wrote a note to the church. You wrote them your note, saying you've been running from the war back home, and they would help you set up your case and bring you a passport so you could leave the country. The church had taken some young kids, some eighteen-year-olds and sent them to Rome, to Italy, or Syria. They didn't want to be conscripted into the Sudanese government's army, made to go back and fight in South Sudan, because that was their people they would have to fight against. So the church helped them to run away. They helped a lot of people. My husband-to-be had run away. He

---

[2] Amarat is a district in Khartoum.

went to Egypt because the Khartoum government had wanted to take him in the military, and he didn't want that. The church helped him, too.

It took a long time to get my documentation. Sometimes they could do your papers quickly, but for me it took, like, a month. Because the government doesn't usually allow ladies to travel by themselves, Majak also wrote me a note explaining that I was going to marry his younger brother in Egypt. I took the train from Khartoum to Halfa. I took the train, and I came to Halfa by bus, by minibus, and after that, another bus to Port Sudan. From Port Sudan, we took the boat to Cairo. The boat ride took about a week through the sea. You could see Saudi Arabia on the other side.

I took the bus to Cairo, where Atak was waiting for me at the station. He knew I was coming, but he didn't know me, and I didn't know him. When he came he just saw we were sitting down and he said, "Abuk Bak?" And I said, "That's me." He just said, "Okay" and I said, "Hi, hi," because I didn't know him. He wasn't really nervous, but I was nervous. I thought, Oh, who is this I am going to be with? I don't know him and he doesn't know me. It was strange thinking that this man would be my husband. It was really hard, but I tried. Maybe it would be different later. Maybe we could know each other.

When I had been there for a week, we went to the church and had a wedding. A lot of Sudanese were there—my husband's friends. They rented a special place to have the party. I had a white dress and we danced. It was happy but I was thinking of my family. When I left Jabrona, I still knew nothing about my family in Sudan. I was still thinking of my mom and how I could find them.

In Egypt, life was hard for a lot of people. You had to wait for a month to find work and you didn't have money to pay for an apartment. You couldn't rent an apartment because it was too expensive. For some people who came, like single mothers whose husbands had died, it was very different. They didn't find a place to live, or they lived in a house with five or seven people, and the landlord didn't want that. They would get thrown out. So some people just went out into the desert and made a tent. Some children got sick.

I stayed in the apartment Atak rented, near Abbassia. It was two bedrooms, and we shared with a woman, her daughter, and her husband. There were five of us. The apartment wasn't very big: just a dining room and two bedrooms, a bathroom and a kitchen. The kitchen wasn't very big, just a small one. Their family had one room, and I had one room with my husband.

Cairo was very confusing. It was a nice city, but when you don't know a place you worry. I didn't speak English or Arabic, so Egypt was really hard for me. I got lost all the time. I didn't know the bus schedule. Some Egyptians were friendly and nice, but some of them are crazy. When you go walking outside they call you *hunga,* referring to your color. That means like chocolate. And sometimes they would just come up and smack you. Some people were nice, but some people were bad.

Sometimes, when you walked at night they could come and beat you. That never happened to me, but some people said that. They hit them, they broke their arm, they broke their head because they didn't want them to walk in a certain neighborhood. I have a friend who was pushed down and punched in her teeth. Some police were no good; they would see you and laugh at you. You didn't walk at night because you didn't know what could happen. At night I stayed in the apartment.

My husband worked in a store that made belts. He worked morning to night, working, working all the time. At that time, I said to my husband, "We need money. I should go work." Some women did work, like doing housekeeping. But working in a house, you didn't know what would happen. Sometimes you would work and they wouldn't pay you, and if you talked back they could even kill you. I heard that one lady was working in a house and they didn't pay her.

They killed her and threw her off the second or third floor and she died from the fall. So when I said to my husband that I should work, he said no. He was scared. He said I could work in a market or a store, but working in a house was too dangerous.

When I came to Cairo, I was pregnant very quickly with my son, Majak. We named him after Atak's brother, who had helped me. He was born in the refugee hospital. The refugee hospital gave me food and checked me every week while I was pregnant. The Egyptian hospital didn't care; they didn't do anything for us, and it was too expensive. When women went to the Egyptian hospital they would give them a C-section and they would take a kidney out; they would steal something. The doctors don't do the C-section like here in America. They start up higher and they take something from inside you; they steal it. A lot of Sudanese who went to the Egyptian hospitals will have another baby here in America, and the doctor says, "Where's your kidney?" So I went to the refugee hospital. Majak was born on June 27, 1999.

At that time, I talked to my husband and said, "Maybe you can keep calling your brother to ask if he can find my mom and brother." After some time, Majak found my mom. When we were separated she had gone to northern Chad. She stayed over there to raise the younger children because she was running with them. My brother was there and my sister.

Now my mom was running back to Khartoum, because when you come to Khartoum they have people that can help you. They have some organizations that give you food and clothes in Jabrona. People over there were always talking, talking; we are Sudanese and we know each other. My mother kept asking people about her daughter, saying that she was missing for a long time from the fight, from the war when the people came to the village to kill. She would say, "My son, my baby is missing, my daughter."

Majak met my mom, and when she asked him, he said, "Oh, I found your daughter. She was here with me and she didn't find you, and she married my younger brother." At that time my mom was so excited, and Majak called us right away in Egypt.

I thought, Oh my God! I found my mom! My husband was really happy, too. We sent money for my mom to come to Egypt with my brother and sister. This was in 1999, around Christmastime. When my mom came, it was a small apartment and we all lived together in that small place.

WE HAD TWO CHOICES

When I had been in Egypt for a year, I got my visa to go the United States. During that year, I went a lot to the United Nations, to the UNHCR, because I wasn't allowed to stay in Egypt. They just gave us visas, like a yellow or pink one, and it expires when it expires.[3] If the Egyptian authorities found you without papers, they could send you back to Sudan, so you had to apply to the United Nations for documentation.

At the United Nations, you had to wait in line to go inside. You went in the morning around three or four a.m. to get in the line. You waited until you got to the door, and at the door they didn't need you to go inside; they just took your passport and your papers. After that they might call you to make an appointment. They said, "On this day you need to come here to see someone." They wanted to know if you deserved to be a refugee.

So I came in the morning and I waited. When I went in for my appointment, the electricity was out, and the man said, "Now we cannot do anything because the computer is not working. You need to go back and come again." They made me another appointment, but I was so angry. I was telling my husband, "It's been really long now. How long do I have to wait to go back there?" It was far from

[3] For more on refugee status determination, see page 414.

home, and you had to take three buses. The buses were crowded, and some days you missed it. You went over there, and maybe you didn't find the number and you missed the bus. Then, when you get there they say, "Now you're late." Some people, they just didn't want to talk to you. It was hard to go over there. They were mean.

I got my interview appointment. The people at the office were Egyptian, but they looked like Christians, you know? The woman who interviewed me told me she was Christian. She was nice. They had a translator, and I told her my story. She said, "Abuk, your case is sad. I'm sorry for you." She said it really touched her heart. At that time I was pregnant and she wished me good luck. She said to come back in three months for my result, to see if they accepted my case. If they accept you, they give you documentation to stay legally in Egypt, and after that they can send you anywhere.

So after three or five months they called me and said, "Okay, you need to choose where you want to go." They said, "We have openings for people in Canada, Australia, and America, and you can go anywhere." To get to Australia you had to pay for your ticket, and we didn't have any money. America paid for your ticket. My husband and I decided to go to America. They said, "Oh, America is good; when you go there, you can work hard and your life will be changed." They gave me papers and made everything ready for me.

My husband had a cousin living in Iowa. I had a cousin in Buffalo. It's easier to go to a place where you have someone when you don't know English. If you have a Sudanese friend, they can help show you how to do the shopping. We had two choices, and we went to Buffalo.

It was my first plane and, God, I was so scared. We left at four a.m., and I was so confused. We stopped in Holland first. We sat for five hours in the Amsterdam airport. My baby was six months old at the time, and he was tired, and so was I. I had never sat in one place for so long. When I tried to walk, I fell down. I fell! Around eight o'clock that night, we went to another airplane and came to America. We flew to New York, to J.F. Kennedy.

When we got there, it was snowing. Oh my God! It was the first time I saw snow. We had a jacket but it was so cold, it wasn't enough. In the airport, they checked our passport and asked us where we were going. They said everything was okay, welcome to America. Then someone came and took us on a bus to another smaller airport. It was night, so we didn't see New York City or anything. Our flight to Buffalo took around one hour, I think.

So when we got there, we saw that people were waiting for us, people from the International Institute.[4] And my cousin was there, too. They had blankets to keep us warm. They had everything for us, and they put us in a nice, nice house. I thought the rooms would be really cold, but it was warm! It was good because it was warm in there, but it was so funny, too, to have heat. The house had one bedroom, and they gave us food and everything for the inside. It was nice. People from the International Institute helped us to learn English and find a job.

In Buffalo I started to work with the American Anti-Slavery Group.[5] I was so excited to share my story. That was the first thing I needed to do, because back then no one knew what was going on in Sudan, and people needed to know. That was my reaction.

I worked a lot with them, and after I was in Buffalo for a year they bought me a ticket to move here to Boston so I could be close to them for speaking engagements. They found a place for my family to stay until my husband found a job, and they helped us rent an apartment. They sent someone to my home to teach me to speak English, and my husband got a job doing banquets in a hotel.

We traveled, and I even went to the United Nations in New York

---

[4] The International Institute of Buffalo assists immigrants and refugees resettling in the United States.

[5] A nonprofit group working with former victims of human trafficking.

to speak out when I heard that Omar al-Bashir was coming. We went in front of the United Nations building to protest and speak out about why Bashir was coming here to tell lies.

I spoke at churches, high schools, and colleges in many cities. I was happy because people sat down and listened to me tell my story. It was good to talk to young people too. I knew they were children and they didn't know anything about Sudan, but it's good to share your story with another person. I told them, "Children are dying. They took our children away. People can go into the village and kill your mother and your grandfather in front of you, in front of your eyes. How would you feel if they took you? How would you feel?"

People got excited because they had never heard what was going on in Sudan. Their hearts were really touched. I gave people our website and told them, "People should know. Your friend, your father, anyone." I told them they could write a letter to the government about civil rights, about how people are dying for nothing.

I think the United States didn't pay attention to us a long time ago, but now a lot of people have opened their minds. I'm not saying all people, but some. When you see what is going on in Sudan, you see it's just because of religion and racism. The Sudanese government wants everyone in the country to follow *sharia* law. For example, if women are raped and pregnant with the babies of the Arab militia, they can't say, "That's not my baby, it's the Arab militia's baby." That's your blood and you have to keep and take care of them, even though it's really painful. No one talks about that in Sudan.

THAT'S WHY WE CAME HERE

In 2003, we saved enough money to bring my mother, my brother, and my sister here as refugees. I had never heard from my father, but my mom said he was back in Sudan after years in Kakuma refugee camp in Kenya. I said, "Thank God, he's not dead, he's okay!"

I spoke to him a few years ago, when he was in Kakuma, and it was so scary. He told me a lot of things about the war and people who died. After our village was destroyed, he married again, to another wife, and the militia came back and killed this wife. They killed my stepmom and her baby, who was three months old. My father thanked God we were okay. We didn't talk a lot because there was no phone over there in Kakuma. We could only talk when he went to the city, to Nairobi, which is a long bus drive away.

When the Comprehensive Peace Agreement was signed in 2005, my father decided he wanted to go back to Sudan. But it's still dangerous. You don't know. You can die. Now my father is back in South Sudan, in the city of Aweil.

People say it is good now in Sudan; that it's getting a little bit better. That's what they say. Even in Aweil they now have a phone. But it's hard to connect when you call.

I'm thinking that I need to visit Sudan now. I'm married, I have three children, and my father doesn't even know my kids. I really need to see my dad. I thank God we are all alive and just hope that we can meet someday.

Now I work in an assisted-living center taking care of old people. I like my job; you feel like it's your grandmother you're caring for. My husband works at the airport, driving the shuttle bus. We have a very nice house. When you work in America, it's very good. When you work hard, you can pay your rent and get anything you need. You work your job, and the kids can go to school to learn. We became citizens in 2005. We're really here in America, our home is here, and it feels right to be a citizen here.

My kids speak better English than me! Sometimes when I say something in English, they correct me. They say, "Oh, Mom, you don't say that!" You work for your children, you know?

I've started speaking with my son Majak about my story. He asks me questions all the time. "Why do they take people for slaves?" He knows the story and he knows why I left Sudan, but it's all so far away for him and hard to understand. We watch news all the time in the house, especially news about Sudan. My kids will ask, "Why is there so much fighting? Why are all the people dead?"

I say, "That's why we came here." I tell them that someday we'll go back and visit. They want to go, but not right now. Not until it's all quiet.

TARIG OMER

AGE: *33*
TRIBE: *Gaaliin (paternal), Rizeigat (maternal)*
BIRTHPLACE: *Khartoum, Sudan*
INTERVIEWED IN: *Cairo, Egypt*

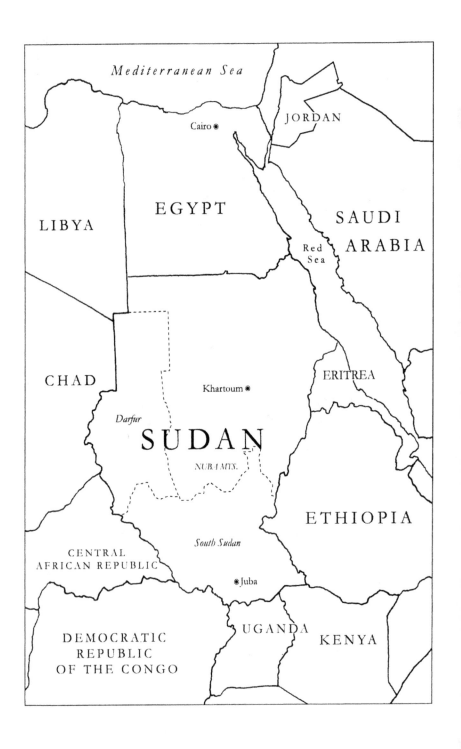

A GOOD ACTOR IN A BAD MOVIE

Tarig told his story in English over the course of several afternoons in the bars of downtown Cairo. He drank tea during the sessions. He never drinks alcohol in the daytime, he explained. Others introduced him as "one of the leaders of the Sudanese refugees of Cairo." He denies this, saying that he simply helps people when they need help, and after all these years he has learned the best ways to survive in Cairo.

My name is Tarig. I'm a Sudanese citizen, and I have been here in Cairo for almost four years. I have been here for no reason.

I feel like a good actor in a bad movie. I'm doing the right thing, but everything around me is completely wrong. I accept that I am a refugee, but I don't even get my rights as a refugee. I mean the basic rights of a human being—education, health service, a life with dignity, a life like any human being should have.

Sometimes I blame myself for being here in Egypt. Many times I think it would be better if I had stayed in Sudan. Sometimes when I'm depressed and disappointed and frustrated, I think, If I were in Sudan, if I had been killed in Sudan or detained in Sudan, this might have been better, because it's my country, and somehow I'd be in the right place. At least I would be at home.

I was born in 1978, in a hospital on Street 17 in the neighborhood of Amarat, one of the nicest neighborhoods in Khartoum. When I was young we moved to Bahri, a suburb in an area called Khartoum North. My father is originally from the north of Khartoum. My mother's family comes from the Rizeigat tribe of Darfur. I have one sister and two brothers. I'm the second of the four.

My mother was a teacher, and then she worked in the Ministry of Education for several years. She was an editor of one of the oldest children's magazines in the Arab world, called the *Sabian*. She was always active in women's rights, children's rights. She's retired now. She's still the most amazing person I have ever met.

It was a fine childhood for me. I went to school during the day. I went to a Christian school. I don't know why, but my parents sent me there. I learned about the Testaments, about Jesus. He's a nice man, a wise man, you know, and I came to love him. I'm still a Muslim of course, but Jesus is great, too.

After school, I would go back home, have lunch with my family, play basketball or football, go swimming, or visit my relatives. My family was happy and very close. We used to joke with each other so much. I mean, I remember how I got hit by a car when I was a kid. I was watching TV and my mother asked me to go to the store.

I told her, "Please let me watch my TV."

She said, "Tarig, go on, buy some bread, and come back."

I went, but I was very angry because I was missing my show, and while I was walking I just looked straight down and didn't look for cars. A car hit me, and now I've got this platinum tooth. But after that time, no one ever sent me to the store to buy anything. "No! Don't send Tarig." They'd always say it. "Please. Anyone else can do it. But save Tarig! No more platinum teeth!"

The first political incident I had was in secondary school. Such a silly thing. I was one of the organizers of "culture week" at school, and someone from the local student union came and asked us to add some Islamic songs to our program. We already had the whole thing set up, and we weren't so interested in their songs. But we didn't want to cause trouble, so we just said, "Okay, we'll do it; just bring us the materials and we'll take care of it." Of course, we didn't do it and just did our original program instead. When I was walking home from school that day, some people pulled up next to us in a car, and asked us to get in, saying something like, "Don't resist us, because that would be trouble for you." We went with them to the high school student union association, and they started asking us, "Why did you lie to us about the program? Who asked you to do this? Why are you refusing? Did you do that for someone?" This whole time I'm thinking, Come on, it's just a song at a high school program. And after three or four hours, they released us, told us keep away, don't make trouble, don't do that again, just do what we ask you to do.

It was silly, sure. But I admit I was a little bit scared.

* * *

I need to tell you about my father now. My father was a politician. He was one of the founders of the Sudanese Communist Party. He also used to work as an editor for the official newspaper of the Communist Party of Sudan.

My father came from a village in the north of Sudan. His father, my grandfather, was a farmer. My grandfather was strong, righteous, and very religious. But my father left this environment and became a very open-minded man. He studied art and English literature at Khartoum University. Back then, in the 1940s, the community was probably asking, "Why waste your time going off to the university?" But he went to Khartoum to learn.

He was elected to the national parliament to represent the town of Atbara, a railroad workers' town in the North with big labor unions. I remember watching him on television making speeches about workers' rights and the right to democracy, about how we need better schools and more hospitals, especially in the marginalized areas in Sudan.

When I was a kid he taught me his ideals. I can tell you one very, very, very good thing that happened in my life. Before he died, my father gave me a book to read about a massacre in Darfur. Arabs had killed hundreds of Southern Sudanese in a battle. He gave me this book to read. It was a testimony of the survivors of this massacre.

Some years after my father died, my mother's relatives invited me to their home in Darfur to learn how to ride horses and how to use a weapon. My mother left the decision to me, and I told my mother, "I read that book about what happened in Darfur. How can I go there to live with horses and guns?" Maybe right there my father saved my life. If I hadn't read those books from my father, I mean, I was just a kid and I didn't know... Maybe I would have just gone along with those around me and become a participant in the violence that goes on in Darfur now. I don't know if it's true or if that even makes sense, but I do feel my father changed my life completely.

I learned that everyone has a right to choose what he wants in his life. My father gave me books to open my mind about what's going on in Sudan. How the people treat each other wrong. How our neighbors can commit great crimes. And also about how no one speaks out, about how no one asks questions. It's horrible. At that time, I started thinking and asking about what's going on, what's wrong, what's right. Why someone would shed his blood in war. It was all very strange to me.

Back to my father—when he was in the parliament he had a lot of trouble with the Islamic parties in Sudan. Now the main party in the country is called the National Congress Party, but it used to be named the National Islamic Front.

As I said, when he was a member of parliament, my father represented the Communist Party. The NIF dismissed all the Communist Party members from the government, and my father stood against the action. He made speeches and protested. He talked about resisting these wrongful ideas. And then he died in detention.

THEY CAME FOR MY FATHER

I was about fourteen years old when they came for my father. This regime was just coming to power at the time, and they were taking away every Communist leader in the country, every big opposition leader. I wasn't at home the day they took him away.

He'd been in prison many times before. My mother didn't tell me that he was in prison this time. She said he had to leave Sudan and he will come back, he will come back. I kept asking, "Where is my father?" and she just said he will come back soon.

It took about a month, and by then I knew for certain what was going on.

I was scared to speak about it. I didn't want to bring more troubles for my mother. I saw how she was very depressed and very sad. She was very sad. My mother just asked me to be strong.

Some men had just come one day, and they took my father away. Then a month, maybe two months later, they took my mother. But just to see my father's body.

Many people came to the funeral. I was angry and sad. But because my mother asked me to be strong, I did not cry. I didn't cry. I just tried to support her. I have a photograph of him still. It's a very nice photograph.

A lot of people in Sudan have passed through the experience of losing family like this. But you should gain from this traumatic, horrific experience, I think. It's given me a power really, a power to do more. To be strong. To fight.

If my father were here today, he'd support me. He'd say, "Do what you think is right. Do what you think is right, and don't be afraid. Don't be afraid." And he would teach me better English, I bet. His English was so much better than mine.

THESE THINGS GAVE US EXPERIENCE

At the end of high school, I was meant to do a sort of military service. It lasts two months, and they teach you Islamic songs, give lectures on *jihad,* on the enemy John Garang, on how he's a part of the American agenda. They would teach you how to use weapons. I paid a doctor to sign a document saying that I wasn't fit for military service. Why should I know how to use a weapon? It's just very stupid.

I gained a high score on my university entrance exams and entered the University of Omdurman. My relatives told me to go into computer science, even though I preferred journalism. "Journalism would just make troubles for you," they said. "Look at what happened to your father," and so on. So I studied computer science, and I loved it. I had good friends, and it was great to talk with them about issues, about the future of our country.

We shared this book written by Dr. Francis Deng. He's an amazing person. He's always trying to find a peaceful way. He told of how his father, a southern man, would have feasts, and they would kill the cow or the animal according to *sharia* law in order for Muslims and non-Muslims to share the meat. This small story gave him an image of how all Sudan could be.

There were students from all over Sudan at the university—Muslims and non-Muslims, from the east and south and west and north—and there are political parties on campus as well, connected to the national parties. You sign up for the political party you like, and then you contribute to their work based on your course of study. I worked in the media department in the Democratic Unionist Party, which is part of the National Democratic Alliance. We are a party in opposition to Bashir's National Congress Party. I would help publish the statements and help speak to the media on behalf of the students. We'd talk about democracy and freedom of religion, of the rights of non-Muslims in Sudan, things like that.

My father's Communist party is still alive in Sudan, but I'm not a Communist. I think that somehow the Communists try to fight nature. They want to make all the people the same, and that seems like an impossible mission. You can fight for the rights of the laborers, of the farmers, of the second-class people, of the third-class people in different ways without being Communist.

My party, DUP, is one of the two biggest traditional parties in Sudan. The other one is the Umma Party. Then there's the National Congress Party, the Islamic party that rules Sudan now. The DUP opposes the regime, stood with Garang and the SPLM, and is part of NDA, the National Democratic Alliance. The DUP stands for democracy and for solving social problems. It was one of the first parties to call for self-determination for the Southern man. They want to try to create a united Sudan; but if the South wants independence, it's okay.

Of course, there are still different opinions between the students and the old generation of the party. Some of the old generation believes that *sharia* can be the source of law in Sudan. Many of the students— I am one of them—want civil rights over Islamic law. Everyone has the right, we believe, to his own opinion. The only rights for a united Sudan should be for a citizen, not just for a Muslim.

We all say we must have free elections to let the people vote and bring what they want. If any change comes through elections, real free elections, then no problem. We will live with it.

The problem is that democracy hasn't found a chance to develop itself. In Sudan there's no environment to grow, or even to think. I mean, even if free democracy brings *sharia* at first, eventually I believe something will change. Democracy has the mechanism to develop freedom by itself.

* * *

In 1996, I was supposed to help monitor the student leadership elections at the university. Our alliance, the NDA, won the elections. The Islamic students were angry with us, and as usual they started making trouble, attacking us, yelling and throwing things at us on campus. When it got to be dangerous, police came and beat the students. They didn't beat the Islamic students, of course. The police don't beat them because they know them. They only beat back the NDA and the other opposition students. They arrested me because I was an election monitor and held me for a few hours. Finally they asked me to sign a form saying that I would stop all opposition activities. They made all of us do that. They forced me to sign it. I didn't care. In a good way, these things gave us experience. It taught us how to deal with these security men, how to answer them, how to avoid answering them.

Each time I would come home from an experience with the police, my family would ask me about every small detail: who detained me, where, what was done to me, what they said. My mother told me to stop the political activities many times, but I didn't stop because I believed in what I was doing. I was doing a good thing. And for me it would have been a shame if I had stopped. I am my father's son. I can't be scared. It's not my culture, not my family, not my personality.

My brother supported me the most. He is still in Khartoum, where he works as a government lawyer reporting on independent corporations. He sees huge cases of corruption. He says every year he tours offices and reports on the problems to his bosses. The next year he goes back and sees the same thing, with no attempts to change. At that point he just has to be quiet. He knows that even if he speaks, nothing will change. He feels very upset about everything around him. Everything is wrong.

I never thought to stop my political activities. But I did think that if I would continue, I would have to do it more wisely. The smart way. More organized.

WE PROMOTED RIGHTS FOR EVERYONE

Our NDA group planned to host a speech one day in 2003 on the topic of the war in the South. The university security knew about it and were going to try to stop us. We knew the guards would have a list of some people to watch out for, and that we probably wouldn't be allowed to enter campus that day. They're not too smart, though. We just borrowed IDs from different students. I mean, the photos didn't even match. But it worked, and we succeeded in making the speech.

The speech was strong and very harsh. We attacked the regime. The leaders of the DUP and Sadiq al-Mahdi, leader of Umma party, had just signed the Cairo Declaration, moving toward peace with the South. The Islamist groups attacked them and even had a *fatwa,* a religious edict, calling the peacemakers unbelievers. We wanted to correct the image for the students. We attacked the regime and the policies. We promoted rights for everyone.

Soon the police arrived at the university and arrested many of the students involved. Unfortunately I was one of them. They sent us to the security office and started to insult us, beat us, and call us names. They beat me in the head with a stick. They tied my hands behind my back and just held me for hours.

You know, these security men really believed in what they were doing. The problem was that they didn't understand what they were believing in. So I would talk to them. "You are Muslim; I am Muslim also. What's wrong? You are practicing Islam, and I also practice. You believe in Allah, and I believe in Allah." That time in detention, there was a really aggressive, violent officer. He kept beating me, and I was looking into his eyes, just looking into his eyes.

I asked him, "Are you Muslim?"

"Yeah," he said, "I am Muslim. I am better than you."

"How do you know you are better than me? How do you know?"

He said, "Because you are against this regime, you are supporting the South, and supporting the SPLA," and so on.

I said to him, "Southerners are living in their towns, and the government comes and bombs them, insults them, rapes them, and kills them. What did they do? They lived in these towns for a hundred years in the south of Sudan until we came, without any reason. They are victims."

He replied to me, "You don't know better than we do. We have a mission and it's a holy mission."

I said, "Okay then, I'm wrong. But right now you are beating me. Why are you beating me?"

He replied to me, "I want to punish you."

"Why are you punishing me? You do not even know what I have done. You are not a judge, you are not a policeman. You do not even tell me your name. I am here without any rights, without a lawyer. It is not your right to punish me. And it's prohibited in your religion. You are Muslim. You cannot harm me like this. It's prohibited. If you are a good Muslim, end this." He just stayed quiet.

At night the officer came back to my cell. "Tarig, I want to discuss something with you."

I was thirsty, so I said, "If you want to discuss something with me, I need a cup of tea."

He took me outside of the cell. We went to his office. The other detainees were very confused about what was going on. We went to his office, and we had the tea, and we had a very nice discussion. I told him again, "If you are a good Muslim, you should stop this. No religion can give you the right to insult or to harm or to beat someone like you have done. Even if you were a prophet you could not do that. This behavior is an insult to our religion. Islam is a good thing, and you give it a bad image." I gave him a lecture! I can't imagine what I was thinking.

The next day, I couldn't believe it, but he was acting pretty nicely to all the detainees. Maybe it was just for that day, but I could feel that maybe his way of thinking had changed. I think you can change their minds, because they do not stand on a concrete ideology or concrete opinions. It's very weak because they only repeat the things they are told. A simple bit of logic could change his mind.

Pretty quickly the officer was taken away. The next day two men came to my cell and told me, "Don't speak with anyone. You are not allowed even to speak with the detainees." I guess they feared I was brainwashing people.

OUR BLOOD SHOULD BE SHED

I was going to university one day shortly after the speech and my time in prison. I came to the gates of the university and I saw a sign. It had my name and the name of one of my colleagues, Mohammed. The sign said our blood should be shed. It said we were speaking against the religion, that we were trying to convert students away from Islam, and it went on like this. It was signed by a group of Islamic extremist students. They believed it was their religious right to call for my blood to be shed.

I went to the DUP party leaders and they said I should be worried, that it was a big problem. They sent me to stay at a friend's house in Omdurman. I stopped going to school. I could go outside only at night.

It only took a few days before they came to my friend's house. Six security men came during the day, attacked the house, and picked me up. Just imagine every bad thing they could do. They beat me, they interrogated me until after midnight. They insulted me, insulted my father and my mother. Twice they threatened to kill me.

They let me sleep only a few hours at a time. They'd wake me in the middle of the night to interrogate me. Sometimes they made me stand for a long time, hours and hours at a time. They wouldn't allow me to go to the toilet. The guards were very aggressive and would never speak to me. They gave me one meal per day. I was all alone.

They would ask me again and again, "What are you doing? Why are you doing that? Who are you working for? Where do you get your money?" They questioned me like I was a spy. I told them nothing, but I was afraid this time. I was worried that I might be killed. Students had been killed before. And they knew who my father was.

They held me about thirty days. I was in very bad condition after the beatings, after being prevented from sleeping, after the long hours of standing at night. Finally I just started acting like my health was really in trouble. I pretended I couldn't walk and couldn't speak. I pretended I'd lost consciousness. They picked me up and sent me to a military hospital.

You know, the doctors at the military hospital were very good. They did their job, gave me some medication and gave me some injections. They even allowed my mother to visit me. She saw me and just kept crying. And then she helped me escape.

The DUP and my mother arranged the whole thing. It was pretty simple really. My mother left me some normal civilian clothes, and I hid them under my pillow. The next day a friend of my family came to the hospital, just walked up to the guards and started asking them crazy questions, acting strange, attracting their attention. They all went over to him, and I changed my clothes and started walking in the opposite direction. I was scared, sure. The guards inside the hospital didn't have guns, but the ones on the outside did. I walked to the part of the hospital that was for military veterans and then just acted like a visitor. I walked out the exit. Another friend named Tarig was waiting with a car. I jumped in, and he drove me to a safe house, this time in the South of Khartoum. When we arrived, I just stood there. It was hard for me to imagine what had just happened. But then we had so much fun! I was acting like, "Yeah, yeah! I fucked them! I fucked them!"

Even now, in Cairo, every time I have an interview about my refugee status, it's difficult for them to believe that I just escaped from a military hospital. But what can I say? It happened.

TARIG, IT'S OVER

I stayed in that safe house for about two months. The DUP prepared a visa for me to travel to Egypt. They bribed someone working with Sudan Airways, and I got a ticket to Cairo.

The main reason I am a refugee is my mother. Not the government. My mother pushed me. The DUP people agreed, but mostly it was my mother. I was making trouble for her, and she had a bad experience already with my father. "Leave, leave, Tarig. At last, you should leave. Tarig, *chalas*—it's over."

They all said, "Leave now, and when the situation has calmed down, you can return again." Of course, even now, I still can't return. I feel this is my destiny—not to suffer, but this time is like a tax. I pay the tax, and I get my life. But four years of my life is missing.

I went to the airport, ready to leave Khartoum. They took me very early in the morning, about five o'clock in the morning, so it was very quiet. My friends came with me and facilitated the procedures. I had some very brief moments to say goodbye to my family. My mother hugged me and asked me to be strong. I said, "I will, my mother. I'm strong enough."

The whole thing took an hour, and I was very stressed. But it worked. Dot dot dot, stamp stamp, Egypt. I got on the plane and looked down at Sudan. Then some tears came out. It was November 2003.

I THINK WHEN YOU TELL THE TRUTH YOU
HELP YOURSELF, BUT I DON'T KNOW

I had great expectations for Cairo. I expected that I would find protection here. But I had no plan. I had one hundred and fifty dollars, some clothes, photos, and one book: *One Hundred Years of Solitude,* by Gabriel García Márquez. Not a very optimistic book for leaving your country, if you can believe it.

When I arrived in Cairo, it was about eight o'clock in the morning. I exchanged my money into Egyptian pounds. A Sudanese man from the DUP was there to pick me up, and he took me to his house.

I had mixed feelings those first days. Happy because I was safe, not happy because I had left. And so many questions. Cairo wasn't like the image that I'd had in my mind.

I got lucky. I got a job quickly. Every day I was going to an internet café in Nasr City, just outside of Cairo. After a few days, the manager, an Egyptian man, asked my name. His name was Tarig, too. We talked for a while, he asked if I had a job. I said "No," and suddenly he gave me a job as a manager. So at least I had money.

For my first year in Cairo, I lived in the suburb of Nasr City, in an apartment with four friends. We had a telephone and a television, so it was okay. We helped each other, loved each other, respected each other. We shared our money to rent the flat. Three of us were working. One had a brother in Australia who would help him. The other had a brother in Cairo to help him also. Between the five of us, we shared the rent of eight hundred Egyptian pounds (US$140).

But a new refugee here in Egypt confronts all these new rules, and organizations, and details. You are confused, you are worried. UNHCR might accept me, might not accept me. Who do you trust? Rumors have strong influence among the refugees. They influence them completely. They say if you mention in your claims that you were with the Communist party in Sudan, then America or Australia or Canada will not accept you because they are capitalist countries and against the Communists. But I don't think that's true at all. People believe everything, because according to their miserable situation here, they want to believe you if you say, "Yeah, I have a *khawaja* friend,[1] and if you give him US$400, you will be in America in four months." Everyone will believe you. We just pay attention to the rumors because we are desperate. I don't know. We're making decisions, and we've never thought about these sorts of things before: telling our stories, seeking protection.

Many people lie to the authorities. But if you lie, you just harm yourself. I think that when you tell the truth, simply, you help yourself. But I don't know. At least there are lawyers in Cairo that provide free legal aid at AMERA, Africa and Middle East Refugee Assistance. If you go to AMERA, they provide you a professional lawyer. They can help you. They can try to provide legal and medical assistance. That's what I learned to do.

A BETTER EXILE

After a few days in Cairo, I went to UNHCR to be registered as a refugee. I had to wait outside with the guards because there was no reception room for us. Really, I didn't feel comfortable at all. They gave me an appointment to come back a few weeks later for an interview and gave me a yellow card to show I was being processed as a refugee. I went home and some other refugees in the community helped me prepare my testimony to give to UNHCR.

It was really lucky for me to have the delay before my appointment. An amazing thing happened just after that appointment, a thing that changed my life here in Cairo. I met a Sudanese human rights lawyer named Drasi Suleiman. I had met him before by

---

[1] Slang for foreigners, specifically white people.

accident at this speech about Sudan—I don't remember exactly what it was about, but many members of the community were there. Mr. Suleiman asked me what I was doing in Cairo and I said, "What do you think? How can I live in Sudan?" He knew the name of my father, so he understood. He was quiet for a moment, just thinking. "Okay, I want to meet you tomorrow."

When I met him again he gave me a memo and told me to go visit Dr. Barbara Harrell-Bond. He said, "She's the right person. She can help you." He told me she would help me get better protection.

I went to Barbara's office in Garden City—she's a small, old, amazing American woman. I showed Barbara my testimony, and she looked at me and said, "Who wrote this testimony?" She told me everything was wrong, the writing was bad, there were no details to make it true. She brought over a lawyer, an Egyptian man named Hassan. He was professional, professional, professional. He asked me about very small details and included everything. He changed my testimony to be strong, to be concrete.

I was lucky, but just imagine—thousands of refugees come and they have to give testimonies, but they don't know what to write or how to write it. It's not their job to be a lawyer, to know the law, or how to prepare a testimony in a good, legal way. Many times I wonder, What if I had not met the lawyer Mr. Suleiman, and if he hadn't introduced me to Barbara? I think I would not have gotten refugee status.

Barbara asked me to come back. She has a big wall of books in her office, and she said, "Come anytime, read from my library." She was very generous. I did go back to her office, became friends with her, did some work for her. I met many people there, many refugees, many *khawajas*.

Some time later, I went back to UNHCR for my appointment. My lawyer came with me. The interview took about two hours. The interviewer was an Egyptian woman, and I think her name was

Miriam. She asked me to come back after two weeks to get my result. They recognized me as a refugee and gave me a blue card.

Again, this was lucky for me. This was the spring of 2004, and just a month or so after I got my card, UNHCR suspended the cases of all Sudanese refugees, due to the Comprehensive Peace Agreement that ended the war in the south of Sudan. They thought everyone would go back to Sudan now because of the peace. Of course that didn't happen—there was nothing to return to in South Sudan, and of course, there's the war in Darfur now. But still, since June 2004, UNHCR doesn't do refugee-status-determination interviews for any Sudanese, except in very horrible, very rare cases. Instead, the refugees get a yellow card which means only temporary protection, no official determination that you are a refugee, no chance for resettlement. But I got here just in time, so I was lucky. They gave me that blue card and an appointment for a resettlement interview. The interview was scheduled for eight months later. From the beginning, I didn't want to go to this resettlement interview.

I didn't believe they would really resettle me, and I didn't believe resettlement would really solve my problem. I mean, you send me to another, better place, but that's not the right way to solve my problem. It's not the end of my problem. My problem is in my country, in Sudan. Resettlement doesn't help to solve the problem in Sudan, and I have dreams about that, not about a new country.

Barbara advised me to go to the interview. I might be lucky, she said, and I might get a chance to leave Egypt. So I went. I blame myself to this day for that decision.

My appointment for the resettlement interview was at the UNHCR office at eight a.m. I waited from eight a.m. until six p.m. Ten hours I waited. Some Egyptian case officer came. He called my name. And then he spoke with me for five minutes. Five minutes! "Tarig," he asked, "do you have any security problems here?"

I said, "No, I don't have security problems in Cairo."

"Do you have a relative in one of the resettlement countries?" I told him I had a cousin living in New York, but I didn't know anyone in Australia or in Canada. I told him I had an aunt in Ireland, but he said Ireland wasn't a resettlement country.

Then he just said, "We have no opportunities for resettlement now. When we find an opportunity for you, we'll call."

I just started laughing.

He told me, "Please don't laugh, it's serious."

I said, "Be finished. You could have just called me, instead of asking me to stay here from eight to six. I've been here ten hours, and you don't offer me food, just this very hard chair. I've been waiting ten hours for you to talk with me for five minutes and tell me nothing?" I was humiliated.

In the end I don't feel good about resettlement. Australia, America, Canada... they would only be a better exile. I would be a stranger. It's not my country. America's not my country. If I have freedom in America, it's meaningless freedom. I should have the freedom in my home. Is it right or wrong? I don't know. A lot of people think that I have strange ideas about freedom. To me, they're not strange ideas. They're very simple and clear.

In the years since, I've had interviews with the Americans and the Australians, and still the same. I hear nothing.

ASK A SUDANESE IF HE HAS EGYPTIAN FRIENDS

After about a year in Cairo I left my job at the internet café. The manager wanted to increase my work hours but refused to increase the salary and that's not fair, so I left. I had no work for months. It was okay though, because that's normal, and I had friends. We share. If any one of my flatmates has no money, he comes and asks me, no problem. If I have money and they have no money, then they get money. They don't even need to ask. We just know when people need money, and we help. We even made a sort of society among our friends and our friends' friends. We contribute ten dollars every month, or as much as we can. We save this money to help the families in desperate need of money. We always say: one fuckin' bucket. Nice, eh? We support each other, and we love each other.

But the Egyptians, I tell you really, they treat you like a third-class person, like you're just coming to their country to steal a job or work. For example, you know, because of my work with Barbara, I've become friends with lots of *khawajas,* lots of foreigners. The other night we were at a bar, a bar I go to often, and it was me and many *khawajas.* It was late at night, and they wanted to close the bar. Okay, fine. When the waiter came over to tell me, he called me *cufar.* That means "faceless people," or "unbelievers," something like that. Me, I'm a Sudanese and I'm with *khawajas*—it's like he questions my allegiance, you know? The idea that you describe me as an unbeliever because I sit with *khawajas,* drinking! You served the beer to me!

All the time, I go to internet cafés to browse. I ask the administrator to give me a headset, and he tells me that it doesn't work. Then an Egyptian man will come and ask for a headset and he gets it. Why? I paid for the computer. It's not free. But these things just became normal.

The Sudanese are very racist people too, of course. In the north of Sudan and for the Arabs of the west, there's more racism than Egyptians, frankly. We have bad names, too. The lighter-skinned people, like many Egyptians, we call them *halib.* This means that his color is white. Not white like *khawaja*—the people from the West are called *khawaja.* I don't know what the meaning of the word is, really. But I know that's what we call people from the West. The Chinese are not *khawaja,* but the Russians, the French, the Americans, the British are *khawajas.* But the people colored like an Egyptian are called *halib* in Sudan. That means he is not a good man. Not a generous man. He's not a person you can trust. Forget about him. But still, Sudan is worse. In Sudan, the Northerners call the Southern man *abeed*, a slave. This is completely antihumanitarian. It's not respectable to describe someone as a slave or something like this. And it's prohibited in Islam, also. Coming from a Muslim family, it's prohibited. If we respect Islam, we should respect others. Simple. Sometimes I call the Egyptians *halib*, and they call me words like *samara*, *chokolata*, or *hunga bunga.*[2]

I do know great Egyptians, though. Like my lawyer, Hassan. I even worked for him for a while, on Fridays, typing testimonies in Arabic. I've had girlfriends here in Egypt. Now I have a girl who is a good friend of mine, named Rasha. We met in Heliopolis, on a bus. She got in and there weren't enough seats. I asked her to come and sit in my place. "Oh, thank you, thank you very much." She was very nice, and she held my bag while she sat. "Are you from Sudan?" "Yes, I'm from Sudan." "Oh. Nice people…" and since then we have been friends.

Actually, she is from a conservative Muslim family. But she has an open mind, really. We meet for dinner, for coffee, sometimes for fish. We smoke cigarettes, but no alcohol. And she has to be home early, before ten. We all know the rules for girls.

The situation for refugees living in Egypt is very difficult and very hard. The Egyptian society increases the suffering of the refugee. You meet the Egyptians sometimes, in a taxi or whatever, and you tell them, "I am Sudanese," and they say, "Egypt is your country. No difference between Sudan and Egypt. We drink from one river, the Nile." All this is bullshit. It's just expressions. Nothing they are saying is true. They treat you differently. They treat you in a bad way. But they keep telling me I am part of their country. Bullshit.

"We are Muslim, you are Muslim. We have one language. We speak Arabic." Sure. But when you start dealing with them, it's very

[2] Derogatory terms for black Africans.

sad. Ask a Sudanese here if they have Egyptian friends, and they'll probably say no.

* * *

I'm also an interpreter now. I took a course through the American University in Cairo so I have certification. I get some work teaching English to Egyptian kids. I've been a typist, a businessman's assistant. I worked for one week selling clothes in a store downtown, but oh, the way the owner treated me! I quit after a week.

It's hard for the men, really. Being a refugee, without work, without security, makes you feel you are a helpless man. You are weak. And in Sudan, the man is the only one who should support the family. The woman doesn't work at all. The man works and provides the money for the family. It's shameful for a Sudanese man to stay at home. But it's so difficult to find work here. You have no income, but at the same time it's not your fault, because you have no legal working papers. And still you have a family. And if you find work, even when you find it, the money is not enough to support a family. To get this twenty or thirty pounds (US$3 or US$5) in a day is not enough. Many times men go to work selling things on the streets, and the police mark them and kick them and take their stuff and they have to start again. It's about weakness and fear for men.

Sometimes, for myself, it's difficult to remember if I ate breakfast or not. Difficult to remember. I need five or six minutes to remember, did I eat breakfast or not. I eat once or twice a day. We lose our appetites.

THEY JUST KEPT DENYING, DENYING, DENYING

I have to tell about the protests that started in September 2005. I heard about the protests from a friend of mine. They said, "We're gonna demonstrate outside the UNHCR building until UNHCR

solves our problems." We wanted protection. Some wanted resettlement. We wanted the end of discrimination by the Egyptian community. "They're gonna protest," my friends said. I said, "Let's see."

I went there the first day. And the second day. And the third day.
I felt safe there. I don't know why, but I felt safe.

On the first day there were thirty or fifty people. Then several
hundred. Soon there were two thousand people there, maybe two
thousand and a half. Not right in front of UNHCR but in the grass
by the street. The UNHCR kept denying that the people outside
were even refugees at all, but we were refugees.

The people stayed there for weeks and months. All Sudanese,
from different ethnic groups all over Sudan. Women, children, old
people. They were sleeping there at night also. They respected each
other, respected the rules, respected the law. I mean, there was no
permission to do this of course. But nobody had problems with their
neighbors in the park. It was a very organized protest.

We had signs: "Stop discrimination." "The UNHCR should fulfill
their mandates to protect the refugees." "We need the real protection."
The refugees had a security team to stop drunk people from entering
the demonstration. They had people cooking food for everyone. They
had doctors doing diagnostic examinations. By October it was cold at
night, so lots of kids were getting infections in their chests. They even
had people teaching classes for the kids. Two or three times, I gave
lessons to kids in the school in the park. Mostly we would sit with our
friends and talk about Sudan, about the new Sudan.

I thought UNHCR would act quickly to do something. But they
didn't and so it lasted three months. UNHCR just kept denying that
those outside were even refugees. They just kept denying, denying,
denying. It's not the right way.

I think it was December 17 when an official from UNHCR came
outside and offered a proposal to do interviews with each person and
review their refugee status. Now most of the Southern Sudanese

refused this, because the war was ending in the South. The southerners knew they would either have to stay in Cairo and wait for the peace, or accept voluntary repatriation immediately. Both were bad options, so most of the southerners refused the offer. Me, I wrote my name on the list for a review, and I left the park.

I was at home on December 28 when a friend of mine called me from New York. They knew about it all the way over in New York. He just said, "What's going on in Cairo?" I didn't know what he meant. He said, "Just turn on the TV and tell me what's going on." When I turned on the TV, I saw a police officer kick an old Sudanese woman and push her into a truck. The police were beating and kicking everyone. There were thousands of policemen surrounding the protestors. They opened the water cannons on them in the middle of the cold night. The refugees were covering their kids in plastic sheets to protect them from the water, and in the end lots of those kids died under the plastic, because when the policemen raided the park, they just ran over the kids. It was horrible. My flatmate was very, very angry. He just started screaming.

Just imagine that night. If an official from UNHCR had come outside and talked to the Egyptian police, he might have changed something, might have saved people's lives. We don't know for sure how many people died in the end. Plus, hundreds went to prison, and were treated so badly there. One committed suicide in prison. Many of my friends were locked there for months, and we couldn't see them, couldn't find them, nothing.

The incident at Mustafa Mahmoud made the gap between the Sudanese and Egyptians even bigger. There's even less trust, unfortunately. Most important, now there's a real lack of trust between the refugees and UNHCR. Now the refugees say to UNHCR, "You should protect me, but when you betrayed me, I lost my kids, I lost my wife. I saw this massacre in front of UNHCR. How can you protect me? You betrayed me. You betrayed me. How can you protect me now?"

Maybe there will be another demonstration someday. Who knows? Because still, UNHCR hasn't learned its lesson. Maybe the solution is to close UNHCR, because they are not able to learn. They say they don't have enough resources. I say: it's not a matter of resources. Sure, you don't have enough resources to fix everything. That's not your fault. But the way you treat me doesn't depend on resources. You're not even offering me a glass of cold water in your offices. Many times there are families inside the UNHCR waiting for long hours. What does it cost you, UNHCR, to offer a meal for the kids? Twenty pounds (US$3) for a whole family? The kids are hungry. They are refugees. They are poor. They might not have had dinner yesterday. Who knows? Imagine if someone from the staff comes and says, "Hey, kids. Did you have breakfast? Here's something for you." This simple thing would mean a lot. Does that make any sense? Maybe I'm very sensitive about this stuff, but when I go to UNHCR, I watch the way the staff treats the refugees. There's just no respect. Like we're criminals. It makes me very upset.

MY THREE Ws

I have my three Ws: war, wine, and women. Hard to imagine the life without wine. Hard to imagine life without women. Hard to imagine life without war.

With women, I have the feeling of missing someone unreachable. A girl I loved lives in Khartoum and I live in Cairo. She used to come to visit me three times a year. Finally I told her it would not work. How difficult! I can't return to Sudan, and she can't live here in Cairo. It was impossible. Now it's a year later, and she is living in Nigeria, where she has her own life, a good job for an oil company, a good salary. Her life is completely different than mine. I do miss her sometimes, mostly when I feel alone. I'm a very strange person, you know. I have many friends. But many times I feel alone, I feel lonely. I don't know.

Then you have the wine. Wine in exile is different than wine in any other place. When you are away from your home, when you feel the unfairness, when you ask why you are away from home, why you are not allowed to return to your home, and you have no answer, it causes depression and a lot of stress. The wine calms you down and makes you feel a little bit comfortable with this strange, abnormal situation. So I drink beer, and I drink *ariki,* a Sudanese wine. The southern women make it at home, from dates—it's traditionally the work of the low-class people in Sudan. *Ariki* is very strong and the men in Sudan like it. I drink much more in Cairo than I ever did in Sudan.

In Sudan, alcohol is illegal, so you buy it in secret—you go to a dark house, you get it in a Pepsi bottle in a small paper bag. It's like buying marijuana in America. And that makes it exciting. Here, some people have objections to wine, but nobody really cares. You know, when you get something difficult, and it's not easy, you enjoy it more than the easy stuff. We don't enjoy the wine so much here. We just need it.

IT WAS PURE CORRUPTION

Some problems started for me in late 2006. I was working with Dr. Barbara at the time, helping her with small projects, doing translation, and so on. She was telling me about a corruption investigation at UNHCR, and I told her I knew cases of people who paid bribes to get fast-tracked for their blue cards and their resettlements. People paid US$300 or US$400 dollars to an interpreter who worked with UNHCR, and they'd get blue cards when nobody else would succeed. It was especially corrupt in the months before June 2004, when they stopped giving blue cards. Some people have been waiting for years. Some were here for what, seven weeks? And suddenly they have a blue card. I had met an Egyptian lawyer who told me that he could facilitate a resettlement for US$3,000. There were many, many examples. It was pure corruption and I knew all the details of the stories.

Dr. Barbara helped me testify to the corruption. I met with a French lady from the United Nations to talk about some investigations inside UNHCR's Cairo office. I didn't feel comfortable at all.

The first time the French lady emailed me, she said she would come and visit me in any place I chose, so I would feel safe. Then she refused to come to my house, and she refused to come to Barbara's house. Eventually we met in a coffee shop, and when I came, she brought a Syrian guide as well. I just didn't feel comfortable with them at all. I don't know why. Maybe after the Mustafa Mahmoud massacre I just didn't trust them at all. But I gave them stories about officials, staff, case files involved in this corruption. I don't know what happened with it in the end.

My involvement in the investigation put me at risk. I was giving information that looked bad for the UNHCR office in Cairo and looked bad for the Egyptians. Who would want to protect me now? Dr. Barbara arranged an interview for me at the Australian embassy. I had my appointment for a resettlement interview in June 2007.

I had a bad feeling about the interview the whole time. I have a weak memory, really, when it comes to the small details. And they were only asking me about my story in Sudan, nothing from Cairo. They would ask things from a long time ago—maybe ten years ago, twelve years ago. They were asking about specific dates. Asking the number of members in the media committee of the DUP student party at university. I told all the important parts of my story, A to Z. But when it came to details, sometimes I had to say, "I can't remember. I don't remember." But they asked me nothing about Cairo or about the corruption case. I saw my file and all my testimonies sitting on his desk, in front of his eyes, but he asked me nothing about the corruption cases. I couldn't say anything. I can't tell him how to do his work properly. I just trusted and hoped.

Months later, I still have not heard a response from the Australians.

GET ME ALL THE WAY TO TEL AVIV

For years, I've been thinking about going to Libya. I have a friend in Libya, and he has a computer company. For years, he was asking me to come work with him. My friend said I could get to Libya and try the death trip across the sea to Italy. They call it the death trip because so many sink in the sea on this trip. I asked Dr. Barbara and she said to me, "Please, Tarig, don't think of doing this." Then my friend faced some trouble in his business. So I never went to Libya, but I still think about it.

Now I also think about Israel. I think about Israel a lot.

Friends of mine have already gone. The Bedouins smuggle them across Sinai for US$400.[3] They sneak across the border at night, and they go directly to the border guards—but that's completely wrong. You never know what can happen that way. Maybe nothing happens to them, and they just get sent to a detention center in Israel. I have a better plan. I want to get straight to Tel Aviv.

I have a friend who used to work with refugees in Cairo and then in Tel Aviv. He sent an email to an Israeli friend, and she told him that if I could approach UNHCR directly, I could get legal assistance and find a way to live and work in Israel. I could be directly under UNHCR protection, and not Israeli government protection. Israel considers Sudanese people enemies by the law. Nobody knows what happens to us under Israeli protection. But I'll go straight to the UN instead.[4]

I have a friend working in a tourist village in Sinai. He tells me that when I want to go, I just have to call him and he will help me

---

[3] Bedouins are a community of Arabic nomads.

[4] For more on Sudanese refugees in Israel, see page 432.

with everything. His Bedouins will avoid the border police, get me through the south of Israel, get me all the way to Tel Aviv.

Getting to Israel would be an amazing experience. I hear a lot about Israel, about all the history of the Jewish people. But you know the media in the Arab world almost always gives you the wrong story about everything. It would be different if I could live inside with them, to know what's going on in that country, to see the world without the Arab media.

Back in the 1990s I loved America, truly. Even now, somehow I respect America. But ten years ago, America had a good image as a state of freedom, a state of democracy. Now, it's difficult to say. In my opinion, American policy has this somehow religious ideology, it's business. And business has its own agenda that's different from the American people's agenda. When I eventually came here to Cairo, I met American people, and they are very nice people. They are cool, they understand the Middle East and Islam. But right now, the American policy in my opinion is just a criminal policy. Especially after 9/11, when everything turned upside down. It's the same with Israel. Israel has a criminal policy that creates crisis for the Palestinians. But I believe there are a lot of Israelis who want to live in peace. And I believe they are peaceful people. Peace is possible. But the policy, the problem is the policy.

I haven't spoken with Dr. Barbara about the Israel issue at all. Never. She would refuse. She would say it's a crazy idea and dangerous. It's dangerous, because all these others don't know the right way to do it.

If Australia rejects me, I'll go to Israel. Definitely.

NO FIRE. NO HELL. NO PARADISE

I'm worried about my future. What's my future? A big question mark. I had a plan for my life before I came to Cairo. Suddenly everything turned upside down. I find myself here as a refugee, and somehow I must face it. I think I'm doing good here in Cairo, helping others. But it's like a self-defense mechanism. Instead of running away from my life, it's like I fall down, fall into the experience all the way. I can deal with things, and maybe help people in a different way because I'm a refugee myself, with the same experience. I'll continue to try to help.

I've read lots of books in Cairo. There's so much time to yourself, so I can read almost a book a day. My favorite character is the old man in the Ernest Hemingway novel *The Old Man and the Sea*. He's a fisherman. He tries to fight nature, to fight something too big for himself, and he loses. Sometimes I feel like this. The same goes for people working to help refugees, people like Dr. Barbara. She's trying to fight nature, too. I just love the character of the fisherman. It was the same end for Hemingway too, I think. He committed suicide. He could not hold on to life. Life's a very big fish that's difficult to catch.

I wish a peaceful life for everyone. People should take care of themselves and take care of others. And I hope, I wish, and I pray for everyone that they never pass through an experience like mine. Really, I ask for nothing anymore. There are other places in the world where people need more help. People who live on the streets, in unbelievable situations, lives that are horrific and destitute. If anyone can do anything, just help them. I'm okay. I'm okay. I can help myself. I can help myself.

Maybe people will read this and think I am a strong man. Maybe they will think I am an unlucky man. You can say that I am someone who has tried to fight, and so far I have failed. My story to this point is not exciting. There's no fire. No hell. No paradise. Just in between.

MUBTAGA MOHAMMED
ALI MOHAMMED

AGE: *32*
TRIBE: *Bija, Ababd clan*
BIRTHPLACE: *Atbara, (Northern) Sudan*
INTERVIEWED IN: *Cairo, Egypt*

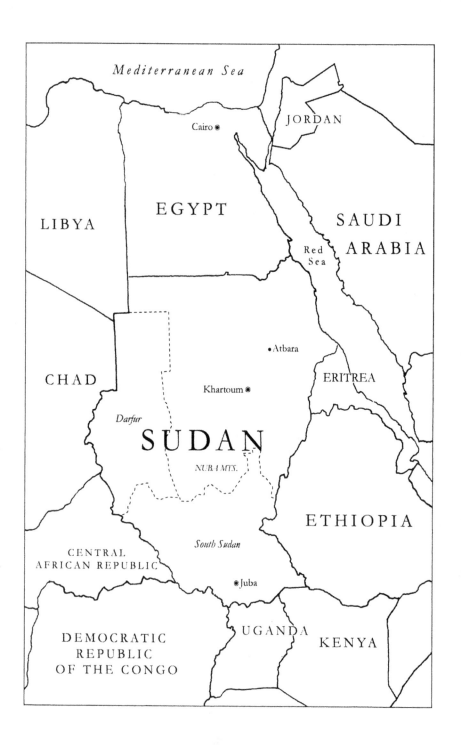

I STILL HAVE A HOPE, EVEN IF
I LAUGH WHEN I SAY THAT

Mubtaga had been a refugee for about a hundred hours when this inter-
view was conducted. In a flurry of impeccable English, she spoke about what
brought her to this point.

My name is Mubtaga Mohammed Ali Mohammed. The first
"Mohammed" is from the prophet Mohammed, and then "Ali" is a
cousin of the prophet Mohammed, and the second "Mohammed" is
my grandfather's name. Mohammed is a common name, you know.
My name, Mubtaga, it means something like "goal," something
you can't reach easily.

    I was born in Atbara, a city in the middle of northern Sudan.
It was very famous for its Communist movement during the forties
and fifties. The town is multicultural, multiethnic and multitribal.
People come there from across northern Sudan, eastern Sudan, and
even from the Nuba Mountains. They are drawn to Atbara to work
as employees on the railways. The city is very famous for its trains;
it's like Birmingham, in England. In fact, Atbara was built by the
British. It was not a city until the British established it as a railway

hub. So you have all of these different cultures, because people were coming from all over, following the trains. They would all get along, because there was this one common workplace, and the labor union would turn them into one unit.

Of course, since 1990 that community has been destroyed. The culture of unity and the rail workers' union was destroyed by the government of the Bashir regime. This regime hates the communist ideas. The regime has this idea that the communists are not believers. Since the sixties, the Islamic Front has seen the communists as an enemy, but this regime brought some of the worst security people to Atbara to break up these communities.

My clan is Ababd, of the Bija tribe, the indigenous people in the east of Sudan. They are nomads who crossed the desert between Egypt and Sudan. And they are located in small, isolated villages in the east. They have the sea close to them, but they put the water behind them and turned to the desert, and nobody knows why. They helped the Egyptian mission, the Turkish mission, and the British missions to control Sudan because they knew the roads and the deserts. The Bija became Egyptianized, really, and still have close ties with Egypt. Most of my family has Egyptian identity cards, along with their Sudanese papers.

The Bija have no voice in Sudan. They're not educated, and they're very poor. People see a Bija coming, they call him Aderoop— that's a common name amongst the Bija, and there are many jokes about men named Aderoop. The woman is very, very subordinated among the Bija. She is just meant for the children. She stays inside the house.

I'M THE ONE THAT RUINS EVERYTHING

I was born on the fourth of May, 1974. My family was not communist, just a very normal Sudanese, Arabized conservative. My father was a policeman at the railway station. A cop. He did not belong to any political party, just to his traditions.

My mother didn't work. No, no, no. She didn't even go to school. When she was a child, an educated cousin tried to give her some schooling. My grandmother came and pulled her out. My grandmother said she took her girl from school because if she went to school, she would learn how to write letters to men. And that's why it was forbidden to her. Girls should not write or read, because if they know to write or read, that means they are going to write love letters. That's why my mother was not so good at school!

My father and mother divorced in 1979. My father remarried, and at first I went to live with him and his wife in a small village. At the age of twelve, they sent me to go to my mother in Atbara, and I was happy to go to the big town.

I have one older brother, and I am the oldest girl in the family. Between both my parents, it's now seven sisters and four brothers. One brother died when he was a kid, from meningitis. He died on the train. There was no hospital where we were. My mother tried to take him to the city but he died on the train.

My sisters are all typical northern Sudanese girls, you know. They wear the veil. They have a room to study, but they are still kept in the house. I'm not close with any of them. I cannot be close with anybody in my family because I have my own way of life. They don't appreciate it, and now they threaten my life. I'm the one who just went against everything. I'm the one that ruins everything.

My mother's very passive because, well, she's a woman. She can't say anything. Now my father doesn't say anything either, because he's become subordinate to my elder brother. My brother is in power in the family because he makes money, he supports the family financially. He has the voice to say no or yes.

When I was at home I did things in a clever way. From a young age, I was a first-class student in school. Same with everything.

I would not confront my family, would not tell them I'm doing this or that. I would find other ways.

I liked to read when I was a kid. There were no movies. Cinemas were forbidden for "good" women. We had a television, but watching Sudanese television is just like going to the mosque. There is nothing to see on the TV. So I liked to read, just to read, even before I could understand all the words. When I was a kid I would read Mickey Mouse books and Arabic magazines. I would save money and go to the booksellers. When I was about twelve I started to read romance novels. We call them *abir*. They're about handsome men who find pretty women, and from the first time they see each other they like each other, and after a while they fall in love. Then there's a crisis, of course, and he saves her from the crisis.

When I was reading those books, did I have my own handsome man in my life? Well, I'll tell you it was forbidden, but that doesn't answer the question. When I was fifteen, we had a neighbor I liked very much. It's funny how we communicated. Atbara is very famous for its bicycles, bicycles everywhere. So when he would drive by, he would ring the bell of his bicycle. I could recognize it among the hundreds of hundreds. I would just go outside so we could look at each other, and that was as far as it went. It was only for like two months, but all that time, I couldn't concentrate on my reading and studying, just thinking about that ring.

I followed my own thing, my own sort of life. I wrote poetry, emotional things about girls playing freely, and destiny coming to stop the girls, to tell them not to play like this. It was around the time I got my first period. I had to behave like a woman now, not a child. From that time I felt like I was entering a different community. I loved dancing but I could not dance anywhere. I wanted to wear trousers, but good girls should not wear trousers. I wanted to be friends with girls and boys—friendship is friendship. But in Sudan it isn't like that. It's like this.

I PUSHED BACK

I had very strong results in school, so at eighteen I was able to study in one of the finest universities in the country, Khartoum University. My sisters and I were pushed to study in Atbara, even the ones who also did well. But I pushed back, and I was finally allowed to go to Khartoum, as long as I lived in a student dorm. I chose to study in the Department of Anthropology and the Department of Sociology and Social Anthropology.

I dreamed of being a great anthropologist. To study at UCLA, in California, to do my PhD there, and to write books. The professors encouraged me. I remember the head of anthropology saying once, "Mubtaga is a smart woman." That's why I wanted to be a smart woman, to prove him correct.

I was living in the student compound with five friends. Most of them are in America now, actually, married to Sudanese men. They came from wealthier families and they found ways to go. In those days we had similar ideas and similar knowledge of the community we were in, and we knew what the community expected us to be. We knew we had to pretend to be good girls. We weren't good girls, of course! We were smoking cigarettes for example, and that's forbidden for girls. I mean, we didn't smoke just because it was forbidden, it was just that some of us liked to smoke. They could have kicked us out of university just for that.

You had to wear *hijab*, the head covering. Even now, you cannot go to university unless you have a hijab. We used to laugh about it, call it our *motomer islami*. You know why? In 1993, the government invited all the Islamic leaders of the world for the Motomer Islami, the Islamic Conference. And that was when they made us wear these big scarves, to impress the big leaders, to show them that we were mad for Islamic ideology.

I would walk on the street, and half of my hair cover would fall, so some hair would show. The police would hit me, and ask, "Why aren't you covering your hair?" It was usual to be beaten by the police at that time.

Wearing it feels like prison. It's very, very hot in Sudan. And it's so hot with the *hijab* wrapped around you. So if you're not convinced of the religion, then of course you don't like the *hijab*. Now, me, I don't believe my body is a sin. But still I have to wear it. You know the red light district in Amsterdam? You know, where women expose their bodies to be sold? I think about those women, and I think about women covering their bodies in *hijab*, and I see bodies that are considered objects of sex, and nothing else. So for me it's the same thing. I know some of the women believe the hijab is a religious thing. But they never ask themselves why it's religious. How should it help you to be religious? God created you as a fantastic human being just like this, okay? And now a human being is telling you, "You are a sin." It's not fair. And I think God is fair, you know? I hope so. Or I imagine so.

Sudanese religion was not always like this. It wasn't always a major part of your reputation, or your behavior. Sufism used to be such a big part of religion in Sudan,[1] and it was about forgiveness, love and acceptance of others. Then in the late 1970s, and 1980s, and 1990s, many Sudanese went to find work in Saudi Arabia, and the Gulf countries, and they brought back this culture of Wahhabi.[2] It is fundamentalist, it is not accepting.

I think it will take some time to solve because it's not just a fashion. You could see it in Khartoum people are really frustrated. Muslims are frustrated. They feel they are subordinated. They're strengthening that identity as Muslims against the West. Me, I don't think the West is against Islam. I don't have these assump-

---

[1] Sufism is a form of Islamic mysticism.

[2] Wahhabism is a puritanical strain of Saudi Islam.

tions. But so many people look at Palestine and Israel, and of course, America in Iraq, America supporting Israel against Muslims. And that's why they have this idea. They see Abu Ghraib, you know, but they don't see the other side. I remember a friend saying to me once, "Look, America is abusing human rights; the West is abusing human rights."

"Where?" I said.

"In Abu Ghraib."

So I said, "Okay, look, who is discovering this, though. Americans themselves. Some Americans abuse human rights and some discover that and tell the world, so that means there are two parts."

Here in the Muslim countries and Muslim governments you can only see the one part. There is abuse of human rights, but nobody says anything about the abuse. You can see it, you can feel it as people, but you cannot say it in the media. So you can say America is abusing human rights. And that's true, that's very clear. But Sudan's government is abusing human rights, and nobody in Sudan says anything about it. TV can't say it. Journalists can't say it.

It's difficult to say whether I am a Muslim now. No. I believe in God, but not really, not in this Islam. This Islam is not mine. I can believe there is a God, but not the God of Muslims, of course. And not the God of Christians, of course. I don't know whose God, but it's my God. And I am sure my God does not say I am a sin, or that my body's a sin.

We used to go out and argue about things like this in university, and I loved it. Still, we had to be clever. Boys can stay off campus after midnight, but girls had to be back by nine p.m. So if we wanted to go to a café or a public workshop in the evening, or celebrate a birthday, we'd have to find another place to sleep, at a friend's house or a relative's house. And all the time we'd wear the veils, and on the streets we'd behave like good girls, looking the way they like us to. We would cover ourselves. We'd go to prayers sometimes. Why not pray with the group, so they see how good you are?

Some of my girlfriends even got involved in politics. They would go to rallies, or labor strikes. I feared it would have been trouble for me if I'd gone public by getting politically involved. So instead I worked on cultural activities, supporting women's events, poetry readings, public symposiums. I worked with a United Nations club, participating in International Women's Day, International Children's Day. It was outside of the political parties, but I could know I was doing something to fight against the ideology by bringing people together, sitting together, discussing together.

The best was a literacy project in which I taught street boys. There are thousands of these street boys in Khartoum. Too many. They're natural outcomes from the wars and the poverty. Most are from the west and from the south of Sudan. They're as young as five, and as old as eighteen, or even older. The first movement of boys came during the drought of 1983 in the West, and then they started coming from the South. They are not educated, but they have their own life, their own communities, they have their own rituals, they have traditions.

If you want to be a street boy you have to respect this culture among them. They live in empty, unfinished buildings, or in sanitation canals, or other corners. They do cleaning, they do housekeeping, they clean people's shoes on the street to get some money. They beg for food; sometimes they steal. The government does nothing for them. I taught a class for them for eight months, sponsored by this UN school in Khartoum. It was fantastic, you know. Some of them were good students. Some of them took the food we offered and left. But I mean, I was still young, practically a kid myself, and I got to teach other kids. It reminded me that I didn't have to be a woman who graduated and then went back to her home, waiting for some man to marry her.

MY FAMILY WAS AGAINST IT, TOTALLY

I graduated from university in December 1996. There were special ceremonies for the students, like me, who got the highest degrees—celebrations, gifts, and even the vice president of the country is there to shake your hand, to take pictures. Of course, many of the first-class students didn't support the government, and didn't want to shake the hands of the regime, so they wouldn't go.

By that time I had already started as a research assistant working on the physical and psychological effects of traditional medicine on women. And it served my part not to go back to Atbara and stay with my family. I could stay in Khartoum, do research, and start my master's degree, work and live in Khartoum.

My family was against it, totally. They'd gotten me a job already, in a bank in Atbara. I never imagined myself as a banker, but my family liked the idea because my older brother worked at the bank. He could watch me. So they ask me to go to interview and I just failed the interview on purpose! They gave this very easy written exam and I wrote all of it wrong, as a joke. They got me another interview. I failed again. So I said to them, "I'm just so bad at this, why can't I go back to Khartoum and stay with my uncle?" They said okay, finally, as long as my uncle was watching me.

I moved in with my uncle in Khartoum, but it was clear his family missed their privacy. Pretty soon I told him about a friend of mine, a medical doctor, who could host me. So I was off to stay with this girl and a whole house of doctors. That saved my life for two years. Somehow I'd become independent, and even had enough money to help support my family a little bit. When you're economically independent and supporting people, you can raise up your voice somehow. Of course we still had to fight the community around our house, because we were girls staying alone.

My parents just cared about me getting married. They never

stopped with that. "You are not married. Why? You should marry, you should marry!" I told them that God is not willing yet. I could at least depend on God to justify why I wasn't married.

Truthfully, I had a boyfriend at that time, Olmert, but it couldn't go further because he just wanted to do the same to me as what my family wanted to do: to make me a "good" woman. Not to have friends, not to have a public life. To be there just for him. And it was not acceptable for me.

When I first met Olmert, I saw him acting open-minded, writing poetry, talking about freedom, playing music. I felt fantastic. But after time, it was different. All that open-minded thinking, playing music, writing poetry, it was something different from reality, and this is the story of men in Sudan. These men have the voice of their grandfathers in the back of their heads, and that's the one they listen to.

AFRICA IS OUR PLACE TO BE

I moved to a job at the United Nations Development Programme in 2003, as the national assistant for HIV/AIDS. The disease hadn't been a public issue at all; the government denied it, saying we are a Muslim community and we behave well, so that disease does not exist. In truth, the first cases had been discovered in 1986 but the media didn't talk about it. Then the World Health Organization says that if something isn't done in the next ten years, we'll be the next South Africa. So suddenly, in 2001, President Bashir says we have HIV/AIDS, and we have to fight it. All the international community brought focus to HIV/AIDS in Sudan because we have a very high rate, because of the war, displacement, poverty, a lot of things. My contract was just for one year. I got a chance to go outside Sudan, to go to Syria, to come here to Cairo, and it felt really distinguished.

I wrote reports on the lack of civil society participation on HIV/ AIDS projects in Sudan. Lots of money was coming in, but they don't give room for civil society to do work on HIV/AIDS. All the money was going to government projects, and of course that was a source of corruption. They would also just teach A or B, not C. C is the condom, you know, and they didn't want to say that word. They wanted to just talk about honor, and how problems in the community were linked to women without honor. It seemed that the UN was actually working to subordinate women indirectly by giving money to the government. So that's what I reported on to the UN staff. I don't know what came of it.

What I do know is it's common to have sex in Sudan, but nobody talks about it. There is prostitution. When I was with the UN they offered voluntary tests to bring people in and get a measure of sexually transmitted diseases. Four percent of the prostitutes had HIV/AIDS. Prostitution isn't formal in Sudan; it's a secret job for poor women, and university students, too. Yes, university students, lots of them. Girls do it for school money, mostly with rich men with vehicles. Most of them just go in the vehicles, doing oral sex.

When I was a student in the anthropology department, one of our professors was doing research about prostitution among students in universities. I was one of the research assistants. His study was funded by the government. The government knew it was a problem, they wanted to know about the problem, but the whole study was secret because of course they would not publicly talk about such things.

I worked with the United Nations Development Programme on this for a year, then I did research on civil society for the European Commission. At the same time I was working on my master's degree research, and a professor nominated me for a scholarship in Germany, at Martin Luther University, near Leipzig.

I liked Germany. I learned a bit of German. *Ich bin eine studentin...* Berlin is fine, other cities were fine, but in Halle, my small town, I couldn't be outside after dark, being African, black. That's what they'd say. I mean, I would go to the nice shops and when I would leave, they'd ask to search my bag. I just got angry most of the time and I gave back what I bought from them. Once I went with a colleague to go shopping for a digital camera, and three security guards came near, just to watch us. I showed them my credit card, and okay, they relaxed.

I went to Austria, to participate in the International Conference for Sudanese Women. It was filled with NGOs, Sudanese women from all over, coming together to form a network. But we didn't build our network. We just chatted, we ate together, and we scattered again. It was a chance, a good chance. But there was no result from it.

I visited Norway and France. It was all nice, but I didn't want to live in Europe. I wanted to go back to Sudan, to do something good. And besides, as an anthropologist, Africa is our place to work. You know, sociologists can study the communities anywhere, and some anthropologists say they study "primitive communities," but I hate that term. Some say "underdeveloped communities," but even that word gives this connotation that it's missing something, like it hasn't done well enough.

Some say "traditional communities," but all communities have traditions. I don't know how I can say it. But Africa is our place to be.

When I returned from Europe, I got a job as a program development officer for the United States Agency for International Development, USAID. I loved working with Americans because they have money. Not for me, of course! I mean they have money for the projects. And they're fast. You're a program development officer, and you say, "Look, this project is good," and they do it. Immediately. To see a need, to develop a proposal, it can take just three days.

I did post-conflict projects in the Nuba Mountains, in the SPLM-controlled areas. As we say, the people needed dividends. They just signed a peace agreement in the Nuba Mountains, and we don't want them to go back to war. But they don't have water, they don't have

MUBTAGA MOHAMED ALI MOHAMED

hospitals, they don't have anything. So we have to get them to trust in the peace.

We built lots of water wells. In that area, nomads just forage wherever they and their animals can get water. And the water is usually near the farmers. So they have these clashes and these fights, especially during the droughts. When you give those nomads water wells, then they will not go to fight with the farmers. The farmers are Nuba; they're affiliated with the SPLM. The nomads are Arab, and they're supported by the National Congress Party. Both sides give guns to their people. So if you don't have enough water, suddenly you have a fight. It's the politics of water.

* * *

The Nuba Mountains are a place of indigenous people who have been living there for thousands and thousands of years. Their history is full of suffering, and lots of exposure to slavery. Enslaved by everyone from outside, and even by Nuba themselves—some tribes enslave other tribes. They're considered inferior people, second-class citizens. And there was just this terrible war against the government.

I spent lots of time down there. It's always been an attractive place for anthropologists. Groups used to flee from one mountain to another, escaping slave traders or invaders, and they would just live in isolation for so long, keeping their language and traditions. So now you have, like, thirty-nine languages, and so many different traditions, sometimes within kilometers of each other.

I tell you, they're very good people. They are very honest. The land is green, even up high in the mountains. If they like you, they give you land, first thing. Even now, the only piece of land I own is in the Nuba Mountains. I built a house there out of grass and mud. I could live with the people, make falafel at home and sell it in the market while I was doing my research. I had my own name in the village and everything. They give you names based on whether you're the oldest, second oldest, third oldest in your family. So me, I'm Toto, because I'm the second. I was happy there. These days, I never miss Khartoum, I never miss my hometown of Atbara, but I miss the Nuba Mountains.

MY HUSBAND SINCE THE FIRST DAY WE MET

I was in Koda, the SPLM headquarters in the Nuba Mountains, for a conference. I saw a man named al-Taher; he was a leader in the SPLM group. And that day I realized he would be something in my life. A friend of mine had a camera, so I asked to her take some photos of me with the leaders. First thing, I went over to him, he was standing and smiling at me, and I asked my friend to take a photo. I still have that picture, of course.

I was at the conference to join discussions on land issues, but al-Taher was in the peace negotiations working group. I just went to the land group for a while, but then I said, Hey, that peace negotiations group, I'm kind of interested in that. At the end of the session, I asked him for copies of papers, copies of the peace agreements, copies of anything. He said, "Sure, come pick it up tonight." At night I went to the building, and his friend was there with a copy for me. So I said, "Okay, thanks, but where is al-Taher?"

He said, "I can't tell you. Al-Taher is a leader; security can't show you his place at night."

I said, "Please, can you, can you just take me? I mean, I have all these peace agreements memorized anyhow. I don't want these papers; I want to meet him!"

The friend finally accepted, and I met al-Taher in one of the huts. We stayed up until the middle of the night, talking about Sudan, about politics, about our lives. He had joined the rebel army when he was eighteen, to fight for a new Sudan.

We met the next day, and the day after. I stayed in that area long after the conference had ended, and we kept meeting each other, and started to know each other. I called my family, and told them I wanted to introduce them to this man. They asked about his background, and when I told them, they said no. They said I could not be with a slave like this man. I am educated, I am pretty, I am an Arab from the North, and my family has descended from one of the prophet Mohammed's clans. I cannot marry this black slave. They said no, and that was it. My troubles started from that day, when my family said no.

In March 2006, I returned from the Nuba Mountains to Khartoum. Al-Taher came with me, because he had been chosen to represent the SPLM in the parliament. It was his first time coming to the North and I was with him.

Of course, we tried to visit my family in Atbara. But it was just an argument. I insisted. My older brother allowed me to bring him inside for tea. Then al-Taher left, and I stayed. When he left, my brother just started to yell at me. "How in the hell can you marry him?"

I argued, "It's my freedom, it's my right to choose who I want to marry. I don't consider him a slave." I said, "Our family isn't really Arab anyhow," and that's when they started to beat me. To hurt me.

So I disappeared.

I could only think, "Why in hell did I try to do this?" I mean, if we wanted to marry in Sudan we would need their approval. So we had to try. But they just made it impossible, made it dangerous. We knew, even if we went to court to apply to marry, they would find us. My father and one of my brothers are police officers now. They could have found us. They could have hurt me in court. They could have hurt me after we left the court. All that mattered was I was marrying a black guy, having relations with him. To them, if you marry a black slave, it means you're not honorable, not disciplined. I mean, he is a Muslim! And if you ask his family, they will say they are Arabs, too. That's the craziness! But my family saw him as black.

Now understand, in Sudan there's this voice of tribalism that's just shouting. The politics come strong, and they just speak with a focus on one tribal identity, like, being Arab, being Arab, being Arab! Arabs are honored people, they say, so the others come to feel subordinated. They have their own identity, they say. They want to protect it so they start to also have their own voice. This makes Arabs cling even stronger to their identity. And then, of course, the violence comes.

My brothers followed me back to Khartoum. One time they came to my office at USAID. They ran in, they tried to pull me from my office, saying they were taking me back home. My colleagues had to control them, and had to pull me away, and my colleagues had to get a driver to drive me away. I went to my man, and he took me to a friend's house, where I could be safe. I collected my camera and my computer that belonged to USAID. I wrote a resignation note to them. I sent the note, the camera, and the computer to the office. My brothers knew the office, so I could not go back.

We went to Kordofan,[3] to meet al-Taher's family. They were not so easy, either. Everything seemed unusual to them. His sisters missed the honors of coming to propose marriage, as the sisters of the groom can do. The family dreamed of their son marrying in a way that everyone would be proud. He was a parliament member. He should marry a famous family not like my family, who would ignore his family, calling them slaves. His family asked him, "Why marry a woman whose family is so unwelcoming? You should fight this," they said, "not marry this."

He just said, "Stop." He said "stop," because he's a man. He never asked for their permission. He just married me.

We went to Egypt, and on the eighth of October, 2006, we were married, here in Cairo. A simple ceremony. It did not have great

[3] A region of central Sudan.

meaning to me, just an official thing. You know, I had felt like he was my husband since the first day we had met.

THEY CANNOT CLEAN THEIR
HONOR IF SHE REMAINS ALIVE

My relatives could have killed me if they had found us trying to marry. I mean it. They just could never imagine me having a son from a black man. They would punish me and the easiest thing they can do is just kill me to clean their honor, because now they feel dirty.

It wouldn't be the first time my family has killed for honor. I remember when I was a child we had a cousin named Selima. She got pregnant, even though her husband had died years before. She had many daughters and sons, but no husband.

Selima was still in the hospital with her new baby when the family came and the police came. They took her to court, with the baby to show evidence. In court they took the girl from her, to put in a house for illegal children, owned by the city.

They took Selima home, with the permission of the court. They shaved her hair. They tied her to the bed, and closed the door of the room. And they just let her starve to death. And you know who participated? Her own son! Her son, her uncles. Her husband's relatives. Even my family, my mother, my aunt, and my uncle gave their support to killing her. They cannot clean their honor if she remains alive, they said. Because, how do you say it? The candle will still burn if she is alive. I am sure if my family would catch me, the same would happen to me. I don't think my mother would accept, I don't think she would agree, but there is nothing she could do. It is my brothers that could do something.

After we married, I went back to Sudan, but not to Khartoum. I went to Juba, in the South. I contacted USAID, and they said they could give me a job in Juba. I asked them to fly me through Kenya instead of through Khartoum, just to be safe.

I was in Juba for about nine months. It's very expensive of course, because it's the capital of the South, you know. Lots of international experts and investors—Italians, Greeks, Ugandans, Kenyans, Americans—so they just raise the prices for everything, especially the houses. A tent is like one hundred American dollars to sleep for one night! But it's very green. My husband would come down from Khartoum to visit me when he wasn't working in the parliament. I had a good job doing peace-building projects with USAID. It was fantastic.

I had to leave Juba when my family found me. They were very clever, I tell you. My brother just targeted me. It was like a game. He followed the links in the social network. I mean, I am a northern lady living in Juba. There are few of us. My mistake was to go to the Nuba Mountains again, to visit. My brother was calling all my friends all the time, and eventually he heard I had visited, had heard I was still with USAID. And there are only two real USAID offices, one in Khartoum, one in Juba. So they figured I was in Juba.

A friend of mine from Atbara called me. "Mubtaga," she said, "you have to get out because your brothers are coming." It was my mother that had told my friend. She didn't want me killed. So she had told my friend, "Please talk to Mubtaga through the computer"—she calls mobile phones computers—"please tell Mubtaga through the computer that her brothers know she is in Juba." So I had to leave Juba.

My husband flew me back to Khartoum. He used his parliament pass and took me through the VIP, without the process of security. I stayed in Khartoum for like twenty days. Not in my husband's house, of course. I hid at a friend's house. I came out sometimes, but only with a veil. No public buses, only taxis. After those days, it was another VIP ticket, and this time I came to Cairo.

This all just happened weeks ago. I arrived in Cairo in June of 2007.

FED UP WITH THESE GAMES

I'm fed up with these games. I don't feel much safer in Cairo. There are so many Sudanese here. That social network is here, and that is how my brother found me last time. In Cairo I can't be exposed much, but at the same time I don't want to hide myself.

And now I've had to quit all of my life, quit my career. What should I do? I cannot go back to Khartoum University. If I go back to Germany, as a researcher, I could someday write my PhD. But my English is the problem. To be an anthropologist I have to have perfect English. My English is good, but not great. I learned it in university classes, and at work, but I still consider myself not so good at English. If I improve my English, maybe I could go to Germany to study.

Now I want to apply for international scholarships through UNHCR. I want to send my application to Australia. I want to go and take the TOEFL if there's a chance.[4] I want to do a lot of things that can help me.

My husband, all he seeks now is to secure me. He cannot protect me by following me every place I go, because he has work. There's little he can do from Khartoum. I mean, he has a diplomatic passport, right? But I'm not in that passport because there is no page for wives in these special passports. Pages for kids, but not for wives. So I cannot really move.

I imagine if I had a different family, or at least if I didn't have these brothers, life would be so good for me now. I could be something in Khartoum. I never imagined myself leaving my country and living like a refugee. Never, never. I was in Germany, you know, and I could have stayed in Germany if I really wanted to. Sudanese were leaving the South all through the 1990s, and I could have asked for

---

[4] TOEFL (Test of English as a Foreign Language) is a required exam for admission to many college and university programs.

refugee protection, for all those times being beaten for having my veil fall from my head. But I stayed. Now I don't think I'll ever get back. I don't know. Maybe God can do something. Maybe a miracle.

There are many categories of Sudanese refugees here in Cairo. I've spoken to them. There are young people: they're desperate people, frustrated, often racist like the Egyptians are, lost, sometimes in gangs. That's one category.

Another one is more educated, open-minded, most of them communist—artists, painters, musicians, seeking freedom to express their life. They're here in Cairo because they have more freedom of expression. They can separate themselves, enjoy their art, drink wine, go out, and nobody asks about them. That's one of the things we lack in Sudan. They can have it in Cairo.

The other category is businessmen, who sell their expensive houses in Sudan for like one hundred thousand dollars, and they come here and buy four apartments, lease three, and stay in one. Then they apply to the UN for protection. They say they were subordinated in Sudan. They maybe say they're from Darfur, but they've really never seen Darfur; they're just telling lies.

So many people tell lies because they want to get out. I think they have the right, because Sudan is a desperate place to live, not a healthy place for many people. People come and lie to live in a better place.

When I came here people told me that if I lie to the UN I won't be caught, and that I'll get protection. They said if I tell the truth I won't get protection. That's what all the Sudanese say. "Say you're from Darfur, or you've been abused by security, or something like this." Since the protests, the UN wants to get rid of Sudanese refugees, they say. So they give us yellow cards and keep us waiting. There are hundreds, thousands of them that are waiting. And people told me, unless you tell a lie, they won't accept you. But I'm not from Darfur, and I haven't been abused by security. I never told a lie.

I hope the UN will understand. They are pragmatic people, I think. If they follow international laws, they will give me my rights. I used to be like them, you know, staff with the UN. I have my case documented. I have a letter from USAID. I mean, I'm not going to sacrifice my career, all the good things I was doing in Sudan, just to be a refugee. It wasn't an easy decision for me. People dream of working with the UN or with USAID. And they'll look at my CV, at what I was doing, "Okay," they'll say, "university in Germany. UN. USAID." If they look and they are fair, they will say, "Yes, this woman would not go, would not leave her career, leave her husband, come to Egypt without a job, unless she has a serious problem."

If they do say no, I thought I could just stay in Cairo, and do junk work. Or go to Libya and work as a teacher in a primary school. Many are going to Israel, but if I go to Israel that means I would just close out all chance to go back to Sudan.

Either way, everyone says I need to find some work, because I'll have to wait at least a year for UNHCR to decide on my file.

HAVE YOU COME TO CAIRO FOR NOTHING?

I started my file at UNHCR two days ago. I left home at seven a.m. By nine a.m., I was there at the offices in 6 October City, and the queue was not very long. I sat there, waiting for my turn to come. I gave the guy my papers. I spoke in English, and I told him, "I'm Sudanese, and these are my papers." I said, "Last week you gave me this file and you asked me to fill it out, and this is a copy of my passport, and this is a copy of the passport of my husband."

He asked me in Arabic, "Is your husband with you?"

I told him, "No, he's in Sudan."

He asked, "Have you come to Cairo for nothing, or has something made you come here to Cairo?"

I told him, "Something pushed me to come here to Cairo; I need protection, and I used to work for the UN." He looked at my papers, and he saw my documents from my work with UNDP. He went to his computer and figured out an appointment for me. He took my file and wrote FIP. He means VIP, I think, but he wrote it FIP. And he said after three days I can come for registration. So tomorrow I will go for registration. I will be registered and they will give me a yellow card.

So I'm waiting. I can't go to the SPLM offices here, even though I want to. I'd love to get a job with the consulate. But my family knows that I'm in the SPLM, and wherever I go that means I have a link to the SPLM, and the first place they can start to search after me is the SPLM office. I like the SPLM, and if I were a politician and I was against the government they could protect me, but how can they protect me from my brother who can come to my house at any time? It would cost my brother two hundred dollars to come to Cairo, and one taxi to go to SPLM offices, and ask them, "Do you know Mubtaga? I'm her brother and I lost her mobile number, can I know where she is living?" Someone might say, "Yeah, brother of Mubtaga, you are welcome to her. She is our colleague, and she is living with Omar. Omar is living in blah blah blah these days; here is his address. Oh, you don't know the place? I will take you." Next thing, I open the door, here is my brother, and I'm flat on my face. I don't want that happening. I mean, the community is so close. Everybody knows where everyone is, knows what everybody is doing. I cannot shake hands with Sudanese people I meet here and tell them, "Nice to meet you, but please don't tell my family you met me here." It's not that they are bad people. But I cannot trust them, because they do not know my story. So I have to keep a low profile in Cairo.

I did, of course, forget myself one time. Rasha played a concert here last week, a beautiful Sudanese singer. And I just forgot myself, just danced until I was at the front of the stage. I did it, and then after a while I just ran out of the theater. At least those people who saw me they didn't see me for long, and if they knew me, they don't know where I'm living.

* * *

I think being a refugee will be hard for me. It was a very difficult decision to make. What can I do? I have no other place to go. I love my husband. I love him very much. I never take a step back and wonder, "Oh, why did I do this? Why did I ruin my family relations, why?" I never take this step back. Whenever I think of all this, I think I am doing good because I love him. He works hard in Khartoum. I hope soon we'll be with a child. I'm going to work for this.

Sometimes I picture my future being in Saudi Arabia. Sometimes I picture it in Egypt, in a small apartment, desperate. Sometimes working in small NGOs here in Cairo, sometimes in America, working like a machine. Sometimes I am in Australia, working doing research in one of the universities, studying indigenous Australian people, Aborigines.

I'm not desperate, by the way. I still have a hope, even if I laugh when I say that outloud. One day I will be a good anthropologist, I'm sure. I just want to be patient.

People must know themselves well, know what they want from the life, and work hard for it. We just stand and adjust to whatever circumstances we go through. Tomorrow is another day. That's it.

{As of January 2008, Mubtaga remains in Cairo. She is a registered refugee with UNHCR.}

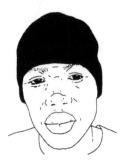

MATHOK AGUEK

AGE: *23*
TRIBE: *Dinka*
BIRTHPLACE: *Aeyid, South Sudan*
INTERVIEWED IN: *Cairo, Egypt*

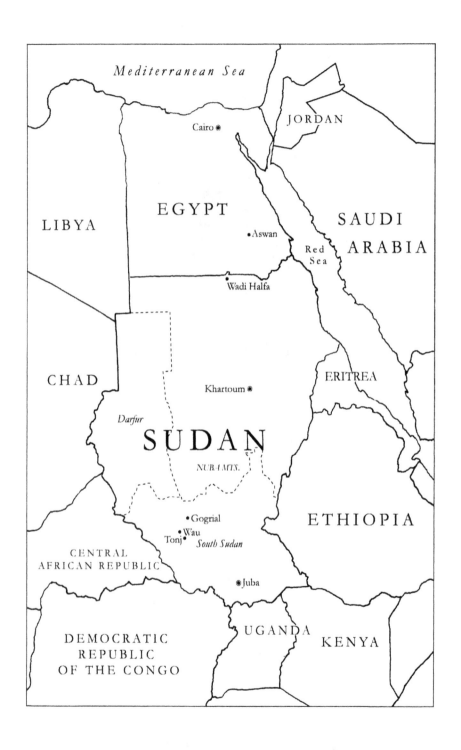

WE LIVE ANGRY LIVES

It took three months to find a member of a Sudanese street gang willing to tell his story. Mathok arrived to be interviewed with only fifteen minutes of advance notice. He spoke Arabic late into the night and left just as discreetly. During the three hours of interviewing, no subject was off-limits.

My name is Mathok. My father's name is Aguek. My family is from the village of Aeyid, in Southern Sudan. I was born in Gogrial, in Southern Sudan, on February 1, 1985. I am Dinka.

I was five years old when my family left the South to escape the war. I only remember cows, plants, huts, and lots of empty space, with mountains and forests. I only know that it was too dangerous for us. I was too young to remember anything else.

When we left our home in Gogrial, we didn't go directly to Khartoum. We stayed in the city of Tonj for a few years and then in the city of Wau for a few years—both cities are in the South. I was about twelve when we finally got to Khartoum. We left my mother in Wau, and she stayed there for five years, until my father brought her to rejoin us in Khartoum.

My mother is a housewife. My father was an officer in the Sudanese army—many southern men worked for the government, because it was a good job. My father is married to another woman as well as my mother. I was always closer with my father. He is a calm man. He is not taken by anger easily, but when he gets angry, he's very tough. There were always many children in his house—I have nine brothers and five sisters—and each of us had problems. He used to be so patient, but things would pile up, and then maybe he would explode over a small mistake. The house worked well, though. When troubles happened, we would solve them together.

In Khartoum, I didn't start school until I was about twelve years old. I hardly went to school because I worked so much. During the vacations, especially, I would work so much to prepare for the next school session, to get money for clothes and registration. I would work in the markets, sometimes selling water, sometimes selling plastic bags.

I loved to play basketball, so I would try to buy shorts and T-shirts. I have always loved basketball. When I was young, everyone used to play football, but I preferred throwing and catching the ball. Then I heard about basketball, and that was it. Basketball is my sport. I play the position of playmaker—I think you call it point guard in America. Manute Bol was a Sudanese man who played basketball in America, and he's my step-uncle.

My mother was very sick for a long time. She had problems with her heart, so she was very weak. After some time in Khartoum, my father saved enough money for my mother's surgery. I remember they had to put tubes in her heart. It was known to be a very difficult and serious surgery. When the surgery succeeded, and my mother recovered, there was momentous happiness for all. She still takes medications, but my mother is doing well.

The years in Khartoum after my mother had surgery were happy years, really. My father decided to have another child. Everyone was nervous, because my mother was still weak, but she delivered a healthy baby boy for my father. They named the baby Motoum—in our language it means something like "experiment."

COMING TO CAIRO

My story of coming to Cairo begins when I failed my secondary school exams. I failed because of money, really—money controls my life. I had to work so much that I hardly went to school. When I failed the exams, it was the end of school for me. I stopped playing basketball, too, and just started working in the markets.

Things got better when I started selling cell phones. I started selling batteries, used phones, and phone covers. I would buy everything second-hand and then sell it. I'd buy something for thirty Sudanese pounds (US$15) and then sell it for thirty-five. I'd take the extra five for my pocket. I did well in this business. Sometimes I could make US$100 in a day. I started buying new clothes, going to new places. I had more freedom with this money.

With the cell phone business, I saved up some money, and I got this idea to come to Cairo and find another chance at education. That was my whole plan—come to Cairo, start school. I told my parents, and they refused. I just kept insisting and insisting. It was all I would speak about. After some time, they said, "Okay, if it is your wish, go." I got some more cell phones and sold them fast, and soon I had enough money to go to Egypt.

I got a visa with the help of someone I knew at the market, a guy who also worked at the passport office. He and my father helped get me out of my military service, too. I came to Cairo on the normal route, to Halfa, then a boat to Aswan and a bus to Cairo. I arrived in Cairo in October 2005. I was twenty years old.

I had this idea that everything would be okay in Egypt. The people in Khartoum who had been to Egypt said that life there was good. I heard I might also find a chance to go to Canada or the U.S., and that made me eager to come. I was also told that when you walk in the street, you might hear some abusive words, but I should just ignore it. That's exactly what happened here. I kept hearing bad words—*samara, hunga bunga, chokolata*—and I ignored it. But it did make me feel uncomfortable.

For the first two weeks in Cairo, I stayed with a friend I knew from our neighborhood in Khartoum. In Cairo, he shared a flat with several other Sudanese guys. Then my aunt came to the city, and she asked me to come and stay with her. I didn't really want to do it, but I took my bags and went to her flat.

As soon as I arrived in Cairo, I discovered that the situation was bad. I went straight to one of the schools near the bus station. They asked me for my certificates, but I hadn't brought any papers with me from Sudan. Someone told me to go to the American University in Cairo, because they have classes for refugees. The problem was that it was far from home, and it would be too expensive to get transportation there every day.

Within a week I got a job in a plastics company. They produced cleaning tools, and my job was to put together pieces of mops and brooms. Selling cell phones in Khartoum was a much better job. It gave me more freedom, and more money too. In Cairo, I would just go to work in the morning, and then spend the night in the apartment.

I only kept the plastics job for a few months before I dropped it.

I arrived in Cairo when the protests in Mustafa Mahmoud had already started. I heard about it as soon as I arrived. After a few months in the city, I went to sit with the demonstrators in the park.

I went because I heard that Sudanese were sitting there and asking for more assistance. By the time I got to the park it was winter, and it was cold. People wore blankets. I had my blanket with me, and I just sat down. Most of the day we would just sit, but I would help to get water and cook food, and I would help to keep order. There was a group of us young men that would help deal with conflicts and troubles within the community of protesters. For example, someone would be sitting in a certain place inside the park, and he would move for a while and then come back, and he would find someone else sitting in his place. They would start to argue, and we would come and intervene. We would make sure nobody fought.

I wasn't there at the end of the protests. I was at home. Friends were calling me from the site, telling me that police were surrounding the place. I was too afraid to go there.

In the end, the protests did not help me at all. They helped nobody. They only created more hate between the city of Cairo and the Sudanese people here. I have no refugee registration card here in Cairo—I am not a protected refugee. And I am not a real refugee, I know. I came to Cairo by choice. But my family had to leave our village in Southern Sudan because of the war. In the past, our people lived in conflict, but I recognize that now the time is different. I just came to Cairo for opportunity. I understand why I am not a protected refugee, but I still think people like me deserve assistance here. This city is a difficult place for people like me.

LOST IN A DIFFERENT WAY

I will tell you about the Lost Boys. The Lost Boys are a Sudanese street gang, like the Outlaws, and the B.I.G. gang. Sometimes you can see them on the streets in Sudanese neighborhoods. My neighborhood of Abbassia is a Lost Boys neighborhood. People used to attack and steal from the Sudanese in Abbassia, so the young men agreed to get together to form a group to protect themselves. They got the name from stories about the Sudanese boys in Kenya who went to the U.S. The Lost Boys in Cairo are lost in a different way.

Until last year, I would just stand with them on the streets sometimes and talk to them. Most of them have no work or school, but some of them are good people. When I was at parties in other neighborhoods, I found people would treat me with hostility, with anger, like I was their enemy. They would say, "You are living in Abbassia, which means you are one of the Lost Boys." I knew there was sometimes violence against enemy gangs and even just enemy neighborhoods.

Last summer they had a free English starter's course at the American University, and guys from the gangs went to the classes. I went along with them. Sometimes when I left the class, there would be guys from the Outlaws gang meeting me in the street, asking me for information concerning the Lost Boys. I kept telling them that I didn't know anything, that I wasn't with them. But I kept getting harassed, and they would chase me away. Eventually I quit the course, because I was too scared to keep going.

The threats got worse and worse, even in Abbassia, when another gang would come to fight. I saw people attacked and injured in front of me, in my own neighborhood. I knew that the Outlaws were sending spies to hang around Abbassia and check where the Lost Boys were standing that day. Those spies saw me with the Lost Boys, and so everyone thought I was a Lost Boy.

It was in 2007 that I finally joined the Lost Boys myself. I didn't even have to say anything—I just stood with them for longer and longer, and they started to know I was with them. Then I started taking swords, and I joined their attacks. With the Lost Boys, I have protection.

NOT JUST A FIGHT

What's going on between these gangs in not just a fight. The reason behind it all is that all of us boys had ambitions and things we wanted to do, but we failed to do them. Some of us want good work, but we can't find it. Some of us would like to study, but we can't find a chance. When you feel that you have nothing to do, and you spend the whole day doing nothing… that's the reason why all of this is happening.

We stand on the streets and speak with each other about normal things, like girls, music, and basketball. We'll make plans about attacks. Sometimes, after that, we'll start an attack. We attack people from other neighborhoods. Sometimes while we are standing on our streets, we face attacks from the other gangs. When they come for us, we have to run and bring our hidden weapons. When one gang attacks another, some get injured, and others run away.

When we attack, we usually attack everyone who's out in the street. I attack people, too, but I don't like to injure them. I don't cut with my sword. I like slapping with the side of my sword. Sometimes I beat people with my hands. We attack gang members and other people; we attack Sudanese and Egyptians, also. We attack everyone.

When we attack, my only intention is to take the other gang's weapons. I don't steal people's things, but some of the other guys do. I'm against the idea of stealing. My calling is for the fighting and the weapons.

I've only had two incidents with the police. The first was to report my lost passport, but nobody ever found it. The second time was when a group of Sudanese attacked some Nigerians. The police came to our neighborhood and took us, but it was a mistake; we had nothing to do with it. They realized quickly that we were not the people they wanted. I spoke nicely to them and explained everything. They realized I'm not a troublemaker, and they released me even before we reached the station. But many other guys in the Lost Boys have been arrested, and we have all been chased before.

EVEN IF WE STOPPED FIGHTING

The Sudanese community in Cairo tells us to stop what we are doing. The Lost Boys did stop fighting for a while, but the other gangs did not. When the Outlaws attacked us again, even the parents and older brothers understood that we needed to retaliate. They understood that even if we stopped fighting, the other side would not stop.

The difference between the Outlaws and the Lost Boys is that the Outlaws get money from the NCP.[1] During the protests at Mustafa Mahmoud, NCP agents from the embassy took some boys and got them drunk, then sent them back to the protests to start fights and make a mess so it would look bad for all the Sudanese community there. The NCP wanted this, because the people in the protests all opposed NCP rule. Those boys who got drunk with the NCP became the Outlaws.

If you ask the Outlaws, they will say that we are the ones who take money from the NCP. But you can just sit with each of our groups. Sit with us, sit with them, and speak about this. Their lies will come out.

We only get help from friends who left for abroad and have jobs in places like Canada or Australia. Sometimes we call them and say we are facing financial troubles, and they send us some money.

Some people in Cairo have tried to help us. There was a guy named Jacob—he was the one who helped start the English classes at the American University last year and asked the gang members to come. Unfortunately, it was too difficult to bring the Outlaws and Lost Boys in the same place to study, so the gang members didn't really come. I went, because at that time I still wasn't a member. Jacob started some smaller classes in Abbassia, too. People thought the classes were good, and our people, the Dinka, need these classes so much. But the classes stopped. I don't know why.

We still have parties for the gang. We play dirty music—crazy, fast music, and rap. I prefer the slower songs, though. It calms you. When you dance slow with a girl, you can dance quietly, and that

[1] National Congress Party. The ruling party of the Sudanese government.

is what I like best. I like to dance to the R&B singer named Joe—that's his name, just Joe. I like Celine Dion, Mariah Carey, R. Kelly, and Bob Marley. Until recently, I had a girlfriend named Abuk. She moved back to Sudan. Right now I don't see any good girls, but there are lots of girls who hang out with the Lost Boys. Maybe there will be a new woman coming to me.

I wear what Lost Boys always wear: a white T-shirt, because white matches with everything, and then a basketball jersey on top. I'm wearing black pants, and basketball shoes. I'm wearing my baseball cap because I just braided my hair, but the braids are still too short. I'm not ready to show it to people on the street. My style is hip-hop. I see singers dressing like this on the television and on the internet, and I want to dress like them. In the Lost Boys, we all dress like this.

I don't drink. Many of the guys in the Lost Boys do drink. Some drink a lot, and others drink with respect. Some smoke weed. I don't like drinking. I never drink at all. Nobody makes that a problem for me.

My life is better since I joined the Lost Boys. With them, I don't feel bored anymore. I feel like they are like my brothers. The thing that bothers me is that now there is peace in Sudan, but here in Cairo we are fighting. It's hard to believe. You know, the truth is we are all the same. We are Sudanese after all. I mean, Outlaws and Lost Boys are from the same tribes! Why do we fight each other here? Why don't we live in peace like before, without fear of each other?

We need a ceasefire among the gangs. We need people who will sit down with each party, listen to their problems and difficulties and start to solve them, separately. Solve Lost Boys' problems and difficulties. Solve Outlaws problems and difficulties. And then gradually join us together or bring us together in a meeting to mediate between us. We live angry lives. If nobody intervenes, the violence will continue.

One problem is that the Outlaws leader and the Lost Boys leader are both in prison right now. We have secondary leaders in charge right now. Really, these days we just listen to anyone with a good idea about what to do or how to attack. With so many leaders in prison, or leaving Cairo, the gangs have now deteriorated. People say our gang is more deteriorated than the Outlaws. But I say, the good thing is that in the Lost Boys we have people with brave hearts. When we go on an attack, we run forward and we don't look back. The Outlaws know this, and that's why they are still afraid of the Lost Boys' attacks.

SOMETHING BAD IS GOING TO HAPPEN

On June 20, 2007, the refugee community of Cairo met at the American University for World Refugee Day. During the event, members of the Lost Boys hired vans and ambushed several members of the Outlaws on the street outside of the university campus. Maliah Bekam, age twenty-four, was killed when he was struck in the head with a machete. Several other people were injured.

I was at the American University Refugee Day. It was a celebration for the whole refugee community in Cairo, people from all countries. Everyone knew about the Sudanese gangs, though. They had metal detectors at the entrance to the event, and many security men to keep peace inside the event. The celebration was in a courtyard on the university campus. There were big buildings all around, and then a field in the middle where we had the celebrations.

Most of the gang members at the celebration were from the Outlaws. For a while, I was the only one around from the Lost Boys, and it was scary, since they were many, and I was only one. I heard threatening words. Guys were saying, "We are ready to kill you." They said it to Lost Boys, and even just regular people from our neighborhood of Abbassia. The tensions were getting high, and some people started to leave, but I remained.

One of the leaders of the Outlaws, a guy named Harvey, came up to me. He knows me, and he is afraid of me. He said to me, "Mathok, something bad is going to happen." He said that the Lost Boys should not be there. I said to him, "Whatever will happen will happen." I ignored him, and when guys came up to me making the hand-signs of the Outlaws, I ignored them, too. Some of the Outlaws starting dancing in a group, and one from the group took off his shirt, which had a photo of Tupac on it. He put the Tupac shirt on the ground, and they all started to dance around it. Tupac is like a hero to the Outlaws—they take their name from Tupac's rap group.

While the Outlaws were dancing around the shirt, one of the Lost Boys just broke into the group and starting stomping on the shirt, on Tupac's picture. A fight was about to start. All the Lost Boys ran to the south side of the field. I found out later that a group of Lost Boys had made a plan to send some of their younger members to the field and then to lure the Outlaws outside the event.

At that point I was far from the entrance, so I didn't see much of what happened. I saw people starting to leave, though, and I started running myself. I ran out of the celebration to the street, and I saw the trap. The leaders and elders from the Lost Boys were out there with swords. There was a fight. A boy from the Outlaws was slashed on the head, and he was killed. Another was stabbed in the back but he lived.

I ran away as fast as I could. In front of me, one of the Lost Boys was running, holding a sword with blood on it. I ran up to him and yelled at him to throw his weapon. He threw it. We were being chased by police, but we were too fast, and the officer just stopped, took the sword from the ground, and turned back. The guy running with me was confused, so some of us took care of him and we all got back home safely.

In the days afterwards, many of my friends were arrested. They are still in prison, and we do not know what will happen to them.

I AM NOT PROUD

I know that everyone will say we are not refugees, that we are criminals killing each other. Everyone will say we have no principles and no goals. You will say, "Refugees are people escaping from unprotected places and seeking protection. But look at you—facing problems and then making problems as well!" You will say to me, "You ask for a solution for your problem, and then you start another problem!" And when you say that, I will agree with you.

I tell you, I am not proud of being in the Lost Boys. But I was compelled to join, because it was my only chance for security. The Egyptian police do nothing for us. They only help if you pay them bribes. Besides, they have enough problems with their own citizens, and that is their priority. I didn't join the Lost Boys because I wanted to be like them, or wanted to fight like them, or because I admired the fame. As I have told you, I simply faced problems, and I could not go anywhere else.

Look at my life: Last month I worked and managed to pay my rent, but this month I don't know if I will have enough. My new job is at an advertising company. I'm there during the day, cleaning the place and making tea for the other workers. It's an okay job, because the people at the office are respectable, and they respect me. But I only make five hundred Egyptian pounds (US$90) in a month. It's not enough for eating and paying the rent.

All my family is still in Sudan. From time to time I speak to them on the telephone, and we speak of normal things. Last time I called, I heard that my second youngest brother had just started the second grade. When I left Sudan, he was just learning to walk. One of my sisters passed her exams and is going to study to be a doctor. Two other brothers are already at university.

My parents don't know I'm in a gang. They would be shocked. I would not dare to tell them about my life here.

I have plans for the future: I want to travel either to Canada or Australia to study. Last year I applied for resettlement to Australia, but I was rejected. I will keep trying though, because I won't go back to Sudan. I can't return to the same place, with no education, with nothing.

I would like to study English. When my father studied in Southern Sudan, all his education was in English. I'd like to learn like that. I like reading philosophy, too. My cousin here has a lot of good books of philosophy. I like reading lessons about life, about how to simplify things, how to understand the world, and to express yourself, and to communicate.

I don't expect anyone to feel sorry for me. But people should understand that some of us need a hand to help us. I have no education, no money, no security. Without a hand to help me, I cannot be pulled up. This is the message that is important. I feel great sadness. I expected to do everything in Cairo, and I have achieved nothing.

I hope my story brings someone to advise me and support me, to help me educate myself, or find a better place. Maybe someone could help me improve my basketball. I play basketball at the big Italian church in Zamalek. We have a team called New Sudan, and we play in the league. It has nothing to do with the gangs. Everyone on our team is at about the same level of skill, but we need better players to come and help us improve our play. Maybe basketball teams in other countries can learn about our players and help us. I would love to play on the national team of my country someday.

{In October, 2007—six weeks after our interview—Mathok Aguek was killed in a fight between members of the Lost Boys and the Outlaws. He is buried in Khartoum, Sudan.}

NADIA EL-KAREEM

AGE: *18*
TRIBE: *Masalit*
BIRTHPLACE: *Greda, Darfur*
INTERVIEWED IN: *Cairo, Egypt*

LIFE, DEATH, THERE'S NO
BIG DIFFERENCE

The outside of Nadia's building is dilapidated, with cement crumbling and bricks scattered in the stairwell. But inside is a clean, sparse, sunlit apartment. Nadia served cups of Sprite and spoke of the destruction of her village, the loss of her family, and her struggles to make a life in Egypt in the three years since. With her two-year-old daughter Sima rolling around quietly beside her on the couch, Nadia insisted that she wanted nothing other than to return to Darfur and to return now, no matter the danger. On the day of this interview, she was in the middle of negotiating a compromise with her husband. They would go back to Sudan, but to the capital city of Khartoum instead of Darfur. Nadia paused throughout her story to ask advice on the most efficient way to get back to her country. She wanted out of Egypt.

My name is Nadia el-Kareem, and I was born on March 7, 1990. My tribe is the Masalit. I was born in Greda, a village in Darfur. I do not know where in Darfur. I have no education, and I don't know north, south, east, or west. I know my village is close to the town of Nyala. It's a small village of normal people. People go to their jobs and then come home again.

My father would go out to the farm and then come back to his house to stay with his children. It was not his own farm. It belonged to an old man I saw only once in my life. My father was not an educated man.

My mother was just a housewife. She had to cook, and she had to take care of her kids. Sometimes she took the cows out to eat grass. She was smiley, she chatted a lot with people, and she hugged a lot.

I don't know where my father is or where my mother is, but on my way to Egypt I met a lady who said she knew my parents. She told me, "Your father and mother died." I have two sisters and people have told me they are also dead. I have one brother. I saw him die.

I had a normal life like any girl in Darfur. I would help the cows and goats get food and water. I would clean the house and help my mother cook. I was happy. People who can stay with their parents should be happy. My cousin Muna was my best friend. We didn't really play together, but we would do chores around the house together, and when we finished we would sleep. Since the conflict, I have no idea where Muna is either.

That is all I can tell you about my childhood. The experiences I have had now are enough to make me forget everything about my childhood.

THE VOICE OF GUNS

It was 2003 or 2004. I was not yet fourteen. My father was coming from the farm, and my mother was outside with the cows. I was cleaning the cows' pen. My mother came back from the field and she yelled to me, "Did you finish?" because she wanted to get the cows inside. At the same time, my father was coming back from the farm. My mother got the cows inside the pen and closed the door. My mother and I went outside together to greet my father. My brother and sisters were inside the house.

Three or four men came, wearing something around their heads. You could only see their eyes. They were armed. They were running on foot and they were holding guns. I don't know if they meant to shoot us, but they did shoot another man and his wife who were our neighbors. The armed men were speaking, but I was scared and didn't hear them. I didn't understand what they were saying. My parents told me I needed to run. They called my sisters and told them to run.

I had heard of armed people coming and shooting before. I had heard the voice of guns many times, but I had never seen anything like this before.

I saw the men shoot children from the village. A boy was playing. They shot him also. I don't know why. All of us just ran away. I was just thinking about how to run away.

It was a messy moment. My father was holding his work tools and running. We were running very fast, and we met another group coming from the opposite direction. It was another group of people fleeing the place. Everyone was confused and I don't know how, but this was when I lost my mother and father. My brother, Mohammed, took my hand, and we started running with the new group of people. We ran away to a quiet place. We tried to hide. I was trying to hide myself, and my brother was watching the area to see if people were coming to attack us.

Two or three people showed up. They looked the same, with covered heads and covered arms. Mohammed told me to hide behind a tree. They didn't see me. I hid myself well. It was a big tree and I made myself small. When they moved to one side of the tree, I moved too to hide myself. Mohammed kept watching. Then they shot my brother from the back, and they ran away. Two shots. Then they ran away.

Mohammed was bleeding. I tried to wake him up, but he didn't move. I tried to hear his breathing—nothing. I tried to make him talk—nothing. So I moved. I ran. I kept crying, running, and crying and running.

I ran for maybe fifteen minutes. I met a man named Mahmoud and his brother. I hadn't seen them before. Mahmoud said he was also from Greda. He asked me, "Why are you crying?" I told him that my brother had died. They asked me, "How do you know he's dead? Maybe he's still living." I explained to them that I tried to hear him breathing and he didn't move.

We started running together. We ran for about two hours. We kept running, and they held me sometimes to keep me running. Mahmoud's brother said we would run to Nyala. It was my first time ever leaving my village.

Mahmoud is not short, not tall, not fat. Darker skin. A very normal, kind person. He's maybe thirty years old. He was very confused and scared like me. They were all afraid like me.

In Nyala, we arrived at the central station, and I met a woman I had seen during the attack. I asked her, "You were with us when the people attacked?" She said yes, and I asked her about my parents and about my sisters. The woman said to me, "I saw that your parents and one of your sisters had been shot."

THEY SAID IT WAS NOT TO BE

Mahmoud's brother had some money to take us on a lorry from Nyala to Omdurman. We just jumped on the lorry and they drove for so long. I remember I was very thirsty. I was traumatized and I just kept crying, but I didn't feel anything really. I can't even remember how long they drove. I just remember getting out of the lorry at Omdurman. Mahmoud and his brother woke me up and said, "We have arrived. We have to get outside."

I saw a big city outside: stores for cold drinks, many people walking in the street, and many cars. The first thing I said was, "Where are we now?" They told me, "You are in Omdurman now." I asked him, "What shall we do here? I need my parents."

We went to live in a neighborhood called Dar-es-Salaam. Mahmoud's brother arranged the place. It was a room made out of mud with a small yard in front of it. Soon we had to leave though. I remember that one of the neighbors told Mahmoud and his brother, "You have to leave this place." Mahmoud went to the head of the neighborhood committee and spoke with him. I don't know the reason, but they advised him to leave the place. So we did. We went to live in a neighborhood called Khartoum Bahri. Mahmoud and his brother knew someone there, and that person helped get them a passport. They planned to go to Egypt.

I refused to go with them. I said, "What's my relation to you?" Also, it's illegal to travel with two men, to sleep with them in a house, and so on. All of this would cause trouble with the people and the government. In Sudan it's prohibited for an unmarried woman to travel with two men who are not relatives. They were definitely going, though. So I said, "Let's do what we need to do for this to be legal." Mahmoud said, "You are worried what the people will say about you for traveling with strange men." I said, "I don't care about the people. It's just not the right thing to do." Mahmoud said he would solve it. He said, "If you won't walk with strangers, then let us marry." Mahmoud was a normal age for Sudanese men to marry, but I had never heard of a girl my age, a thirteen-year-old girl, getting married.

We met a Sudanese man in the neighborhood and explained our story to him, and he agreed to act as my father for the ceremony. Then we went to a man responsible for making a marriage contract, and I was married to Mahmoud. The man gave Mahmoud a copy of the contract, and he gave a copy to me. But we stayed as normal. Mahmoud and his brother slept in one place, and I slept in a different place.

It was just in order to help me flee the country. Then they could put my name on Mahmoud's passport as his wife. If his passport says

I'm his wife, then it's okay; there's no problem for me to travel or to be with him.

In total, we were in Khartoum and Omdurman for less than a month. Of course, I was still scared. Sometimes at night I couldn't sleep. I recalled all the experiences. I saw images of killing, and I had nightmares. I heard the voices of the guns, and I would wake up and cry at night. No one ever explained to me why it all happened. I couldn't understand a reason for myself.

Still part of me wanted to return to Darfur, to search for my parents. Mahmoud and his brother reminded me that the woman in Nyala said that my parents and a sister were dead. I said I could search for my other sister at least and stay with her. They said if I returned I might be killed also. They said it was not to be.

We went to the railway station to take a train to Halfa, on the border with Egypt. While we were waiting for the train, this businessman came up and asked us, "Why are you going to Egypt?" We said, "We flee Sudan to be safe." He told us that there is an office there called UNHCR that could help us a lot.

We got to Halfa and then took a boat to Aswan. Then we took another train from Aswan to Cairo. We arrived at Ramses station and took a bus to the suburbs. Mahmoud and his brother were happy to have me with them. They treated me in a very good way.

We rented a flat, and Mahmoud told his brother to start searching for work. Then, just immediately, the next day, the flat owner kicked us out. I went to stay with a Sudanese family nearby, some people who knew Mahmoud's relatives. Mahmoud and his brother stayed with a group of single Sudanese men.

At the beginning, this family was okay to me. But after a while, you see, their place was very small, and I could feel they were not happy with the situation. It was difficult for me, because I was increasing their suffering in that small home. I told them I wanted to leave.

I told Mahmoud I could find work to help pay for a flat. Mahmoud said no, that I was too young. Mahmoud was working in a milk store, but the manager was only paying him two hundred Egyptian pounds (US$35) a month, and that's not even enough for transportation to the factory. Soon Mahmoud left the job, because it was better to just stay at home than lose money. His brother had a small job, earning three hundred pounds, but still it wasn't enough. That was when we went to UNHCR.

The first thing UNHCR did was ask Mahmoud, "Why did you marry Nadia?" They saw I was underage and that the marriage was illegal. The UNHCR worker took a copy of our marriage certificate, showed it to some other worker, and came back to us. He was very upset and he told Mahmoud, "This is a crime. How did you do this?" At that time, I tried to explain that I asked Mahmoud to marry me in order to flee from Sudan. Eventually he told Mahmoud to come back after two days and bring the original copy of the marriage contract.

We came back two days later with the original marriage certificate. The same man took the paper and our passport. Then an Egyptian woman came in and called my name. She took me outside and she told me, "I want to speak to you frankly." She asked me if Mahmoud treated me well. She asked about Mahmoud's brother—did he treat me well also? She asked me many questions. I was resistant and tired, and she gave me the impression that she just wanted to make sure I wasn't lying. After a while, the UNHCR man brought us yellow cards and asked us to sign them. They told me the yellow card was protection.

I HAVE NOTHING TO BE AFRAID OF, BECAUSE I'M COMPLETELY DESPERATE

We moved to the suburb called 6 October City.

Some people here treat me well, and some people treat me very badly. Some Egyptians say, "You are coming here to make trouble.

Life became very, very expensive after you refugees arrived." Sometimes men follow me on the street until I arrive here at my house. Maybe they just want to know which flat I live in. I don't know why they follow. I never speak to them.

For a while, Mahmoud got work as an assistant to a painter. We lived in basements, moved from one apartment to another. We lived simply like that for two years. On January 29, 2006, I gave birth to a daughter. Her name is Sima Amal Mahmoud. She's a very good girl.

When Sima was just a few months old, she became sick. At the time, Mahmoud had no job, so we had very little money. We were taking care of a building, and in exchange, the owner allowed us to live in the basement. Sima was having trouble with her eyes. They were red and infected. I went to UNHCR so I could add Sima's name to my yellow card and get some help for Sima's eyes. A lady at UNHCR took down the information. I told her that Sima was sick, and my husband had no work. She told me to go to Caritas, the Catholic relief services, and they would give us some financial assistance and care for my daughter. She said, "Go right now to Caritas, and I will email them to tell them to help you."

I went to Caritas with Mahmoud. The security man outside the office asked me, "Are you Nadia?" I said yes. He took me and my husband inside, and interviewed me, and made a file for me. Then they told me they couldn't give me any money now, but that I could come after a month for financial assistance. I told them that the lady at UNHCR had said we would get money immediately because our daughter is sick. After a long discussion, the Caritas lady told me, "Okay, we can give you some assistance now, but you have to go away. And don't come back here again." She gave me a name of a doctor, and two hundred or three hundred pounds (US$35, US$55) of financial assistance. I met the doctor and he gave me medication for my daughter.

Then things got worse. My daughter started having bad allergies and problems with her chest. We had to take her to the emergency hospital a couple of times at night, so she could get oxygen to help her breathe. The man who owned the basement where we lived kicked us out.

When I got kicked out of the flat, Mahmoud wasn't home. He was out looking for a job all that day and night. I walked for hours, and then I had to sleep on the street with my daughter. I woke up when the sun came up, and I went to Caritas. I waited in line for hours, and then Caritas told me to go to UNHCR. By that time it was after two o'clock or so in the afternoon, and when I got to UNHCR, the Egyptian police officers told me the office was closed for the day.

I asked the policeman outside the building to please give me UNHCR's phone number so I could call them. I asked if they would call inside on their radio. I explained that I had slept on the street last night. The officer just said no. I asked again and he hit me with his hand. I fell down on the street and he even kicked my daughter. He put one foot on top of me and kicked me with his other foot. Another police officer came over and tried to separate us, but this man just said, "No, keep away." He took my feet with one hand and pulled my hair with the other hand, and kicked me. He insulted me with every dirty word you could imagine. Then, the last thing he did was kick his boot in my face.

I went back to our neighborhood to find Mahmoud. I could hardly hold Sima because I was tired and starving, and my daughter was vomiting. Mahmoud took us to live with a Sudanese family who offered us a room, but after just a few weeks we couldn't pay the rent and they kicked us out. I went back to UNHCR.

I met the security man outside of UNHCR, and I explained to him that I wanted to meet with an official employee. The security man said, "I'm the responsible man here. If you have anything to explain, explain it to me." I told him my problem, that we had nowhere to stay and no money. The man told me, "Take your daughter and go away. You can't meet anyone official."

I became very upset at this point. I just told him, "Take my daughter. Take her and take care of her because I cannot feed her, and I am failing to give her the fundamentals of life. Take her." I gave him my daughter and started walking away.

I was really ready to leave her, in a way. I thought there was nothing I could do anymore to keep her from dying. I just couldn't take care of her. As I walked away, she started crying and I just started crying, too.

A man stopped me as I was walking away. He told me he was Dr. Ashram, the UNHCR medical coordinator. He gave me two pounds, and the phone number for inside the UNHCR office. I went to a phone booth and I called UNHCR. Dr. Ashram waited for me with my daughter.

When I called inside the office, the girl who answered the phone was very rude to me. I tried to explain to her that I wanted to meet with someone who could do something for me. She kept saying, "Why?" and "For what?" I tried to explain my problems with living and housing, and after some time she just hung up on me.

I went back to Dr. Ashram and I explained everything to him. He asked me to take my daughter back, and that he would try to find some solution and call me himself. I explained to him that I had nowhere to go, that all I really needed was money.

He said, "I understand, but I have no time, I can't help you now. I have so much work to do."

I said, "If you are going back into the UNHCR office, let me go with you, and let me just meet anyone to explain my problem. Let me talk to the chief, let me talk to anyone." I was being loud, and the policemen outside the office came over and stood next to me, trying to scare me. I told them all, "I have nothing to be afraid of because I'm completely desperate!" The police officer started shouting at me.

I shouted back, "I have nothing to lose, I have no house, I can't feed my daughter!"

I guess Dr. Ashram finally saw that I was facing a serious problem. He asked me to come with him. He stood me at the door of the UNHCR office, went in, and brought someone out to meet me. This man told me to go to Caritas for financial assistance. I explained to him, "I went to Caritas before, and they told me, 'Don't come back here again asking for money.'"

The UNHCR man did something very nice then. He walked with me to the Caritas office. He brought me in, and we met someone named Sammy. Sammy said, "We can offer you a place to live in a neighborhood called Badr City."

I went and asked some Sudanese people about Badr City. They told me it's very, very far away from Cairo, that it has no hospitals, no strong Sudanese community, no nothing. It is just an area of factory buildings. People told me, "Imagine if your daughter gets sick again. You won't be able to find a hospital." We were scared she would get sick one night with influenza or some bad infection, and we wouldn't have a hospital close to us. Mahmoud and I discussed it and decided we would not go to Badr City.

We stayed with friends for a few days, and then a good thing happened. I met a woman with a villa here in Cairo, and she needed a cleaning lady. She offered me work, and I continue to work for her to this day. Mahmoud gets some work from her also, working as a guard, or a driver, or helping to fix things. Sima comes with me when I clean. It's a good job, and the lady that hired me is a nice lady.

IT'S JUST BETTER TO DIE IN MY COUNTRY

Right now, in August 2007, the lady with the villa is in Sharm el-Sheikh on holidays. Before she left, she gave me three hundred pounds (US$55) until she returns. But she said after she returns to Cairo, she will soon move to Kuwait. When she told me this, I explained my problems to her, told her about UNHCR and everything. When she heard it, she said, "If you want to go back to Sudan, I can buy a plane ticket for you and a train ticket for your husband to travel to Khartoum. And if you stay here in Cairo, I will give you about six or seven hundred pounds." She tried to advise me: "If you make your mind up to go back to Sudan, please stay in Khartoum. Don't go to Darfur because you might face the same fate as your family."

Just last week Mahmoud and I went to UNHCR one more time. This time we went to close our refugee files. If you repatriate to Sudan, they say UNHCR will give you train tickets, and maybe one hundred dollars each to help you in your first few weeks.

At UNHCR they asked us, "Why do you want to close your file?" I told them there is nothing here for me and I am suffering. They asked us, "Where are you going to live in Sudan?" My husband said in Khartoum. I said I would rather go back to Darfur. The officer—Hisham was his name—Hisham said, "If you will go to Darfur, I cannot close your file." And then Mahmoud said, "For sure, we will go to Khartoum."

Hisham asked us to sign some papers. He said to Mahmoud, "Call me this afternoon, and I will give you an appointment to go to the interior ministry." Finally, two days later, we got the appointment. Mahmoud had to go to the Ministry of Foreign Affairs first. They gave him a paper to take to the Ministry of the Interior, in order to get us an exit visa.

Now Mahmoud has a job for a few days, helping an old woman move some things. The job finishes tomorrow, and he will go to the ministry to see if we have a visa. We will go to UNHCR again to get assistance for closing our file. The lady with the villa will be back in a few days, and I will find out if she will help. It will be difficult, because she wants to give me tickets to travel, but UNHCR wants to give us train tickets also. The lady has given me a lot, and I don't want to press her to change her offer.

I am very ready to go back to Sudan. There are no benefits to going back, and I know there could be risks. I still want to go to Darfur, even though it's dangerous. Even in Khartoum there might be security risks. But it's just better to die in my country, in my home.

I have no feelings about UNHCR at this point. They did nothing for me. They didn't offer anything. They didn't help me. That is all I think. But I feel nothing. The same for Egypt. I live here, eat, and sleep like any eighteen-year-old. But Sudan is my country. What happened to my family was the work of criminals. It was the Sudanese government's mistake not to secure the lives of the Darfurians. But Sudan is my country. I hope the Sudanese government takes care of its citizens, and I hope UNHCR pays more attention to the refugees.

In Sudan, I will live in the same circumstances as here in Cairo. Nothing new will happen. I think my daughter's life will be the same as mine—no education, no nothing. We will all just stay like this.

I guess I still have some hope. I haven't been there before— I have no experience about this—but I have hope to go to America or Australia. Everyone tells me that you can find a safe life there, and your daughter can find a good education. That would be a hope. Education and a stable life. I know in Sudan that will be impossible. And I know if I go back to Sudan, I will not get to Australia or America. But now it's all the same to me. If I can find work in Sudan, I will work in Sudan. If I can find food, I will feed my daughter. If I die, I die. Life, death, there's no big difference. God will make it easy.

{Several weeks after these interviews were conducted, Nadia returned to Sudan with her husband and child.}

MOTUZ SALAH AL-DEEN

AGE: *25*
TRIBE: *Shwai (Paternal), Gaaliin (Maternal)*
BIRTHPLACE: *United Arab Emirates*
INTERVIEWED IN: *Cairo, Egypt*

MY DECISION WAS WRONG, BUT IT WAS ALSO RIGHT

Motuz Salah al-Deen, or al-Limbi, told his stories in a café on a summer morning in downtown Cairo. He wore a knit rasta cap and smoked cigarettes along with his Arabic coffee. The café's other patrons watched as al-Limbi spoke into the microphone in Arabic. He paused occasionally to turn and stare back at them. Again and again he paused, saying, "I'm not a real refugee, you know?" The interpreter reassured him: "Just tell the story. It's the funniest story in this whole city."

Everybody calls me al-Limbi, but it's just my nickname. In a famous movie here in Egypt, the hero of the movie is called al-Limbi, and he uses a homemade bong to smoke weed. What can I say? After that movie, they started calling me al-Limbi.

I was born in September of 1982, in the United Arab Emirates. I lived there for fourteen years. My father was working in the Emirates as an electrical technician, as the guy who connects cables. He was working for the government in Ajman province. Of course, my family is from Sudan; my father is Sudanese, and I am Sudanese; I am really from Sudan. My father is Shwai and my mother is Gaaliin.

These are northern tribes in Sudan. Just like you can find in any group, there are good people and bad people in these tribes. We are all Muslim, and I'd say my mother is religious, but the rest of us are not so much.

In the Emirates it was me, my parents, and my three brothers. Two are older than me and one is younger. I was very close to my father. I even look like him. We looked the most similar of any two people in the family. He felt close to me too, and I guess that made me love him even more. My father had been in the Sudanese Army until 1978. When we were young, he told us he decided to leave Sudan because he was upset with the system there, the lies there, and he wanted us to grow up in a different environment, far away from that system. He wouldn't explain details, because we were too young.

Still, every year we would go back to Sudan and visit. Once we actually stayed a whole year, and I even studied in a school in Omdurman. It was a lot more fun in Sudan, because we could visit relatives every day. Just being in the neighborhood felt like being around family. But for some reason, we turned back again. I think my father couldn't find a good job, couldn't find money for us, so we returned back to the Emirates again. I was not happy to go back. In Sudan, no matter my circumstances or conditions, I was never humiliated. Sudan is my country, no matter if it's for the best. In Ajman, in the Emirates, it wasn't really humiliating, but people just give you the impression that you are less than them. The Arab students in the school, from the Emirates or Syria or Jordan, they would look at us, treat us poorly because we are black.

Once my father died, we returned to Sudan for good. He was bleeding in his stomach. An ulcer maybe? A hole in his stomach. He died from this. We knew he was sick, but still, I wasn't prepared for him to die. We took the body back to Sudan and buried him there. In Sudan, the mourning process takes three days. The people come and comfort you, we receive the body, we bury him, and everything is like the custom. A family friend in the Emirates closed my father's life there. He sold my father's car, took the pension from my father's work, and sent the money back to us in Sudan. My mother took responsibility. She bought a new house and leased part of it for some extra money. Then she started working as an employee at the University of Khartoum. Even now she teaches computer programs there, things like Excel and Word.

I was very happy we were staying in Sudan. I had friends and enjoyed my life, and everything was cool. I had a girlfriend, but nothing serious.

FIND A WAY TO LEAVE CAIRO

When I finished high school, I looked at my mother working so much, taking care of me all this time. I thought I had to do something to help her. Some people get good jobs in Sudan, sure. But those people have a university certificate, and I just have a secondary-school certificate. And for me, in that position, it's difficult. I had already been accepted in the university. But I couldn't accept the idea that my mother would have to keep working to pay for my school and for my college. It's not even a matter of how much it cost. What mattered was my mother working and giving me my pocket money to go to university. I couldn't imagine it. I decided to leave.

One of my brothers had left, too. He moved to Saudi Arabia to work in a construction company. He works as a security guard. He's not officially working for this company, but he helps them somehow, and so they give him money. Me, I chose to go to Cairo. I was really hoping for a future in Canada, or Australia, a place with good housing, and good work, so I could send my family some money. I thought I could go to Cairo and then find a sponsor to help me at the embassy. Unfortunately, I failed.

When I told my mom I was going to Cairo, she told me not to

go, to stay and finish university. She told me, "We don't need any help from you right now. Just stay, and go to your university." But I just couldn't stay. I was insistent. Finally they respected my desire. My mother said, "Just go."

I got a passport and a visa, and I came to Cairo on January 24, 2002. I knew some guys in Cairo who had lived in my grandfather's neighborhood in Sudan. They were in Giza, near the pyramids. I got to the airport and called them; they gave me the address, and I went to see them. They were very happy to see me. Those guys aren't in Egypt anymore. One made it to Australia, one to Canada, and the third one returned to Sudan.

My plan was to find a way to leave Cairo. On my first day I went to the UNHCR and they gave me an appointment. My friends gave me advice for how to prepare my testimony. They said, "Don't forget what's written on your testimony. If you miss a date or you look confused, it might mean rejection for you." They sent me to a Sudanese lawyer who could advise me.

I left Sudan searching for a job, but when I submitted my testimony, I submitted it like those people leaving danger, leaving war. I wrote that I had problems in Sudan, and that if I returned, there would be a huge danger that I would face death. I told the UNHCR I was a student activist and an opponent of the Khartoum regime. I told them about Islamic students making speeches, and how I stood against them, and about how security detained me because of this and tortured me.

None of it was true. Lots of people do this, you know. So many. I don't know, but I would say 90 percent of the people who go to UNHCR mention a story like this. And none of them faced a serious problem in Sudan.

The thing is that the government of Sudan is a disgusting government, and that causes people to get desperate. The government makes the people want to move from Sudan to other countries for another life. In my opinion, anyone willing to come to Cairo and submit a case to UNHCR has a problem somehow. Maybe it's not directly with the government, but somehow he faces a problem in his life. They make the conditions in Sudan so bad, the government somehow forces the people to do this. For me, going to UNHCR didn't feel like the right thing to do, but on the other hand, I don't feel like I made that big a mistake.

Anyway, they didn't accept me. I received a letter from UNHCR, saying that I did not have a "well-founded fear of persecution."

GIVE ME A CHANCE, GIVE ME A CHANCE

I've been working many jobs in my years in Cairo. I worked in Sinai, near the Red Sea, doing hotel service work. The best job was in a computer store. I started working with them as a cleaner. After a while, I gained their trust and was one of the managers, working on sales and stuff. But one of the secretaries there did some dirty things under the table. She wanted to get me out, because she had a friend and she wanted this friend to have my job. She started telling the owner that I was coming late, that I was arguing all the time and not being respectful. It wasn't true, but she succeeded. The owner lent me some money when I left, to help me out. When I came back two months later to pay back the money, I saw the secretary's friend working there in my position.

I went to Alexandria with my friend, and we tried opening a hairdressing shop. We didn't want to work under someone; we wanted to make our own business. We set it up and started working but unfortunately, nobody came. It didn't succeed. I went back to Cairo.

I was in touch with my family this whole time, and they asked me many times to return to Sudan. I asked them to wait for me. Give me a chance, give me a chance. I tried getting resettled through the Australian Embassy and got rejected. A Sudanese friend of mine in

Canada promised to sponsor me to go there, but he never sent the papers. Now I've finally decided to leave, but I can't do it legally, because of the problems I now have here in Egypt. The problem is, I have no passport.

It sort of starts with the protests at Mustafa Mahmoud. I visited the protest in late 2005, heard them talking, and found out it was serious. I joined it, because I thought it might be a hope for me and for the refugees. Maybe to find some solution for me, maybe reopen our UNHCR files. So my friends and I left our flat, and we stayed there, made it our home.

During those protest days, we were out in the neighborhood of Dokki one night. We were drinking, and one of my friends was really drunk. Suddenly I look up and he's fighting with three Egyptian guys. I ran over to help him, to try to stop the fighting, and my jacket came off in the mess. There was some serious fighting. And soon an Egyptian police car showed up. The Egyptian guys ran away and one of them took my jacket. And oh shit, my jacket had my documents! My passport, papers, everything. We didn't know these guys that ran away. There's no way I would be able to find it. There was nothing to do. I was very frustrated, and I had to find a way to get a new passport, but I didn't know how, and I knew it would take months, especially since I was in Cairo illegally by then. My residence permits had run out.

It was a few months later, maybe February 2006. Still I had no ID. It was late at night, close to my home, and there's a checkpoint on the roads; I don't know why. The police asked me for my ID, and I told them I didn't have one. They took me to the police station and asked me my name. I told them my name is Motuz Salah al-Deen. They told me "No, your name is Motuz Salah al-Deen Al-Tejani, and you have been sentenced to three years in jail for using a false ID."

So you see what happened here? They thought I was this other guy, because our names were similar and I had no ID. And they wanted to put this other guy, Al-Tejani, in prison for using a false ID. Kind of funny I guess.

LIKE THEY WERE ENJOYING IT

I denied all their accusations. They didn't believe me and they kept me in prison. It was twenty-seven days in prison in the end. Every day they would take me to the investigator's office, asking me the same questions, maybe changing the questions a little bit to catch me in a lie. They were absolutely not nice. They treated me like a dog. Sometimes when I was thirsty, they didn't provide me with water. We were about a hundred detainees in the cell. One very dirty toilet that smelled very bad. Two pieces of bread per day. I didn't just lose weight, I felt like I was about to die. Sometimes friends used to visit me, to bring me cigarettes, or some food. But no lawyer. My friends' conditions were like mine. They were poor, and they had no money to pay for a lawyer. I just told them to make sure not to tell my family.

Everyone in the prison cell told his own story. There was a guy called Sayeed, from the Zeitoun neighborhood. He'd stabbed someone in the stomach, and he admitted he'd done it. Something about a fight over girls. Then another guy, Ali, he was so nervous; they'd accused him of stealing something and he kept denying it, day after day. He was just waiting for a decision. None of us had money, so none of us had lawyers.

It was about the tenth day, and this police officer inside the station woke me up and started insulting my mother, talking about my mother's genitals. So I repeated the same thing back to him. He asked me, "What did you say?" I told him, "If you can't hear me, bring a paper and pen, and I will write it down for you."

Look, if the police insult me, it's okay. I can accept it. But he insulted my mother also. That's completely unacceptable. The policeman knows me; he knows I'm here for a reason. Fine. But how does he know my mother? Maybe she's dead, maybe she's sick, you don't know her at all. Why would you insult someone you don't know?

Of course, he beat me and I tried to fight back. Five more policemen showed up, and they took me to the interrogation room. By this point, I was very upset and angry and frustrated, and I just started insulting them. I didn't care about anything, and I didn't give a shit. The police officer I'd shouted at first was very angry, but the other policemen seemed pretty happy, like nothing personal, they were just doing a favor for their colleague. They were enjoying it. Eventually they tied my hands with a rope, and then they tied my hands to my legs, from behind. They burned me with cigarettes in my chest and beat me until I lost consciousness.

All day, it was running through my mind—how do I prove I'm not Motuz Salah al-Deen Al-Tejani? They told me I'd be in jail for three years, and I'm not guilty. Any day they were going to send me to the judge, and then they'd forget about me, just send me away for the three years.

I was taken to court after twenty-seven days. Not really a courtroom like on TV, but just a room. They told me, "This is the judge, and he's going to ask you some questions, and after that you'll get your sentence." I had no lawyer. If I'd had money, they would have given me a lawyer.

They sent me to the judge, and they introduced me with this other guy's name. Before the judge could even ask me questions, I started to speak to him. I said to him, "If you know your position, if you respect your position as a judge, and if you're an honest person, then please just save me." Then I gave him my UNHCR file number, and I told him, "Go to those files, they have a copy of my passport, you can find my ID there." Thank God, the judge was a nice man, and he postponed my sentencing to the next day.

The next day they didn't send me to the court at all. They sent me to the Mugammah, the huge interior ministry building in the middle of downtown. When we got there I saw an official, an employee from UNHCR and he had brought my file, including a photocopy of my passport. That saved me, really. Suddenly I was innocent.

After that they looked up my name in their records, and it's funny, they see someone has already left Cairo using my name. I guess after I lost my jacket, someone used my ID to travel somewhere else. But this was a problem for them, because here I am in Cairo, but according to their immigration database, the holder of my passport has left Cairo. So to avoid any confusion, the security people and the immigration people decided to deport me to Sudan. They wrote the letter and approved it, and they sent me back to the police station.

So I had to deal with the same policemen again. One day we'd go back to the Mugammah, the next to the security office. No solutions, and they return me to the same prison. After some days they finally figured out the procedure. They sent me to the Sudanese Embassy.

If they deported me, they would have sent me on a train and a ferry, and then the Sudanese authorities would have taken me, interrogated me, and who knows? Maybe they'd release me after a few days, maybe not. I couldn't know. And I was just so tired at that point. I didn't want to go that way at all.

I JUMPED

They sent me in one of those huge black police trucks, in handcuffs. When I got to the embassy, they took off the handcuffs. They said I couldn't be handcuffed by Egyptian police inside my own embassy. They sat me down on a couch to wait in the reception area, and the policeman took the deportation letter to the desk. The Sudanese secretary gave the guy some paper and told him we had to wait for a stamp from the immigration officer. Fortunately for me, they said it would take an hour until the immigration officer returned. We were sitting there waiting, and I asked the policeman if I could go to the toilet down the hall. I needed a plan.

I went inside this toilet room, but it had no window. So I turned the lock, and I went back to the policeman and told him, "The toilet's locked. I want to go to the toilet upstairs." He took me to the upstairs floor and waited for me outside the toilet room. Inside the bathroom there was a window looking out to a back alley, and I pushed it open. I jumped out and grabbed the water pipes that were on the outside wall. I slid down until I was a few meters from the ground, and then I jumped. Then I came back into the embassy reception through the back door. I crossed the room looking really normal, really natural. And all that time the police officer was still upstairs! There was one girl waiting in the hall who looked at me, confused—she'd seen me before when I was in handcuffs. I walked a little faster, got to the entrance, and then I just ran. I ran to the big street nearby, Qasr El-Aini. I jumped in a taxi, and we drove. The taxi drove me to my friend's house, and they paid. I was scared and confused, but my friends were so happy. After a few days, I felt normal again.

These days, I'm busy. One of my friends came here from Sudan to get some special medication and I'm trying to help him. And just recently my aunt was here also for medical treatment, so I was busy with her. At night, I just get drunk. And I see my girlfriend almost every day.

My girlfriend's name is Manal. We've been together one year. She's twenty-one and very, very pretty. I met her through a common friend. She is Egyptian, and from the first time I saw her I felt that I liked her so much; too much, really. We felt attached to each other and gradually we started to love each other.

She lives with her family and actually, her family doesn't know anything about me. I don't want to meet them because now I have nothing. I have nothing I can give their daughter, and I would be embarrassed.

I've told my girlfriend all of this. I mean, I've told her everything about me, everything since my birth. She just said, "You have to find a solution." She wants me to go back to Sudan for two reasons. First, she wants me to go get a new passport, come back legally. Second, I have an inheritance waiting for me—some farmland from my father. My mother has agreed that now I'm old enough, I should take my piece and sell it. I can get some money, come back, and marry her. She said if I do that, she'll return with me to Sudan.

I have no job right now. I'm searching for a job, but more than that, I'm trying to fix my problem in order to return back home. I'll need to smuggle myself through the Sudanese border, probably take the train down to Halfa and then see from there. There are many possible solutions. They're not legal, but I need to help myself. I do know it's possible to take someone else's name from his passport and use a fake travel document. But after all my troubles, I don't want to use a fake identity and make trouble for someone else. So I need to find a different way.

My decision to come to Cairo, it was wrong, but also it was right. I tried to do my best and sure, I feel regrets. But I'll continue to try my best, and I'll thank God.

I hope to return to Sudan in the next few months. I hope I will not stay longer. I've decided it is time to turn back to Sudan again. I'll try to work and hopefully to study at the same time, because I know a university degree is so important. I am ready to start from zero.

ALWEEL KOL

AGE: *33*
TRIBE: *Dinka (Nor)*
BIRTHPLACE: *Mulmul, South Sudan*
INTERVIEWED IN: *Cairo, Egypt*

I JUST WANT TO SEE
IT THROUGH

Alweel's smile shone and her voice chirped in Arabic as she told her story deliberately and in deep detail. We took breaks for chocolate and tea after difficult episodes. It took two days for her to unfurl all of her experiences, reaching back to the village in South Sudan where she was born, to the Nile in Khartoum and then, years later, following the river north to Cairo. Listening to her speak, it was difficult to comprehend how this beautiful, gracious, intelligent woman had undertaken such a journey. But Alweel remains luminous.

I can close my eyes and paint a picture of Mulmul, the village where I was born. I can see houses made of straw and children playing on the way home from school. I remember how much I loved school— I was an excellent student and my teachers loved me. I loved math and English the most, and I can picture the English books. I would read the English words out loud, even if I didn't understand their meanings.

I remember playing with my dolls. I put a cloth on a brick to make a bed for the doll. Some of my cousins were lazy, but I was always helping in the house, washing and carrying things for my mother when she would take her cooked foods to the market. I can hear myself singing all day long, dreaming of being a famous artist and celebrity.

I remember my large family, my parents, my two brothers and five sisters, my aunts and uncles. My two parents were Muslims, but the town was Christian. When we were growing up, my friends would go to church and I would go with them. I would go every day, and they would tell us stories about Jesus and the crucifixion. I used to have my cross to wear, and we used to pray before meals. My father was a very democratic man. He used to say it's a choice, and you choose your belief, and everyone should go with what his heart believes. I believe that God exists and he loves me. I like the story of the crucifixion. Everyone was standing around Jesus waiting for something to happen, and he said, "Please, Father, forgive them, because they don't know what they're doing."

My father was big and tall, but he was a kind man who would laugh and play with us so much. He would solve people's problems. He was a leader of our tribe, and a worker on the bridges and roads. I don't remember much else about him. My mother was always a very sweet person who took good care of her children.

I remember that there was a cat in the village named Endewah, and I used to get upset when the children would tell me that my eyes looked like a cat's eyes and call me Endewah. I used to cry every time! But I would go to my mother and she would help me. She would remind me, "No, you are not Endewah, you are Alweel."

SOMEWHERE ELSE

I lost my parents in 1985, on the day when people came to our village and burned it. My father and uncle died that day, and I lost my mother.

I was only ten years old, so I didn't know anything about a war.

One evening, armed men came to our village to catch certain people. They attacked our home, tied up my father, and threw him to the ground. I saw him get killed. My uncle was killed after my father, and then my aunt threw herself on my uncle's body and they killed her, too. There was so much blood everywhere, and I was so scared. My mother used to tell me to become a doctor, and I hated the thought because I couldn't deal with blood like a doctor should. But when I saw my father get killed and I saw all his blood, I couldn't think about anything else except blood.

My mother was far away from home, at the market in Abyei. They took me and my two brothers, Farid and Deng. They put us in a Land Rover car and inside were other children I had never seen before. They told us that the one who runs away will be shot. They drove for an hour or so. They took us to a faraway place with tents and houses made out of hay and with lots of other kids. It was a camp where they kept many cattle and many children. There were policemen in charge of the place. They wore uniforms and called themselves officer and sergeant.

They made us herd sheep and small cows. When they took me to the cattle, I asked, "Where are those other children running?"

The man said, "They are running to go to school." I did not believe him. Of course not. These men had killed my father. I knew at that time I was not safe.

At night they put us in a big tent so full of children. They served us very bad food and gave us blankets like the ones from relief workers. They separated me from my brothers. I had no idea where my mother or my sisters were.

I stayed like that for maybe ten days. Then a cow stepped on my foot, and it started swelling; then I wasn't walking, I was limping. We had to walk early in the morning and come back at night with the cattle. There was no medication for me, and I showed them my swollen foot and they didn't do anything. They pushed me to the floor. I found a couple of stones, a small pile of hay, and salt, and a small pot of water. I heated the water and the salt, and I started putting the water and the salt on my foot. In a couple of days it became better. I had learned this from my mom. I saw her doing this.

When my foot healed, I ran away. There was a family traveling with their camels; I saw them, and I walked up behind them. They were riding their camels and I was walking on foot, but when I came close, they knew there was a child behind them. The man saw me, and I told him my story and he was kind to me. He took me to his children, and they gave me milk and food and my stomach felt good. I remember the son's name was Almer, because he was so nice to me and so cute, and didn't make me feel like a stranger. They took me to the city of Abyei.

The sultans in town—the local leaders—told me that they knew my story and they knew about the people who died in my area and about my father. They knew stories about people being taken, like me. I told them I wanted to go somewhere else. They put me in a truck and gave me money in case of trouble, and they gave me a letter to give to the church in El Obeid to the North. El Obeid was the biggest place I knew, so I went there. I was trying to find my mom.

The truck drove for many hours. I wasn't afraid of those I was traveling with in the truck. I was afraid of the people who attacked me before. I was afraid they would come and take me again.

I went to the church and there was a missionary and a priest; I talked to the priest and I talked to the missionary and told them my story. They listened to me. They gave me two choices—either they would send me to Khartoum or take me to school here. At the time, I did not know what a "Khartoum" is. We had it in the books, but I didn't know what it is, so I asked. They said it's a big, big city. They have many churches and organizations, and there are many priests there and it's a bigger city than here. I chose Khartoum.

ALWEEL KOL

OH, THAT'S A GOOD GIRL

There were many people on the bus to Khartoum, but I was traveling
alone. The road wasn't good and it took two days to go two hundred
miles. It was a nice trip, but I was a bit tired so I would sleep sometimes. When people would take a break to pray or to eat or anything
I would just go down with them for air.

I didn't know anything about my destination, but when I arrived
I felt a bit safer. It seemed like a clean city with nice buildings, not
those huts we had in Abyei. Khartoum is bigger and nicer than the
South. Once I got off the bus, I asked where to find the Roman Catholic church of St. Peter and Paul. It was in Amarat, close to the airport. I went to the church and gave them the letter. They didn't say
anything. To this day I don't know what was written in that letter.
They just kept asking about me and my family and what happened.
They said they were very sorry, and they would take me to school and
take care of me. The church had a school in it, so I went to school
there. They got me money to buy some food and clothes for myself.

I met a girl from the Shilluk tribe named Angelina, and we became very good friends. She was the same age as me. I showed her
where I lived, and she showed me where she lived, and then I moved
and lived with her, east of the airport. They lived in a hut covered
with plastic sheets and a big room built with mud and a big space
outside.

Angelina was living with her family. Her father was dead and
her mom was married to another man. She had younger siblings and
older ones—a younger sister called Regina and four boys. I was very
happy at school and with this family of nice people. I became another
member of the family. They spoke a different language than me so
I didn't understand them. But Angelina knew Arabic so I could
speak to her.

School was good; I was happy; the teachers loved me; it was excellent. The other students were a mix of Arabs and people from the South, but I don't remember them. Angelina was my only friend and the only one I talked to. We wouldn't say much. She didn't want to sit and talk about boys, and I was very shy as well. The kids would make fun of Angelina. She would get upset and angry. Angelina is a bit tough, and sometimes she would beat other children. Sometimes when many of them would come and beat her back, I would defend her.

After school, we would work with her mom and try to make some money, and help ourselves. We would go to houses and clean and get paid a few pounds. We would brew alcohol and sell it in the home. You get a big plastic container, cut the top off, and you fill it with dates, water, yeast, and sugar. You heat it with fire, punch little holes, and let the water go into a pot underneath. You leave it for three days and it's ready. Everyone would come drink it—Southerners, Arabs, people from Darfur. When Muslims would come, they would take it and drink it at their home. I never tried it myself, even to taste for cooking. If I wanted to know if it was strong, I would put it on a plate and light a match. If it flamed, it was good. If not, it was bad.

I was happy then. I used to talk a lot about my family, but I couldn't find anyone to guide me to them. Part of me wanted to go back to the South and just find my brothers again or just run into my mom. I was almost eleven years old then.

I went to a government school for middle school, and to church for Christian education and to pray. I lived with Angelina's family still. People would see me living without my family, and they wouldn't say, "Oh, that's a good girl." They would look at me badly.

GOOD FOR MARRIAGE

When I was sixteen, I was in love with a guy name David. He was very good-looking, and went to university, and was smart, but his life was very complicated. And he drank. His two parents were dead and he was raised by his paternal aunt. His financial situation was very bad. Sometimes I think I should have waited for him. One of the reasons I lost hope was because his family wouldn't agree for me to marry him since I had no family.

I was seventeen in Khartoum when I met my man, Akaich. He was Dinka like me. After I finished middle school, I went to high school. I went to a special school called Agrazella for IDPs from the South, because our Arabic is different from the other students'. I met another girlfriend in the new school named Nimera. Nimera's family is well off, and her father had his own workshop where they did metal-work and artwork; they had a big house with many rooms. The man I'm married to is Nimera's uncle. Through Nimera, he married me.

I was in Nimera's kitchen and I was helping her cook. It was a big household. Nimera's father had five wives; each of his women had many children, and I was helping to cook for all of them. Akaich saw me and was pleased by me. Dinka men like women who are hard workers, and he saw me as a hard worker and he liked me. He told Nimera, "I like this woman and I want to marry her." He said that to Nimera the day after he first saw me. He said she is good-looking and hardworking, and I like her. And that was it.

For the Dinka, the most important thing is that the woman is hardworking. If she is hardworking, knows her responsibilities, and can keep the family under control and keep things going according to the norms and the traditions, she is good for marriage. Beauty and height are good as well, but they are extras.

When Nimera told me the proposal, I thought she wasn't serious. I said, "No, because he looks old." He was about forty at the time and I was seventeen. I said, "I don't want him." But something happened that made me marry this man: I wasn't able to pay the expenses for my schooling. Akaich started giving me money, with no relationship actually happening, just as Nimera's friend. He bought me a uniform for the high school and gave me money to buy things. After two years, he asked me again to marry him. And I told him, "Well, I cannot say anything. I will ask Angelina's mom." She acted as my mom and invited Akaich to talk to her. Akaich went to Angelina's mom and he asked for my hand in marriage, and they agreed and I married him.

I was not very happy. I did not love this man. He was a liar. I had my conditions for marriage. I wanted to finish my high school education and go to university. He promised me he would support me. But after I got married, he said no more schooling and no more going to school and no more education. He used to beat me up and fight me over it. He used to hurt me, but he didn't break any bones. When we grind garlic, we use something with an iron handle to smash it, and he hit me with it in the leg and caused problems with my knee. Sometimes when I would walk, my knee would pop out, but now I'm better.

IT WAS ALL LIES

Akaich was very jealous when a friend would come to visit me. He said, "No, they're only coming to see you and take you to another man." At the very beginning, Akaich said he was not married, but it turns out he was married to another woman. She was Dinka as well. In the house where we married there was a woman with her two children. He told me it was his brother's cousin, but it turned out that it was Akaich's wife, and those children were his children.

Nimera never told me about the other wife. She didn't tell me about the other children. After I married, she got married herself and left for Nairobi. She was not a good friend.

I worked at home. I was the one cleaning and washing and doing everything. I would go to the supermarket to buy flour. The same month I married I got pregnant. I had to leave school. I thought about running away, but where would I go?

After I had my son, Deng, I became pregnant again less than a year later. It was 1995. I stopped breastfeeding Deng, because they say that it's bad to breastfeed a child while you're pregnant. One day, I came home from the market and saw the other wife with her breasts out feeding my child. The wife was pregnant and she said my baby was crying. I thought that because she was pregnant and breastfeeding it might harm my child. At that moment, I decided I didn't want to stay in that house anymore.

When my Akaich noticed I stopped breastfeeding, he asked why and started beating me up. I told him I was pregnant. He said if I was pregnant, the child was not his. It was not true. My husband was jealous. Even when I would speak to his cousins, he would get jealous and say I was sleeping with other people.

When I argued with Akaich, he went to the court and filed a complaint against me. He got an arresting order, and I was arrested by the police for being pregnant with a man other than my husband. The punishment for something like this is prison.

I was detained for three days. My husband kept my son, Deng, for those days. They took my statement and there was an investigation. I said my husband was a jealous man. I said I'd had a relationship with a boy before I married, and my husband thinks I still have a relationship with him. It was all lies. Nothing had happened. After they finished the investigation, they appointed a guardian to speak for me to officials, because I was not important enough to defend myself. Nimera's father spoke for me. He wrote a letter to local sultan leaders telling my story. One of the leaders came and took me out of the prison. Everyone in the neighborhood was talking about me. I was given a very bad name.

After that, I had to go to the court. When we went to the court they spoke to my husband first, because he was the one complaining. He said this is my wife, and she is pregnant from another man. The judge asked me for my say. I told him, "Your honor, it's a lie. Akaich is my man, I am living with him, I got pregnant with him, and

I have been pregnant for several months with his child." The court asked my husband to bring witnesses to show I was pregnant with another man.

When we left the court my husband started beating me in the street. My back was hurt very badly, and my whole body was traumatized. When I got home, I lost my babies. A midwife came to take my babies out. They were twin girls; one of them was dead already and the other lived for five days.

After this, the house was so full. People came from the neighborhood to give me the evil eye and feel happy about my loss. When someone would come, they would say, "Oh yes, she deserves it." Everyone was surrounding the house demanding to know the name of the other man. It is a tradition that when a woman goes with another man, she should say who the other man is. When the twins were born, people were saying the man should come and sacrifice two sheep or else I would never have children again. I told them I don't have a man. I was bleeding badly, a whole tub-full of blood. All day I was so tired, and I'd lost my babies, and there was lots of blood, and I was so thirsty and so weak. I asked for water and they said, "No water for you unless you tell us the name." I was so thirsty that even talking was hard. My tongue would stick to the top of my mouth. They said, "No water unless you talk."

They brought local Dinka sultans to the house. I told them the father of the children was a northern Arab from across town, but it was a lie. It was not true. My husband became so happy, and everyone was so happy because now they could go to this man and take cows or property from him as compensation. The neighborhood would get to share this compensation to right the wrong. This is the tradition in all of Sudan. Those uneducated people had ancient traditions, but I was just so thirsty and I wanted to live. I said it to save my neck. They gave me water.

It was evening, and I told them I would give details about the man in the morning. That day my husband came with a sultan and two witnesses and asked me about what I had said yesterday. I started lying to them. I told them the man was a trader from another neighborhood. I wanted to keep them happy. They took me to court with the witnesses. I told the judge I had lost my babies. They gave me twenty-one days in prison. The judge asked me, "Is this all true?" I said that I had only said what I said because I was thirsty. The judge asked my husband if it was true that they had kept water from me. My husband said yes. The judge said the session was over. He said he was finished until there was real evidence, and I would not go to jail. He said he would call us back to court in two weeks.

My husband had a lawyer, but I didn't have one. When we were in the court that time, a lawyer came up to me and said he wanted to support me if I paid him. I told him, "I have no money and that's why I have no lawyer." He gave me some free advice: He said in court I should ask my husband if he's ever seen me with another man. He said that was the most important question to ask so the judge could see my husband was lying.

When we came back two weeks later, the judge asked for my husband's witnesses. My husband said he could not find them. The judge asked if I had anything to say. I asked my husband if he had ever seen me with another man. My husband said no. The judge decided I was innocent of adultery. I went back with Nimera's father. Even though my husband was his cousin, Nimera's father was very supportive of me.

I wanted a divorce. Akaich only wanted to separate but not divorce. I went to the special family court for non-Muslims and asked for a divorce. Then my husband converted to Islam, because in Christianity I could get a divorce for what he had done, but not in Islam. They took my case from the non-Muslim court to the *sharia* court. The *sharia* judge said this man was my husband, and he doesn't want to divorce you so you must stay with him.

I had lost all my defenses now. I couldn't do anything. He was a criminal. He was evil. I just gave up. Now I was not really married, but not divorced. The elders of the neighborhood decided we should stay together. I asked for a home of my own. My husband agreed. He said he would slaughter two goats in memory of my lost children. He said he wanted to sleep with me again to make new children. I said no.

He left for Singa, the village of his childhood, and took his other wife and my child, Deng. I followed him to Singa to get my child. When I went to his house, he beat me up. I went to the police station to file a report, and I was taken to the judge. My husband came to the court; he said he was a Muslim, and I was his wife and I belonged to him and the child belonged to him. He told the judge that I just wanted to roam around and not stay at home. I knew nothing about *sharia* law, and I just lost. The judge said I was married to this man and I must stay with him.

I returned to Khartoum and lived with Angelina again. My husband stayed with his other wife. My husband came back six months later with my son and some money. He stayed for a week. This was when I became pregnant with my second son, Bol.

Akaich did not give me my own house. He took me to Nimera's father's home and put me there. He gave me about five Sudanese pounds every day (US$2.50). I used to go out and work to support myself. I would wash clothes and iron them. I would get paid by the dozen, about two pounds (US$1) for a dozen pieces of clothes. For about six months, I was happy there. My fun would be to sit and chat with the many wives of Nimera's father, maybe have some Sudanese coffee and eat. Soon I moved in with Akaich again.

Eight months later I had my second son, Bol. I was imprisoned for fifteen days for making alcohol. They came in and arrested the women for brewing. We always hid the alcohol in the ground, but the soldiers found it by poking with their rifles. I was in the shower.

They made me get dressed and take my son because he was breast-feeding. I went with them. The prison was really dirty and smelly, and people slept on the floor.

After fifteen days in jail an officer came to me. He asked who had brought me to jail and I said I don't know. He said he would talk to a judge to set me free, because people looking like me should not spend any time in jail. This officer was nice, and very cute really. The nice officer took me out of jail and put me in his office with my son. I wasn't sure if he was trying to have a relationship with me, but he just gave us tea and milk and desserts for my child. I was able to sleep in a bed that's usually for officers. After three days I was allowed to leave.

Akaich was an army soldier, and I knew that the war in the South was becoming very severe. People were evacuating and coming to Khartoum. They would all talk about how they lost their families, like me. Sudanese television would never say anything about that. There was a TV show called *Sacrifice and Battlefield.* They would show the brave northern soldiers as heroes—coming and conquering, and being brave and noble. They were not showing the truth about the fires they set or the kidnapping. They only showed brave heroes.

The southerners in Khartoum were treated so badly. In the past, the graveyards would be mixed with Muslims and Christians. Now they didn't let the Christians get buried in the same places. They burned small huts in the city, the places where people like us would live. They would start burning it down, not caring what's inside. Shortly after I left Angelina's hut the second time, it was burned down. They besieged the area, and every small house they saw they burned. Angelina's family was moved in trucks to a faraway place called Jabrona.

Akaich was upset about this because he was southern, too. In March 2000 he decided to leave work. When he tried to leave, they detained him, imprisoned him, and said he was part of the SPLA rebels. We were at home when they took him. The people who came weren't even from the army, they were from security. They don't wear uniforms, and you can't report on them, because they don't even exist. They are secret.

They came to the house at three a.m., tied my husband up, and started beating him. They told me that if I reported them, then my husband and I would just disappear. My husband was a big, tall guy, but they were bigger and awful. They took him away.

After five days, the same men came back again, also at night. One of them threatened me with his gun and said, "If you file a report you will die in the same way we killed your husband." Then I knew that they had killed him. While they told me to keep quiet, they raped me. I only saw three of them, but I am not sure how many it was. My children were in the small room next to mine, but they were asleep and did not come out. When the men finished, I ran outside after them to see their car. I saw a big Land Cruiser like the state security uses. It's a very expensive car, so only state security or a rich businessman would have it. After they drove away, I took my children and I left.

My feelings about Akaich did not change when he died. He was a liar. But I never wished him to die. If he had died naturally, it would have been fate. But he was killed by men, and they hurt me in his name after he died.

OUT OF SUDAN

As a result of the rape, I had become pregnant. I brought my children and went to live with a woman I knew. She was living in a building that was still under construction, and she was getting paid to keep strangers out. One day on the street I met a German man named Andreas. He worked as an engineer. I started cooking and cleaning for him. I told him my story, and he helped me and was very supportive and gave me lots of money. While I was working for Andreas I had the baby, a son named Ashweel.

Andreas gave me the idea to come to Egypt. He told me that if I come to Egypt and tell the United Nations my story, I might get to go somewhere else. I wanted to do it. He helped me get official papers and documents. I had to pay lots of money for passports and documents and it took months, but Andreas helped me. Even after the first agent just stole my money, Andreas gave me more money to try getting papers a second time. That time it worked. I remember I got the passport on September 11, 2001.

Once I had my passport, I went to the airport to buy my exit visa. It was the last step before I could leave. Ashweel was seven months old, so he was old enough to travel. When I came back, I couldn't find my oldest son, Deng. At that time, Deng was only seven, so he would not have gone away himself. My son Bol said his grandmother had come to take him to the market and then they would come back.

They did not come back. I was so afraid and I was confused. I didn't know what to do. I thought maybe to stop my traveling plans and look for my child but then I didn't know where to look, and I was so afraid to complain to the police. I called my mother-in-law. She said she didn't want Deng going to Egypt. She had taken the child away to her home village in Singa.

The next day I went on a seven-hour journey to Singa. I don't know what they told Deng while he was there, but when I saw him he didn't want to talk to me. Maybe they told him they would hurt him if he talked to me, but Deng is my son, my son, and I couldn't understand. The family said they didn't want me to take the child. My husband's cousin tried beating me up, and I just ran away because I was afraid they would kill me. I left. I was emotionally destroyed.

I could not stay in Khartoum. If I stayed longer, my visa would expire, and getting another visa is an issue in itself. I was thinking that I would come to Egypt and then come back to take my son. Then I found out that when you talk to the UN, you are cut off from Sudan. I could not go to the Sudanese embassy, and I could not go back to Sudan. I had to find another way to get my son to Egypt.

I left Khartoum with two of my sons. I took a train to Halfa, on the border. It was a tiring trip. I was carrying two babies. The trains broke on the way. Everything was very cold and dusty. I had to squeeze onto seats, and there was no place to move. I spoke to the other people, and everyone was talking about Egypt and Sudan and about their own tragedies, so I found out that other people had bad things happen, and not only me.

INTO EGYPT

I dreamed that I would go to Cairo and find my family and live with them again like when I was a child. I arrived in the city on a bus. We arrived at night. I was feverish. One woman traveling with me told me to go to a doctor and get some medication. Another said no, if I went to the doctor, they would see my passport and put me in quarantine and send me back to Sudan, because they were afraid of malaria. I didn't go to the doctor.

I went to the church at Abbassia because they receive refugees there. The bus stopped near the church, and many were there to pick up other passengers. I had nobody to pick me up. I had no blanket and it was very cold that night. It was November 16, 2001. I slept with my children in the church and slept near a woman called Abuk. I don't remember where she was from. Abuk had a big blanket with her from Sudan. It was really big. I shared with her and my children.

In the morning there were people selling tea and sandwiches, so I ate. The church people brought more food and juice and milk for the children. Abuk had a family in the Ardeliwa neighborhood, and I went with her to that house. I stayed there for a week, and then Abuk and I got our own flat. Her family helped me get a job in the Zamalek neighborhood cleaning for seven hundred pounds (US$130) per month. I worked for Egyptians. It was a tiresome job for many hours every day. I would leave at eight-thirty and come home at ten at night. The food they gave me in the day was not good, and they were not very nice to me. The mistress was merciless; every day I had to polish the wood and metals in her very big house. I worked for her for four months. Abuk would watch my children at home, because she had family in America so she did not have to work.

I was not making much progress. I made seven hundred a month, and I paid over five hundred just for rent. I was safe, but I was very tired all the time from long work and my babies.

Andreas had told me to go to the UNHCR as soon as I came to Cairo, but I couldn't. At the Abbassia church I had met a woman named Flora who said she would give me fifty pounds (US$9) if I let her borrow my passport so that she could use it to buy alcohol and cigarettes from the duty-free shop. She kept my passport for a week. When I got it back, I went to the interior ministry building, the Mugammah, first. People said I had to go there first for an entry visa or else I would be kicked out of the country. I got a stamp there, and then I went to the UNHCR.

In 2001, the UNHCR was different than it is now. They gave me a piece of paper that proved I had visited them, and they made an appointment for me two years in the future, in 2003. In two years they would interview me, they said.

A DREAM

When I got to Cairo I contacted my sister-in-law, Lena. She lived back in Singa, where my son Deng was being held. She was sympathetic about my lost son. I sent her money and put her in contact with the same guy who helped me get my passport. She was afraid and was telling me maybe there would be a problem, and I said, "No, it's okay, I just want my child." She took Deng from Singa, and he went to Khartoum with Lena to get his photo taken to finish the documents. He stayed with her in Khartoum for about a month. At the border, Lena pretended Deng was her son and brought him to me in Cairo at the close of 2001.

It was like a dream. I never imagined I'd find him again. He told me lots of bad things happened to him in Singa. He used to shepherd the sheep, and after school he had to polish people's shoes on the street. His stepmom would beat him, treat him badly, wake him up early, and he would work all day. He told me he had wanted to come to me when I saw him in Singa, but my husband's other wife was beating him up and treating him badly and he was so scared.

I WAS NOT BROUGHT THERE FOR A GOOD JOB

In 2002, I got a new cleaning job with a German man named Michael. He was so sweet and tall with black eyes. I started out working for him, but it became a romantic relationship. We dated for two years, but no marriage happened because he was already married. His wife was in Germany, and they were sort of separated and still together only for their kids. His job ended after two years, and he went back to Germany. He paid me very well, though, and took care of my children. He still calls me to this day to check on me.

Michael was good to me, but in the first Cairo year I had so much trouble. A friend of mine named Ragah was walking with me in the Agouza neighborhood at eight p.m. We were crossing the street, and a Saudi guy in a car stopped near us. He asked me if I wanted a good job and I said yes. He was dressed like a Saudi in long robes. It was just after I had left my cleaning job in Zamalek so I wanted a job. He said his house was across town, and he needed me to start today. I told him I had to go tell my family, and he took Ragah and me to see Abuk so I could tell her I had found a job. Ragah didn't want to come with me, but I told her, "Ragah, you have to come with me so I can show you the house because I don't want to go alone." It was a BMW and the glass was tinted; two men sat in the front and we sat in the back. I didn't know they were criminals because they looked like wealthy Saudis and they talked like Saudis, so I thought they were Saudis.

Inside the car, everything was dark from the dark windows. Every once in a while, a driver would get out of the car and make a call on a pay phone. I began to get nervous when he stopped driving. They took us into an empty apartment. They sat us in a room on a couch. The Saudi guy was beside me, and then me and Ragah and then the other guy. They closed the door and locked it. I felt my heart beating and something wrong was happening. The apartment was not even as good as my own.

I was not brought there for a good job.

One guy told me he wanted me to sleep with him. I said, "Me sleep with you? Did you bring us here so you could use us?" He slapped me and he had a knife. He said if I opened my mouth, he would cut me into pieces. He took me to the next room. There were other men in there standing in a line. It was on the third floor of the building, and all the doors and windows were closed. The man who slapped me said, "Take off your clothes." I tried to pull away, but he took out his knife and then he raped me.

The other man originally with us was still in the other room with Ragah, beating her up very hard. After I was raped, I went in there and saw an open window. It was the third floor. I thought that if I threw myself off I could die. The same guy who raped me raped Ragah.

A man from the other room came for Ragah. He told Ragah to go sleep with him. The man beat her up and dragged her away. Then I saw the men in the other room run out of the house quickly. I ran to the other room and saw Ragah hanging out the window and screaming. She was only holding onto the wall of the balcony. The neighbors turned on the lights and they saw. People came onto the street in their underwear. Some brought mattresses so Ragah could jump. Ragah let go and fell onto the mattresses.

When the first Saudi ran out, the neighbors grabbed him by the robes. Ragah was screaming. She was naked like the day she was born. Everyone came around with wooden sticks. I didn't know if people wanted to hit me or hit the man. I grabbed Ragah and we ran to the Saudis' BMW car, because I was afraid to stay in that neighborhood—it looked bad and strange. We got to a bridge, and the driver opened our door and said to get out. We told him to take us to the police. He said he would not and tried to give us money. I said, "I don't want money, just take me back to my home."

A car stopped close to us. An Egyptian man got out and asked if something was wrong. I said yes and told him what was happening. He went to speak with the Saudi and then got back in his own car. The Saudi driver started grabbing me to get me out. I said, "I will not get out until you take me to the men of law."

He drove me and Ragah toward our neighborhood. I saw the Egyptian private car driving behind us, so I felt a bit more trusting. He stopped once and said he was going to get money. He came back with a folder. When he drove again, we went to a construction site. He stopped the car and pulled Ragah and me out. Ragah was still not wearing anything. The Egyptian came. He took the money. The Saudi and the Egyptian beat up the two of us so badly that Ragah and I were lying on the ground and couldn't move. The cars left. It was very dark, and I wasn't able to see the license plates. There was no point in complaining to the police. They left us lying on the ground by the street.

The men had dropped two hundred pounds (US$35) next to us. I took off my shirt and gave it to Ragah for a cover. We took a taxi home. I never went to the police. I had no evidence and I was new to Cairo.

THEY DID NOT GIVE ME A REASON

In November 2002, I got a telephone call to go to UNHCR for my refugee status interview. A man named Ahab interviewed me and a woman was there. They asked me questions. It was a bit weird, because they would ask me a question and then go out of the room. When they came into the room again, they would ask me how I felt after being raped. The entire interview lasted half an hour. I really didn't get to tell them anything. They were not compassionate. When I would cry in my story, they would not comfort me. They stopped and asked if I wanted to move the appointment to another day. I said I just wanted to get it done. They got bored, and the woman would leave and come back again. It ended. I went back in two weeks to get my results. I found I was rejected for refugee status. They did not give me a reason. They gave me a month to appeal.

I was upset. I wondered why I came to Egypt. Now I was very upset. I think that the laws of UNHCR are good, but the people there do not care about refugees. We come from Sudan, and we only know about the UN for help. We go to their office and the security guards outside treat us like shit.

I wrote an appeal in December 2002 and gave it to the UNHCR office. I received an answer in October 2003 telling me I had an interview appointment for an appeal on May 5, 2004. When May 2004 came, I was working in Alexandria, because the family I cleaned for had moved there. I told them I had to be back in Cairo by the fourth of May at the latest. The madam told me she didn't want me to go, and if I wanted to go, I should leave and never come back. I told her to give me my money and that I would go, that the only reason I worked was to support myself while I waited for that interview so I could get away from Egypt. She said no, because she didn't want me to leave. I did not have enough money to travel back to Cairo and I knew nobody else in Alexandria, so I missed my interview. I made it to Cairo two days later. The UNHCR gave me another appointment for June 6, so I was lucky.

When I returned on June 6, I found out that there was a decision from Geneva. They had stopped giving interviews to all Sudanese. I asked why. They said it was because Sudan now has peace as a result of the Naivasha negotiations.[1] They said to wait until December and then we would have more news. They gave everyone there a yellow card, which means your case is undecided. Yellow only keeps them from deporting you. When December came, there was no news.

At All Saints' Cathedral, they had a meeting and said there would be financial aid for yellow-card people. I had my three kids, and I needed the money. To get the money, I had to register with Caritas, the Catholic Relief Services. The security outside the building was absolutely awful. None of the clerks inside would come and talk to us. They treated us like wild animals. They said come back another time. I needed to make money. I gave up.

A SMALL FAMILY

I go to the church in Abbassia, and the sultans sometimes meet there. Anyone who doesn't have a family goes to them for news of their family. In 2003, I was invited to Sakakini Church, and there in the office, they told me they had found my brothers. My brothers didn't look the same as when they were children. Their faces hadn't changed, except Farid became fat and huge, his face chubby and big. Deng is still thin, so his face did not change. When I met them, it was a beautiful moment. I cried a lot. I kept them with me at my home. It was a very good time. My brothers would sell hair creams in the market and help out in photo studios. That is how we got money and

---

[1] Discussions in Machakos and Naivasha, Kenya led to the signing of the Comprehensive Peace Agreement between the government of Sudan and the SPLM/A in 2005. For a timeline of independent Sudan, see page 382.

supported ourselves. Me and my children and my brothers were like a small family.

Deng and Farid told me about their time in the cattle camp when we were separated. They told me they ran away as well. They went to another city, not Abyei. Then they walked to Abyei, and then to Khartoum. Deng told me that Farid was very young at the time and got sick on the way. They were both under ten years old. They reached Khartoum. From Khartoum they came to Egypt.

They told me my youngest sister is in Dallas, Texas, and married with twin girls. She's very happy there, and I would love to meet my nieces.

They told me my mom was in Australia. She had taken a different route to Khartoum, then to Cairo, and now she was resettled. My brothers had signed papers to meet our mother, and Australia had accepted. They were ready to see her soon. My mom sent me a form, so I filled in the form, enclosed my case, and sent it in a letter. A lawyer went to my mom and delivered the news that I was rejected. Maybe it is because of my failures with UNHCR.

The foreign lawyer helping my mom is a very nice person and used to call me every day from Australia. My mom went to the refugee affairs office and complained and said, "This is my daughter, and I want the right to have her here." The lawyer was a very good person, and they sent me another form. Australia didn't reply to the second form. There is nothing to do now. My brothers were resettled in 2005. They are with my mother, and everything is good in Australia.

I found another person here in 2004—my friend Angelina from Khartoum. She heard of me, got my phone number, and called me, and now we see each other all the time. Her mother is dead now, but she's here with her four kids and she has another in her belly. She was married, and she had a dispute with her husband who got married to another woman. He took the money, the car, the house, and everything, so she came here. I am lucky to have my friend Angelina again.

There is a man named Abdel Monid who I met in Cairo in 2005. I had met him in Sudan years ago. He is a Muslim from Darfur. When I saw him in Cairo again we recognized each other. We started to see each other in a relationship. He is a short guy and I'm taller than him. I couldn't find a man tall enough for me! He is a nice man. He was nice to my kids and would come visit us. He manages a cybercafé. I helped him start it by lending him a little money. It was a good job for him. We got married on September 1, 2005. When he asked me to marry, I thought having a man in the family would make our life better in Cairo. Eventually I came to love him, but only eventually. Then it turned out he is not so great. He stopped treating my kids well, and they hate him now. One day last year he disappeared, and now I hardly see him. I have not heard from him in months.

THE LAW

This year, 2007, on January 11 at four a.m., I was on my way back home in a taxi from a friend's birthday party. A police car stopped us. There was an officer inside and two younger police also. The officer got out of the car and asked the taxi driver for his license. The officer found the driver's license had expired. He came to the back and asked me for my ID. I showed it to him. He asked for my residency permit. I told him it is attached to my husband's ID. He told me I had to get out and go to the police station to answer questions, and then I could go home. He put me in the police truck. Only the officer would talk to me. The other two looked nervous. I wasn't nervous.

I sat in the middle seat and one man was on either side. The officer said to me, "Listen, I got you in this car because I like you."

I did not expect him to say that. I respected him because, when he was asking for my identification, he was very professional. I said, "What do you mean that you like me?"

He said, "It means we can be friends, and I can help you with problems, and you will never regret knowing me."

I told him, "I am sorry, but I am a married woman, so I cannot sleep with you. We can be friends, but we cannot have a relationship."

He told me we could be friends and talk on the phone, but he would take me to the police station first. I hoped he would just take me to prison for ten minutes and then let me go.

They did not take me to the police station. The officer took my hand and put it on his penis. I started shaking. I told him I wanted to go home, but he said, "No, just five minutes, and then we'll go to the police station." The officer pulled me to the back of the car, and the other young policemen went up to the front so it was just the officer and me in the back. They drove to a dark area by a bridge. All three left the car and they smoked. Then the officer came back and sat beside me. He said, "I want to sleep with you, and then I can take you home."

I told him, "No, take me to the police station or leave me here; kill me before you sleep with me."

He said, "There is no way out. You must sleep with me."

I said, "I cannot sleep with you because I am on my period."

He said, "Okay, if you can't have sex with me, then you can give me oral until I come and that's it." He took out his gun and said, "If you don't do this on your own, you will do it against your will." He pulled my hair and made me do it.

Then he opened the window to talk to the other guys. There was a box of tissues in the front of the car, so I got some tissues and I wanted to keep some of the officer's sperm. Then he put on his clothes and he left. He ordered the other two men to do the same to me.

Then came the big, fat, lower-ranking policeman. He told me to do the same to him as I had done to the first. He took off his trousers and his underwear. He held me by my neck and he made me do it to him. After the fat one was done, I cleaned the sperm with a tissue and this time I hid it in my shoe.

The fat one left. The third guy was a nice guy. He came in and sat beside me and found me crying in the car. He said, "Don't cry, I wouldn't hurt you," and he didn't do anything. He sat beside me for about fifteen minutes to make the others think we were doing something, but he didn't do anything.

The morning was coming. When I saw the place in the light of day, I took note of where I was. The two that abused me went in the front, and the kind one joined me in the back. I had a small black bag with my phone and passport and 440 pounds (US$80). The men in the front took my bag; they took 400 pounds and left me 40. The officer told the man beside me to hail a taxi and pay the driver ten pounds. I told them I wanted my money back, but the officer pulled me out of the car. I shouted and shouted and screamed for my money back. The officers were nervous because the taxi driver was watching. The kind officer went and got my money back and asked me if I was still upset. I told him no. When they drove away, I memorized the five numbers on the license plate of the police car. I thought of their faces again and again so I would not forget them.

I told the taxi driver to take me to the police station in my neighborhood. The driver asked why and I told him. The driver said it would be safer to wait and go with a lawyer. He took me home.

IN THE MORNING

At home in the morning, I called my friend and told her everything that had happened. I asked her if she had the phone number of the protection office at the UN. There was no answer when I called. I sent him a message to please call about something urgent. Ashraf at the protection office called me at ten a.m. from his office. I told him everything, and I told him about my evidence. He said it was good that I acted bravely. He gave me an address for a women's rights organization. I went there and told them my entire story. They referred me to a lawyer named Mohammed Bayoumi.

It took a week for me to find my husband to get our residency document from him. When I told my husband what happened, he was very upset. Then he went to the district attorney's office with a report. One attorney read the report for an hour and then said he could not do anything, and we would have to take our case to a higher level. We went to the chief of the district attorneys, and we worked with their office. I described the men, gave them the tissues, and gave them the car number. The lawyers asked me questions, and I answered until they were done.

I can trust the district attorney. When I went to file the report, the office was serious about it. He asked questions and summoned people and confronted them in front of me. He was very harsh and upset with the police. I trust the attorneys, because they took the tissues with the sperm and analyzed them and they have taken blood from the officers to analyze it. They showed me a lineup to identify the officers, and I was able to point them out. The three police have been suspended from their jobs since January of this year, 2007.

The day after the attorneys confronted the police, there were police cars all over my neighborhood. They were asking for me. They wanted to take me to meet the head of the station and settle the matter now. I was not in the neighborhood when they came. A neighbor called my phone and asked if I had seen the police outside. I told her I was away and did not know. Another friend called and said the police were going through the buildings looking for me.

The soldiers found my son Deng. They asked him about his mother. Deng's friend whispered in the Dinka language that he should not answer. Deng does not really speak Dinka, but he understood and he shut up.

My friend Asunta called and came to where I was, outside the neighborhood. She told me I had to hide, and I became very scared. I called my lawyer Mohammed Bayoumi. Mohammed Bayoumi told me to hide anywhere I could, that police wanted to erase my case. I hid in Asunta's home and thank God they did not find me. They knocked on the door, but Asunta opened the door wide and smiled so they trusted her when she said she was alone. If they had done a good search, they would have found me.

FAST TRACK

Mohammed Bayoumi took me to the UN. I had an interview and the UN said they would get me a blue card for full refugee protection. A month later I got the blue card. Mohammed Bayoumi gave my case to the American Embassy, the Canadian Embassy, and the Australian Embassy. The Americans and Australians said they would only consider me for resettlement if my file was referred by the UN. So far the UN has done nothing. But the Canadians are considering me for resettlement. The process is called fast-track resettlement, because I am in danger here. They could take me any time, but I have no news yet.

If I traveled to another country, I might have protection from another government. Right now, nobody protects me. The United Nations does not protect me, Egypt does not protect me, my husband does not protect me. My husband told me that according to Islam, what happened to me means that I am no longer his lawful wife. I know he is just a coward and irresponsible and doesn't want to support me in my ordeal, and so he is finding excuses for himself. Without protection, my life is in the hands of God.

Now I am trying to get residency stamps, so I will be allowed to get copies of my police report and give them to the UN so they can help me get resettled. But the residency stamps are controlled by state security, and I think the officer's family has a hand in stopping me, because I still have no residency stamp after nine months of this.

PLEASE FORGIVE HIM

One day the officer went to Mohammed Bayoumi's office and said I should go to the district attorney's office and say I was lying about everything. Bayoumi took him close and said, "Between you and me, man to man, did you do this?"

The officer said, "Yeah, I did it."

Bayoumi said, "You're telling me you did this, and you want me to go tell my client to lie? If she denied everything now, I wouldn't allow her! I would let her go and pursue the case myself!"

We found out that the officer's father is a lawyer in the Court of Appeals, and his uncle was once head of national security. He seems to be a guy from a very big family. But I don't care. I just want to get my rights, and I just want to see it go through. I don't care if I get killed.

Somehow the officer got my phone number. The first call came from the officer's mother. She called and said whatever I want, if I want all the money of the Queen of Sheba, she would give it to me if I end this now. She admitted yes, her son had made a mistake, but it was just a simple one and that now he could lose his career, so please, please forgive him. I said your son should pay for this. If it was my brother and your daughter, I'm sure you would find justice for your child. She cried over the phone to forgive him for the mistake. She said Allah would never forgive me if I did not forgive him. I said that if it was only her son that did this to me I would have forgiven, but he also ordered other men to do this to me. He thinks he is the master of the world. He thinks everything belongs to him. But it is not so. The mother cried and I hung up.

The officer called. His other relatives called. I met the officer and his family two months ago. The officer's father comes to my lawyer's office all the time to bother him.

His mom came and met me in Bayoumi's office, begging for me

to deny the charges. She told me her son's wife wants to divorce him now, and he can't see his baby—please forgive him.

I said, "Madam, I'm a grown woman with children. If you think about what your son did to me, and if I had fought back, and they had killed me, what would have happened to my children?"

She said it was a mistake but promised Allah would take care of everything. She said I should forgive because Allah will take care of me.

I HAVE TO BALANCE

My children are beautiful. They go to a good school, and I only pay three hundred pounds (US$55) for the year. They have become afraid of the police. Every time my youngest son Ashweel sees the police, he runs to me. Every time I go out, he says, "Mom, don't go away; the police will take you." My boys are now thirteen, eight, and six. They are not so tall yet, but my whole family is tall and soon they will be tall. They don't mind about Sudan so much. They want to meet my mother in Australia. Sometimes they speak to my sister's children in Texas, and they want to visit there. For my boys, it is more about family than land.

These days I work as a hairdresser. For a short time I worked as a hairdresser in a Kenyan woman's shop, but now I work at my home and go to people's houses when they ask for appointments. Sometimes they pay me a hundred pounds, sometimes a hundred and fifty pounds (US$15–US$25). I enjoy the work. I have loved hair since I was a child in Sudan. I am good at the job.

I am grateful to God that I am here and I am alive. When my mind needs peace, I go to my friends and we chat and we have a coffee. We use a special mix of ginger and cardamom. We boil it several times. We sit and drink and chat. Sometimes I listen to music with my children. I listen to Bob Marley, and I share it with my children. "No Woman No Cry." My children like 50 Cent and R. Kelly, and

I sort of like them, too. I am a single mother, so sometimes I am a mom, sometimes a dad, sometimes I am a sister, sometimes I am just a friend. I have to balance.

I have no idea what will happen in the future. I don't even have an idea of what is happening now. I do not know if Canada will take me for resettlement. Even if they do, maybe I should not leave Egypt yet. I do not want to end my case against the officers. Maybe I will get justice. People should be strong in such situations and never weaken or give up. They should stay strong.

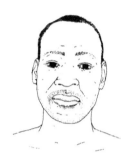

BOB (AHMED ISHAG)

AGE: *28*
TRIBE: *Fur*
BIRTHPLACE: *Kuro, Darfur*
INTERVIEWED IN: *Cairo, Egypt*

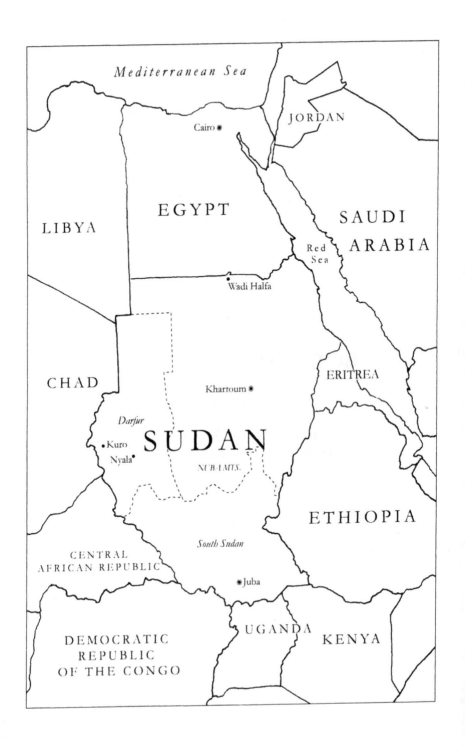

WE WANTED ISRAEL'S
PROTECTION. THAT WAS ALL

The interview sessions with Bob took place after midnight because he works well into the evenings. He sat shirtless on the couch in his hot, dimly lit apartment and spoke English in a deep voice that is made for radio. His flatmates chimed in intermittently to fill gaps in stories or prod him to tell some of the more sordid ones. Bob was energetic, infinitely patient, and laughing throughout the long nights of storytelling. At the conclusion of our final session, he said, "One day maybe I'll buy your book and read my story. I'll remember everything I've told you, and remember what I've forgotten, and then maybe write a new book of my own."

My name is Ahmed Ishag. I was born in Kuro village, which is outside the town of Zalingei in West Darfur. I was born in 1980, and on my papers it says I was born on January 1. We don't know my real birthday. I am from the Fur tribe. Now people call me Bob, because until about two years ago I had long Rasta hair, like Bob Marley.

My village in Darfur was beautiful. It was close to mountains, a valley, and a river. There were lemon trees, guavas, and mangoes.

We planted okra and sugar cane. There were many animals around—donkeys, horses, camels, cows, goats, and even savage hyenas. It was a beautiful place to live.

There were no schools in the village, just a *kalwa,* a place where children could go to learn the Holy Koran and religious traditions. My family sent me there because we are a Muslim family. My family believes in the Holy Koran and in praying. We are truly Islamic, but not strongly Islamic, I would say. The difference is that some people will say they believe in the Koran and then add stuff to use the Koran for bad things. But we just use it as a way to believe in God, to pray and obey its orders.

I have three brothers and two sisters. I used to have three sisters but one died from malaria during the rainy season of 1988. Darfur has almost no hospitals, so it's very difficult to get medicine from Khartoum all the way to Darfur when the heavy rains come and flood the roads. For that reason, we didn't get any medicine before she died.

My father was a farmer in Darfur with over seventy-five cows and lots of goats. Everybody had these animals—at least three or five. You can drink from them, you can use the meat at celebrations, and you can sell them for money to live. My mother is a very quiet, strong woman. She worked on the farm, too, and had a big garden she inherited from her own mother. She kept mango trees, guava trees, and lemon trees, and she loved that place.

My father's a short man, but he works hard—he's a strong man in his heart. He would care for us, provide for us, and protect us from invaders. Janjaweed militias have been coming for a very long time, long before the start of the war in Darfur. When I was a child, there were men coming on horses, stealing cattle, goats, food, and guns. We called their guns "Jims" because the gun model was GM3, I think.

These days the janjaweed are mostly Arabs, but when I was a child they were not only Arabs—it was a mix of different tribes, all desperate people from the bottom of society. *Janjaweed* were a problem, but the men of the village councils would come together to secure the lands. The sheikh—the village chief—would gather all the men, and if the janjaweed would come and attack, the men would shoot back and kill or arrest the thieves. If they were arrested, they would have to give back what they stole, and then they would be let free. When the attackers would come, the women would hide the children in the backs of the houses. My mother would hold me to keep me from seeing anything, but sometimes I could kind of sneak around the corner and see people on horses.

YOU COME TO KHARTOUM

I was about twelve when my father first left for Khartoum. He went by himself to the big, modern city. At first, he thought he would just look around and bring back some nice things like a radio and good clothes for the family, but he saw the life in Khartoum and decided to stay there. He called to my mother, "You come to Khartoum." My mother followed him. My grandfather and aunts weren't happy, but my father had discovered that Khartoum was really something else, and he wanted that.

After three months, my parents came back with new clothes, new shoes, and many things we had never seen before. Man, it was something else! Darfur is an undeveloped place, you know, and I'm talking about 1992 now, just when people were starting to go to Khartoum a lot to trade, to move there and build nice homes in the city. Back then, to see those new clothes was a big deal—the people in our towns were just wearing big wrapped cloths, nothing like the American clothes you can get now.

My parents came back and showed us their gifts for us. My father said he'd gotten a job in Khartoum, working as a mechanic's assistant for Naz Safari, a big company with planes that would take people on hunting trips. We would all move to the city, and it would be good for money, and also good for the children because we could study in the city schools. It would be a big change for all of us, but my father was so happy. I just saw those new clothes, and I knew that the president lived in Khartoum, so I thought it must be a good place.

We traveled on a truck to Nyala, and then on a train to Khartoum. I wasn't really excited for the trip. We always saw those trucks bringing loads of things to Darfur—vegetables, things like that—and the people would be up on top, outside of the truck. When it was our time to go, they just put me up there. They said, "Stay here," put stuff all around me, and then we were off. Not the safest thing—one big bump and you go flying. But we made it to Khartoum.

When we arrived, we didn't go to the big buildings and cinemas I had expected. We went to Mayo camp, where all the houses are broken, and when it rains there's so much mud that they cancel school. Mayo camp, where there's no electricity, no hospitals… and I just thought, shit! This is the same as Darfur, except without the trees or the rivers, just desert and puddles of mud. We did get to see the center of the city, of course. I remember seeing the huge buildings and just wondering, "How do people get to live in those things?"

My father went to work with the mechanics, and did little jobs on the side here and there. My mother started selling tea. In Khartoum, everywhere you see a tree, you see a Darfurian lady or a southern lady underneath it selling tea. They have these metal cans and coal and bottles of water and spices, and they find a spot and sit and brew tea for the daily workers. That was my mom.

There was a little school in the camp. It was just a mud hut really, and it was run by a church. I had trouble at first—I knew how to read a little Arabic, but only from the Holy Koran. This woman teacher was really good to us. She saw that my siblings and I were very clever and she tried to help us. She made us some birth certificates and took us to the government school. The people at the school looked at us and said we were too big to be in the lowest class, but we didn't qualify for the higher classes. They told us to go back to the little school in Mayo, work on our Arabic, and come back in a couple of years. I said, "Okay, I can wait."

There was so little in Mayo for us—imagine a whole city of just dust. Every time I would go and play football, I would be running and I would have to stop in the middle of the field because of the dust. There was no grass to play on, you know, just dust, and there were cars driving all around making dust, and I would get this cold in my chest. One time, it was like I got kicked in the chest, and I leaned over and couldn't breathe. Friends brought me home and told my mom, "Your son is gonna die if he doesn't stop." I met this doctor from Canada who was working for the Red Cross, and he gave me some stuff to make it better. When we were lucky, we would find organizations like that coming to visit and help a little. There was the United Nations World Food Programme, too, but in general they weren't helping, because the government stopped them with their rules and orders. The good people could not help us even if they wanted to.

IN KHARTOUM I SAW THE TRUTH

For a few years, I worked as a water seller in Mayo. There was no running water out there, so I'd buy a big jerry-can of water at the market in the morning, and I would walk around yelling, "Water, water, water!" all day. It gave me enough money to eat some breakfast, eat some dinner, and then save enough to buy another big can of water. All that time, I was working on my Arabic too, learning the grammar, learning the words.

After a while, I heard about a school in the center of the city at the church of Saint Peter and Paul. And I heard the school was free. So I took my money the next day and I went to the school, and as soon as I got in they said I have to bring someone bigger to be my representative. I just went outside and went to the first man I saw and asked him to come back into the school to sign something for me. When I brought him back in, the teachers just started laughing and told me to go get a man from my family, not some guy from the street.

I came back the next day with my older brother, and he went to go see the master, and I went with one of the teachers. They found that I would be a pretty good student at this point, and they said, "Class three would be good for you," but I said, "You know, I want class four! I want to go fast! Ah, come on, put me in four." I lost. They assigned me to class three. They sent me straight to the class, and that first day, that first time, they gave me papers and pencils for free. Oh my! They gave me a new T-shirt for free. Oh, it was very exciting. From that moment, I was just very happy. My parents were happy I was studying. My father and mother would even come visit the school sometimes to see how my studies were going.

Most of my classmates were Christians from South Sudan, but around the time I came—we're in the middle of the 1990s now—there were more and more Muslims at the school coming from Darfur. There were maybe fifty or fifty-five of us in the whole school. The church did a nice thing for us. They brought in a Muslim teacher to teach us Islam, so we would go out for that when they would teach Christianity and read the Bible. It was so considerate. They never put religious pressure on us. When Christmas was coming they would pray, and we'd sit and smile and then there would be a party for everyone. Nobody was saying, "You're a Muslim, and we're Christian."

Even when they opened a new school in Mayo, I stayed at the church school. From school and the market I met many southerners. The civil war was still going on at that time, and I would hear talk about the Southern rebels, about John Garang, their strong leader, and I believed in his path. Back in Darfur, they would just wash our brains with talk of *jihad*. They'd tell us that the Southerners want to bring in the Jews, that the Israelis used to be in South Sudan a thousand years ago, that the Christians wanted to bring back the people from Israel to take over the land. For real!

We were like goats back then, you know—no education, no nothing. If you tell a goat, "Go and throw yourself in the sea, and you'll go to paradise and meet beautiful women," then the goat will go and do it, even if he's just going to a sea of shit. I started to see the difference between Islam and the words of the imam. I stopped going to the mosques on Friday, because they'd just push and push and push with words like this, and I didn't go back until I found a mosque that spoke of open minds and peace.

You see, in Khartoum I saw the truth. In Sudan we have, like, five hundred different tribes, but the government is run by only three or four of those tribes—so what happens to the rest of us? If you go out into Khartoum and talk about politics, they catch you and beat you. Then you see the leader Garang, fighting for our rights, and you just have to say, "Oh yeah, he's a good man; he has to change this fucking government."

WOMEN FOR BOYS

In 1997 I entered the Khartoum Academy for secondary school, and got jobs washing cars, doing mechanic's work, and other little things like that to pay my tuition. Studies were still good, and I was dreaming of becoming a big engineer. I stayed out of fights—the only fighting we did was study-fighting, to see who was the most clever. The Academy was only for boys, but it was right next to the girls' dorms at Khartoum University, and in between classes the boys would just sit in the yard, drinking tea, watching the naked girls walk from the dorms to the toilets. No, they weren't really naked, but they weren't always wearing a *hijab,* so for us it was like being naked. They'd walk to the toilets and see us watching, and the shy ones would yell at us, but some of them would wave. We loved it—university women for secondary school boys. One day, though, they put up a curtain, and it was like a big wave came and washed our girls away.

That was as close as I came to girls in those days. I had a girl-friend, in a way. Her name was Lubna, and I would buy her gifts, and speak with her, but nothing else would happen until marriage. Of course, some guys would have women to sleep with. There were places to go when you wanted to relax your body. You would go and find a girl, pay, and that's all it was, business. I just looked forward to university, where it would be girls and boys together.

My mother and father divorced around that time. My father is a good man, but he likes women, and he found a younger woman that loved him too. He asked my mother if he could take this woman to marry as well. My mother said no, so they divorced and now my father has remarried. It's okay though. I still love both of my parents.

SALAAM ALAIKUM

In my second year at the Academy, I came home from school one day, and I saw this big group of police at the bus station asking everybody for their ID. The boys without IDs were picked up right there, and they took them to the military camps for training, to give them guns and send them to the South to fight in the war. I had a school ID, so I was okay that time, but they were just waiting for me to finish my exams. After that they would send us to the South to fight, and if we lived, we could come back and go to university or get a job. It really was like that—you'd give the teacher your final exam, and he'd give you a ticket with the name of your training camp and say, "Salaam Alaikum," Peace unto you! There was no peace where you were going, though.

My two older brothers had already been assigned for training, but they didn't go. They kept running away from the training camps and hiding from the police. One of my brothers went to jail for this twice. My other brother saved some money and went to a doctor who changed his medical forms for him. The doctor wrote down that my brother had problems with heart attacks—not a weak heart, but heart attacks! It was bullshit, but it worked. My brother kept that paper in his shirt pocket, and when they found him the next time, they just took him for an easy job guarding the camp for three months.

My time came for exams. I got first-class marks, by the way. But I remember the last exam was in history, and when I turned it in, they gave me that paper, and said "Salaam Alaikum!" I smiled at them, signed the paper, and yelled out "Allah hu-Akhbar!" Then I went straight to the schoolmaster and begged him, "You have to rewrite my school ID." So we made a deal. I still owed tuition money, so he gave me a three-month extension and told me he would extend the ID until I paid. Then he gave me a second card, a brand-new one to last me another year. It was great—the police were stopping me those days, and I could just say, "Oh no, sir, I'm still studying, but the day after my exam I'm going to go fight, Allah hu-Akhbar!"

I was working hard those days, making money. I wanted to go back to Darfur, really, but I found out the roads to Darfur had checkpoints, and if they had caught me on the way, they would have sent me to those training camps. I didn't want that kind of trouble. My brother was already hiding from the police, my sister was trying to save some money to finish her education, my mother was selling tea all day, and my father was working like always. We were always running around for work. I would go to different neighborhoods washing and driving cars for people. It was just small work, and really I still had nothing. I was always worrying that they would pick me up at the bus station one day and send me to the fucking war.

It was like that until my friends came to me one day with some money to lend me. They said, "You don't have anything. Go to Cairo. Work, study, leave this government behind, because they're gonna catch you. If not today, tomorrow they're gonna catch you, and if you don't obey them, you'll go to jail."

I told my mother I was leaving. She was upset because she didn't want her child to leave her. But she knew I had no choice. She said, "We know you don't want to go south, that you don't believe in this war. You know we don't want you to go, but if you go, you study." With my father it was easier. He was eager for me to go. He knew my situation, and he was also scared about what was happening in Darfur at that time. He was always sending a little bit of money back to Darfur—groups of men would collect money to buy a mill or a water pump or some medicine for a village. They kept in touch with home.

Through that contact, he knew that the janjaweed were becoming a bigger problem than ever before. More cattle were being stolen. They were cutting off people's hands to make an example of them. The government was acting suspiciously—shootings in the police stations, new police coming in, things like that. He knew that the people of Darfur consider that land their ancient kingdom, and he knew there would be fighting. He wanted me far away from all that. He told me, "Go to Cairo, but try not to stay there. Try to get to another country. Get to America or Europe to study. I hear that there's nothing in Cairo. Get past there. Get an education; come back and solve these problems here. Take your time," he told me, "because this isn't going to change in one day, but it's your generation that is going to change this situation."

I didn't tell my girlfriend, Lubna, that I was leaving. I thought it would be better just to get to Cairo, send her a big gift, and call her on the phone to give the news. I thought that if I was already gone, if she didn't see me in front of her eyes, it would be a little bit easier. But the day I was leaving was just too difficult. I told Lubna I had to go to Cairo. Then I asked her mother if I could marry her. I didn't ask in the formal way, but we were all talking and sitting and I said,

"Yes, I want your girl. I love her; I'm gonna marry her." We all knew how difficult that would really be.

JUST A CITY LIKE ANYWHERE ELSE

I took the train to Halfa, in the north of Sudan. I actually got stopped there—a guard was suspicious of my papers and took me in. When the boat was leaving, though, they said, "He's just one person. Let him go." They asked me for *baksheesh*—a little bribe—and they let me go. I don't know why it happened. I guess they got lazy. They let me onto the boat, and I sailed to Aswan, Egypt. It was the winter of 2000. I was twenty years old.

On the boat to Aswan I met some guys from Darfur, and some from the Nuba mountains. They were in even worse shape than me. I had a bit of money from my friends and my mother, but they didn't even have enough to eat. I said, "We'll share until we get to Cairo, and God can help us from there." When we arrived in Aswan, we went to the train station for tickets to Cairo, but we found the tickets were much too expensive.

Instead of a train, you could hire a microbus to drive you, but I was nervous—we didn't know these drivers. They had a plan that worked for us, though: they would take our passports, drive us from Aswan to Cairo, and then when we arrived, they would go to the duty-free market and use our foreign passports to buy cheap alcohol and cigarettes. They said they'd even give us fifty Egyptian pounds (US$9) in the deal. We said okay, and they drove us. But look what happened: When we got all the way to Cairo, they looked at my passport, and it said I was only eighteen years old! You have to be twenty-one to buy alcohol. "Ah, man," they said, "you're too young!" But we'd already arrived. "Pay us for the ride," they said, but I only had a hundred twenty pounds left at that point, and that wasn't nearly enough. They threatened to keep the passport. In the end, they just bought lots and lots of cigarettes and took all my money, except for five pounds—one dollar—that I had kept hidden. I had a dollar left when I finally started life in Cairo.

People had told me to go to the Agouza neighborhood once I came to Cairo, because lots of people from the Fur tribe lived there. I saw a coffee shop in Agouza with lots of Sudanese sitting around. I guess they knew I was new, because someone asked, "Where you from?" That first day, someone took me in to stay with them. That's how we behave in Darfur.

I'd seen Cairo's big buildings on TV many times. But to see the streets in reality was different. It's nothing special, just a city like anywhere else, and the life was just like Sudan.

In my first week, I got lucky. One of the other guys in our house quit his job. He had been washing and cleaning a woman's house, but he got in a fight with the woman because she was always shouting at him. Of course, I said I would take the job for him. I wasn't afraid of any type of work.

The lady was from a big political family in Yemen, and she was crazy. I had to work from seven in the morning until eight at night, cleaning her huge villa in Zamalek, the fancy island in the middle of the city. Every day I would clean everything, and then the next day she would make me come and clean it all again. And it wasn't just me—there were twelve of us servants! The Sudanese would clean, and the Egyptians would cook. The salary was really small, but at least she gave us good food to eat.

I kept searching for new work all the time, but it was difficult to get work in the winter. It's easier in the summer, when the rich people go to Alexandria or Sharm el-Sheikh and take extra servants with them to their summer homes. In the winter, though, they only keep the Cairo homes clean.

After six months, I had to leave the crazy villa lady. She had me working twelve hours a day, and I was too tired to even try to study.

I had promised my father I would try to study. The problem was that the lady really liked me and didn't want me to leave. When I told her I was leaving to go to Cairo University, I don't think she believed me. She even had her driver take me to the university the day after I left. He drove me to the front gate and tried to follow me in. I told him to wait outside, and I'd get him a pass. Then I ran away through the exit on the other side. She was right when she didn't believe me. I still didn't have any money to study.

I did find better work. A man from South Africa and his Egyptian wife hired me, and through all my time in Cairo, they've always given me some work when I needed it. At first, I just did some cleaning, but they helped me get a driver's license, and now I drive for them also. The hours are better, usually from nine-thirty in the morning until eight, or noon until midnight.

I've been a driver for many clients. Sometimes they're good, and sometimes they're bad, and sometimes I'm not so great either. I was a driver for this Egyptian woman, and late at night I would go and sneak down into her office to use her computer. Her password was her daughter's name, so it wasn't difficult to open. I would use the computer to chat with Americans, asking for lyrics for songs like 50 Cent singing "In da Club," Tupac, Ja Rule, Jay-Z, hip-hop music like that. And of course, my favorite, Bob Marley. One day the woman caught me at the computer: "Hey! What are you doing?"

"Ah, I'm just chatting with my friend in Canada. I'll be finished in five minutes." She was angry, mostly about the bill. She checked the bill and saw that I was chatting online for six hours sometimes. I didn't work for her much longer after that. But I still love American music.

On the crazy side, I worked as a driver for a very famous Egyptian actress here. She had this big new BMW. Her husband was this big businessman, and he was gay, a homosexual. Sometimes I would drive him, too. One day he took me to this big house, and inside there was a huge room with big paintings of naked women, a bed

big enough for six people, lots of pillows, two TVs, and lots of beer
bottles. He took out these sex videotapes and brought some beer and
hashish. He asked me if I was okay watching the tapes. I told him
I had seen this sort of show a long time ago, before Cairo. I told him
that for me, it wasn't a bad thing and it wasn't a good thing either,
that it was nothing for me. Then he started saying, "If you feel hot,
you can take off your clothes." I said, "I'm very cold." He talked
about how Africans have big dicks and fuck really good. I just said,
"Every country has weak people and strong people." I was ready to
get out. The man would do things like this often. He would walk
around naked when I was the only one home. He would kick his wife
while I watched, calling her a bitch, accusing her of cheating, even
though he was the one cheating. I couldn't call the police, because
I knew they would only arrest me and not him. He took me to a
club, and when we got there I realized it was one of the gay clubs,
with men wearing makeup and acting strange. He kept saying that if
I was good to him, he would get me out of Cairo someday, and take
me to France, and buy me new clothes. I wouldn't be good like that,
though. It's not for me. It's okay for others—there's lots of gay life in
Egypt, and even Sudanese do it when they come to Cairo, because it's
more open than Khartoum. But it's not for me.

When I came to Cairo, I stopped going to the mosques. When
the imam would speak at the services, I heard him saying things
I did not believe in. They would talk about violence like it was *jihad*.
They talked about the situation in Darfur, saying that the people of
Darfur were not truly Muslims, and that the Americans wanted to go
in to attack the Muslims. They would say the same about Iraq. You
know, this is politics, not religion. But at the mosque, they would try
to hide one inside the other.

I felt like I was a guest in the Egyptians' mosque, and I could
not say anything. If I was in Sudan, maybe I could have done something, spoken out, said, "I'm here, I'm from Darfur, I'm a Muslim."

But in Cairo I'm a refugee first, and I'm in the middle of this old, closed community. I can't talk about politics in public. If I stood up and said, "Islamic nations are blind. You hear the news that the government tells you, and you believe it without going back to the Koran..." Well, you just can't say that. So I could not pray with them anymore.

If I'm in a taxi and the driver asks me about Darfur, they'll feel comfortable if I say, "America wants to come and take the oil." But if I say that it's the fault of our government, then it's a problem. Often Sudanese refugees will just say that we're from Aswan, in the South of Egypt, so we can avoid these discussions.

It's a trick of the mind when it comes to life and politics here. Every news program starts with a good story about President Mubarak, or his wife, or his son, Gamal. And the people think this is a lie by the government media, because the people know the real life in Cairo. But then the second story will be about Sudan, or America, and their minds will switch off and they will think, "Oh, this one is true." Goats, I tell you.

NOTHING UNTIL TOMORROW

My life in Cairo is lots of work every day, very little money, and a little time to sit around with friends. I make maybe five hundred pounds (US$90) in a month. I don't eat three times a day; sometimes once a day, sometimes twice. In the morning I might take a sandwich, and then in the evening we gather in groups to sit together and eat. You sleep, and you get nothing until tomorrow.

Because of work, I've never had a chance to go to school. Even the free classes at places like St. Andrew's United Church and the American University are too difficult, because they're in the afternoons, and I work in the afternoons.

There are six of us sharing a flat now; we've been in the flat one year. There are two rooms, a common room, and a kitchen. We're all from Darfur—no matter which village or which tribe. We are brothers now. We spend money on rent, a few clothes, telephone calls to family in Sudan, and then you find the money finished. We share a satellite television subscription, so we can watch the news about Sudan, watch movies and football.

I also play a little bit of football with a club at one of the neighborhood gyms. I'm really good, you know? I got recruited once and invited to a professional club for a tryout. I didn't have shoes, though, and I was working so much, and I really didn't believe that they would ever put someone from Darfur on their team. It was months before I saved enough money for equipment and got the courage to go. When I did go, they wanted to take me. They asked for my residency papers. I told them I was a refugee. The coach was very nice, and he even called the Sudanese sports ministry to try to get help. In the end, he just called me one day and said, "Sorry, I can't do anything." Now I just play on Fridays sometimes at the Jazeera club. Maybe it's not the end of my football career, though. I'm twenty-seven now, but I can still play. If I could get out of this place and go anywhere else, I could start in the lower leagues and work my way up.

LOC

I went to the UNHCR offices pretty soon after I arrived, to try to get refugee status. I went to the office and they gave me an appointment—they said come back in one year and two months! This was in 2001, when there were still lots of southern refugees coming. But ah, man, what was I supposed to do for one year and two months? They gave me a small paper to protect me from the police, but I'm nervous about police. I thought they could take me to jail and then back to Sudan anytime.

I waited the year and two months, working all the time, still no studying. I finally went to give them my application. I had written out my whole story, about the problems I had with the government, the troubles that were starting in Darfur, and the life I was living in Cairo. I requested help. They took the application and told me to come back in two more months for an interview.

In Sudan, the only time you see a woman's breast is when you're going to sleep with her. When I went to UNHCR for the interview, this Egyptian woman interviewed me, and I swear her breast was hanging outside her shirt! I could see her nipple and it was the scariest thing. She was wearing this short skirt and kneeling down all the time, acting like she wanted my attention. I must have been distracted because she said to me, "Your mind is not on your case. Where is your mind?" My mind was on her breast! I think she was doing this to distract me and catch me lying in my story, but I don't know, maybe she was just strange. She didn't ask many questions in the end. She asked weird things, like, "If the Sudanese government was fighting against the Egyptian government, and they gave you a choice, where would you stand?" She spent more time doing her hair than asking me questions.

When she was done, she asked me if I had anything else to say, but I just wanted to get out of there and get some fresh air. When I told my friends about the whole thing, some of them recognized the woman. One told me that she had shown him her underwear, and he got so upset that he made a big fight, yelling at her for acting that way, and she was so nervous that she accepted his application right there.

The next week I came back and saw the results posted on the door. I was rejected. I had told them my whole story, and I was rejected. Next to my name was LOC, which means "Lack of Credibility." They didn't believe my story.

I wrote for an appeal. I wanted another chance. It wasn't until 2004 that they called me back for another interview. In April 2004 I came back, and it was a new woman interviewing me this time.

Her telephone would not stop buzzing. I would start talking and she would pick up her phone and start talking. I got upset: "You know, last time I was here, the woman was doing things like this. If you don't want to interview me, I'm leaving! Finish my interview and then get to your telephone!"

I went back two weeks later, and they had closed my file. I was rejected again.

Without UNHCR to help me, I started going to all the embassies here in Cairo—Portuguese, Italian—to ask them to take me. But the security at the front were all Egyptian men. They wouldn't even let me in. I wrote notes to pass to the embassies. The guards would tear them up and throw them on the ground.

Every day I saw more and more Darfurians coming to Cairo. As the years went on, and the war in Darfur got worse, I realized that I was one of the lucky people who got out early. The government was closing all the roads out of the region. I figured there would be the liberation army, and some rebellion against the government. But I never expected that the government would retaliate like it did in 2003, going into the villages, killing the people, destroying the homes. My village was destroyed in 2003. All the villages in my area around the Tululu river valley and the city of Zalingei are now destroyed. There's no life there. If I had been there, I would have fought. I remember thinking when I was still in secondary school in Khartoum, If they take me to fight in the South, I would just take the guns and go to Darfur to protect the land there.

A PACKAGE OF REFUGEES

My Israel story begins with my passport. I carried my passport everywhere in my jeans pocket, and one day it was really crowded on the bus and my passport was gone. I went to the police station and told them, but they didn't care at all. They just said, "If you want to go away without trouble, then go. But don't come telling us your passport is lost." I said, "How come? I was on a bus and my passport was lost!" They said, "We don't believe you. Maybe you sold your passport for money. We can't do anything for you."

Now I had no passport and my file was closed. I had nothing, no protection at all. If I was picked up by the police, they could take me to jail. What happened next was pretty simple. I was speaking with my friend Mohammed Omar, and we said, "Ahh, let's go to Israel."

I knew Israel already. I saw it on the map. I saw news on the television. I know it's a democratic country with human rights— I know there's a fight between Israelis and Palestinians, and I read the stories about it, but if they put me in there as a judge, I would keep those Palestinians out of Israel, because they don't understand how the world works.

In my Sudanese passport it was written, "You can go to any country except for Israel." Why can't I go to Israel? What's the problem between Sudan and Israel? Yes, maybe, in the war between Israel and Egypt, the Sudanese fought with the Egyptians. But it was a war and it's now finished. Even Egypt has relations with Israel now. It was like a parent pointing at a mysterious box, saying "Don't open that box." I really wanted to open that box.[1]

I had heard that two Sudanese had snuck into Israel, but there was no real news, just rumors. Even if people in the refugee organizations would have talked of it, nobody would have advised going, of course. So my strategy was don't ask, and don't tell your friends until you get there. If I found the way was dangerous, I would call and tell people. But if I found what I wanted, I would call my friends: "Come on, I will tell you the way to go. Leave that fucking life there and join me."

A friend of my friend knew people from the Bedouin nomadic

---

[1] For more on Sudanese refugees in Israel, see page 432.

tribes on the Sinai peninsula, on the Egypt-Israel border. Mohammed Omar and I got the Bedouin's telephone number. They didn't give names in case we were ever interrogated by police. They just told us the plan: They would come to Cairo and take us in their car. "From there, you don't need to know anything," they said. "You'll just keep quiet in the back of the car until we tell you to go ahead and sneak." Simple plan.

They asked for money—two thousand Egyptian pounds per person (US$370). I took my savings and sold my things—my radio, my extra clothes—to get all of my money. My friends lent me some money, too—a hundred, three hundred at a time. They lent me money, even though they didn't know what it was for. Mohammed Omar and I told nobody. It would've been bad if someone had said, "This is a great idea! Let me come with you!" I had no idea what I was doing, really, and I couldn't think that someone else would risk their life for something they heard from me, when I didn't understand it myself. I was scared of dying—I mean, I knew it could maybe happen—but I had no life. When everything is lost, you have to go take the risk.

When I saved enough money, Mohammed Omar called the Bedouin and said, "We are ready." Six weeks later, in June 2004, they called back and told us a place to go meet. They picked us up in a red taxi, the type of taxis that are based in Sinai. They were very nice and sat us in the backseat. We picked up another Sudanese man along the way, and the two bedouins drove us out of the city. They were smugglers, and we were a package of three Sudanese refugees.

SNEAK

At the town of El Araish, we switched cars to a pickup truck. They put us in the back of the truck and covered us in blankets. We couldn't see anything. We just kept quiet, thinking. I was keeping track of the time in my head—if something happened, I would know how far we would have to walk to the closest city. Mohammed was quiet, too. I remember him lighting cigarettes under the blanket and lifting the blanket once in a while to blow out the smoke.

As the sun set and the moon started to shine, we came to a mountain in the middle of the desert. The bedouins stopped the car and helped us out. They said, "You go directly straight, not left or right. Even if you see a mountain, go over the mountain, not around. If you go straight, you'll reach the border, and then you sneak."

We walked straight for three hours. It was dark by then, hard to see anything clearly. We were dressed in black, wearing no shoes. We carried small little black backpacks. We knew we were at the border when we heard the sound of a military jeep. We dropped to the ground. We all just dropped straight down like we were marines.

The police jeep came near to us—maybe twenty meters—but they never saw us. We crawled bit by bit and saw the tents at the border. There was a fence. We threw our backpacks over the fence, and snuck underneath it. We took a deep breath.

Maybe seven or ten minutes later, we heard a big airplane coming from the Israeli side and saw three jeeps coming. They had huge lights flashing. We hid in the dirt again. They crossed right by us but again they didn't see us. We didn't show ourselves yet—we weren't totally sure that these weren't Egyptians. It was dark, and maybe we were in a space between the two borders or something. But then as they were driving away, we heard them shouting in Hebrew. "Mah? Mah? Mah?"—"What? What? What?" Mohammed knew some Hebrew from working in Sinai, and he said to us: "These are Israelis." Still, we weren't certain we were actually on Israeli land yet. We decided to wait until the morning when we could see where we were and who we were talking to.

The Israeli jeeps drove away to a hill, and for about half an hour they shined their lights in the area. Then they disappeared. We walked up to the hill they had just left, because it was a good point to see what was around us. We laid down on the hill. Mohammed and the other guy slept for a while, but I didn't sleep. I kind of kept watch.

When the sun came up, we saw a dirt path and started to follow it. We saw nobody—just Hebrew signs, and old broken vehicles that looked like they had been destroyed by bombs. We were dirty, thirsty, hungry, and tired. At that point the third guy was falling over from exhaustion. The summer sun was making him worse. We shouted into the air for anyone to come at us. We gave up after a while and decided to go back to the hill we'd slept on the night before. We figured the Israelis would pass by that point again eventually.

From on top of the hill we could see all the way back to the border. This time we saw Egyptian soldiers on their side of the fence. They started yelling to us, "Hello! Hello! Come back here! We'll give you water." We stayed on the hill. We didn't need their water.

Night came. The third guy was really, really weak. He came up with a plan to run back to the fence, shake on it, and run back up to us. He figured the Israelis had some sensors on the fence and that he could attract attention like we did when we crossed. He ran to the fence and then came running back, saying there were Egyptian soldiers at the border. I said, "They're not going to shoot us in Israel." I walked to the fence and started throwing stones at it, and banging things, making noise like I was trying to sneak through or something. In about ten minutes, the Israeli jeeps showed up again, and this time they were driving really fast. We waited until they sped past us. We didn't want to show ourselves when they were driving at us. We wanted to be as calm as possible and make sure we didn't get shot before the soldiers knew who we were. So once they passed us we stayed low, but then we started shouting out for help. The jeeps turned around really fast, like in the movies. We stood up slowly, still shouting, "Hey! Hey! Hey!" We could hear them loading their guns. They were ready to shoot.

They called out in English, "Who are you! Who are you!" We yelled back in English, "We are refugees! We are Sudanese refugees!"

IN ISRAELI HANDS

The soldiers got a bit closer, and then they smiled and relaxed. "Aw, man—look at these guys. They're black!" They put their guns down. One guy called immediately to the truck, "Bring these guys some water!" They brought us water and cookies. We told them we were the ones that they were looking for last night. They brought an ambulance for the third guy because he was very sick. They took us to a military camp nearby, and gave us showers and new clothes, and let us sleep all night.

Wow, we were happy! We knew they were going to ask us questions and there was a long way to go, but now was the time to sleep and get better. Everything was fine.

The next day the commanders started asking us for all the details. We told them everything, and again we said we wanted to become refugees. It was all very relaxed, and they told us they didn't know what would happen to us, but they would see if they could help.

I tell you this: we lied to the Israelis. We told them we had all walked from Khartoum to Egypt to Israel on foot. We didn't tell them we had been living in Egypt. No, we said we came directly from Sudan and only crossed Egypt quickly. We told them stories we knew from the news and maps to support the lie, but everything else was true. We told how our home villages in Darfur were destroyed, how we didn't want to be drafted into the army in Khartoum, and that was all true. We only lied about our stop in Cairo, and we gave false names so they could not trace our time in Egypt. The Israelis never found out we were lying.

Why did we lie? Because we thought that with the truth they would send us back to Egypt for sure. When you come from Sudan on foot and go straight to Israel, they're going to be nicer to you. Everyone was always asking about Darfur and *janjaweed,* but nobody asked about the normal problems for Sudanese.

Our first day at the border camp, two more Sudanese were brought to join us. They had come the same way as us. The next day, we were all taken to the immigration office in Beersheba. People from the immigration office and national security office interviewed us with the same questions, over and over and over. It was relaxed. They weren't asking difficult questions, just asking about our problems, about why we came to Israel and what we wanted there. They asked what they could do for us. We said we wanted their protection, and if they couldn't give us that, then we asked them to take us to the UNHCR. That was all. They said, "Okay, we hope we can do what you want."

They took the five of us to the jail somewhere in the Negev, the South of Israel. It was a military prison for Palestinian fighters. I don't know why they took us to a jail. We thought it was just temporary, while they were investigating our sneaking across the border, and then they would take us to a better place. At the same time, we are Muslims, and even though we're African and not Arab, we expected that they would put us in a place like that. The guards asked us if we wanted to be in the open air with the Palestinians, but we said no. We were put in small rooms that they used for punishment—each one was not much bigger than a meter squared. We could see the Palestinian prisoners sometimes, when we were going to the kitchens or the toilets. Some of the other Sudanese would speak to them in Arabic, but I lied and told them I didn't speak Arabic. I didn't want to get into discussions with them.

Once I was taking a shower in the bathroom, which was next to the prison kitchen. Some Palestinians who worked in the kitchen approached me after a shower and asked me, "Why did you come to Palestine?" I told them, "I didn't come to Palestine, I came to

Israel." They said, "Why do you say it like that? The Israelis are our enemies. We are Muslims." I repeated, "I am in Israel. I'm in Israeli hands. I am not on the Palestinian side." They were very angry, and started shouting at me. They wanted to fight. They were going to the kitchen, trying to get knives from there. Thank God the guards came back at that point, or who knows what would have happened.

After that incident, the guards moved us to another part of the jail. After about six weeks, the Red Cross came and interviewed us. They took our names and photos, our files and interviews. They gave us some fresh clothes. They said they would go to Tel Aviv and speak to some officials from other countries about resettlement. They never said we could just stay in Israel. One of the interviewers asked me, "Where do you want to go?" I said, "I will go anywhere that gives me freedom, protection, and a place to build my life. If the Israeli government will take me here, I will be with them. If they want to take me to any other country, that's fine. Even an African country is fine. Just not an Arab country."

The Red Cross took our papers, gave us their business cards, and they left.

JUST WAITING FOR NEWS

The guards were very kind to us in the prison. They taught me some Hebrew, which is very similar to Arabic, so it's easy: water is *mayim* in Hebrew, and *moya* in Arabic. We played cards and volleyball with the soldiers. We wanted a big football match between the guards and the refugees, but the big commander said it wasn't possible. He told the officers to wait until we were free and then to organize the match when we were free men.

We stayed in jail for another six weeks, always just waiting for news. Almost every day new Sudanese would show up. They heard the news, because when we arrived the Israeli newspapers wrote about us, and the Egyptian newspapers showed up, and even television—Israel Channel 2, the BBC. We weren't the first to come across the border, but we were the first that didn't just sneak across and stay underground. We asked for protection from the Israeli government or the UNHCR, and I guess that's why we made news. I think even Omar al-Bashir was asked about our case—he said that we weren't really Sudanese, that we were from West Africa, from Nigeria or Cameroon or something. The media asked us mostly about Darfur and the *janjaweed,* and then we told our whole story, without Cairo of course. We kept saying we just wanted anyone, except the Arab countries, to take us.

The number of Sudanese in Israel was growing and growing. After a couple of months, we had our own unit in the prison. One day some northern, white, Arab Sudanese showed up in the camp. They had been working in Sinai and heard the news about Israel and decided to come. One said he was homosexual, and risked persecution in Sudan. Another said he disagreed with the Sudanese government and was at risk of political persecution. They both said they wanted to go to Europe. But they were Arabs! When they put those guys in our unit, at first I thought it was like the Israelis were putting the rats in with the cats to see what would happen. But then I realized, it was because we were all Sudanese, and not only Darfurians have problems. Maybe these guys were suffering, too. Maybe they had their reasons. Mohammed Omar and I didn't speak to them—they would sit in one place, and we would sit in another. We wouldn't eat together. But there were never problems. After two or three weeks, the Arab Sudanese were taken somewhere else. The Israelis told us they had sent them back to Egypt. We never learned any more about them, and we didn't ask.

After three months in Israel, they took us to the UNHCR office in Tel Aviv. It was very different from UNHCR in Cairo. A woman named Sharona interviewed us in Israel and was so nice to us. She asked the same questions as usual, but she spoke to us in intelligent, human ways. In Cairo, I was always feeling confused and rejected. That lady in Israel made me feel like she really wanted to help us. She said they might transfer us to an Israeli civilian jail, with better food, and televisions, and better living conditions.

Then, two bad things happened. There was that school incident in Russia,[2] and there were two buses bombed in Beersheba, in Israel. All the bombings were by Muslims. This raised the tensions in the country, and when I was reading this news I knew it would complicate our case. No matter what, I am still from a Muslim, Arab country. I figured the Israelis wouldn't want us, because if we stayed in Israel we might meet Palestinians, have our brains washed, and go join the fighting.

AN ENEMY OF GOD

A few days after the bombs, the guards came and said, "Okay guys, we're taking you to the border today. You're going back to Egypt." We said, "No, we don't want to go back." They said, "This comes from high in the government." We were very upset. We started begging, talking about the life in Egypt, saying, "If you take us back to Egypt, they're going to give us to the Sudanese government. And we're traitors to the government, because we told our stories to the press!"

I knew the law in Sudan—anyone who goes to Israel is a spy, and the punishment for spying is death. We wouldn't even make it to Khartoum. As soon as we would cross from Aswan to Halfa, they would shoot us on the spot. Spies from Israel! In Sudan, Israel's not just an enemy of man, it's an enemy of God.

The soldiers were crying on the day we were taken away. They had no power to stop this. We were friends by then. You know, these

---

[2] In 2004, armed Chechen rebels stormed a Russian school, taking 1,200 children and teachers hostage, and eventually killing 338 people.

orders came from the Israeli authorities, not from them. They would have kept us if they could have. The day we left, the big commander of the jail came to say goodbye to us, and he cried in front of us. He gave me a card with his phone number and the number of Sharona, the woman from UNHCR in Tel Aviv. He told me to call him if I ever needed help. He let me call Sharona. Sharona told me she had sent our case to UNHCR headquarters in Geneva and that Geneva had said we had to go back to Egypt, that the Israelis didn't want us, and there was nothing UNHCR could do. I don't know if that was true or not, but that's what she told me. We were given a piece of paper that had government stamps. It was supposed to protect us—it said the Israeli and Egyptian governments agreed that we should not be sent back to Sudan.

I absolutely knew that the Egyptians were going to send us back to Sudan, because of the partnership between those two countries. But the officials kept saying there was an agreement and pointed to that paper. To me it was just paper.

YOU'RE JUST DEAD BODIES

In a prison bus they took us to the border in Brava. They called out our names and we waited for the Egyptian commander to take us. The Egyptians took us to interrogation rooms and started asking us questions about how we managed to sneak across the border. They asked us about whom we spoke to in Israel, and what we learned there. I told them the same old answers, but I was very cold to them. I wasn't afraid of them anymore. If they had beaten me, I would have hit back. In my mind, I was sure we were getting sent to Sudan anyway, so I didn't care anymore.

A man from Egyptian national security came to speak with myself and Mohammed Omar. Mohammed started speaking harshly to him: "The crisis in Darfur is killing people, and you Egyptians are making it worse." The officer started arguing back, but Mohammed pointed at him and said, "You are making this problem! And now look at where we are!" He kept yelling and pointing, talking about all the destruction in Darfur, about how our villages have been destroyed, and our people killed. This officer was a big, fat man, but I swear to you, by the end of it he was crying! Things calmed down and the officer brought us tea and Coca-Cola. We drank, and then we were taken to the jail in Rafah, which is just across the border from Gaza. We spent three days there before we were taken to Cairo in the back of these hot, horrible trucks. We couldn't breathe for the whole trip, and we were so upset.

We were taken straight to the Mugammah—the big interior ministry building in downtown Cairo. We were expecting someone from UNHCR to pick us up, but nobody showed. We only saw one guy from the Sudanese Embassy, who walked up to our group, counted us, and left. We waited in that office building all day, and then that night we were sent to the Attaba appeal prison. For the next three days, we were taken around to different offices—interior ministry, national security—asked those same dumb questions over and over.

At night, we'd go back to the prison. I'll describe that prison by saying: If someone offered me a choice between one hour in an Egyptian prison or ten years in an Israeli prison, I would go to Israel. In Israel, even the Palestinian bombers were treated well, with good food and showers. If you didn't see the guards, you wouldn't have known it was prison. In Egypt, it was filthy, and we were treated like animals. The food was shit. They'd take a pile of rice and soak it in cold water, put in a couple of old vegetables, and maybe some salt. The bread they would give was the worst bread ever—you could actually choke on little stones inside the bread. We drank our water from a tiny dirty faucet in our rooms. We never got a real shower. And the worst part is they never, ever let us sleep. Every five minutes, all night, they would come in, make you stand up and count you, or bang on the doors. All day and all night. Oh man, it was something else. It would be better to live in hell than an Egyptian prison. I was never beaten, but the guards slapped me on the head a lot and beat other inmates in front of me to scare me. They said terrible things to me, calling me an African monkey, a motherfucker, calling me stupid, calling me a spy. It went on like this for thirteen days.

After thirteen days, a commander told us we were being taken to Aswan, on the Sudanese border, and then we were going to be sent to Khartoum. He told us, "You're not even men anymore. You're just dead bodies." We screamed and yelled and begged to go to UNHCR. He said it was out of his control. We absolutely refused. I held on to the bars in my cell and wouldn't let go when they tried to pull me away. They had to handcuff us all, chain us together, and drag us out of our rooms, because we absolutely refused to go. I kept fighting, swinging my arms and kicking around. We all fought, and each of us was jumped on by five or six guys with their kicking and their sticks. I fought until I couldn't move. I started feeling like a dead body.

They drove us to the train station, and when we got there, there were so many soldiers waiting for us that you would have thought President Hosni Mubarak was coming. They threw us onto a train car that was packed with a hundred other prisoners. It was filthy in the car. There was no light, no seat, nowhere to piss or shit, so it smelled horrible. We sat on that train for hours going down to Aswan.

We were taken to a little prison in Aswan, and on the second day Mohammed Omar and I were taken to the Sudanese consulate. When they interrogated me, I told them my only problem was that I'd lost my passport, that I'd been taken to jail, and that I'd gotten into a fight in jail so they were sending me back to Sudan. I said nothing about Israel. I knew that they knew, but they didn't say anything about it either.

They tried to take our photos, but we refused. They were going to use the photos to make emergency visas for us to travel to Sudan,

BOB (AHMED ISHAG)

but I was ready to fight them every step of the way, and Mohammed Omar just kept shouting at everyone.

They took us back to the jail. The warden there held us down and took our photos. They brought in a man from the Fur tribe, and told us he was there to find out if we were really Darfurian, or just making it up. The man started speaking to us in the Fur language and asking about our stories. We spoke back to him in the language. Mohammed Omar said to him, "Why are you working with these men?" He said, "I just want to help you." We didn't believe him at all. We were so angry that a Fur man would work against us like that.

TURNED AROUND

We stayed in prison there for four weeks. Our day came to take the boat to Sudan. We were so close we could see the boat, when they suddenly stopped the car, turned around, and took us back to the prison. I had no idea what was happening.

Two days later, a manager of the UNHCR office in Cairo came to see us in jail. He spoke to me first and asked me the old stupid questions. He spoke to us all and said, "I'm going to help." Two weeks later, they released us.

To this day, I have no idea why we were released. Some people have said that John Garang, the Southern commander himself, heard of our story and he called the Egyptian president to intervene. I believe Sharona from Tel Aviv followed our case and contacted the Cairo UNHCR to save us. The Egyptians took my card with Sharona's telephone number, so I can't call her to find out what she did. I guess that to this day she is still waiting to find out what happened to me.

The officers gave us some papers and pushed us out of the jail, saying, "Go to the UNHCR office in Cairo. Get out of here." We didn't have any money for the train back to Cairo. We were still wearing prison clothes. We had no other possessions, not even our bags from Israel. But at least we were released.

At the Aswan train station, we managed to call a friend of a friend who knew somebody in town. This man came to meet us and loaned us four hundred pounds (US$70) and bought us a meal. We took the train back to Cairo and went back to our old neighborhood. For about two weeks we rested, and of course we told our whole story to all the Sudanese who would come and visit us. When I left for Israel I didn't tell anybody, so all my friends were shocked to see me again. They couldn't believe the story I told them.

We went to the AMERA office for refugee assistance, and the people there helped us deal with UNHCR. Within a few weeks, we were registered with yellow cards that gave us temporary refugee protection.

Would I do it again? Look, if I had four hundred dollars right now, then I'd be in Tel Aviv tomorrow. Since I was kicked out, the situation in Israel has changed. Many more Sudanese have gone to Israel and they're not being deported anymore. A close friend of mine is there now, working and living in Tel Aviv with a good salary, and he's so happy. There are about a thousand still in detention there, but they're going to be released soon and allowed to stay. There's been more attention to the life of the Sudanese in Cairo, and so the Israelis won't send the refugees back here any time soon. If I could go again, I would, and I wouldn't be afraid at all. Put it this way: I'm still practicing my Hebrew.

I am not angry at Israel at all. I think they misunderstood my case, and they didn't understand the life of the Sudanese. Israel couldn't believe that Egyptians would treat Muslims as they treated us. But after the violence at the Mustafa Mahmoud protests, when the world reported that, everyone knew for sure. Israel lives in fear of terrorism, so they have to be absolutely sure about people like us. Now they have enough evidence to know that our stories are real.

BOB (AHMED ISHAG)

OUR ELEVENTH OF SEPTEMBER

To understand my second period in Cairo, you must simply know about the Mustafa Mahmoud protests. This is the story of all the Sudanese community. The protests started in September 2005 when a group of Sudanese sat in the park in front of the UNHCR office and demanded their rights. The movement grew and grew. I helped them by doing reporting—the leaders needed people to post news on the internet sometimes or send letters to the news. I would write about what was happening with daily life. I would help to draft lists of requests from the protesters to UNHCR and the press. By the end, as it was getting bigger, they were people from other countries asking. We would send our stories to organizations around the world—the Red Cross, UNHCR offices overseas, places like that. Whenever I was free from work, I would go there and sleep there sometimes, too.

The people at the protests were very happy. They thought that one day good things were going to happen to them—believing that maybe UNHCR would remove them all and take them to another country. They had heard stories about Nairobi, when planes came in 2001 and took many Sudanese to America. They were hoping for things like that.

In December, on the day when the protest was destroyed by the police, I wasn't there. I was at work, driving to the airport late that night. When I came to the park the next morning, I found no people, only police. When I looked at the television and I saw images of protesters being beaten and killed, it wasn't like news, it was like a movie.

My friends were beaten and put in prison or military camps for a week, or a month, or more. After the protests, four of my six housemates were detained in jails. The other two of us waited and tried to believe this was happening. It was a shock; it was like our community's eleventh of September. Our big concern was finding our friends, to find out how they were and where they were. It wasn't very safe for Sudanese on the streets those days, either. The Egyptians were saying that the people in the park weren't really refugees, that we were sent to fight against Egyptians. The day after the protests, I went to the market and people were spitting on me, and the shop-keeper didn't even want to sell me food. I don't blame the people, though. Everybody knows how it is in Egypt. In the press, they're never going to say anything bad about the government or the police. Instead, they said the protesters weren't really refugees. They said we all had AIDS. They said we were having sex in the park. They called us dirty people. They said twenty-seven died, but I heard really it was more than a hundred, including old women and children. Even the opposition leaders were lying. There was nothing we could do. If I spoke to Egyptians, they wouldn't believe a black man like me. They're going to believe their televisions.

After the protests fell, the street gangs started to rise in Cairo. These were just Sudanese boys who were angry and had nothing, like me. I used to play football with a couple of the guys from the gangs, but now I don't know where they are. When they stopped showing up, I didn't try to follow them, because what they're doing is bullshit. Those people are crazy. They try to look like niggers in the United States, and they imagine they have some bond with the Americans. They're beating each other, killing each other. In the end, we are still guests in Cairo. We're not in Sudan—and even in Sudan, this is no way to live.

Maybe these boys have ideas about going to the West. But they don't know what's going on in America. I mean, nobody in America acts like these people here. In America, nobody kills each other like they do here in Cairo. Maybe people kill each other over business in America, and you've got those rap and R&B people, with the West Coast and the East Coast. Maybe those people shoot each other, but it's because of business. And there's politics in America, too. Maybe some of the black people don't like to work or do good things, so they throw themselves into selling drugs. And there are lots of Americans out of control from smoking and drinking maybe. But why do you have to do that stuff here in Egypt? You have no food, so you're going to act like you're in America? We're refugees here! If we act like those people, it means we don't need help!

If it was about protecting our homes, I would be with those guys in the gangs. But they're not protecting themselves, they're killing themselves! The stupid names—the Out of Law, the Lost Boys, whatever they call themselves—if they were protecting themselves, why would they kill each other? Those are not refugees. It's a shame for all Sudanese. If someone's going to help the gang members, I think it has to be their families first, and then the UNHCR. Sit with them, talk with them: What do they need? What do they want? At Mustafa Mahmoud, the Egyptians responded to us by beating and killing. Now we are responding by doing nothing when our own people beat and kill. It will only get worse this way, I am certain.

SEVEN YEARS

Last summer I got a job in Sinai, working under the table as a waiter in a beach resort. It was a job with long hours, and at first I thought the pay would be good, but it shrank when I had to bribe the Egyptian police so they wouldn't report me. You won't believe this, but one day I was in the restaurant, and a voice called out to me, "Hey!" I turned around, and a man asked me in English, "Have we met before? Did we meet in Jamaica?" I still had my Marley dreadlocks then, so he must have been distracted by my hair. I just kept walking, but he called me closer and said, "You're from the jail!" It was one of the guards from Israel! We laughed and laughed, and the guard started telling the story to all his friends. I wanted to follow him back to Israel, you know. Instead I stayed in Sinai, served meals and paid bribes to the fat police officers.

If I keep staying here in Cairo, what's going to happen to me? Look, it's been seven years here. Seven years! I have no permanent protection, no education, no good life. I hate my boring work as a driver, and I barely make enough money to survive. I can barely afford to call my mother in Sudan, and even when I speak to her, I'm ashamed of my life here.

I've lost touch with people in Sudan. No news from my best friend, Garan, since 2004—he was like my brother, you know? And nothing from my girl, Lubna—I don't even know where her family lives anymore.

My aunt in Sudan found a good girl for me and has been bugging me about this girl for years now. But I'm not ready to get married, because I don't have a life yet. I can't go to meet this girl in Sudan, and if she came here I couldn't support her. I would come home from work at midnight every night and she would be asleep. I couldn't rent us an apartment. If she were sick, I couldn't give her health care. I could only take her to the public hospitals, and you know, they steal organs in those places.

Now I'm applying again for a blue card at the UNHCR to give me official recognition as a refugee, but I'm nervous when I deal with their office because since the protests they're so suspicious of everyone. I even managed to get on the phone with Ahmed Mohsen, the UNHCR man who came to Aswan. I asked him about my blue card, and he just said, "You must thank God that we released you," and then he hung up the phone.

He showed no respect. I don't feel like I'll get a blue card, and even if I get it, what does that mean? Thousands and thousands of people in Cairo have blue cards. Maybe I can try knocking on the door of the Portuguese embassy again.

There's no way I can go back to Sudan at this point. They have a list of charges against me: I failed to go to *jihad* in the Southern war, I violated my passport, I went to Israel, and the worst, of course, is that I'm from Darfur. Being from Darfur is enough for them to kill me right there.

If I could go back seven years, I would not leave for Egypt again. I would go to Darfur. If I had been in Darfur all this time, I would not have gained the same experiences, but I would have been able to fight for my land. Just give me one sniper rifle and get me to Khartoum, and I'll find the president and change the history of my country. The people of Sudan are so afraid. They know the president, Omar al-Bashir, is lying when he yells "Allah hu-Akhbar! Bush! Bush! Bush! America, Israel, America!" The press is too afraid to disagree. The people are so afraid that they're like goats. They need something to wake them up and open their minds.

Sudan is in the center of Africa, full of resources. How can we be in this position in 2007? We could be a first-class African country. But the world doesn't care about us, and our leaders don't care about us. Even here in Cairo, we see these expensive villas that are owned by Sudanese government officials. Why are these guys taking their money to Egypt, to Switzerland, to Taiwan, or donating it to Hamas? In Darfur, people are dying from thirst, and these leaders are stealing our money. Everyone knows this is going on, but the common people like me have no power to change this.

Some nights Mohammed Omar and I will just sit all night and discuss what to do about our country. We want so badly to do something, but we have no good ideas. I know that first I have to get out of Cairo.

Of course, I'll get back to Sudan someday, as soon as we have a new government. It will be soon I think. If a UN force went into Darfur today, I would fly to Chad and walk back to Darfur. But if there were two planes waiting for me, one going to Darfur and one going to London, I would go to London. If I go to Sudan right now, I can help, but if I go to London first, I can learn to help in a more important way. If I went to England, I could study, get some work, save up money and learn skills, maybe even play football. I could take that money and that skill and bring it back to help my family and my people. If I return back now, though, I would add nothing. I would only be a burden to them. It would be cool to see them— when I speak to my mother she always says, "I'm going to die and will never see you again"—but from the UK I could send money to get her medicine. If I went to Sudan now, I would just be another hungry guy from Cairo looking for help.

If I went to fight in Darfur tomorrow, I would die, and then another uneducated person would come and die. And eventually one side will win and put another uneducated person in the leadership. This is how it works in Darfur. We should learn from what John Garang did in South Sudan. He fought and fought, but he also sent many children to the United States, Canada, and Germany to get education. Now the South has good minds to develop their land. We have a few of those minds in Darfur, but we need many more. If the UN decided tomorrow that the Darfurians could control their own land, we would not be ready. Our Darfurian leaders care more about their own power than about the people. If they gave me the power, I would take all the young generation outside of Sudan to get a first-class education. I would say to the children, "I don't want you now. Come back after fifteen years and help build our future."

Someday soon, I will get out of Africa and build my future. The first time I was unlucky. Next time I will make it, God willing, because my hope is dead in Cairo, and nobody is coming to help us here.

MARCY NAREM

AGE: *18*
TRIBE: *Dinka*
BIRTHPLACE: *Chokulu,*
South Sudan
CURRENT HOME:
Kakuma, Kenya

ROSE KOI

AGE: 20
TRIBE: *Dinka*
BIRTHPLACE: *Chokulu,*
South Sudan
CURRENT HOME:
Kakuma, Kenya

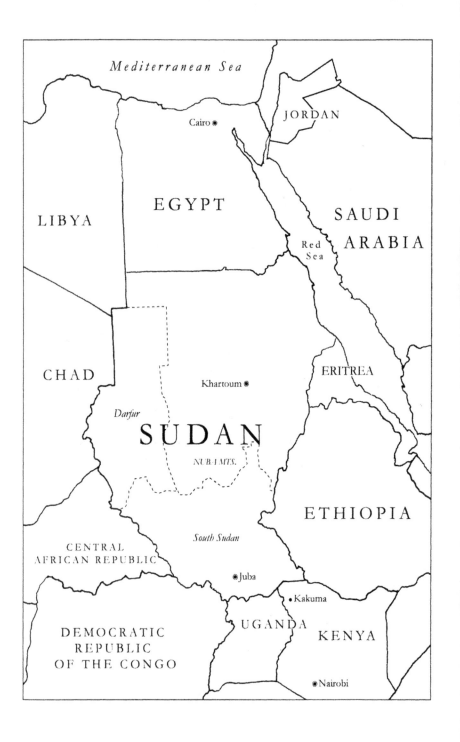

HAPPY ARE THOSE
WHO ARE MERCIFUL

The interviews with Marcy and Rose came along by chance. They had tagged along with their boyfriends, who were eager to tell their stories. Marcy and Rose sat quietly in the corner of a cockroach-infested room at the Kakuma Guest House. When asked to speak, they were hesitant, and agreed only if they could tell their stories together. Kakuma camp is their lives, they said.

MARCY: SUDAN IS FROM A TIME BEFORE MY OWN

My name is Marcy Narem. My father's name is Keng. My tribe is the Dinka, and I was born in a place called Chokulu, South Sudan, in the year 1990. I have two sisters and two brothers. My parents have passed, so I am in charge of the family. I look after us all, and I keep us all together.

In my mind, I only remember my home, but not the country of Sudan. I remember a big tree of mangoes, and all the land was very green. I remember being happy there, but that's really all. My father was a farmer—growing potatoes, cabbage. He was a nice man, very sociable to all people. He died when I was two.

I came to Kakuma Camp in 1995, during the war. I was five years old when I left Sudan. We took a truck from our village to here in Kenya. When I would ask my mother why we were here, she would say, "Because of the war with the Arabs." Everything that happened in Sudan is from a time before my own. After twelve years, I can say Kenya is my home, because this country has supported me for so long. Sudan would not do that for me.

When we ran from Sudan, my mother became sick, and I think she never recovered. I don't know what happened—I was too young to understand anything. Mother passed away three years ago. At the time, I was fifteen, and since then I've had the responsibility.

ROSE: I LOOK AHEAD, NOT LEFT OR RIGHT

I'm called Rose Koi. I am Sudanese by nationality. Like Marcy, I am Dinka, and I was born in Chokulu. This is how Marcy and I came to know each other.

I am twenty years old. I was born in 1988 or 1989, something like that. I don't have a birthday. I don't even remember Sudan or the place where I was born. I lost my mother when I was two years old, and my auntie took care of me after that. I have no idea about my father. It is impossible for me to find him, and I don't want to find him. My auntie told me that my mom was just a young schoolgirl when a man came and confused her and tricked her, and then she was pregnant; the man just ran away. When my mother died, I was left with my auntie. If she was a good auntie, I would have asked her more. But when I asked, she would answer so rudely that I was just too afraid to ask anything more.

My auntie took me to Kenya because of the war. I arrived in Kakuma Camp in 1997. From the beginning, my auntie would not allow me to go out and play with the others. She would just overload me with work and give me no time to read for school, or go to games.

She would have me work all day, so there was no school sometimes. And she would beat me. She loved her own children, but she would beat me. Sometimes when I would try to read, she would beat me and tell me I should go fetch water. She would even tell me to go fetch water while her own children were eating and then sometimes I wouldn't get to eat anything myself.

I've never had books of my own, because I don't have enough money. Sometimes other students would let me borrow theirs. Once I tried to get my auntie to give me money and she yelled at me: "I'm not the one who killed your mother! I have no money, even for my own children! Find your own money for your own books." I just cried, and I never asked again.

Life was like that for many years. It was 2005 when my auntie was beating me the most, and I think that was when I started to dream about my mom. I just dreamed I was at home with my mom. But when I woke up, there was nowhere to go.

My friends would tell me, "Don't even think about it. Just stay in school. Do what she says. If she beats you, just turn your mind away." Once my friends took me to a support group, though. It was when my auntie had told me to fetch water, and I refused, and she brought a stick that time and beat me on my head. You can see on my head where I had the bruise. I went to the support group, and they let me stay in the clinic for three weeks to heal. I enjoyed it a lot. I could invite my friends to visit, and we could just play, even at night. There was a counselor who talked to me and said that I could go back to the support group if my auntie beat me again. She did beat me again, but I didn't go back—there was nothing else to do, and it was most important that I just kept going to school. School is always my safe place. They say, "You go to school, you make yourself a life." I've got to finish school, so I look straight ahead, not left or right.

When everyone started talking about voluntary repatriation, things changed. So many people are going back to Sudan now! Last year, my auntie decided to take her children and go back, too. I insisted: let me remain here! It was no question, I wanted to stay. And she let me. Two months ago she left. Now I live by myself in my auntie's old mud house. Now I am free to play and to read sometimes. I don't miss her, and I don't feel like I need to go back to Sudan.

If Kenya allows us to stay here for good, I will stay here for good. Only my auntie is waiting for me in Sudan—and when she was here, I wasn't comfortable. She's been gone for two months, and now I feel much better.

The life in Kakuma is quiet now that I am alone. I go to school most days. I like it—I mean, nobody supports me, so of course I like school. It is the best way for me to help myself and my future. My teachers are very nice to me—I am a dedicated student, and I keep coming, and I never fight. Other kids will steal pens and get in fights, but not me.

I like mathematics, although it is hard. But biology and chemistry—these are my best subjects, the ones that are the most interesting. If I could find a job in biology or something like that—wow!

Other than school, I just have to get my food. We follow a long line to get the food. You can't try to cheat in the line, because police are there and they will beat you if you cheat. You stand in line, sometimes for an hour or more. You show your cards, and you get your food. Neighbors sometimes will cook and share food together. My neighbor is Madeline, but she doesn't need to care for me really. I take care of myself. When I need help, my friend Agnes advises me—she has a mother, and she repeats her mother's advice to me about work, about boys, about the home and family. She is a good person to learn from. She has a mother and father, so she enjoys everything.

MARCY: I'M A STRIKER

I wake every day when the sun comes up. I wash and help my brothers and sisters prepare for the day. Sometimes we eat a little for breakfast. When we are ready, we all leave for school. We come home around one o'clock in the afternoon, cook lunch, and prepare dinner using the staples that they give to us. We eat together—we pray for the food to be blessed by God, and we eat at the same table. Some people will disagree, but I like the food here! Sometimes they don't give enough—if there's not enough, what can you do? I can go to my neighbor and ask if she will share some, and sometimes she will help. Of course, the family helps each other most of all. My brothers and sisters respect me, and they listen when I advise them. They help me in many ways. I was sick with typhoid once, and my siblings took me to the hospital and cooked for me.

If there is time in the afternoons, I will go to the fields to play sports. When I play football, I strike—I'm a striker. I score. I know that in Sudan the girls aren't allowed to play football, so I feel lucky. In 2001, we flew in an airplane to Nairobi for a football match and a basketball match against a girls' secondary-school team. We lost both matches—they were so tall and we were so short, so we just had to foul, foul, foul! I think it was 108–52 in basketball, and in football we lost 7–2. I was crying! But I loved the plane ride.

I go to church every week. I read the Bible. I have my own Bible in my house. I read about Jesus, and Noah and his ark. Religion is very important to me. They say, "Happy are those who are merciful, and God will be merciful to them." I think about this a lot. I want to be with God in his mercy.

Jacqueline is my best friend. We play basketball and football to-gether on the camp teams. Jackie had a boyfriend, but in 2001 the boyfriend flew away to Australia. Before he went away, though, they met together, and she became pregnant. Jackie came to me and told me, "I missed my period this month." She asked me if it meant she was pregnant. I said, "I don't know. Let us go and check with the doctor." The result was positive. She was pregnant. I went to the boy and asked, "Are you the one that made my friend pregnant?" The boy denied it. He was angry and about to slap me, and I just said, "Oh, oh, excuse me." It was three days later that the boy flew away. Jackie was alone to have her baby girl. There were difficult years that followed, but Jacqueline will be okay. Her parents take care of the child. Recently she has even started playing football and basketball with us again. Since the boy left to Australia, we have heard nothing—not even greetings. But Jacqueline will be okay. I believe she will be able to find a husband.

Love can be scary for lots of reasons, not just pregnancy. The staff here makes HIV-awareness projects for us all the time. In Kakuma, many are infected by the disease. They say that AIDS has no cure—the only solution is to wait and to die. There is a place for testing. I went there one day and was tested. I am HIV-negative, so I know my status. It's better to know your status, and when I went, I told my friends to go also. When I get married, I will tell my boyfriend that we have to get tested first. If he is positive and I am negative, I will tell him to go his way, and I will go mine. A negative person and a positive person cannot be together, or else I will become positive also.

Kakuma hasn't really changed much over the years. There are more trees around the houses. They have changed the foods they give us—we get more flour, more oil. If you don't have another thing to support your salary, you only get what they give. And where would I get more money? I cannot work.

Sometimes I don't feel safe in Kakuma. I understand that we are refugees here, that we are visitors. But the hosts—the Turkana people—at night they will come and attack you and take what you have inside the house.[1] Clothes, food, they just take it away. I saw

---

[1] The Turkana are indigenous people of northwest Kenya. Kakuma Camp is located on their lands.

it with my eyes in 2004—Turkana came at night and attacked a woman who was my neighbor. They came in and they shot her in the arm with a gun. We started begging, please don't hurt her. The woman lived alone, so she was poor, with no food and no clothes. The attackers saw nothing they wanted, so they left.

Since I've been here, nothing has happened to me. Nobody notices me. I see UN staff, and people from the International Rescue Committee, but I never talk to them. I'm not one of the people who is quarrelling or fighting. I am just silent. If I am with my friends, I like joking with them and laughing, but I won't fight or quarrel. We tell stories about boyfriends mostly. I just say that I have a boyfriend and I'm proud of him—that he's a nice guy and good to me. It's best to stay out of trouble. One girl named Sophie was smoking and taking alcohol—there is a proverb, if you are walking with someone who is taking alcohol, it is like you are taking alcohol also. She doesn't respect her elders or her parents. Because of this, we cannot be friends any longer.

Life is different for girls here, of course. You find that girls drop out of school every year because of forced marriage. They can be fifteen years old, or even younger. Your family can just take you out one day and force you to get married. You will have no choice. The good thing about nobody taking care of me is that there is nobody to marry me off. I control myself. I improve myself.

I don't want to get married! Someday, yes, I would like to marry, but right now I'm not ready. If I got married right now, I could not take care of my brothers and sisters—I would have to care for my husband. So for now I go to school, and I help my brothers and sisters. Maybe I don't have to get married at all, ever! But you see everyone else living in marriage. If you see everyone carrying on in a group, and they're without you, how do you feel? It's like that.

In the camp, there are signs everywhere about women's rights. We learn women can do anything, even tell your husband to cook!

A man can even be in the kitchen, helping to cook while a woman is doing something else—washing clothes, or even just relaxing. The men don't understand, of course. Sometime they'll even argue and say that women belong in kitchens. I say, yes, I need to fetch water, wash clothes, and prepare food. But what if I need to see a friend sometimes? I hope that when I marry, my husband and I will share the kitchen. In a good marriage, there is no reason to quarrel about such things.

We learn about women's rights, but even if they didn't teach us, we would understand these things inside. During the celebration for Women's Day, they made speeches and celebrations for us, and they told the men: "You cook today! Let the women go for celebrations, and you stay and cook." Some men helped and prepared food for the women—some, but not all. Some of the men, oh, if you said, "You cook," they would slap you, or beat you. This happens a lot in Kakuma.

There are times when women come together to discuss life and news. But when that happens, they won't accept me—if I come to join, they will chase me away! They say, "We are women, and you are just a girl!" Even though I am responsible for my home, I am only sixteen, and I am not married. So they tell me, "Go search for your friends; there is no reason for you to be here." It is okay when they say this. I am able to take care of myself.

ROSE: I AM READY TO CHOOSE LIFE

The culture is changing—for so long, we never had these discussions. You could not get a man to work in the kitchen or to clean the compound. He would just be sitting and waiting. The men here don't work, so they're lazy—sitting, waiting for the food. If a man wants to drink water, he calls you and says, "I am thirsty." But now, it's really changing.

We are an important generation. In old generations, the dowry would keep people from marrying, or families would match people who had no interest in each other. Now it will be different. It is our generation that will bring new things. We are trying to change things for Southern Sudanese people. We will bring education and health. We are the right people to change things. The traditions, of course, are very important. But we know some traditions are harmful to us.

I feel free now—I am ready to choose life. After school, people will offer me work, and if it's good, I will take it; if it's not, then I won't. I'll get married sometime after I finish my school, and I'll go to college, and after that I'll marry. When you are a girl, it's only about marriage. It's a must!

My boyfriend's name is Amos. He's happy that I go to school. We are both doing our best, and when we finish, we will get married, and I'm happy about that plan. My husband will understand me—he will fetch water when I'm busy in the kitchen, and when he is in the kitchen, I will fetch water. We are going to help each other. Neither of us will work alone.

If I get work here, I think I will stay in Kenya a long time. But in the end, I depend on God. I pray, and I go to school, and if God hears me, I will be fine. I read the Bible sometimes: "Love your neighbor as you love yourself." If somebody tries to abuse me, I will think of the Bible, and I will love.

I just want to be in my home, to take care of my children, to have a good family, to get good work, and to be social sometimes. Mostly to have a good family.

I will not beat my children! Never, never, never. If I have children, I can only tell them stories about Sudan—I can tell them that when I was in Sudan, I was really in bad conditions. I will tell them that in Kakuma my auntie would restrain me and abuse me. This is really everything there is to my story.

Maybe I would go to Sudan if there were really peace. But I wonder, if I go, who will care for me? I have nothing to take care of myself. Where am I going to stay? I only know my auntie, and she abuses me.

Right now, I will remain in Kakuma thinking about my future. I won't think about the problems or even my auntie—just about school. If they allow some of us to stay in Kenya, I will stand in line to register to be a Kenyan citizen. Really, I do not want to go back.

MARCY: MANY ARE GOING BACK, BUT I DON'T KNOW

Now I am in my second year of secondary school. Two more years and I will be finished with my degree. Then I will choose whether to get married. I would choose a traditional marriage ceremony, not an official one. The people will come and dance, and celebrate, and maybe I will cook something for them. Normally in Sudan, there would be cows for a dowry, but here, they are just using money. If I marry a wealthy man, maybe the family will buy a cow or bull from the local Turkana, but that is rare.

I hear about voluntary repatriation to Sudan. Many are going, but I don't know. Even if I do go back to Sudan, where do I go once I get there? I don't know the place where my parents lived before. Who am I going to know in the country? You know, with repatriation they just pick you up, take you to a city in the South, and drop you there. What if you don't have anybody waiting for you? In Sudan, you can go to school if you pay money—but who would pay for me? They do not let girls play sports, but at Kakuma, they mobilize us to play. Here in Kenya we have everything—school, and food, and hospitals—they give us everything. In Sudan, you have to have land and cultivate food for yourself, because nobody will give you anything. If I went now with my brothers and sisters, we would not survive. I would like to go to America, but it's very difficult for us. If I had a chance, I would go. But it's not likely.

I don't know if I will be happy in the future. Actually, I am thinking about my future—what am I going to be? I dream of being a nurse or a pilot. I remember flying to Nairobi, being high up in the sky, and I think it would be so great to be a pilot in a plane like that.

JOHN MAYIK

AGE: *31*
TRIBE: *Dinka*
BIRTHPLACE: *Maquatch, South Sudan*
INTERVIEWED IN: *Nairobi, Kenya*

WE WILL BE VALUABLE ASSETS

John told his story in his office at the Sud Academy. For four years he has served as principal of this school, which provides free education to Sudanese children living in the slums of Nairobi. The school building is no more than a set of corrugated iron shacks. Stagnant pools of rainwater and sewage mix together by the side of dirt roads. Theft and violent crime are rife in this neighborhood, and there is no security presence in sight. John has lived through worse than this. Here he tells of his life as a refugee and a child soldier in South Sudan, and of how he escaped that life not by running, but by being, as he says, "clever."

I am John Mayik. I was born around 1977, but that is a rough estimation from my uncle, based on battles and floods at that time. My tribe is Dinka. I was born in a village called Maquatch, in the area of Loatch, in Tonj district. The home where I grew up was remote, though. It was far from any village. When I eventually left home I couldn't actually tell where I had come from. Up to now, I've never gone back to that place.

My father was a polygamist. He was working class, one of the few guys who went to school during the British colonial era. I was told he was a senior councilor in the government.

My father was jovial, contrary to my mom. My mom was a very serious lady. If you joked around, you'd get a slap within a minute. People say I'm more like my dad, talking to everybody, making them laugh. I would get in trouble a lot as a child, eating when it was not my turn at meals, saying impolite things to adults. My mother would ask, "Have I given birth to a witch?"

Our family had a farm, but I preferred taking animals out to roam around the forests. That was far better than digging on the farm all day, which just made me sick.

My dad sent me to school from a very young age. I think that was one of the things that distanced me from my mother. I would go to a school that was three or four days' walk from home. During the school season I would stay with my father and with one of his other wives. I would only come to my mother's house during holidays. My stepmother near the school became my friend. She treated me like a real son.

In school we were taught in Arabic. We were mostly taught by learning songs. When you teach in the form of singing, the students can remember better. We still teach that way when we teach Arabic, but English is mostly learned in a spoken form. There are fewer English songs to be sung.

My father died when I was young. I don't really know how, but I was told he was poisoned by other colleagues at his government office. The day before he died, he was okay. At four o'clock in the night he went to pass urine. When he came back he sat on a bed outside, and that is where he died. It was the first time I saw a person die.

Things could happen like that. My father was an educated man from the South, and the government was not friendly to educated people. It was the educated ones who would tell others that there are wrong things being done by the government and what those things are.

I think back to that time, and I remember my mom saying, "You know, one day there will be a war in this country."

When my father died, my uncle took my mother as a wife. I have a younger brother, Aleyo, born from my mother and my uncle. According to our culture, it is accepted that he is my brother, so he is not called by my uncle's name, he is called by my father's name. I went back to live with my mother in Barial Dat, her home village.

When I went back to my mom, life took a different turn altogether. For three years or so, I was sent to the cattle camps. Boys would go and keep cattle and rear them. To go to the camp, I had to leave school. I would care for more than a hundred cattle every day in the forests. If one got lost, we would be beaten. I lost several. Many, really. It was three years of rearing cattle, and they were so many and so wild. If I was lucky, I could go a week without losing one. But many times I was unlucky, and every time I lost one, my uncle's eldest son would beat me. When he was young, he was beaten, too, so he had to do the same.

THERE WAS NOTHING TO SAY

In the 1980s, war broke out. Our area was attacked and that was the second time I saw people die.

I left my village when I was about ten years old, around 1987. My uncle took me away. He thought I should be taken back to school. He knew my father had a brain, that was the one thing he knew, and so he thought that maybe I have the same brain. By then, the war had become intense. There was fighting erupting every week, and there were no good schools left in South Sudan. So one day he took me and we walked to Ethiopia. I said goodbye to my family, and to this day I don't know what has happened to them.

My uncle said we had to walk, and we left with a large group of men and boys. I took only a walking stick and a blanket. On our

OUT OF EXILE

way it was dangerous. There were enemies everywhere, so we had to avoid human settlements and we had to avoid water, because people live near water.

Many died along the way from lack of water and lack of food. It was too hard with all the walking. We would walk from early afternoon until midnight and then rest until two a.m. We would walk again from two until noon, rest for two hours, and then walk again. We used that rhythm so we could rest in the hottest and coldest parts of the day. When we stopped, I would just fall to the ground. After so much walking, you could sleep anywhere. I remember how I would even sleep when I was walking. I'd be listening to the other people's footsteps, and close my eyes. I would wake up again when I hit a tree or a rock, and the pain would hit me.

We would hear wild animals coming, and people would run, run, run, and the lions and hyenas would pick off people and you could hear the cries in the forest at night. Once the lions tasted human flesh, they got used to it, and the lions preferred humans to gazelles, because it was easier to chase us. The animals were clever. It was like they could tell when one of us was tired, and they would pick them off. I was always wondering if I would be next.

We would come across settlements of people sometimes, even if we tried to avoid them. Sometimes they would start shooting at us, and nothing could be done except run away. We became used to it. What killed so many people in the war wasn't just the fighting between the armies, but the impact of the war on the rest of the people. What I mean is that tribes became wild to each other. They were killing each other over clothes. Clothes became more important than the people wearing them, and tribes had different languages, so it was easier to kill than to ask.

My uncle hardly spoke to me the whole time we walked. There was nothing to say. We would have talked about where we were going, or how long it would take, but even my uncle did not know about where we were going, so what could we talk about? Talk about the family back at home? He did no know how they were doing, so we could not talk about that.

I would walk with the other young people in the group. Maybe we played sometimes when we weren't too tired. Actually, kids were stronger than the older people on the walk, because it would take us longer to feel hungry. And it was easier for us to forget about home, about tiredness, about everything. The big people remembered the wealth they had, and their women. I was only ten; I'd never had a girlfriend. I didn't know who was missing me. So I didn't have anything to think about.

WE WOULD SING ABOUT OUR STRENGTH

It took three months to reach Ethiopia. They say the journey was about 1,500 kilometers. It was funny when we arrived in Ethiopia. We thought it would be a good place, well-constructed, nice, and lively, with no problems. When we came, we realized it was only the beginning of our problems. The place where we settled was called Pinyudo. It was in Ethiopia, just inside the border.

Many other Sudanese were already there. We were taken to a place in the forest where no humans had ever settled, and the people in charge told us, "Make this place your home." We were told to clear out the trees and build houses. There was water nearby, but there was no food. We would eat like chickens, picking things off the ground and cleaning them. Stomach problems came, and diseases, and people started dying again. They set up a clinic, and sick people would sit in line waiting for treatment. Some people in the line would get very sick, and others would remove them so the line could move forward. The so-called doctors would look at people, and they would have a bag of pills, and they would take one out and take a bite of it to test it and see if it was the right one. I know the doctors in the United States can't test medicines first and then tell you like that.

After some time, my uncle left and returned to Sudan. Some months later—it was around the middle of 1988, I think—I was taken to the military training center of Pinyudo. The leaders of the camp trained us. Those people were the Sudan People's Liberation Army, the SPLA.

The training was tough. There were about five hundred, or even a thousand boys in my task force, my group. At two a.m. the leaders would wake us up, and in the dark we would run around and sing. At six a.m. we would come back and do some exercises. At seven we would go to lectures. Somebody would stand by a chalkboard, and all the boys would squat, and we would have the lesson of the day. Sometimes it was about operating a gun, sometimes it was about theories, like how to make formations and hide to ambush an army unit. After the lesson we would go and practice these tactics in the forest. At lunch hour we were brought back for food and a bath. Then we had more singing sessions, where we would sing about our strength, about how we would crush our enemy. After the singing came more lessons and more practical exercises. By six in the evening we were done. It was like that every day for six months. It was training, but no background. All we knew was, Arab. All this is against the Arabs. That was the plan.

The seventh month, we relaxed, and then we went back to Sudan. This was in 1989, or 1990. We went back to where we belonged. I didn't ask myself why; at that point you think you are strong and powerful enough to do everything, to do away with everything that is supposed to be done away with.

We went back with guns. We had these AK-47s. They gave guns to those of us who were tall enough. You had to have a good physique and be strong to be picked. It didn't matter how young you were as long as they could see you could hold a gun. We walked for around two months, back into Sudan. We were strong this time.

THE RED ARMY

In Sudan we walked from town to town. We were called the Red
Army, the army of children—some ten years old, some younger. I was
twelve or thirteen. We had no uniforms, of course. Our shoes were
made from pieces of rubber tires, and we would tie those on our feet,
and they worked fine.

We had to defend towns, stay around them and defend them. We
did not go inside the towns. I never knew anyone in the villages we
defended. We only guarded them from outside. We had no homes,
only holes in the ground. The leaders would give us food, though it
was not enough—a big cup of cooked maize or sorghum would be
lunch for ten or eleven people to share.

I became friends with the other children. Some of them are alive
now, and some are not alive. Over the years I would be told that so-
and-so died, so-and-so was killed in the war, and there was nothing
I could do. As time goes by, you adapt to new situations. I become
used to you, you are taken away, I remain. You make new friends.
You would never remain an island. They would form new groups and
move us from place to place, and we would make new friends.

There was not much fun to have. There were no ballgames. At
night we would play music and sing when we had free time. We
would leave our minds and not think of anything. That was the good
thing about us, particularly me. We would not think of anything.
We had forgotten our families. We would never think of anything.

Those years influence me today in one way. The tough things we
did, the lifestyle, the lack of food, those experiences gave me a lot
of strength. I saw that there was nothing I could not do. If I could
survive that, I think I can do anything. When I have a problem now,
I compare that time in the army with all I have now, and I find that
my problems are very minor.

I continued like that for years. Soon I was fifteen, sixteen, seventeen. I was a soldier in the army. And you could not just leave. If you were caught leaving the army, you would be shot dead.

We were encouraged to take marijuana and alcohol. It was like it was a policy of the army, though nobody would speak badly if you didn't take any. We could get it from the villages that we passed through. With alcohol or marijuana you get to the front lines and you don't have fear, because you don't realize what's happening. You just lived for the day, survived, waited for tomorrow. So some people would take anything that came to them. Groups of friends always formed—people who would smoke certain types of tobacco, or drink certain types of alcohol would meet together. And then there were those of us who didn't take anything. Nobody told me, "don't do it." I told myself I didn't have to do it, even though others did. I did not take any because I had seen people die from using these things. Sometimes the drink itself would harm them; sometimes they would drink and then do something stupid. These were the days when you could be shot dead for sleeping with the wrong woman or committing a crime. I had a friend named Theop who would get into trouble for that sort of thing, and one day I was told that he was gone.

YOU GUYS LOOK SHARP

I do not remember exactly when, or why, but one of the elders in the army came to me one day. He took my friend Angelo and me and said, "You guys look sharp. I think you can do something better." He started sending us to classes in a village.

We were living in barracks at that point, near the town of Kajo Keji. We were in a reserve rotation, so we only had to help protect the town, and not do any attacking. We were lucky, really, that the town had educational activities. So during the days I would go to school, and at nights I would sleep in the barracks. Some days I couldn't go to school because of special army assignments.

The highest risk at that time was airplane bombings. On mornings when the sky was clear, we could expect bombings at seven a.m. to wake us up. Then again at three p.m. the bombs would come. And we had to lose *somebody* on a daily basis. On an unlucky day, the town would lose twenty or thirty people. The town was always afraid. Our school was bombed one day, but luckily the students were outside at the time. After that, the teacher taught us under a tree. After some time it grew so dangerous that we would only meet for thirty minutes or an hour a day, and the teacher would simply give us assignments and send us off to work independently.

I did not go through systematic education in those years, but I progressed in my classes very quickly. I did so well that my teachers thought I was cheating. I wasn't cheating, of course. I simply asked them to let me do my best. At the same time, I remained in the army—I was doing all this part-time while I was still a soldier.

I took the big high school entrance exam along with about four hundred other students, some of them from fancier schools in bigger towns. When the results came in, I had the eleventh highest score. Others couldn't believe that was my name in the eleventh spot.

As I continued learning, I always felt threats. If you were rich, people would want to get rid of you. If you were popular with girls, people would want to get rid of you. When people saw that some of us kids could do well, that we were clever, that we could do well in our studies, that we had proven we could make it, that was threatening.

We continued to take exams and progress in our classes. I remember at one exam, my friend Angelo was sick with guinea worm, and worms were coming out all over his body. Still, he managed to take his exam and had the number-one result of all the students. I was number six. People were asking, "Where are these guys coming from?" It was a big threat to some people. Word was spreading. The elders, the military leaders, came to us and said, "You kids, don't be number one. Don't do too much. Don't be too good in school. You'll get poisoned." Then they told us, "And don't talk to those girls." Our first reaction was about the girls—it wasn't until then that we realized that girls even liked us! We had always just been polite when girls came up to say hello after lessons. But people talked and said the girls liked us.

By then I had become good in English. I could score 95 on exams. Angelo was a giant in mathematics. He would help me in math, and I would help him in English. He would help me in geography, and I would help him in history. Both of us were good in science. By exam time, it was like we were of the same mind. What he knew was what I knew.

OUR OWN FAMILY NOW

After some time, one of the military policemen, a man named Tokyok, began to take care of us and exempted us from service to concentrate on studying. He wanted to send Angelo and me back to our homes, where we had come from. But we said, "Now that we have some schooling here, we want to continue here." Tokyok gave us a small hut in town.

Angelo and I were glad to be in town, on our own, to concentrate on studying. Eventually I sort of had a girl. Her name was Edith. She was a girl in the town and a fellow student. She was not a lover, just a friend. She was sympathetic to Angelo and I, and wanted to take care of us. She was well off since she had a brother-in-law who was a doctor. Sometimes she would bring us food. We would get annoyed—we were too proud, we did not want to depend on people—and we would say, "Why do you bring food?" but of course we would eat it. We were just nervous that people would talk about her visiting us.

A general in the army, a man named Mario, came to us one day. He had heard people talking about us, the boys in the hut, and he worried about us. He sympathized with us. He talked about taking

JOHN MAYIK

us away, to some place safer—perhaps to Uganda. We said we wanted
to stay and study. He offered to move us to his general's compound.
We said no, because we wanted to stay on our own, to depend only on
ourselves and not the army. We knew our lives in the hut were better
than when we were in the army.

A woman named Norweech joined us along the way. She had had
trouble with her husband and had been imprisoned. When she left
prison, she had nowhere to go, and asked to stay with us. She had a
little baby, too. So we had our own family now. We built a hut for
Norweech, and we had a hut for guests. Norweech would cook if we
had food. But usually we would just go out and search for mangoes.
We would cut the mangoes, add a little bit of salt, and that would
satisfy us.

Those were fine days, but another problem came. A new major
from the army came to town. He was named Kichner. When Kichner met Norweech he became interested in her. He asked Norweech
about her relationship with Angelo and I. She simply said, "These
boys are my people. I live with them." Kichner was a big man, with
many wives, but he needed another. Kichner offered to take care of
her, to feed her. She refused, and Kichner was furious. This brought
us a crisis.

We were home one evening, Angelo, Norweech, and I, just
laughing and talking. Kichner came to the hut with his bodyguards.
A bodyguard asked, "Who is this lady?"

I said, "She is our sister."

He asked, "Your sister in what sense?"

I said, "We all live together, take care of each other. In that sense
she is my sister." I said to Kichner, "We greet you as an elder."

He insisted that Norweech should not be living with us. He said,
"I hear how you speak of each other." And I saw Kichner's men, and
they looked like they wanted to pull us away, kick us out, and throw
us in the garbage. Luckily they didn't. They went away again.

I spoke with Angelo, and said, "You know we are having troubles because of the lady. It is not her fault; it is Kichner's fault, but we still have problems." We were scared that the men were coming back. We took our guns, and we were ready to shoot anything, even if it was just a bird flying in the wrong direction. Our soldier roots were suddenly revived.

We came outside, and we yelled, "We have the same training as you! We have the same knowledge, the same minds! We know how you think!" But they were gone.

HAVING PEOPLE EVERYWHERE

Some days later Mario, the general, came back. We told him everything that had happened. Mario was very angry; he wanted to go and arrest Kichner and his bodyguards. I don't know what happened in the end, but I know they were taken away.

By this time many people were not happy with us. Even the others in the army were jealous that we were being exempted from military service.

After the trouble surrounding Norweech, it was decided that Angelo and I had to be taken to Kenya. Mario gave us money, and arranged for a car to take us to Uganda, and from there we would go into Kenya. Norweech went to a neighbor, who eventually married her. He was a good man, who understood her. We were very happy for that. I have not seen her since we left the town.

Angelo and I were driven to Uganda, and it was difficult there. The Ugandans sympathized with us, but we had no money. When we tried to cross the border to Kenya, we were denied. We were seen as a problem by the Kenyans. We went to Kampala, the capital of Uganda. We then went to a refugee camp. It was full of people from the Acholi tribe. The Acholi did not like us Dinka—they believed the Dinka had caused all the problems in Sudan. The UNHCR told us that we could only register as refugees if we stayed in the camp, but it wasn't safe. We had to leave quickly. Angelo and I got onto a public bus and headed toward Kenya again. And this time there was a good Samaritan who helped Angelo and I, along with some other ladies and young children. This Ugandan man took us to a quiet place on the border and helped us walk across. We walked until we found a bus, and took it all the way to Nairobi.

When we came to Nairobi it was my first time in a big city. It was morning when we were approaching the city, and we saw so many people moving toward the city center, and I remember thinking there must be a great migration going on since so many people were moving. I remember arriving at the bus station and going up to people and trying to talk with them, asking why everyone was moving toward the city center, but they would just look at me like I was strange, and they would walk away. One man kept walking, and I tried to run after him, and he just ran even faster! He must have thought I was coming to rob him.

We didn't know where we were going, or who could help us. We just stayed near the bus station. By a miracle, a man named Akol came and found us—he was Dinka. Mario, the general, had sent Akol to receive us. He took us to his house and arranged for us to travel to Kakuma. This was in 1994.

I was so happy to go to Kakuma camp. After all that had happened in Sudan and Ethiopia, I was ready to appreciate anything peaceful and any chance to go to school. I felt good about all of that when I came to Kakuma. I saw old friends from Ethiopia who had come to Kakuma as well. We shared many stories and experiences. People were warm and received us—it was like a family reunion.

My home in Kakuma was in zone 4, group 47. But thanks to Mario, I was soon able to go to school in Nairobi and live there with Mario's family, in a neighborhood called Lanata. Mario's family cared for me. I only went back to Kakuma for holidays, or important things like headcounts of the camp residents. It was a good thing to have lives in Nairobi and Kakuma. Nobody will deny that having people everywhere is nice. Wherever you go, you feel you are at home.

I got a disease in the first year in Nairobi, something you get from insects, and I was bleeding from everywhere, from my nose, from everywhere. The treatment was very expensive—daily blood transfusions and medicines—and I was in the hospital for three months, but Mario paid for everything. Mario's family is still in Nairobi and I see them often. They are proud of me, and I am proud of them for all they have done.

I enjoyed school in Nairobi, of course. But I enjoyed the freedom in Kakuma, the open spaces, where I could walk for long distances without disturbances, and so many friends around.

All this time, Angelo was with me. We were schooled at Karura, a Seventh-day Adventist school, one of the best schools in Nairobi. I became a Seventh-day Adventist there. That place changed our lives. We grew spiritually. My religion is important to me—it taught me how to live in humanity, how to accept the situations around us. In the bush, we had lived for the day. But religion taught us that we have tomorrow, too, and showed us how to plan for tomorrow. When I was in the bush, if I had found 10,000 shillings, I would have just called all of my friends together and we would have spent it and finished it that day. We didn't care about tomorrow. I mean, something could have happened that evening, and we could have easily lost all we had. My thinking was changing.

Seventh-day Adventists are not so different from other religions. Religion is religion. The most important thing is acceptance, and the hope that the church offers. I am proud of my religion, and I am proud to be part of it.

After I graduated from high school in 1999, I went back to Kakuma and worked for the UN, teaching for a year at the Kadugli Primary School. I taught classes in the morning, and took teacher training classes in the afternoon. I taught history, science, and English, but not math, because I still don't like math. I liked the children at Kadugli School very much and they performed very well. After a year, the staff at Kakuma wanted me to stay, but I returned to Nairobi to further my own education. I got a college degree in public relations at the Strategic Management Institute in Nairobi. Nairobi is my city these days, and the one thing you must know about Nairobi is that it is very expensive. If you have money, then it's okay. But the difference between rich and poor is too great. Even the working poor make less than a dollar a day. They cannot afford daily meals. The little people, with no money, can only live in slums, and the worst part of these areas is the security problem. People turn to theft. People are being robbed day and night, and dying on a daily basis.

I am used to life in Nairobi and I know how to live. I don't mean that I have money, but I know how to live a cheap life, eat a cheap meal, rent a cheap place, and find friends who can direct you with good advice.

A PLACE TO LEARN

At the end of 2002, one of the schools in Nairobi, Sud Academy, went on a search for a new teacher, and somebody at my church suggested me. When the committee met me, they were suspicious— they thought I was too young. But I had teaching experience and I was ready. They gave me a chance. Quickly the students liked me, and so the committee asked me to stay.

The Sud Academy was founded in 2002 to cater to the needs of the Sudanese children in the city who could not find a place in the public schools. Some of these children could not go to public schools because they were too old, such as the twenty-year-olds who did not even know how to read. We called them "tall trees in the desert." Others had families with no resources. The school was founded by a group from Germany called Sign of Hope. They hoped to give these Sudanese refugee children a place to learn.

When the school was founded, they brought in Kenyans to act as a principal and teachers, and several Sudanese women served as a committee of advisors. Little did the women know that this arrangement would cause them troubles someday.

You see, the management committee was being badly influenced by some people. See, we were not getting money directly from the donors in Germany. The donor would give money to some white person in Nairobi who worked at the Konyonya Community Center. This guy would connect to the Sud Academy community. But he was not good. He would talk about documents from Sign of Hope, agreements that had to be signed. And the advisory committee of women would go to his office to sign the documents, and they would be told that the documents would refuse to come out of the computer, and the man didn't know how long it would take for the documents to be ready. These women on the advisory committee were from a war zone in South Sudan, so they didn't understand how long it should take for a document to come out of a computer. This man stood in between our community and the donor, and the rest of us were told not to talk with the man, but just to deal with the women on the committee. We teachers were not to play any role in management. The man knew that we teachers were more intellectual, and we would not believe him when he would say the documents would not come out of the computer, because we know computers. We knew it would only take a second to print documents. But the women did not know, and they were told by the man, "Don't listen to the teachers. They will overrule you, they will overthrow you, and you will see how your children will suffer." So the women were made to worry, and they were confused.

By the time I arrived, large problems had come to the school. At the end of my first year, when the financial accounting was being done, it became clear that many things had been lost. People had been taking supplies from the school to use in their homes. When the financial report went to the donors, the donors were very upset. They felt betrayed. The principal was told to leave.

At the same time, the donors visited from Germany and came directly to the school. They started asking, "How much are you paid?" We were paid 3,000 Kenyan shillings (US$45) a month. "And do the children eat food?" No, they didn't eat at school. It was so bad that one of the Germans even started laughing, and asked, "How can you live in Nairobi if you're only getting 3,000 a month? We sent a lot of money! Where does the money go?" We teachers said we didn't know.

We told them there was an advisory committee in place, but that they were confused. Soon we found out that the white man from Konyonya was inviting different members of the advisory committee on different days, and giving them little bits of money to use, with no receipts. That way nobody could keep track, and when they came together, the man would say, "No, she took the money, and she did," and there was no clear answer. And who were the victims? The kids and the teachers.

There was confusion and problems. Some people didn't want me to take charge. Others thought I taught well and would be a good principal. The women from the committee, the ones who had been manipulated, did not want me to take charge. But the students and many parents did. Some who sat down and analyzed the issues realized that the committee and Konyonya were playing a game. I went to the donors of Sign of Hope and told them that from what I understood, a lot of money had gone to the white man at Konyonya but it had disappeared somewhere. I said that we needed direct reporting to Sign of Hope. I said that the teachers needed a place where they could go directly to get paid, and have records, receipts.

Even though the advisory committee realized that most people wanted me in charge, they resisted, and there was no fast resolution.

After some days, the women of the committee wrote letters of resignation. They were frustrated and not happy when they left, and said they didn't want to be involved anymore. But by that time it was too late, really. The Germans from Sign of Hope had already left, and they were frustrated. They figured we didn't care about the school or about the children. And so for nine months, the teachers had to keep the school running with no money at all.

When the ladies resigned, they said, "Fine, let the boy take the school." So I took over the school. We had no money. Our rent on the property accumulated. To this day we have not paid back all of our debts from those nine months. Teachers were not paid for nine months. But the children kept showing up—every morning the school was full of children expecting to learn. So I had two problems: the landlord who asked for money, and the teachers who needed salaries. How can you wake up in the morning and work all day and come home in the evening with no money? Even me, I needed food, I needed clothes. Every morning I would get to school and have to convince the teachers to work the day, to give lessons, to be loyal to the children, and not show the children that we were facing such problems. For nine months I had to keep telling stories to the teachers about how it would all work out. And the landlord, too—every month I had to tell him, "Hey, you just wait. The money will come. I'm telling you, you'll be given your money and everything will be fine." Teachers were telling me to sell the benches in the classrooms so at least we could have a few shillings. I would say no. I could only say, "God knows. Something will happen someday." We stayed that way from April until December of 2003. In those months, I really felt it. It was a pain I felt in my blood.

It was a day in December 2003 when the landlord came and locked all the rooms of our building. That month, when we gave the semester exams, the kids literally sat on the side of the road to take their tests from eight until five p.m. The teachers sat on the road and marked the exams outside. And remember, December is summer in Nairobi.

I pushed and pushed my friends to try and find help. A friend named Nuna finally connected me with a group called Canadian Aid for Southern Sudan. They offered to pay for food for the kids and for rent for the building, but not for teachers' salaries. I pushed and pushed some more, gently. Finally they agreed to pay our teachers 2,500 shillings (US$37) a month. For all of 2004, we were paid 2,500 a month. And that's how the school started coming back, slowly, slowly. In 2006 salaries increased to 5,000 (US$75), which is what we're still being paid now. That's still nothing compared to the average teacher's pay in Kenya. The average Kenyan teacher is paid at least 11,000, and some make thousands more than that, plus they get pensions. We get 5,000. But we appreciate it. What we are doing is for the sake of the children, and no one else. It's still a problem, of course. We have good teachers, people with degrees, and when they are being paid 5,000, they're very often tempted to get a job teaching in another Kenyan school.

My friends often tell me that I should find new work, find a place where I am valued. They say, "How foolish are you? With all the knowledge you have, you are not doing much." I keep quiet, because I know what I am doing. I want to overcome problems. Even if only two or three students can overcome the problems here it will be a beginning. I know there are kids in Nairobi who want to be like those who read this in the United States.

In Sud Academy we now have around 420 students squeezed in our small compound. We have sixteen teachers. We have eleven classes. We are by the side of the road, between the slums of Kawangware and Dero. It's not a nice neighborhood. It's largely Sudanese living in these slums. It's not safe, but we chose this place so we could access children from both neighborhoods. It takes about forty minutes for the children to walk from either direction, from Kawangware and from Dero. Last December, thieves came into the school, broke into the office, stole our books and a table from the teacher's office. There is no water supply or electricity. It would cost 100,000 shillings to connect water but we cannot afford that. We are waiting and saving and trying to convince the city council to help us, but the city council is taking its time. They don't have much money either. The building is made from corrugated iron, and there are ponds of sewage and drain water running beside it, pooling from the hill above us. Everything is rusty, and not clean.

The children come to school, and we feed them a meal every day now. They are happy students, and they do very well. They read very well. They do very well on the national exams every year—better than the national average. They like being at Sud Academy, because Sudanese often get harassed in the Kenyan schools—their classmates will come up to them, poke them, say, "Hey! You are a refugee. You create problems in your country and now you want to come here to make trouble for us."

The kids will wonder, "What is a refugee?" because most of the young ones were born here in Nairobi. They'll come home to their parents at night and ask about this word. And that's not a good way to find out. The government and the culture gets better bit by bit, but still these things happen. At Sud Academy, it is safe. It is like home. Nobody will ask them questions about where they come from. We can be together and safe.

I know the future of the Sudanese community in Nairobi. I know someday they will go home. They'll go back to Sudan. But I also know that there will be problems in South Sudan. There are problems with infrastructure, medical care, particularly schools. If there are no good schools, you'll find it will be a threat to the Sudanese community. If you take a child from sixth grade here in Kenya to South Sudan, that child has no future because there will not be schools waiting for him, and he won't yet have enough knowledge to build his future. Right now in South Sudan, so much of the curriculum is still in Arabic. The East African curriculum we have here in Kenya is strong, but it still lacks in South Sudan. It is possible to bring the curriculum back with us, and teach in Sudan. But the problem is that teachers are not being paid well in South Sudan. Someone told me that teachers in South Sudan are being paid eighty dollars a month. And these are people that need to be motivated to teach. That's not enough to build a life in Sudan. The future of South Sudan will depend on people using their brains, not guns. If the teachers are not treated well, there is no future for the country. But if they are treated well, then I have high hopes for these children. It's so easy for them to forget, forget about parents who die or places they leave. When you are young, you can live with anybody. These children can live with friends, they can live with cousins, they can live with people who are not even their relatives. They can easily adapt to any situation. I worry more for the old people. For them it is not easy to adapt. I look at my students and I see that the young ones know the languages of Kenya better than the old ones. It is very difficult for the old ones to change, but easy for these young people to change and adapt. That gives hope.

I have a Kenyan wife now, and a daughter. My wife is Kahzia, and we have been married two years. We have a child, named Akuche. She is less than a year old, and she is a very beautiful one, almost as beautiful as my wife. We have a life and friends in Nairobi, but even as we speak, my people need me back at home in South Sudan. They send word from Sudan. They say, "If you really exist, you must come." I have to plan. I cannot just wake up one day, pack my things, tell my wife, "Hey, stay here with your job and the child, I have to go to Sudan." I must organize myself, so I can know that when I get to Sudan I will be able to support the family. Plus I am taking more college classes now, and they will not be finished until December of 2008.

The people here, we have been away for so long. When we go back to Sudan, it will be strange, especially for the children. It will take time to get used to the place. So I need to plan for the long term. The good thing is that my wife is interested to go, too. She is a teacher also. We will be valuable assets. She's told me that it's one of her dreams, actually. She's said she always dreamed of being married to someone who is not Kenyan. She never wanted to die in the same place as she was born. She wants to go somewhere else. It is a dream for me.

There are many things one can learn from being in exile. You can learn different cultures. Every culture has its own goodness and its own badness. In your own culture there are good things and then there are bad things too. Being in Kenya we can leave our bad things and take new good things and combine them to have a new sense of direction. That's why, if we look at people like the Israelites, or the United States today—they have brought together different brains from different backgrounds. And then you grow a multicultural community where everyone can feel at home. We must have a place where people can come together from different backgrounds and not point at each other, not care where we come from, but simply be somewhere together. It's a difficult experience, but can have its own benefits. It can be bad if not handled well, of course. But I am hopeful.

MARGARET IBADYO
BAGET YON

AGE: *42*
TRIBE: *Belanda-Bor*
BIRTHPLACE: *Nazret, South Sudan*
CURRENT HOME: *Khartoum, Sudan*

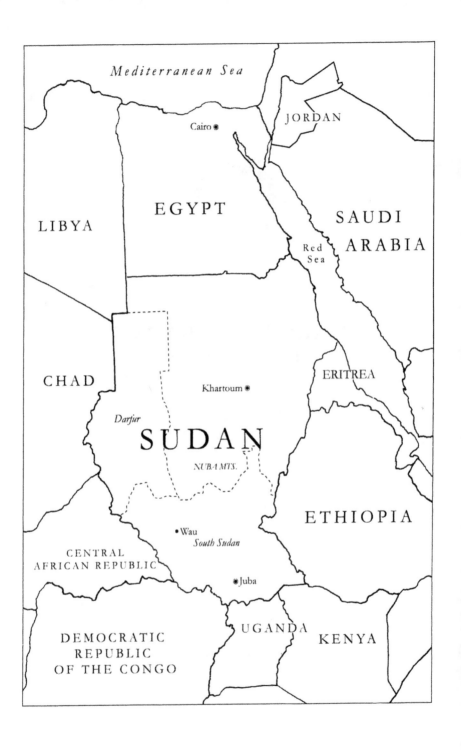

IT IS PAST MY TIME

A group of thirty women from the Mandela neighborhood of the Mayo Internally Displaced Persons Camp were sitting together. Margaret volunteered to talk about her life. She walked to her home nearby. Its walls are made of mud. Inside it was dark and much cooler than the desert sun outside. The single room was filled with old chairs, a table, and a large glass-windowed cabinet holding cups and plates. She spoke in Arabic.

I am Belanda; my tribe is Belanda-Bor. My people come from Bazir, in the South of Bahr al-Ghazal state. My village is called Nazret, close to the town of Wau. I was born in 1965.

I grew up with no father. I really don't know how he passed away; I only know I was still little. My mother raised the family. She had eleven children and, thank God, there are six of us left. We were raised with trouble.

I say I am Belanda—really, my father was from the Belanda. My mother is Ndogo. We are all southern tribes in my region, so we all just marry each other. My mother was Muslim and my father was Christian. So when they got married, she converted to Christianity, and nobody said anything. I am a Christian as well.

I can tell you we didn't have enough money to go to school, even though it was pretty cheap. So instead of money, my family would just donate a bit to the school, a chair or something instead of tuition, and buy some school clothes. At first, only my older sister Christina could go to school. She's the only person you could say was really educated in my family. After my older sister graduated, the rest of us could get a little education, too.

My mother built a house for us herself. She was a farmer. We ate most of the food, and the rest we sold. She also brewed alcohol in the home. The money that we made from that supported us. My mother is a strong woman, and she taught us to be hard workers. We would help her out during farming. At the end of the day, we'd usually search for wood and bring it back home.

My mother planted peanuts, and I have a funny story there. When we collected the peanuts from the field, we'd leave them out in the sun to dry. Under the sun, my friends and I used to go eat them. Take a little bit here, a little bit there. Then we would put them in sacks, in storage, to be sold later on. And then, too, we'd just eat peanuts all the time.

My mother knew, and she didn't want anyone stealing her peanuts. She hid the peanut bag in a big barrel and put books and boxes on top of it. For days I was wondering, "Where did she put those peanuts?" I was just thinking and thinking. One day I found my mom taking stuff from the barrel. I made a mental note—I knew that was the spot. So right after she left, I took all the stuff down from the barrel, opened it up, and I started eating. Of course, my mom came right back in, and when she caught me, I started crying, crying, crying! She taught me a good lesson in that situation: "If you want something, just ask for it. Because if you keep this up, you'll end up being a robber."

All the women in the area were in the alcohol business; the drink we made was called *merissa*. Every night, after all the kids would finish farming, we would spend time at our neighbor's house and help to make *merissa* all night. We would break down the yeasts and the dates to make the ingredients. We would sleep over there. Then the next time, when my mother would want help, the children would all come and sleep over at our house.

There was one kind of alcohol that they would give the children to try. The women would mix it with milk and give it to a child, a poor child, and make him happy. Yes, I tried it myself. And I did get drunk!

Everyone drank. But when my father died, my mother started drinking a lot. I remember a night when she became very drunk, and she kept crying and crying all night, crying for my father.

Like I said, once my father died, we were just in trouble. We didn't have enough. But once my sister graduated, she got a job as a teacher in a school in Wau, a big town nearby. She sent us money. We started dressing like normal people.

At eight years old, I started school and I studied for eight years. My mother would wake us up early on school days. Right until I hit puberty, I used to pee my pants at night, so my mother used to prepare hot water for me to clean myself before school. It took two hours to walk to the local school, and all the kids from our village would walk together, there and back. We played tag every day along the way—you tag me and I'll tag her, you know? The school building was a bunch of classrooms just stuck together. It was all made of sticks. There were maybe seventy of us in the school. They taught us how to read and write. There was a knitting class for us and a cooking class. Those are the things I learned, and I loved it.

I remember my best friend at school, Lucia. We spoke the same dialect, and she understood me so well. We lived really far from each other, so we played mostly in school. We used to play soccer, and we would jump rope. That was our favorite.

I was a good student, and I would never get into trouble. I was very patient, very calm. Those days, once my sister had started working, things were really better. But time has passed, and now my sister has become an old woman.

DON'T HURT HER, HURT ME

In my later years at school, I fell in love with a teacher. He taught at a neighboring school, but he lived in the same village as me. He was older than me and very, very handsome. He started giving me private lessons, and books, and money for lunch. That's how we kind of met. I loved him, but we loved in secret. I loved him until God gave us a child together. I was sixteen.

I first guessed I was pregnant when I started being really sick. I kept going to school because I didn't want to arouse suspicion. But I was scared. In the mornings, when the class sang our anthems, I'd be in the washroom and I'd be scared. Mostly I was scared of my mother finding out I was pregnant out of wedlock.

Once during that time I went to visit my aunt at a hospital. I went to visit her, and secretly I wanted to see if they could test my illness. I still wasn't certain I was pregnant. My aunt saw me and said, "Wow, I'm sick, and you're sick too." She questioned me: "What do you have? What's your illness?" I couldn't tell her. So she said, "Okay, let me see your chest." I showed her my chest and she said, "Give it a couple of months and your illness will be gone. After that, you will be all right." She knew.

Of course, after a time my mom noticed that I was tired, and I was growing. She was angry, for I was now a blemish on the household. And my mother beat me. The whole household beat me a lot. They beat me until I confessed who did this to me. After I told them, they went to my lover and he said, "Please do not hurt her." He told them he was the problem. He said, "Don't hurt her, hurt me."

In the end, all that happened was fair. My lover paid a dowry and my family gave me to him. The dowry was three pounds. When he had paid the full price, I was married to him, but it was only a traditional ceremony, and not a legal one. There were no officials. Because it was not a Christian wedding, I stayed in my house and did not move to him.

I had the baby and named her Teresa. From then on, it was like I couldn't do anything else except care for the baby. Sometimes I would walk to the school to see my friends. During the day I would hide in the washroom, and at lunchtime, my friends would knock on the door of the washroom and take me and we'd go eat. Then I'd go back to the washroom until they were ready to walk home.

Soon after Teresa was born, my man found another woman and got married to her. Honestly, I wasn't thinking of him a lot, because I was living with my mom and taking care of my child. It was okay by me.

Everyone loved my girl. She was always happy. She used to call me by my real name and call my mother Mom. We were happy at home.

At eighteen months, my child became very sick and entered the hospital. The first time we went, she was sick and then we brought her back home. The second time we went to a German hospital, and the German people loved Teresa so much and she loved them too. The German people were kind. They would take her on trips to the river, and she would always have her medicine on time.

Teresa healed and we left the hospital. But after another year, she became tired again and we brought her back to the hospital. This time we stayed only one day and she passed away.

I did not know why it happened. I asked my sister how my daughter died, and my sister said she didn't know, but she had seen many people dying of chest pains in the hospital. She said there was a good chance that your daughter caught a sickness from them. I do not know.

When Teresa died, it was the hardest thing ever for me. But it wasn't as bad as when my father passed from my mother, because in my mother's situation, our father was our main support. For my daughter, at least, we could just move on. I didn't have time to mourn because the war was starting, and I started moving.

IT WAS LIKE MY HEAD OPENED UP

When the war started, I remember that there were not many radios in my village. The SPLA had their own radio station where they would bring out news. So everyone would just come to one house and listen to that radio station. They used to sing songs on the radio station. All they had were their SPLA songs. I never really paid attention to the news, but I did pay attention to the songs that they had. SPLA was something new, and promising change for us, so I was pretty happy. But I didn't know then what would come with it.

After some months, SPLA soldiers started coming at nighttime and stealing things. If you had a nice watch, they'd take it from you. If you had a nice bike, they'd take it from you. Anything that was valuable to you, they'd take it from you, and they'd take the men to go fight.

My mother's land was destroyed in 1984, in the nighttime. Just burned. When we woke up in the morning, we saw the fire, and went to a big square near our home. We found dead bodies. My friend Lucia's brother had been shot. It was like my head opened up. I started crying. I couldn't think properly. I couldn't go to work, I couldn't go to school, I couldn't do anything. I looked for my child, but I didn't have a child anymore.

I don't know who did the killing. And soon it just became normal. When you wake up in the morning, you hear about dead people. It happened a lot.

We were all girls living with my mother by then, so we were

in even more danger. The people warned my mom. They said you should just move, just get out, because they'll do something to your girls. So my mother took all my sisters and me, and we moved to my dad's old house, in the middle of the town of Wau. We went to my mother's family to take some crops for money, and then we moved to this big town of Wau.

It was no better in Wau. Still, we would wake up in the morning and hear about dead people.

I LEFT WITHOUT A GOODBYE

At the end of 1988, or perhaps the beginning of 1989, there was a caravan of cars. They were all going to the capital city of Juba. My friend Lucia told me she was going. I wanted to go and I wanted to do it secretly, because I knew my mother would not approve. I had no money, I had no good clothes, but I packed my stuff early the next morning, and I left without a goodbye. I wasn't feeling anything at all.

When I arrived in Juba I met a woman from Wau. Her husband was from the same tribe as my father. She asked me to stay with her and care for her children, and soon they were like my little siblings: Joseph, Bengara, Dundu, and Pong. Four children. I stayed with them for a year, and I was happy. The woman of the house gave me freedom and allowed me to earn some money as well brewing *merissa* in the home, as my mother had done. I had learned the recipe well, and I became known for making good-quality drink. My business started to grow.

After a year with that family of the four children, my cousins in Juba invited me to stay with them. But soon I found they did not treat me well at all. They made me pay rent for my room. They saw my success at selling *merissa*, they saw that I had started making money and buying some better clothes. I even got a bed. They hated me for it.

Quickly I moved out from there, and I rented another house. I met an old woman, a neighbor, named Burutan, a Meru woman with a Dinka husband. I came to her one night, feeling scared, telling her I could not sleep alone by myself. She said she would be like my mother, and she would look out for me. Burutan brought her daughter to my home, and her daughter slept with me for comfort.

In those days, the war was getting more intense. People started moving out of homes and living in these trenches that they dug outside the city. They used to put all their food, equipment, and furniture in these holes. Nothing was really safe. There were no straight routes. I could not walk from home to the market without sounds of bombs or guns scaring me. Sometimes they would be shooting from above, and I would have to run fast to get water and run back home.

Most bombs would drop in the night. Often when dark was coming, I would take some food and go out to people's trenches—friends or relatives—offer some food, and ask to share their trench. We wouldn't sleep, really. Sleep would only come if we were really tired.

I stayed in Juba until 1993. That was when one of my cousins came to get me. He came to me and said that my mother and sisters in Wau were all crying over me, thinking I'm dead or injured because they were hearing so much news about bombings in Juba. He was also worried about HIV and AIDS, which was spreading fast. He wanted to send me to the North, to Khartoum. His mother had recently died, and he had been stationed in Juba by the army, so there was space in his home there. I agreed to go.

My cousin bought me a ticket for an airplane. He gave me a piece of paper and a bit of money for a taxi, and he told me, "Once you get to Khartoum, give this piece of paper to a taxi driver, and he will bring you right to my house."

The plan was for me to go on a cargo plane. My first airplane. There were no chairs. It was just a huge space, and it was filled with dead and injured soldiers being brought back to Khartoum. The injured were screaming. I was so scared—my stomach was quickly empty. I felt that we were going to fall at any minute. But we made it to Khartoum safely.

I got out of the airport, I saw a taxi, and I got in. The taxi drove for an hour, and I stared out the window. I saw buildings and so many cars. It was a big change. In Juba, I felt rich from selling *merissa*. Now, suddenly, in the middle of this city, I went from rich to poor. But as the taxi drove on, I saw changes. The houses started getting worse and worse. Soon I thought to myself, these homes are in such bad condition that I would never see houses like this in the South. I asked the taxi driver, "What is this place?" And he replied, "This is Mayo."

He stopped in Mayo Camp. And that is where we are sitting right now.

THAT PICTURE WAS RIPPED APART

I had thought I'd be living in a nice apartment in a big building, with a refrigerator, with fruits and everything. I had a picture in my mind of Khartoum and that picture was ripped apart when I came here to Mayo camp.

When I first came to the camp, I stayed with my cousin's wife. I had no work. I sat in the house most of the day. I tried to brew a bit of alcohol. There was nothing for me here.

A year later, the same cousin put me on another plane to see my family in Wau. I went home to see my mother.

Everything had changed. It wasn't like the place where I was raised. It was not that the land had changed, but that the people had changed. The people that I left there had all grown up. The class-mates I should have graduated with had... well, I don't know where they are right now.

I did see my mother, though, and I ran to her. She said, "I hope God gives you a girl like God has given you to me." It meant so much to her that I had come from Khartoum to Wau to see my family. She just repeated those words again and again. I stayed with her for six months, until my cousin asked me to return to Mayo to help care for his family. I have stayed here for the thirteen years since.

Mayo brought troubled times again. Sometimes I have nothing to eat. Our homes are made of mud and sticks. In the rainy season the roof leaks. Right now it is the end of the rainy season, and the roof is about to collapse. I have not tried to repair it this year, because I know that this is what happens, no matter what I do.

This part of Mayo camp is called Mandela. The people here are all from the South. God has brought us together, and now we're really close neighbors. During the day, the women will all be at work, to earn five, or six, or maybe eight pounds in a day. It is easier for us to find a job than it is for the men. We clean houses mostly. I took a course on first aid once and a course on knitting, like I did when I was a child.

During the afternoon, we sit down and talk like normal people talk, about family and our pasts, and the news we hear every day. I learn things from members of different tribes. We would do henna together. Eat different tastes of food. It is a good community. This became my life.

IT'S JUST LIFE, AND THIS IS WHAT HAPPENS

As the war was ending around 2002, my cousin, his wife, and their children went to Canada. They left me here. I don't know how they got a ticket. He didn't even tell me. He just told me right as he left.

I moved in with another cousin and his wife. He died in 2005, so now I have his children that I take care of. So I live with my cousin's wife and her kids. Six boys. All boys. It's difficult to have a house full of boys, but thank God, they respect me. The youngest is seven years—he is ill right now; there is a swelling in his hand, and we are trying to find a doctor for him. The oldest boy should be in university, but we don't have the money for him. None of the boys can get enough work, and even when they find a job, doing construction or something like that, sometimes they don't have enough transportation money to get there. So they just stay at home. It is difficult for the boys.

I used to make *merissa* here in Mayo. We make two or three times as much money from *merissa* compared to cleaning houses, and this way we do not have to pay for transport to the people's houses. I earned enough to buy clothes again and another bed. But the Islamic law in Khartoum says that I cannot make alcohol. In 2004, the police came to the camp and searched the houses for women like me. At midnight they came, searched my home, found the *merissa* and took me to jail. The next morning, I went in front of a judge, and they sent me to Omdurman prison for two months.

In jail, we could only eat when the people from the church would bring us food. Sometimes they gave me soap. There were no real beds, and it was all very dirty. For two months I was there, and I was very tired and very scared. I had a couple of friends from Mayo who were with me in the jail. They told me to be patient. We'd go to church together. They would tell me, "It's just life, and this is what happens in life."

Since the arrest, I have stopped brewing. I clean houses sometimes instead. Right now, I'm working for a petroleum company. I clean for them, cleaning the floors, cleaning the tables. The money is not enough at all. I have problems with broken teeth, and they give me cotton balls. In some months, I get a lot of periods, lots of bleeding. I went to the hospital, and they said I have a disease that stops me from getting pregnant. It's still small, but it's getting bigger and bigger and bigger. I have to have the surgery to get it taken out. They gave me a paper with instructions for surgery, but I do not know when I will have care.

TO SEE MY MOTHER, TO SIT WITH HER

I thank God for the new peace in this country. Right now there's a chance that I can go back to my home in the South. The government will let me go back and I want to go back, but I can't find a way to go back. I don't have money to travel. I signed up for a government project to send us back. They have a tent right here in Mayo. When your name gets called, you take your furniture and clothing, and you go to the field at the edge of the camp. That's where the car comes and transports you. A car will just take us to Wau. Right now, they don't call, because during the rainy season it's really hard to transport. I hope they will call me in the next season.

I don't think I will ever marry or have children. No child—this is the greatest sadness of my life. I have become an old woman now, older than thirty-five. It is past my time. But when I go home to Wau, life will be easy for me. I can start farming like I used to. I can start my business, grinding dates and brewing *merissa*. All my family will be with me. And when I go back, all I want is to see my mother, to sit with her. My mother raised us with so much trouble on her hands when she had so little. Sometimes I love her so much that I don't want to face the pain if she dies. I want to tell her, "I wish I would die before you so I don't experience the pain of your death."

Now I have told everything. It is all part of God's plan.

APOBO KALIFA

AGE: *35*
TRIBE: *Dinka*
BIRTHPLACE: *Khartoum*
INTERVIEWED IN: *Marial Bai, South Sudan*

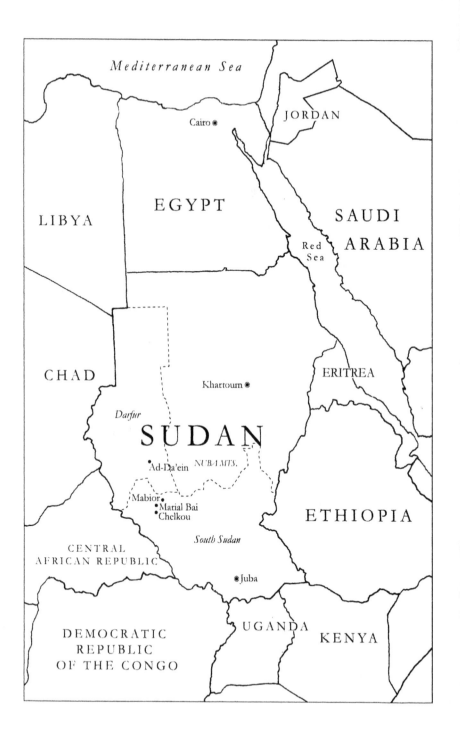

WOMEN ARE THE
MARGINALIZED OF THE
MARGINALIZED

On a warm sunny day in July, Apobo Kalifa told her story while sitting at a plastic table in the compound of an NGO operating in Marial Bai. She talked steadily, waving a few times to women-friends she knew who were cooking for the Ugandan NGO workers. Apobo had only recently returned to Marial Bai to live; she had spent most of her life in Khartoum, and she and her five children were slowly becoming accustomed to a much smaller town with far fewer conveniences.

I was born in Khartoum. My father went to school there. The marriage between my father and mother was arranged; she was sent from Marial Bai to Khartoum to live with him, her new husband. I was born there and spent almost two years there. Then my mother and I left Khartoum to return to Marial Bai.

Then the war began. During the war my mother fell sick and went back to Khartoum to join my father. I was left with my grandmother here in Marial Bai. When the *murahaleen* and the Sudanese army began attacking the region, my grandmother took me to a place called Chelkou, south of Marial Bai. Many people were running in that direction. Nobody went north because the *murahaleen* were coming from that direction. We spent some days in Chelkou, running every day while the *murahaleen* took away our cows and everything we owned.

At that time, in 1986, my maternal uncle was in the Sudanese government army. He communicated with my family and told them that he was coming to get me, to send me to Khartoum. But to do that he had to escape from the army. He put on civilian clothes and took a jerry-can of water, and then the moment he left he was spotted by the government; they started shooting after him.

My uncle managed to meet me in a place called Mabior, northeast of Marial Bai. We began walking. We would walk at night, going to Khartoum now. My only choice was to go to Khartoum and join my father. We couldn't go anywhere else. We were part of the movement of many, many people.

And so we walked. One night I was fetching water and people started running. I ran into the bush and I accidentally jumped on an animal. It ran away; I didn't know what it was. Later on, people said that they had heard a lion roar. I am almost sure that I had jumped on a lion! I didn't know that it was a lion! People thought that I had been eaten.

THE MASSACRE AT AD-DA'EIN

Eventually my uncle and I reached Ad-Da'ein. My father had prepared me a train ticket from Ad-Da'ein to Khartoum. At Ad-Da'ein I met many other relatives. Everyone was going to Khartoum. My extended family was there, including the two sons of my grandmother and their wives, and many others.

I was sent ahead on a train to Khartoum. I forget why I went ahead, but the rest of my family remained in Ad-Da'ein, meaning to take a later train. It turns out that the train I was on was the last one to leave Ad-Da'ein safely. After I arrived in Khartoum, I met my father at the train station. He was living on the banks of the western Nile, working at a bottling company.

A week later, we received a letter about what had happened. There had been a massacre at Ad-Da'ein, and my two uncles and aunt were killed.[1] Of my family, all of the children were killed in that massacre. So there was no one left in my family except my father and his children already living in Khartoum. The uncle who brought me to Ad-Da'ein died there, too. My father was the only one of his family left in the end.

KIDNAPPED WHILE LEAVING SCHOOL

I was enrolled in school the next year, 1988. It was a Comboni Missionary school, mostly Christian students. There were many more boys than girls at that school. There were a few Northern Sudanese, but most of the students were from Southern Sudan.

I liked science and history. English was not my favorite subject. At Comboni they teach two languages. Some Comboni schools focus on Arabic more than English; in some parts the focus is more on English. And for my part, I was speaking Arabic, and English was not my favorite. I failed most of the tests on English. I couldn't speak English well because not many people spoke English at that time, and I didn't take it seriously. If it were now, I would try with more effort.

In 1994, I finished my last day of fifth grade and then began the upper primary school. I remember that year because I was in a car accident. My family was going to a party not too far from Khartoum and they forgot to close my door. So the door opened and I fell on the street. I was lucky, because the driver of the car that was coming

---

[1] For more on the *murahaleen* and the massacre at Ad-Da'ein, see page 397.

behind wasn't so close. If he had been closer, I would have been run over by the next car.

And then two years later, my life changed drastically. School ended. My girlhood ended. I was leaving one school one day when two men ran to me, grabbed me, and threw me into a car. I was taken to an apartment and kept there. This is when I learned that one of the men, named Mohammed, wanted to have me as a wife. This is how things were done at the time in Sudan. You kidnapped the girl you wanted to marry. So Mo [he went by this shortened version of his name] and his cousin kept me against my will. I did not know this man Mo, but apparently he had been interested in me for a while. He had asked my father for my hand in marriage, but my father had refused. My father said that I was too young. I was at school, and he was not ready to marry me off before I completed school.

But then, as they do in Sudan, Mo decided he didn't like that answer, and so he took me by force. And because we were southerners living in Khartoum, it was easy to do anything like this. The rules were bent and broken. So even though my father had refused to marry me to this man, this man ran and got his car. He got his car, and he and another man, a relative of his, parked the car at the corner of my school. When I left school that day, they appeared and grabbed me, threw me in the car and drove away.

Then the next day, the man who abducted me let my family know that they had taken me. This was customary—that the abducting family would let the girl's family know. Usually, the girl's family would simply succumb. The assumption is that the girl has been spoiled by that point, and the girl's family has no choice but to accept the marriage. Presumably the girl will have no other marriage options after such an abduction.

But when my father heard that I was taken into someone's house to be a wife, he sent the police to catch Mo. He wanted the police to put him in jail and bring me home. But Mo didn't want to give me up. Instead of releasing me to my family, Mo and his cousin changed their location. The police went to Mo's house and couldn't find me.

The police were angry, so they took every member of Mo's family to jail. They said, "Unless you show us where you took Apobo, you are going to be detained. And then if you don't do this within a few days, you will face more consequences."

When Mo heard that everyone in his family was taken to prison, he decided to turn himself in. The police forced him to reveal where he had hidden me. When he did, the rest of his family members were released. I thought I, too, would be free.

The problem for me was that my uncle, my father's older brother, was a friend of Mo's. My uncle was the eldest of the family, and so he was permitted to make the decisions for the family. And he wanted my father to grant the marriage to Mo. After some discussions, my uncle convinced my father to allow Mo to take me as a wife. It was my uncle's influence that changed my father's mind. I was crushed.

This situation would not have arisen if all of my other uncles had not been killed at Ad-Da'ein. If they had not been killed, they would have been alive to intervene in my case. I would never marry if I did not marry Mo, he said, and my father eventually believed him. So my family negotiated a bride price with Mo's family, and my fate was sealed.

AN UNHAPPY UNION

I was Mo's first wife. He was young, no more than thirty years old. Mo did not have a job at that time. He was a day laborer. He was part of a group of men who would go to the market seeking work each day. Ideally someone would employ men like him, and they would work for a day. That was the kind of job he was doing.

Mo was dominating. He insisted on being the decision maker in almost everything. Even with cooking, which is not his business, he would decide all that was to be cooked. And always he said a lot of bad things. He was verbally abusive, physically abusive. Sometimes when he was mad he would kick me. Even when I was still a new wife! He didn't want me to talk with the neighbors. If I did that, he would accuse me of seeing other men. When he became jealous, he became violent. A lot of things happened there that I could not stop.

After we began quarreling, I had hope that it would not go on for long, that maybe it was some mistake and maybe we were trying to know each other. I had been taught to be tolerant toward my husband, to forgive him for the sake of the marriage. But the abuse did not stop. He began drinking and drinking. That changed everything; the abuse became worse. He hit me often. He yelled at me. He treated me like an animal.

THE END OF THE MARRIAGE

We had two babies. If I had given up early, that would have not happened—we would not have had two babies. The first baby we had lived for six months and died. It was a very sudden incident. We never knew how the baby died. And then we had the second baby a year later. That baby did not die.

After the second baby was born, I had hoped that Mo would cease being violent, and also being irresponsible, but it didn't happen. At one point the baby was admitted to the hospital and he had to spend three months in the hospital. During that entire time, Mo never visited once. I started wondering, "How could my husband not come to the hospital to see the baby?"

This is when I first proposed divorce to my father. Because he had never favored Mo, my father agreed to a divorce. He said that he didn't want his daughter to live in that condition. I adored my father for letting me leave. He felt bad about agreeing to the marriage in the first place, and realized that divorce could be a solution.

My uncle, the same one who had convinced my father to give me to Mo, intervened again. He said that I was not going to divorce Mo. He repeated that three times. He said that while he was alive, I was not going to divorce Mo. I told my uncle that he would rather Mo hit me than have me stay in a place where I was safe. I told him he was committing me to an imminent death. Staying with Mo was an imminent death.

To punish me, my uncle sent for a policeman. I was taken to a court, and the judge said that if I wanted to divorce Mo, I would be beaten one hundred times with a cane. It was an official proceeding. At that time, women had no voice. They made their threat, but I would not back down. I accepted the punishment to be caned.

At the police station I was caned a hundred times. Some on the leg, some on the bottom. At times they would beat me on the back, just where they knew it would hurt most. While they were caning me they made me say, *I am not going to divorce him.* It was torture.

After I was caned I was taken back to the court, and then was asked if I was still considered divorcing Mo. I still wanted to divorce Mo, but they said that if I still wanted a divorce, they would beat me again. I knew what I believed, but had no energy to resist more beating. So I gave in. I said I was going to go back to Mo. After I accepted that, that was the end of the trial. They sent me back to Mo.

ESCAPE

I returned home. Mo was drunk, and he was very angry about everything. That very night he picked a fight with me. He rolled our mattress up and insisted I lift it. It was a silly demand. It was just something he wanted me to do to show he could order me around. When I refused to do it, he grabbed a knife and said that if I didn't pick up that mattress he was going to stab me.

I refused. I told Mo that there is only one death. I said, "I've been caned a hundred times, my body is full of pain, my soul is full of pain. I would rather you kill me than have you abuse me by having me carry something that we are not taking anywhere."

I tried to run. He grabbed me from behind. We struggled. Mo dropped the knife and the knife fell on my leg. I got cut. I picked up the knife, and while we struggled over the knife, Mo also was cut.

I ran out at that moment. I ran back to the police station and told them, "You beat me a hundred times! You sent me back to that man but you should have asked him not to hurt me again. I cannot live with him. I would rather be divorced or killed instead."

After I went to the court, my father came to the court to testify that he didn't want his daughter to go back to Mo. Finally my uncle arrived, and said that if my father agreed with me then he was washing his hands of that marriage. And from that day on my uncle was never to be consulted for anything by the Kalifa family, my family. And then he left the court. And the court finally granted a divorce.

After we broke up, Mo never remarried. After that I went home with my son and stayed with my family. I was seventeen.

A NEW AND BETTER MAN

I spent four years at home, four years without dating anybody. I went back to the same school I had enrolled in and starting working as a cook. I would cook at school in the morning, and after the school closed, I worked at a tea shop.

There was a man who would come every day for tea. He was a friend of some of my distant relatives. This guy was good. He spoke very well, very eloquently.

A year later, this man began to approach me and ask for a relationship. I said no. I told him that I didn't want a man again, that I didn't want to be slapped or shouted at unnecessarily. I didn't want anybody who will hurt me emotionally. I just wanted to live alone and be happy. I didn't want anybody to accuse me of adultery when it didn't happen. I didn't want someone who was jealous of anything.

This man insisted that he was not going to do any of this. That he was in fact married and that he'd never had kids with his wife. They had problems conceiving, and he really wanted a second wife because he wanted babies, children to love. And he was ready to provide what I needed.

I refused. I refused, so this man did a very unusual thing. He spoke with my mother first, alone. He asked my mother first for my hand in marriage. This was very unusual, and my mother was impressed. Then he spoke with my father, and he spoke with every family member. To everyone he was saying that he heard of how I was hurt by my husband, and that he was not going to do that—that in fact he was going to provide the opposite of what Mo had done to me. And that it was important that the family understood all of this.

So everyone saw his seriousness and honesty and transparency and they agreed. Then he came back to me and he told me, "I have talked to everyone. You are the last." And then I agreed. The marriage was arranged, and we were married.

THE MARGINALIZED OF THE MARGINALIZED

We have four children, and my husband has fulfilled his promises. I don't know what will happen in the future, but he has never insulted or beat me. We've always been happy. I feel like I have the right husband now.

The way I broke up with Mo, and the way I was forced to marry him and stay with him—these are some of the primary reasons I wanted to fight for the rights of women. In Sudan it's much worse than anywhere else to be a woman. There are no rights for women. There are none. No matter what happens, no matter what the consequences of the war were, the woman has always remained the marginalized of the marginalized. Women's voices are not heard anywhere.

The war was a problem, and the woman were central victims of that. The women are the ones whose husbands have been killed. And the ones whose children, whose sons and daughters, have been killed. Or raped. Or tortured. And everything that happens during war comes back to women. We are victims of all that has happened, in the North or the South. It all comes back to women.

My organization was founded in 1989, long before the Comprehensive Peace Agreement. Before the CPA we called ourselves the Southern Sudanese Women's Association. It was a group meant to make women politically aware and to empower them economically.

I wanted to make women aware of the things that happened to me, and at the same time I wanted to talk about the Khartoum government and how they treated women. It was so bad. For example, in Khartoum, the police would come to your home and accuse you of adultery, or of brewing wine illegally, and they would take you to jail. But you haven't done anything. So while they interrogate you, they get you to say something they don't like. They beat you and interrogate you, and when you protest, when you fight back, that becomes the case against you. Women are raped and abused in custody. And there is no protection for the women.

So first we mobilized and we made people aware of women's rights. Seventeen of us were identified as the leaders. We called this "the formation step." And then came the "action" stage. Our first step was to generate income. We needed to have money to do the things we wanted to do, to empower ourselves. So we started making and selling chairs. With a bit of startup money, we employed carpenters and upholsterers, and we trained others. We began manufacturing chairs, selling them to friends and on the open market. We did upholstery, anything like that. And we were successful very early on. We made a good deal of money and were able to give it to the needy women in our neighborhood, and were able to expand the business.

We were very active in our work. But we suffered many, many problems because there have been no rights for women in Khartoum under Islamic law. Members of the association have been jailed, have been beaten. Advocates for women have to operate underground. Even at home, the husbands of some of our members refused to let them participate. They said, "What do you want? This war was not for women. This group is just going to learn about prostitution and how to run away." So of the seventeen, nine members of the group could not come back due to those problems. And only eight of us remained to pursue the goal of the women's group.

All along, it was difficult to be Southern Sudanese in Khartoum during the war. There was suspicion about anyone meeting anywhere. Groups of people were suspicious. And groups of women were especially unusual. Whenever Southern Sudanese formed groups or met regularly or in large numbers, there was suspicion that they were plotting against the government of Sudan.

Sometimes there were retributions in Khartoum when there was an SPLA victory. It was done in very secretive ways. They would kill people in prison, or they would say you were an SPLA spy or an SPLA sympathizer and you would be killed. You couldn't even listen to the radio announcing news about the SPLA—even the BBC. It was prohibited. You could not play SPLA songs on your radio. Nothing of that kind was allowed. You couldn't wear anything saying SPLA. That was a huge crime. The Southern Sudanese people, especially the educated and the outspoken, became the target.

During wartime, when SPLA radio was operational, their news reports came at three p.m. And that time was when the security would be outside, and anytime you were seen sitting around at that time, listening to the radio, to that channel, you would be caught and punished, even executed for treason. That was the solution. If

a group of people was caught and none of them were executed, that
was a miracle. There were people who were forced, through circumstances, to denounce supporting the SPLA. To speak against the
SPLA. In their heart they knew who they supported, but they had to
survive. And people who spoke against the SPLA were favored by the
government. So our group could not be pro-SPLA. We had to seem
neutral—interested only in the rights of women.

A NEW DAY, POST-CPA

After the Comprehensive Peace Agreement in 2005, we decided to
identify with the party that supported the rights of women, and the
Sudan People's Liberation Movement was that. The SPLM began to
erect many offices and began many projects in Khartoum. We wanted
to align ourselves with them and work with them.

Our group decided to invite the SPLM and many of the leaders
in Khartoum to a party. We spent the little money we had to bring
in people who were powerful—politicians and so forth—to make
them aware of what we were doing, and to request that they build
an office for women. It was a big party, a very festive event. We
showed our chairs, our upholstery, and we also got to show every
kind of food we could cook. At the party, all the dignitaries were
singing and dancing. We gave all of the big guys opportunities to
talk. All the leaders wanted to show others that they were promoting women.

After that, the political leaders were supportive of us. And seeing
that we were legitimate, the husbands who had previously forbidden
their wives to be part of our group now allowed them to do so. We
were proven now, and from then on, all of the women in the group
were allowed to come. Soon after that party, the other nine of the
seventeen were allowed to come back. Just so long as no one stayed
out too late.

A PERSISTENT DANGER

Khartoum was not our home and it will never be our home. After the CPA, the authorities there are still hostile to Southern Sudanese people. For example, when John Garang died in July 2005, the incidents that followed convinced every Southern Sudanese that they could be wiped out at any time.

When Garang died, some Southern people went on strike. It was difficult in the city at that time, and many Northern Sudanese took this out on Southern Sudanese. There were random lynchings and killings in Khartoum. People who worked at different companies, people who worked at different homes, people who worked in the street, even the homeless—a lot of people were killed in Khartoum following Garang's death, and still are being killed now. If you are alone on the street and you are surrounded by Northern Sudanese, they could kill you and throw you into the Nile.

Some neighborhoods are heavily populated by Southern Sudanese; some neighborhoods are not. In the places where the Southern Sudanese population is bigger it was better, because anybody who penetrated with the intention of killing Southern Sudanese knew of the consequences. In my neighborhood there were so many Southern Sudanese, the assailants would only shoot people who went outside. Or they'd throw handmade grenades. They would be scared in those districts. But in other districts in Khartoum, where there were fewer Southern Sudanese, worse things could happen. They would just surround your home. And then your people are gone, killed. These things go unreported.

Whatever the news said about the number of people who died, that was just on the news—that number is not even close to the reality. It was more than that. Incidents like that have taught us that it could happen again. A second genocide could take place in Khartoum.

THE WOMEN COULD BE ORGANIZED SOMEHOW

I've been in Marial Bai for three months now. I came back in April 2007. This year the governor of northern Bahr al-Ghazal state went and spoke to the internally displaced people and anyone who went to the North during the war. The governor knew that three quarters of the IDP population in the North are from northern Bahr al-Ghazal, and he came to say that the Government of South Sudan would help anyone who wanted to come back to South Sudan and could not afford to come back. After hearing him speak, we went and registered and were brought here by a convoy of cars and trucks.

For many people who return here, it's just survival. You begin from scratch, building a house, buying all the materials that you need, and then you cope with the environment. It's so challenging, because the years that many people have spent in the North have changed their way of life, their way of coping. It's more modern in Khartoum. There are roads, stores, conveniences. So the comparison is drastic.

But for me, I cannot compare my situation with the others. My husband came back with me; many women who have returned have lost their husbands. My husband is a professional builder and makes a good salary. He is a family man and a provider, and I help him to make some money for the family. But for many of my friends it's very difficult. It will take a while.

When I came here I looked around, I called some neighbors and asked what they do here. They told me that they don't do anything except be housewives. That is who I am, too. But I also thought that the women could be organized somehow.

I have discussed the possibility of a group of women contributing one pound per month to a common cause. If we get a thousand pounds we can begin a business. We could make locally made perfume, which is what I do now—I sell it at my house. We could make it a larger business, and have our own place in town. Men will come and buy the perfumes, and the women will come and buy, and we will make money. It can be done.

We could also begin a small restaurant. If we make it clean, people would eat there. They won't say, "Man, we're not going to eat there!" They will eat. So we could do that and we could make revenue from it, and if that worked then we could also begin making handmade crafts. We could do things like that and sell them, and slowly but surely the group will grow. And when you grow, you have goals. That's what my group used to do in Khartoum. With more money comes more possibilities, more ideas, progress.

It could be done here. I'm happy because there is a good business mentality here. You find that everybody wants to involve themselves in trade. What people need to do is to open shops, because that's where people spend money. That's where we would begin.

I think I'm naturally someone who organizes people into groups to work together. I am an only child. When I was growing up I was always looking for brothers and sisters, so my friends and neighbors became my brothers and sisters. I would go and spend a long time playing with the kids from other homes, and I would invite my friends to play with me at our home. My mother and father one day told me that because I was their only child, I should consider all of my friends my siblings. And to this day I try to create family from friendships. If that is a way of leading people—bringing friends and neighbors to make a family—so be it.

PANTHER ALIER

AGE: *31*
TRIBE: *Dinka*
BIRTHPLACE: *Kolnyang, South Sudan*
INTERVIEWED IN: *Newton, Massachusetts*

WE WERE NOT OLD
ENOUGH TO BE THINKING
LIKE GROWN-UPS

Like many dedicated graduate students at Brandeis University, Panther spends long days on campus moving between classes, lectures, and study rooms, where he often orders a pizza to keep him going during late-night study sessions. Over the course of several interviews in various study rooms at the Heller School, Panther explained how he came to be here in Waltham, Massachusetts, a place very different than Kolnyang, the Sudanese village where he was born. He described his journey, his current work as an activist, and how he hopes to use his education to create lasting, positive change for future generations in Sudan.

I'm from Kolnyang, a small village outside of the town of Bor in South Sudan. I was born to a family of five: two sisters, two brothers. I am the youngest. My father died before I was born. I think he died of disease. My mother and my aunt told me that he was tough, that of all his brothers he had the skill of negotiating with people who owed a dowry for his sisters and things like that. You didn't want to mess up with him. My mom died later, when I was about five or so. When my mom died, I was taken to live with my mother's sister in another village called Makuach, also outside of Bor. My brothers and sisters remained in my father's home with my uncles and aunts. My aunt took me into her family and raised me with her children.

A typical day in the village where I was born began in the morning with the happiness of being a child, getting up to go play with friends and enjoy the whole day of running around in the neighborhood. We just played all day. We climbed trees, made small huts or molded cows from clay. Cows were basically our lives, so we began as children making cows of clay. Cows would show that you were wealthy and could marry someone's daughter.

My cousins and I would play every morning while the adults started to work. The women prepared food, and the men went out to hunt or to farm, or they went to the cattle camps. For us, it was just a time to eat and play. It was the best experience for me, being among my family and knowing that my sisters and brothers and all of my relatives were going to be watching out for me. When the food was ready at my cousin's house, their mother would call us all to come and eat, including the wives and mothers of our uncles; we ate as a community, with a very strong sense of communal living.

When I went to my aunt's village and I was growing up, I began to assume some chores, like taking care of the goats, making sure they got enough to drink and didn't get lost from the herd when I took them out to graze. As I grew older I started taking care of young cows. But still, we were always playing. We were not old enough to be thinking of grown-up things.

In 1983, I heard the war had started, and some of the young men from our villages went to fight with the SPLA. In fact, two of my aunt's sons went into the army with the SPLA. I knew that the war was happening between the army and the rebels, but we always saw it as something that was happening in the big towns. It had not affected us, because our livelihood was centered in the villages and we did not trade in the modern towns. We had cows that gave us milk and meat. The elders grew sorghum for us; we had nothing to do with the modern towns, and that was where the fighting was always happening. So it didn't affect us that much, except for those young people who had gone to sacrifice their lives in the war. Once in a while, you heard that someone had been killed.

When I was younger, I didn't really understand what the issues were, or think about going to fight with the SPLA. But as I grew older, I realized these young men were sacrificing their life for something they thought was noble, for the people of the South. I realized why the boys were going to join the army when they could have made their life in their village, just like their parents had done, without bothering about what was happening in the towns. I understood perfectly that what they were doing was a noble cause for us all. I could have contributed and gone to fight as well if I had been their age.

It was fascinating to me when they came back from fighting. They had AK-47s and uniforms. We were always fascinated with their guns. When my cousin came back we wanted to touch his gun. But he was always cautious for the few days he was there, telling us not to touch it, that it was dangerous. He didn't really tell us any stories about fighting or being in the army, but he talked about wanting to go back to the army after coming back home. He said he got the gun to fight, not to come home and stay. When he said the gun could kill, I was really curious about it. But I never had a chance to see it working until the village was actually attacked, and it became real.

EARTH COMING TO AN END

In 1987, the government decided to actually go into the villages. I'm sure that, at this point, they realized the villages were the supplying source for rebel soldiers, so this was their only way to break the supply. At this time, when the whole region was in this upset of war, the village I was living in, like the rest of the villages in the region, experienced a very aggressive attack from the Northern government.

I was about ten years old. Like so many Southern Sudanese, I did not know when I was born, because so many of us were born in the villages, not in medical facilities. So we just kind of estimated. One of my cousins who had gone to missionary school actually said he could almost say for sure that I was born in 1977, judging by some of the events that had happened around the time of my birth. But he did not know the date.

My cousins, my friends, and I were outside in the nearby bushes taking care of the young cows when all of a sudden we heard this rumbling sound. Although we had heard gunshots before, this was more frightening. You heard this rumbling sound and then it just abruptly became continuous shooting. In an instant, there was so much confusion and we got frightened. All of a sudden, I saw people running from different directions, and you couldn't tell exactly where the thing was happening, because people were running in a confused manner. Later on, I sensed that some people, especially our parents, were running to find their kids and then the kids were running to find their parents, and that became a whole mess. The kids who were nearby at the outskirts of the village were running back to their parents, even though the village was the source of danger; they felt like if they could find an adult, someone in their family, they would be more secure. I got separated from my aunt and all my relatives, so I was by myself with friends. There were so many bullets, you heard them whistle as they were going through the air. And you saw people just falling to the ground.

I couldn't see any of the Arab militiamen who were attacking us, because I was on the outskirts of the village. But I saw people who had been injured in the attack, bleeding and running, helping one another to get out of the village, carrying each other. I saw people falling. It was like the earth was coming to an end.

I remember one of the elders who was known in the village trying to signal for people not to run toward the village, because it was under attack and was being burned already. He wouldn't bow down for the bullets. He and some of the other elders started to sit us down and calm the sense of fear that we all had, that feeling that this was going to be the end. I am sure they wanted to give us confidence, to make us quiet and to keep us from panicking. But the fact that there was so much shooting and burning was alarming. You could see the smoke rising into the air already. I remember feeling like it didn't make sense to just be sitting there and not going somewhere, although I didn't know where to go. There was no place that was safe.

While we were sitting there, the elder who took charge of us said it was the Arabs who had come to kill us. So I got a feeling from him that they were our enemies and that they had come to hunt us down. I understood immediately that our village had been attacked by the enemy our people were fighting in the SPLA. The village was literally brought down to nothing. The elders tried to give us the feeling that things would be okay, that soon we would go home. We never did.

That first night, the elders told us that we shouldn't go now and that they would let us know when we could; they sent people to check. You could still see the flames, so it was hard to even think about what the next step would be. But they told us late in the night that the SPLA was going to come to our rescue soon, and that we would be fine.

They decided to collect all of us together, and we started walking. They put us in line and we all held hands. Southern Sudan is a grassland, a savannah, so we had to make a path. We just walked barefoot, and the elder ahead of us just tried to clear a way and push through the grass himself.

Most of the people who left were either boys or elders. There were women, of course, and some girls, but not a lot of them. Not many of them had the courage to go to unknown places. Also, many of the girls were home with their moms when the village was attacked, and so if they didn't escape, they were captured. We picked up people as we went; we would be going along when all of a sudden we would find a few people from here and there, also mostly boys. You would hear voices, and people would come from where they were hiding. And so we became a collective. As we continued going along, the number of women and girls began to decrease. I think some women just gave up; they could not go any longer. Some women had young kids, and no one was there to carry them, and they just remained behind. The walk became too long.

We never knew where our elders were taking us or how long the walk was going to be. We just knew they were leading us to a place that was going to be safe, and because the enemy was going to hunt us down, we should always stick to them. They kept telling us that it was close, that in the next few hours we could arrive. Of course, as we were walking, we did come to some villages, but they were different tribes than our Dinka tribe. I remember when we arrived at one village, the chief gave us some cows and killed them. That was the first formal meal we had since we left. It was really great, but we were exhausted.

Our journey started on a very dry path. People actually lost their lives from thirst and not having enough water. And then food was an issue. The night before we left our village, a few of the elders who knew that leaving was not going to be an easy solution snuck back into the village and got some food from any houses that were not burned down. But there were just a few of them, so we ate everything we had pretty quickly. While we were walking, the water was drying up, but they started getting sticks from the woods and going to fish in the pools that were left. If we were lucky, we caught fish with just our hands. We also sometimes happened on small animals, so we would try to catch those, like by throwing a stone at a bird. We also ate some edible leaves. But sometimes we had no food for a day or two, and that contributed to young people remaining behind.

We were getting closer to Ethiopia. After crossing a really dry desert and having people die from thirst, all of a sudden we came to this area that was muddy and we were faced with floods. Sudan is a very large country, and it has different geographical conditions. You had to walk through the mud, and many of us were just too young to be pulling along that much water and mud. And people were left behind because of that. There was this river that was filled with crocodiles, alligators, and things like that. In one place, we spent two days going through mud and water, and the water would come up to your neck sometimes. The elders were tall enough and could just walk through it. We crossed that area and came to a big dry area. There were some edible fruits, and we started eating all that; we came to a village where they supplied us with some corn they grew.

WE HAD ALWAYS THOUGHT THE
WORLD WAS REALLY SMALL

While we walked, I thought about my family and wondered where we were going. I had gotten separated from my aunt and most of my cousins. I did not know if the same thing happened to my sisters and brothers in Kolnyang. I was thinking about whether they had actually survived or if their village had not been attacked, and if I could have had a better chance to survive if I had gone to the other village instead of leaving with the elders. But, as we were going along, you could sense from the influx of people that there were coordinated attacks through all the villages. The one cousin from whom I had not been separated was with me the whole way to Ethiopia. He was about my age. And many of us knew each other, so we started collecting ourselves by villages as we walked.

We always walked at night and rested in the day, because the elders said the enemy would easily see us if we walked in the day. We encountered a lot of animals attacking us at night, even simple snakes on the ground; we didn't know what our feet were going to step on. People would get frightened all of a sudden, and then one cry would just create a mess in the whole group; people would run in all different directions, and it would take hours for the elders to collect us together.

There was the feeling of, When exactly is this journey going to end? Where exactly are we going? For us, we had always thought the world was really small; we never knew of other places. Then, the term Ethiopia became part of us, and we were always looking forward to the day we would arrive there. We thought it was going to be something beautiful. We all held to that feeling, thinking that anything could happen. But there was always the feeling that maybe, at some point, we were going to run into the enemy that we were running from.

We never really saw the Arab militia while we were walking. We would hear that people got attacked, and at certain points the elders told us to stay where we were, or to go around some places because the enemy was waiting there. I always wondered where they got that information. All of a sudden, they would tell us we had to spend two days in the same place and be quiet. Then suddenly you felt like something was going to happen soon, and they would tell us to move. I don't know whether they told us this to encourage us to keep going, but we would always hear that the group behind us was attacked and that many of them were killed. As we were going to Ethiopia there were a few incidents, but at no point did I see the enemy with guns. I had never seen an Arab up to that point, because our lives were so centered in the village. I knew how people described them, how their skin was lighter than ours and about the clothes they wore. But I never saw them. We kind of made fun of Dinka people who were lighter-skinned like them; they were suspected of being of mixed race.

THIS IS ETHIOPIA?

The only time we got attacked by the government militias was when we arrived at the border. As we were crossing the river into Ethiopia we got attacked, but it wasn't as massive as what happened back in the village.

When we arrived in Ethiopia I said, "This is Ethiopia?" It was just bush, another jungle like we'd been going through for the last one and a half months. I wondered, what tells you this is Ethiopia and not Sudan? I thought Ethiopia was going to be villages like the ones we had left, that life was going to be back to normal, and we would find cattle and things like that. All of a sudden, they told us that we were safe now, that we would not be attacked and, of course, that was true. We would spend a few years without being attacked. But there was nothing there for us.

After we got across the border, we walked for another five to seven days. When we stopped, there was really no refugee camp yet, just trees and some people who had arrived before us. The Ethiopian government had created a kind of reception area in a space under some trees where new arrivals were all put into one place before they were distributed to different groups by the elders. While we were there, the people who had arrived first came to see if any of their relatives had arrived with us. That's when I saw my cousin, who told me that my brother was also there.

At the encampment, we just waited and waited and waited. We were surviving on plant leaves and fruits, and we would hunt small animals and birds. We had to clear the trees, and I didn't know what was going on and why we needed to be there in a place that wasn't even home. It was always a puzzle. I didn't understand until we started building a life there, and they started calling it Pinyudo refugee camp.

When we had been there for about a month, the Ethiopian government came with a tractor loaded with about four bags of corn. By then people had come from different parts of Sudan, South Sudan in particular. It had quickly become a really huge number of people, so that's when they gave the corn to our elders for cooking. People would wait in line for the grains. The Ethiopian government also brought some medicine, because people started dying from different diseases and poisons from the desert itself. A few months later, the United Nations delegation came. It was my first time seeing white people. A few of our elders knew some English, and they would translate. The UN delegation went back, and three days later there was a convoy of food for the first time. Food and other things we did not have were distributed. There were actually things to serve it with, and people would use the corn sacks as bowls.

The food they supplied took care of the hunger, but you still had to eat and sleep on the ground. When it rained it just rained on you. We didn't have any kind of house whatsoever. Not even tents. Our life still had a homeless feeling. I always wondered what would happen next and whether I was going to go back to Sudan. I wanted to go back so badly; there was nothing in the camp for me, but we were always told that our villages were destroyed and many of our relatives were killed. There was nothing to go back to. So we would play in the day, but still, we didn't know what happened to our other life. It was a hard transition.

There were a lot of disease outbreaks killing a lot of people. One major disease that killed people was measles, because once it touches one person it just spreads. Back in the villages, you just had to be exposed to it, and if you were lucky to survive it, you didn't get it again; there's a natural immunity after you have suffered it. But so many of us in the camp were young and had never had the chance to have that disease, or to become immune from it. Back in the villages, when one person was suspected of it, the elders would take care of it so that it didn't spread. But in this case, it was basically like an outbreak of cholera. One person passed it to another, and you just had to be lucky enough to survive it. The UN brought tents for us and made a medical clinic with antibiotics, so people who were sick would be taken to those places.

Then people started to show symptoms of trauma. People were losing their senses. They had to create a really big, big area for people who had gone mad. When someone was taken to those tents and didn't come back soon, you kind of knew that they'd died. Many of us were later surprised by people who had spent months and months in those tents and still survived. A cousin of mine was admitted to that tent, and people were not allowed to go and visit him. He spent a lot of time there, and we thought he had died.

They started making groups under the trees. At first, we were grouped by our villages. They would want an older, bigger person to be the leader. Then they started asking people to go cut trees and grass and to thatch places for us to stay in. That began the camp. The elders would instruct us what to do; we made our thatch houses and we were able to stay in them for the first time. Then the elders split us up, and we formed groups of boys who were from different tribes. It was really amazing to be with people you did not know and to become a part of them. I can only guess why they did that, but I think it was to make sure that we learned from each other, to teach us to think not just within our own village but about other people. I think they wanted us to build a relationship and become friends, to know that we were all one. For the first time, we sat with strangers and ate with them. It was awkward at first. I don't really remember, but I think all we talked about was our life back home. We talked a lot about cows and the way things used to be.

Then, while we were thatching our houses, the elders divided us so that some people would go and cut grass, and some would remain at home. In the morning, they would take those who remained at the camp to the trees and teach them the English alphabet. The group that went out in the morning would come for English in the afternoon, and the other group would go out to work. The UN would later continue this by distributing some writing materials, but we started just from leveling the sand and improvising; we used the cartons that the oil came in as a chalkboard, burned charcoal and used it as a chalk.

The elders told us that education would be the only way we could succeed. They said the life we had lived was destroyed and that we were not going to go back to that life. We had nothing back there to hope for, so we had to look for a new way to survive and make our living. Many of the elders had some English background from missionary school, so that was the only thing they could help us with. So they started with English, and they kept telling us it was the only way we would survive. People started learning from one another, and I was very interested. I was curious and I liked learning new things. To be able to know the letter *A* was a big deal.

We would stay in that camp for another four years. Life began to transition to a better one. We started getting more supplies from the UN, and they gave us chalkboards, exercise books, and pencils for our classrooms. We got more food and more medicines, and we kind of settled in. We would hear once in a while that the SPLA was winning in the South and that we were going to go back to our villages soon. And then they also told us that if we learned enough, we could go back and be leaders, take charge of our country. That idea was motivating for me, and so was the fact that we were going to be like our teachers. They kept telling us about doctors and pilots and things like that, and you wanted to be all those things.

WE WERE USED TO LIVING
THAT DANGEROUS LIFE

Four years later, Ethiopia went into its own civil war and we had to run back to Sudan. The new Ethiopian government was friendly to the Sudanese government, so they were quite motivated to pursue us and inflict a lot of casualties on us. We sustained a lot of tragic atrocities when we were crossing back. There's a river called Gilo that we had to cross, and we were caught in this situation where there was river ahead and the army was attacking us from behind; we had to remain and be shot or jump in the water. People were so frightened by the attack that they just jumped in the river. Those who did not know how to swim were carried off by the current. Those who knew how to swim but were unlucky were caught by the crocodiles. That was terrible. That was probably the first time I was very, very close to an extremely traumatizing event where I had to actually see the soldiers who were running and killing and shooting. I remember when I was just at the river bank in the water and kind of hesitating. I knew how to swim, but I wasn't sure whether to swim and be shot or to just stay there and hide and hope that someone would find me. I don't know what I did then, but I found myself on the other side of the bank. I don't even remember how I got to the other side. All I remember is that I was running, and there were people everywhere who were running and dying, and carrying or pulling a child or someone who was much younger. I didn't know whether some people being pulled had been shot or whether they were just frightened.

After a few hours of hiding, one of our elder caretakers who had gotten to the other side of the bank started collecting people together. I had gotten separated from my brother and my cousin in the attack, so I was by myself again with friends. We started walking and joined the other groups that had collected. When we arrived at the border, the government had already heard we were back and the aerial bombardment started. The government just started bombing the town we were in, so we had to run again. We went to another town where they said it was safe, because there was SPLA around. Then the International Committee of the Red Cross started dropping some food, and we started eating. It was a rainy season and there were mosquitoes everywhere. There were no mosquito nets; you couldn't sleep from it. I think they started dropping some mosquito nets along with the food, and we settled in that town and stayed for a few more months.

Later there was an attack, and we had to run to northern Kenya and that journey took a while. The travel was dangerous and terrible, worse than before. The climate was dry and the Sudanese government was paying militias to hunt us down. The good thing about that journey was that the Committee of the Red Cross kept track of where we were going and dropped food from one station to another, so every two weeks or so we would find food and water. Otherwise, I don't think anybody would have survived the journey to northern Kenya; it was so dry and so long. It took us almost a year to finally arrive. We would stay in little towns along the way until we got attacked and then run again.

My friends and classmates were five or six years older than when we first left our villages. We were adolescents, and we started to understand the complexity of our situation and how to survive, so it wasn't as bad as when we first fled. We were used to living that dangerous life and we adapted. Even now, we still talk about how, when we hear a news helicopter, the first thing that comes to mind is that it's an attack. Then you realize that they're just media trying to take pictures of something. In Sudan, when you hear the sound of a gunship, the first thing you do is find a place to hide, because sooner or later they're going to drop bombs. You just pray that they don't fall on you.

When we arrived in Kenya, the UN was waiting for us. They

knew there was a large number of children coming to northern Kenya. It was years from when we'd first fled our villages, so we were kind of getting used to being away. But we were also always hoping we would one day go back home. We lived life expecting that one day we would go back. I never thought about getting refugee status and going to America. It was always about going back home. We never felt at home anywhere, you know? America was not even something we thought about. We did not even know about America. There was not any place we thought was any better than the home we fled from. Every year we said, "Next year we will go back, next year there is going to be peace; the SPLA will win and we will go back." We never did.

YOUNG MEN

I was in Kenya for nine years. For the first few months, we were in a place called Lokichoggio, and then we were taken to Kakuma camp, Section 1. In the beginning, things weren't that good. Just like when we arrived in Ethiopia, it was just another area where there was nothing. We had to put down our tents in this empty space. The environmental conditions were challenging; there was a lot of dust and sand. Later on, the UN brought building materials and equipment, so we started thatching our houses. Then the food came, and water. In the beginning, the water supply was really scarce, but a few months later, our group was given a pipeline for running water so the supply increased. Things really improved. We had utensils for cooking and food was abundant.

But then, as the population increased, resources began to decrease dramatically. We had to share the same resources with more people; we had the pie, but it was being sliced in different ways to feed all of the refugees. Food became so scarce that it was just a question of survival. Life started to be really painful. Some other nonfood items were cut off as well, like sugar, soap, and the clothes that had been distributed in the beginning. Things began to decrease to the point where we only got grain, which was usually corn.

Some of us were finishing high school, and school was the thing that occupied our time, so even if you had no food you thought about school. But then people who had graduated from high school, or those who finished primary school and didn't want to go to high school, they had nothing to do and so they were bored, from the beginning of the day until sunset; this started a lot of issues in the camp. People began fighting a lot. They didn't have anything else to do with their time.

Most of my friends were Dinka, but in my group we had people from the Nuer, Morlei, and Mondari. The family groups were pretty much separated by tribe, but the groups of minor boys who had come alone were all mixed up. Sometimes we played games. I played soccer, but I wasn't good; I just played for fun. Once in a while I would go to one of the traditional dances in the camp with other Dinka. In Ethiopia, we had been too young for the idea of girls to even cross anybody's mind. But in Kenya, we really started to behave like young men. Around 1997 or 1998, the boys and girls in the camp started going to dances to meet. It's not like the American dating system. We call it engagement, but it's not as serious as engagement here. At the dance or at school, you and your friend would talk about how you are interested in one of the girls you see, so you would go as a group and talk to the girl about one particular guy. She will have her cousins and friends as well, and the negotiation would begin to convince them that you actually like her. If she likes you, too, she will convey the same thing to her cousins, and they will relay back that the answer was yes and you would be dating. Then, once in a while you would go to see her, or you might stop her when she was going to fetch water and just talk a little bit to keep up with things. In 1999, I started dating a girl, but it wasn't serious. It's not like dating here, where you have a very intimate relationship; dating her wasn't a guarantee of marriage, because there were other people dating her at the same time.

While I was in high school, I took on a teaching job in an adult education program. I would finish school at two p.m., then walk for about an hour to another section of the camp, Kakuma 3, to go teach. It was a struggle to finish school and go work in the baking sun without enough to eat. It was challenging, but when I finished high school I was recruited to teach in the grammar school, a job that would actually pay me. I was paid by the Lutheran World Federation, an agency that is under the UN. Later, I began teaching literacy classes, because they paid better than the regular primary school.

My English wasn't that good, but in the camp there were not enough materials to learn from, so in our groups we spoke in our own languages instead of English. There was no practice, there were no books to read; you just copied notes from the teacher. It wasn't that good, but I knew how to write and speak, so I was helping with the literacy classes. I used that money to supplement my food with more nutrients; people got only corn to eat at that time. Those of us who were lucky to have some income from the UN bought lentils, oil, sugar, things that were considered luxury goods to supplement our food. In 1995, my aunt who I was separated from during the attack in South Sudan came to the camp, so I was living with her, supporting her with my income as well. She cooked for me and other relatives from my extended family who were also in the camp.

HISTORY WAS IN THE PAST

This is how life was until the resettlement started. I had heard about America before in my history classes, especially about slavery. People talked about how history had not been good toward black people, so I really never thought of coming to America. I didn't think it was such a pleasant place to go. Not many of us thought about leaving Africa to go to other places and make life better; we still always wanted to go back home.

But then, between '93 and '98, some people started leaving the camp to go to cities in Kenya. They got themselves exposed to the idea of resettlement, and so people started to learn about making a life outside of Sudan. I had a friend that was resettled in Dallas, Texas, in '96 or '97. He started sending us some information about America, especially pictures, and some of them were really beautiful, with tall buildings, nice chairs, and things like that. He was able to work and he talked about education. In the pictures there were lots of books on his shelf. He didn't talk about the things that I had learned before about America; I saw that the history was in the past. People started sending money to the camp, and the image of America was changing. Even the elders started encouraging us to go, and I also learned that the leader of the Southern Sudanese Movement had gone to America to be educated. Those things changed my perception of America, and I wanted to go.

In 1999, the U.S. State Department came to talk to our caretakers, or maybe it was the Conference of Catholic Bishops or the UNHCR. The leaders of the camp met with them and discussed the process and that there were quite a number of us. Many of us were unaccompanied minors, and the ones who were in really horrible condition were the groups of boys; our traditions had disadvantaged us because we didn't know how to manage household chores or food. There was a prevalence of malnutrition among the boys, because we didn't have cooking skills; we just boiled food and ate it. So when the UN decided to resettle people, they looked particularly at the boys.

We started talking about people being resettled in the United States and hearing that the process was about to begin. It became real when the Kenyan workers from the immigration office started coming to the camp and posting names on the signboards. I have no idea how they chose the names, but everyone went to check for their name; if you saw your name, you went to the area they called the office. They would give you a card with an appointment date for your interview. At that point, I wanted to go to the U.S., but I didn't know how. They only resettled a small number of us, not even a quarter of the people. I was among the lucky ones who had their name posted on the board, and so I started the process.

The first interview was pretty much about what had gone wrong, what had forced us to be refugees, basically tracing our life history. After that, there would be a second interview with the actual U.S. immigration lawyers. They asked pretty much the same things, but in a very detailed format. You had to pass each step in the process in order to move to the next one. I don't think many people failed at the first level, because it was reconfirmation of our life history. But I think some people failed during the interviews with immigration officers, because many of us had to answer legal questions about whether we had ever been in the military or whether we had left the refugee camp at any point and had gone back to Sudan; if you went back to the country you were fleeing from and then came back to the camp, somehow that disqualified you from being a refugee.

There were some language issues as well. They had interpreters but some of them weren't that good. It wasn't so much about language as it was about accent; these interpreters were part of us, and they had as much difficulty understanding American accents as we did. I remember one point when I asked my interpreter to let me just talk freely with the lawyer, because I realized the interpreter was saying my words in the present tense, and I was narrating something in the past. Since I knew as much English as he did, I realized that it would be more helpful for me to just talk to the lawyer. I took over the interview from that point.

After I passed the second interview, I was sent to the International Organization for Migration for the medical exam and orientation, which was all about American culture. They told us about people in America and different issues, like safety.[1] They were basically placing our minds in the American setting, because we came from a very different background; they wanted to bridge that gap. They talked about cold weather and how to dress warmly. They brought ice for us; it was so cold! It was amazing. They told us the emergency number to call if there was a fire, and what to do when you're sick. They talked about the working environment in America. Orientation was about three days long. We just listened; there was so much information. After you passed and finished your orientation, the INS, now part of the Department of Homeland Security, gave you a small permanent residency card and some papers that said you were admitted to the U.S. and granted liberty to work and stay there. They assigned me a birth date of January 1, 1977. Everyone who comes to the U.S. without a birth date gets January 1.

When orientation was finished, I was excited. I was excited for the opportunity to come here and go to school; that was my first goal. I was excited to work and be able to support myself, to move from dependence to independence. I was also nervous and sad about leaving the camp, and Africa, and my relatives. I never imagined that it would be possible for me to come back to Africa any time soon; I saw it as a long-term separation. So it was strange. I had one friend who I had always been with; we'd lived the same life, been in the same class, taught in the same school. And now we were being separated. I also had my girlfriend, who I had been dating for two years. Even though it wasn't serious, it was hard to leave her. It could have been a much more serious relationship if the resettlement hadn't started. I had finished school and had an income, and the next thing I would have done would have been to get married. I would have had to make a decision, and her family would have had to decide if I was the right

[1] For more on refugee resettlement in the United States, see page 416.

person or not. I never had any offers for arranged marriages before that, because my relatives and the other people around me understood that I was very serious about going to school. Plus, two of my older brothers were not married, so I had to help them get married before I could. It's a superstition in our culture that you have to wait for the people older than you in your family to get married. Even though they weren't with me, I still had to wait.

The night before I left, I went around and said goodbye to everyone. I had to say goodbye to my aunt's family, and to so many relatives from my extended family. Even though they were distant relatives, they were from my mother's clan and they were still part of me. One of my very special friends gave me an embroidered bedsheet that I brought with me, and I have always kept it.

The day I left, my cousin came to the airstrip with me. At the airfield, they had a barbed-wire fence, so people would come with you to the airstrip and then the workers would call you in line to go inside. When I was boarding the plane, I looked back and saw people on the other side of the fence, including my cousin. I realized, looking at the people who were watching me take off, that I was not going to be coming back to Africa.

BREAKING BORDERS

I didn't know much about the rest of my family when I left. I knew my brother was in a camp in Uganda, and I heard my sister was in Khartoum, but this was third-party information. I never heard from someone who had come from those places directly, so I didn't really know what to do with it. It wasn't until around 2003 that I got to talk to my brother. He was able to come to northern Uganda and somehow found a number for my cousins in South Dakota. They relayed the message to me, and I was able to call him and talk. He basically told me everything about my family. I went back to Uganda in 2005, but I didn't see him because he had already gone back to Southern Sudan.

We landed first at Heathrow, I think. They said we were in London. When I was in Kakuma, my cousin gave me the phone number of my distant uncle in London, so at the airport I was thinking about him and his family. I told a British Airways agent that I had an uncle in England. I gave her the number and she called for me. I didn't talk to my uncle, but I spoke to his wife. My uncle was still in school, studying for his PhD in geology and mining, or something like that.

After London, we landed in New York. We stayed there for a few hours; I think they were taking care of some immigration issues. When we were in New York, we were all taken to different places. We thought we were going to see each other again, but that was it. Some of the friends I came with went to California, and we never got to say goodbye to each other. We were just spread all over, depending on where there were agencies with the space and the resources to resettle us. We had been assigned to different places at some point in the process.

I was brought on a plane to Boston with two of my friends. It was March, and we were not prepared for the cold. Even though we knew from orientation that it was going to be cold, it was hard for us to imagine. We didn't have warm clothes either. I was wearing a sweatshirt with no coat. When we were going to the parking lot where our case manager from the International Rescue Committee was waiting, it was just cold. It was unbelievable. Our IRC case manager took us to a hotel and gave us some food that he had bought for us. He said we would be staying there for the night, and the next day he would take us to the IRC office and to the apartment where we would live.

In the hotel we talked and ate before we slept. We were tired. Our case manager had gotten us some milk, which was great because we came from a cattle-rearing community. But it was milk in a container, so we weren't sure it was actual milk. Then there was a roasted chicken and bread, which we also ate. We talked about how cold it was; it was just hard for us to imagine we were going to survive it. That night, the case manager had turned the heat up really high in our room. And so, almost at midnight when we were sleeping we found ourselves hot and sweaty. We could not figure out what was going on, from how cold it was to this extreme heat. He didn't tell us where the thermostat was, so we couldn't turn it down.

The next day, he took us to the office to sign some immigration papers and then he took us to the apartment in Chelsea, which had just been renovated. The water system was not working, so there was only cold water. I don't even remember taking a shower for about two days. There were five of us in a two-bedroom apartment, so it was overcrowded. But we were just happy to be there. We had shared everything anyway, so it wasn't a big deal. The apartment was furnished by the IRC.

Shopping was another thing we had to get used to; we had a volunteer who was assigned to take us grocery shopping. The grocery store was fascinating. The only thing that I wasn't sure about was how to find the products that I wanted. Then I saw that they had signs that named the products in the aisles, so being able to read was helpful. But then we were not sure about things to buy. The groceries were strange to us, especially the vegetables. We bought things we recognized, like bananas and pineapples, and of course rice and beans, milk in containers, chicken and beef. We were always unsure about the things we were eating.

It was hard living with four guys from Sudan. We had never really learned how to cook; we only knew how to cook rice, boil beef and beans. It's not like we made it to be really good or nutritious. We just cooked things that were practical and basic, that we were able to do. It was a mess. We did not know how to diversify food by having some vegetables and some other ingredients or spices and things like that to make it more attractive. We just had to eat what we knew how to make.

When I started working, I started to go food shopping at small stores and went to restaurants, and I started experimenting with foods I had never had before. I was also observing what foods my friends and workmates ate. I had a mentor who was also helping me cook vegetables, although I did not like it. She cooked a mix of cauliflower and broccoli, and I just didn't like it. Now I love broccoli, though. It's my favorite.

My first job was doing security in a parking garage in Chelsea. It was overnight, so it was really hard. I wasn't sleeping. My body was used to sleeping at night, but I was supposed to be awake, working. So, when I managed to be awake the whole night, the morning would come and I wouldn't be able to sleep, because my body didn't want to sleep in the day. So I was having a hard time. I worked nights for a while though. The first security job had no health insurance, so I found another security job at the Prudential in Boston. It was overnight as well, and I did that for a while. Later on I got sick, so they had to change my schedule. I switched to the day shift, doing security at a bank, so that was much better.

While I was working, I was thinking about school and studying for the GED tests, because they would not take my certificate from high school back in Kenya. I was also doing a program through AmeriCorps that helped disadvantaged and at-risk youth. I had a tutor who was part of the program, and our supervisor was helping us with the GED. The only things that were challenging were American civics and government, and English, because of the essays. But I felt comfortable so I signed up for a test and I passed it, and I thought of going to college.

I asked my mentor to help me find a way to go to school. She had taught at UMass-Boston in the ESL department, so she told me about a program called Directions for Student Potential; you do the program for six weeks in the summer, and if you complete it successfully, you enroll in the College of Arts and Sciences in the fall. I applied for the program, got admitted, and successfully matriculated in the four-year program in the fall of 2002. I majored in political science and economics, and also did a program in international relations.

Going to school was extremely hard, because of the difference in the educational system and my prior experience in learning before I came here. It was the first time I had to actually read and think critically; I had to be able to synthesize the literature I was reading and produce my own argument assessing the author's point. I didn't have the educational preparation to succeed in this system, so I had to work extra hard. However, most of my classmates were in the same shoes; they were non-native English speakers, and we had an ESL class of English 101 together. It's the same material but taught in different terms by someone who is trained in dealing with English as a second language.

We were always struggling with using English, and many of us were immigrants so we had the same stories of breaking borders. There were people from the Caribbean, South America, Africa, Brazil—it was a very diverse group. It was very interesting in that I felt I was part of people who were in the same situation. I could really relate to their experiences, so it was good to be able to talk about that, even in a language that wasn't our own. We had to really double our time and resources to match the work of English-speaking students. My first teacher there was very supportive. She's like my adopted mom now. I went to her house this year to have Thanksgiving with her family. I also had classes with the American students, such as political science and a pop culture class, which was really hard. So I had my American friends who I was really close with. They were really supportive and friendly as well.

I graduated in 2006 and started looking for a job. At first I was doing more short-term jobs here and there. I worked for UMass for about four months. Later I took a teacher's assistant's job at North-eastern University, then got another job with a document-processing organization. I got an internship with an environmental consulting firm in Cambridge and transitioned into a research analyst position within that organization. Before I got that position, though, I was applying for the Masters program in Sustainable International Development at the Heller School for Social Policy and Management, at Brandeis University. I had to decide whether to defer the program for a year and work for money and experience. I was leaning toward that decision, but the consulting work began to be more challenging. I was working late hours, and it was a salaried position so I didn't get paid overtime. The work was just incredibly difficult. So, while I was trying really hard, I felt that I wasn't successful in my work. I wasn't feeling a sense of accomplishment. To be a consultant, you have to sift through a lot of things to be able to get information for your client. It takes a lot of energy, and I was getting so stressed out. I had no time to socialize with my friends. I also thought about my long-term goals; even if this was an incredible work experience, this wasn't something that I was going to pursue as a career for the rest of my life. I want to go back to Sudan and contribute to the reconstruction of my country. I decided to start at Brandeis this past August 2007.

SUSTAINABLE DEVELOPMENT

I've always had an interest in community building and development, and I think that to have skills in sustainable development would be an asset for me in finding a meaningful job in that area in Sudan. Most of the development projects that are being done in developing countries leave a blank space where the locals end up not knowing what to do with the projects that are initiated. It's very easy to work as a fundraiser, to write grants, and go start a water project, for instance. You dig the hole, you introduce the people to clean water, and then, in a year or two, you leave. But, if you don't introduce the ability to sustain that project, you might worsen their life; to get a new life with clean water and then to have to go back to your old life would be a hard transition. Learning the sustainable development skills will help me be able to do that in several villages in Sudan, not just in water but in other development projects. Some schools are being built, and people don't understand that in order to continue the process you need to build in a way that will regenerate income for the school to sustain itself. I am at Brandeis to gain all the possible skills I can so I can apply them when I get where I want to go. Working on a project that will have a long-term lifespan will fulfill my interests in doing something that is good for the community. That's why I chose this program.

I'm very happy with the coursework and the other students I'm working with; they have so much passion for what they're doing. There's a really wide range in terms of the work they have done and their wealth of experiences. I was surprised by the level of enthusiasm about sustainable development. So, I'm really happy with everything, but the classes are a little bit challenging, a little bit overwhelming. School has become like my home. I leave school around eleven at night and go back at six or seven in the morning. But I think it's great. By the time I finish, I think I'll have the tools to be able to practice everything I've learned.

When I finish, I'm hoping to be able to intern in Sudan. I don't see myself moving back completely, but it's possible if there is a sustainable peace, if conditions are conducive to having a certain level of confidence and comforts. It's one thing to have a passion, but it's another to have no liberty to practice it. I just don't see myself resigning to my inability to practice what I want to do. I'm a person who likes actions, and I like things done correctly, in the right way, and genuinely. If I don't see any of those elements, that would frustrate me. It might affect my idea of going back. I'm not just talking about the war between the North and the South, or the war among the Southern Sudanese. I'm talking about issues that could get in the way of my ability to practice my work. For instance, if I'm working with a group of individuals who have different self-interests and corruptions, and I'm not able to practice in a free manner with peace of mind, those things might affect my ability to go back for good. But, if I go back to intern there, and I realize that everyone is interested in the welfare of the community and working together to raise our community of Southern Sudanese and that is the goal everyone has in mind, I'd be more than happy to go back. I was born there. It will always be home to me.

I have no idea what the situation is like in Sudan at the moment in those terms. I have tried very hard to familiarize myself with what is going on back in Sudan, and in Southern Sudan in particular. But it has been hard to find information. I can't go to bed without checking the news on the internet, without reading something about Sudan before I go to bed. I turn on my computer and check the news every single day and night, just to see how things are going. There's not much in the American media about Southern Sudan. The *Boston Globe,* the *New York Times,* they don't talk about Southern Sudan. They only talk about Darfur, when they talk about Sudan at all. But there are international websites that write about the South.

I'm really excited that people in the media and the public arena are talking about the issue of corruption and that possible culprits are even being identified. It gives me confidence to see that someone out there is also working toward a better environment. I really hope that becomes a motivating point and that everyone uses their power well to be able to deliver services for the public and not just for individuals.

All my family and friends are back in the South, but it's hard to communicate with people there. It's easier to talk to someone from Khartoum, which is in the North, or Uganda or Kenya, but Southern Sudan is just landlocked in terms of communication. Sometimes people arrange to go to the radio station and use the satellite phone, but if it's rainy or cloudy, it doesn't work. The last time I was able to communicate with my family was about three months ago, and it was only for a few minutes. I haven't had a chance to actually connect for a long time, so I haven't had any nuanced conversations with people about what's going on there. But I think my decision to go do my practicum there might be a testing point. If I do my practicum there and realize that's the place I want to continue contributing, I'll be happy to move back. But, if not, you know, I'll just say I had the heart and the will, but there's no way. I hate to resign myself to the idea that I cannot make a difference, but sometimes there are conditions that will not let you do what you want to do.

My brothers and sisters, who were all displaced during the war, are all back in my home village, with families of their own. One of my brothers just had his first child, I think. And the others all have children. So I have a lot of people to see when I go back, some of whom would not know me. I don't think any of them want to come to the U.S. It's hard to even think about that; I don't even think they understand the idea of here or anywhere else. It would be hard for them to come here, too. They basically speak just one language. Life would be challenging for them. So I'm not even thinking about bringing them here. If I had money, I'd have them visit for sure, but that's not something I can afford at this point.

A SUFFERING THAT DID NOT DISAPPEAR

I started talking about what was happening back in Sudan right away when I came to America in 2001. Our story was in the news a lot. It was first broadcast on *60 Minutes* with Tom Brokaw. People began to get interested. My first talk was at a community center in Arlington, Massachusetts. We talked to people about our experiences, and the audience was saying that they did not know anything about it. Some of them didn't even know what Sudan was. I went to give a talk at Concord Academy, and my audience reacted the same way; they did not know what was going on.

Most people had positive reactions. Some were emotional. Some were just crying. Some were asking what they could do. They were shocked beyond belief that they could live in this world and not know that this was happening. So I told myself that my goal would be to educate people and to share with them the suffering we were going through, a suffering that did not disappear now that we were in America. It was a suffering embedded in our life, and the people we love are still suffering. I started talking to the media as well. The *Boston Globe* and some other papers interviewed me, and I went on National Public Radio.

I started like that, and eventually the momentum shifted from individual people to leaders and to the government. In fact, the peace negotiations between the Sudanese government and the Southern rebels in 2002 basically started because we were talking about everything that was being done, and the public officials here in the U.S. were beginning to get pressured by their constituents. It became something to rally behind. Even those in the Bush administration were pressured by their evangelical constituents and became influential in pushing the peace process forward. The evangelicals felt a sense of responsibility in that the suffering we were going through was related to the Christian religion we had adopted, so they became politically involved.

Then the situation with Darfur came. They were signing a peace accord in Southern Sudan, and war was beginning in Darfur. It wasn't right; you don't sign peace in order to create another war. So I started speaking against that. Even now, with my busy schedule I still find time to do it, because I feel like there are people there who could not be here to talk for themselves. In a sense, I'm obligated to talk on their behalf. In fact, there are people who have died among my group who could have survived if someone had talked on their behalf. So, I think, this is not stopping the killing, but it's making a difference. I feel a sense of responsibility and obligation to continue doing it. I don't spare anyone when I speak; I talk of the governments who are supporting this, and I make sure that the media will expose their actions.

I go to many places to speak: high schools, middle schools, community groups, and many churches and synagogues. I really have no boundaries. I'm a community educator. I speak to anyone who is interested. In fact, I spoke to a group of nurses at a hospital in January. I don't know what their particular goal is in having me speak, but whatever they decide to do afterward is their decision. I'm there to teach them and educate them on the reality of the problem.

WE ARE NOT SILENT ANYMORE

People sometimes ask me if I am one of the Lost Boys of Sudan, and I say yes. I'm part of the story, but I'm not a boy at this point. I don't consider myself a Lost Boy, but I have no problem with the term being applied to the story. The term describes the journey, the way we fled and were never reunited with our relatives; it summarizes what happened to us in a way that makes sense and can help people understand. But applying it to the personality, the experience of one person, is to demean the individual. The term was adopted when we were boys, but since the time of the resettlement, none of us could be described as a boy. It's not relevant to us at this point.

When people ask me what they can do to help, there's usually a gray area, because you never know what people are capable of doing. One thing that I knew from the time I came to America is that this is a country that is ruled by people. I mean, the leaders are there, they disobey and they obey, but it's ruled by people, by vote. So one thing that I told people from the very beginning was, use your vote. Talk to the people you voted for, help them understand that this is something that you are gravely concerned about and you want action. That's first. Second, the individual level is to be part of the activism; if people are rallying, join them. People are wearing *Not On Our Watch* wristbands; wear it. Things like that, and, of course, monetary help as well for those who are able to do so. That's basically what I tell people, but ultimately, they have to make their own decision about what they are able to do. I have no way of knowing what people do after they hear me speak, but from my own observation I'm pretty sure that people have become more aware of the situation. I see people with signs about stopping the genocide in Darfur, and I see a lot of students becoming activists. Things aren't moving fast, but they're different than when we started; we are not silent anymore.

IN OUR SPIRIT, THAT LAND IS OURS

In the future, in Sudan, I would like to see a community that lives in peace and harmony. I would like to see a generation that has a place to grow, a generation that is able to play, a generation that grows among their loved ones. I want our people, my children, my children's children, to have a place that they call their home, and that they call their ancestor's home, a place where they live proudly, a place where they consider themselves citizens of that country. And of course I want to see a society that is also competent, a society that lives with its neighbors and will also be respected by its neighbors, a society that is able to provide for their disadvantaged—the people who cannot provide for themselves.

I want to see a united Sudan. But, if this means oppression of one region by the other, I would rather see two different Sudans. Unless the people of northern Sudan recognize what they have done and change their thinking, I would rather see a Southern Sudanese nation. I'm a person who is always optimistic and always believes that something can change, but I don't see that happening any time soon. So, if all it takes for my children to live in a peaceful Sudan is for the South to become a separate country, I will work for it. Peace is hard to negotiate and living together is hard to do, so someone's got to change their thinking. Someone's got to change their beliefs and ideologies in order for us to coexist.

I think all of these things will be hard to achieve because of modern greed. All people have in mind these days is the principle of acquisition, to be able to have more. And now, people are really going away from truth. They're creating a gap between recognizing the facts to being people who just live within their own reality of greediness. I didn't have to suffer, you know? I don't know how human beings were created or where we come from, but I believe that I didn't have to suffer in my own home, at the hands of someone who came there. Someone did not have to call me a second-class citizen in my own home. In our spirit, that land is ours. It doesn't matter what's there. It is our land and we will always identify with it.

I hope for a time when I can stand up proudly, look into the eyes of those people who hurt us, and tell them that they made mistakes. We didn't ask them to enslave us. We didn't invite them to oppress us. No sane human being would ever want to do that. We underestimated their greediness.

I do believe that the world can come to its senses and recognize that we don't have to live as greedy people to be able to survive. I think we've got to understand the need to live as human beings and with a sense of humanity. The whole southern region of Sudan was always seen as backward; people were less educated, there were fewer people who could compete, come and stand before the Arabs in the North. The Arabs were well developed, they knew how to get the oil from the South. I think it's time for them to realize that we actually do see it. Even those people they call primitive, they were intelligent in their way and they knew. They always knew what was going on. They just didn't have the ability to say, "This is not right."

I always find it hard to believe that it has taken our people this long to finally rise up and demand dignity and recognition. These are just simple elements that any human being deserves. I just wish that somebody had done it before so that I could have lived in a peaceful world and didn't have to move and assume the responsibility of being an elder even before my age. Many of my friends and I have just been the unlucky ones. If history had been different, this could have happened earlier. We could have enjoyed the life that people had before us. But, the fact is that we are the ones to experience it, and we just have to deal with it. I find it hard to forget. There's something in me that makes it much harder to relate to other Americans who had a history of immigration in their life and just let it go. I find it very difficult to believe that I was meant to move to America and just forget. As long as I see people around me, I'm always going to be jealous of not having the relatives I call my own.

I'm always thinking about home, about my siblings, my relatives, and everyone else in Sudan. There's nothing more painful than losing the privilege of growing up around the people who can give you love and caring. Having been away for a while, I still feel like there's a lot that I'm missing in my life. I wake up every morning and feel that my life is incomplete, that my relatives are somewhere else, that I came from Sudan and a part of me is still there. It's torturous. I'm a U.S. citizen now, but Sudan will always be home. I will be home when I have all of my relatives around me, when I'm in the culture that I was born into, when I have the privilege of being loved by everyone around me. Only then will my life be complete.

Someone could say that the life I lived was primitive and needed to be changed, but I don't think the way it happened to me is the way to go. To have to spend the rest of my life homeless is something that comes back to me every day, and it just increases the amount of resentment and hate I have for whoever did this. It's one thing that my mind never recovers from. There's no reason for me to be living the life I have lived for the last twenty years.

For the last five or six years I've been trying to get myself used to the culture here. Life is still strange for me. I have dated Americans and some girls from other communities in Africa, but when it comes to thinking deeply and talking about life in depth, there are things that come back to me and sometimes I think, Why do I need to be in America? Not many Dinka girls came here, girls who I can speak with in the language that I was born in. Sometimes when I get angry, I start talking in Dinka, because that's inherently me; that's the flesh, mind, and spirit in me. That's what my spirit is centered in, and it will always be.

Your life is fulfilling to the extent that someone truly understands it. My life would be fulfilling if I were just around the people I was born with in my village in Sudan. I would have the respect of my community and be recognized as an important member of my family, important to the decision-making of my relatives. I don't have to be driving a car and in a brand-new building with electricity. I have a wonderful, wonderful family, and a wonderful, wonderful culture. It's a culture that's centered around communal living, and it really supports its people. I feel so deprived of that.

I hope to heal some of those feelings by going back home and spending at least some time in the culture I was born in. Every single time I think about my internship in Sudan, I think, just do it now. I need to be there now. I would probably be settled after that. I will know exactly how to live my life after that.

ACHOL MAYUOL

AGE: *28*
TRIBE: *Dinka*
BIRTHPLACE: *Marial Bai, South Sudan*
CURRENT HOME: *Marial Bai, South Sudan*

I WAITED FIFTEEN YEARS
TO BE FREE

Achol told her story while sitting on a bedframe outside her home in Marial Bai. Her five children sat with her, and sometimes went in and out of the hut behind her. She spoke very quietly, and with visible disgust toward the man who had kept her for many years as a slave-concubine.

I was born in Marial Bai around 1980, the second of nine children. My father was a farmer with many cows; he was relatively wealthy. As a girl I was just like the other children. I would build toy houses with sticks and mud. We would play house. We girls all wanted to grow up and be mothers someday.

When I was very about three years old, I saw the *murahaleen* attack Marial Bai and burn it to the ground. My parents didn't think it was safe to keep me there, so they sent me to live with my grandmother. My grandmother lived near a Government of Sudan military post, so we thought we would be protected. I was about six years old when I went to live with her.

I had spent about two months there when the war came to us there, too. One day I heard gunfire and cannons, and we ran into the bush. I was hiding with some other children when we saw horses—people on horseback—all around us. They shouted at us, and they reached down trying to grab us. They grabbed many children and threw them onto their horses. When a child ran too much, the men jumped off their horses and beat those children badly.

I was running through the grass, away from a man on a horse, when I felt a large hand under me. I was lifted up so quickly I lost my breath. And then I was taken away. We were all taken away. They gathered us in a nearby field and they divided us up that day. The different horsemen would take the people they wanted, and we would go in groups to different parts of the North.

My group walked for many days. The slave masters were on their horses while we walked. I was barefoot and the paths were so hot. My group was about thirty boys, girls and women. Some of the women didn't make it. They would get tired and the murahaleen would simply kill them. This would get rid of the dead weight and would motivate the rest of us to walk faster.

We walked for many days until we reached a clearing under a tree. They had set up a fence around a tree, the same kind of fence used to keep cattle. This is where they put our group. We were combined with many other groups until there were a hundred or so of us. There were many adults, but mostly children and teenage girls. The men who had captured us left, and the men who remained to watch over us were older, and were armed with knives and guns.

On that first day we were given orientation. The men were speaking Arabic while another man who spoke Dinka translated. We were told, "Your homes have been destroyed. Your people are gone—your fathers, mothers, parents have been killed. The village is gone, there is no life back there where you're from. Now the only choice is to accept the person to whom you've been given. Accept them as your father and mother. Do what they ask you to do. Anyone who does not follow this order will be killed, just as you've seen many of your fellow Dinka killed."

We stayed there for six days, sleeping on the ground and being fed meager things. Some of the captives did not survive the six days in the fence. A few women complained about our situation, and they were killed. They were shot. They shot one pregnant woman who had not complained. I think they thought they had made a mistake by abducting a pregnant woman, so they fixed that error by killing her. They killed an older woman for the same reason. It was the young boys and girls they really wanted. We were worth something.

Eventually the buyers came to see us. Older men, farmers mostly, came in their robes to see us. A man would come and say, "I need some boys to take care of my cows and my goats." Some would come and say, "I need girls, young girls, to help me take care of my housekeeping." Some buyers would take a teenage girl for other reasons.

For six days people came to buy us, divide us. They were buying and selling cattle at the same location. We were the same as the cattle.

BOUGHT BY A TEACHER

The person who bought me was an elderly man named Abdul Karin Mohammed. He took me to his farm, and along the way he avoided big towns. They did not want the interference of the government or any other slave owners.

We arrived at his farm. It was a big farm, a plantation, where he kept cattle and other livestock. The man had two wives. With one wife, he had ten children. With the other, he had nine children. It was a huge compound—nineteen children of various ages, much activity.

There were other Dinka children, abductees, already there: three girls and five boys were kept by the same man. The boy slaves were mostly older, so they were always used to take cattle to the pasture far away. The girls would take care of the goats and sheep closer to the compound. When we grew older we girls were made to clean the home and take care of the children. We were shouted at every day, always called *abeeda*—slave. We were always reminded of who we were. "You are here to work," they told us, "Do whatever job you are asked to perform. You are a slave."

We ate leftovers from whatever the owner and his family had eaten the day before. It was never enough. We slept on the ground every night, while the slave master's children slept on new beds. When the slave master bought new clothes for his own children, the old clothes were given to us.

If one of the master's children wanted you to do something, you had to do it. The kids were worse than the master. You had to do whatever they pleased. If you didn't, these children would beat you, tie you with ropes, and leave you lying there for hours.

We were all given Arabic names, and were taught Arabic and the Koran. I was forced to do away with anything that was of my culture. I was forced to study Islam and Islamic ways. I was forced to undergo different rites of passage than the Dinka ways, including genital mutilation. I was forced to abandon all my beliefs and customs. I grew up there, from age six to sixteen.

ADUT SHOWS THE WAY

There was one older Dinka girl who lived at the compound. Her name was Adut and she was my close friend and hero. She was tall and dark and strong. Every day she talked about escape and made plans to leave that place.

One day she tried to leave, and was caught and beaten. She had scars all over her body from disobedience and trying to escape. They had beaten her with a cane and with other instruments. But Adut was still determined to leave.

She came up with a plan. She planned to take the goats out to pasture and lead them far enough away from the houses that she could then run. When the day came to try this method of escape, I was not part of Adut's plan. I was too young. But she did escape that day. She walked the goats far away from the compound, and then she ran. She ran for three days, and we thought that she had successfully escaped.

But on the fourth day, she returned on the back of a horse. Our owner had hired horsemen to track Adut, and they found her soon enough. She was brought back and she was tied up and beaten. She was tied up for many days, outside, so we could all see her. The owner wanted to make an example of her.

After that, Adut did not try to escape again, but she left soon just the same. She was sold off as a wife to another farmer nearby. She became one of the wives of this man.

She would come back to visit us every few months. But she had changed. She now advised us not to try to escape, that it was impossible and that we would just be bringing punishment upon ourselves, that we could be killed. She told us that the only way out of this slavery was to wait. To wait until a day came when the war was over and the SPLA had triumphed. The day would come, she said, when we would be redeemed. Someone someday would find us, she said. Someone would recognize us.

SOLD AGAIN

I stayed with this slave master and his family for ten years. I was six years old when I was brought to him, and sixteen when I was sold again. Usually a slave kills himself or herself, being enslaved as long as I was. But I did not. Then he sold me.

One day I was told by my slave master that I would now go to another person, that I was to be wife to a new man. I was told that I would have to obey him, and stay with him, and not attempt escape.

I was told to remember that whenever I tried to escape, there would be nothing to go to, that there was nothing left of Dinkaland. He said that because Dinkaland had been destroyed, I must accept this new man as my husband. I had watched Marial Bai burn, so I did believe some of this.

He told me about this new man over many weeks, and I waited for the day the man would come. When all the details were agreed upon, a car arrived. There was a man and a woman in the car. I was put in the backseat and was driven away. The man was one of the brothers of the man whose wife I was to become. The woman in the car was the brother's wife.

We drove for two days. The man who bought me lived close to a city. They had a farm, and they kept cattle. The home was a compound of several houses, with each of the man's brothers occupying one home. Each brother and his wife had their own house, and each had many children. The man's mother and grandmother each had their own house, too. It was a large complex, all kept by this one large, wealthy family. They were well-educated. All of the man's nieces had gone to school.

After I saw the property, I met the man who had bought me. He was a very old man, perhaps sixty years old, named Akil.[1] He was a well-educated man, a teacher in the secondary school. He had no other wives and no children; I am not sure why. He told me that he had paid money for me, so he had the right to keep me. He told me that I was his property, and that he could do anything he wanted with me.

My duties were to fetch water from the reservoir, wash clothes, and cook breakfast, lunch, and dinner. I had to keep the house clean and cook for guests when they came to visit. I wasn't treated well, but I wasn't treated like a slave. There was a lot of work, but the other

---

[1] Achol never referred to her second captor directly, being unwilling to utter his name. For the ease of reading this narrative, we will call him Akil.

brothers' wives did similar work. We all worked for the men. If I was productive and worked hard, I was treated decently.

And though life settled into a routine, I never felt any love for the man who bought me. I never accepted my situation. Always I dreamt of escape.

I had been living at this man's home for about two years when I became pregnant by Akil. I gave birth in the hospital to my first child, a baby girl. She did not live long, only two days, and then she died. I don't understand why she didn't live.

I had another child the next year. This one, a boy, he survived. Eventually I had three more children by Akil. They were treated well; they were treated as the legitimate children of Akil. They slept in beds and were fed well. I was always treated as something less than a real person. I was still a slave, but the children were considered the proud offspring of this man. They were sent to Arabic school and were being groomed to take over the farm when he died.

Even with the children under my care, I was not allowed to go into town. The family had big homes in town, but I was kept away from that. At this time in Sudan, keeping slaves was not accepted by all people. Someone who wanted to keep slaves had to do so out of the public eye. If I needed something, I had to ask one of the other wives, and she got it for me. I spent all my time on the farm, caring for the children and cleaning the house.

ESCAPE AND REDEMPTION

One day Akil told me to get dressed in the best clothes I had, and to get the children dressed in their best clothes. He planned to bring us into town to have our picture taken. This was the first time he ever wanted to bring us all into town.

We arrived in town, all of us dressed up. We walked to the photo studio, and just outside the studio, I saw three Dinka men. They were tall, and they looked familiar to me. I caught the eye of one of the men, and he asked me if I was a Dinka. Akil looked at me; he was afraid. I was not afraid. I spoke to the Dinka man and said I was a Dinka, from Marial Bai. I told him that this man had purchased me and was keeping me against my will. I said this in a mixture of Dinka and Arabic, because I could not remember much Dinka.

One of the Dinka men said, "Aren't you the daughter of Achokuth?" He recognized me! This man was related to me, and could discern my lineage from my physical features. This man was an uncle of mine, named Ny Nyang. And among the men there was another distant relative of mine, named Deng Mul.

Immediately Akil was aware there was trouble. He said that it didn't matter that I was taken when I was young, that he had bought me legitimately, that I was his wife. The Dinka men did not accept this. They told the man we were all going to the police station immediately. And we did. Along the way Akil realized that he would not win this battle. He began to protest, telling the Dinka men that he would release me if they would allow him to take his children. But my uncle and the other Dinka men were not satisfied with this, either. They insisted that we all go to the police station, and said that I had suffered enough and that I was entitled to keep the children I had birthed and cared for.

My case became a big court case in the town. It took about twenty days and involved many of the powerful people of the town. There was also an agency working in the area called Christian Solidarity International; they were working in Sudan, redeeming abducted people. They helped to free me—because there were Westerners there, attending the court hearings, nothing corrupt could happen.

All along, Akil tried to trick everyone. At one point he said he wanted to take the children home for a moment to get some clothes. But the court and my relatives saw through this ruse. Akil planned to take the children away and never come back. But the police kept me and the children together in the courthouse. All along my relatives, the Dinka men, fought for me. They said that they had lost Achol once, and would not lose her again.

When the judge finally ruled in my favor, Akil was not around. He was working that day, and one of his brothers was in court that day to hear the verdict. I never saw Akil again, but he sent word that he was not finished with me. He made threats, sent through his brothers, that someday he would find me and kill me. But I don't worry about that now. I waited fifteen years to be free and I need to feel free.

BACK IN MARIAL BAI

I came back here to Marial Bai in 2004. I had forgotten Dinka, all of it, but I began to learn it again. It took me about two years, but now I speak the language again.

My family is here, and they help me. But they have a lot to do, and they have their own problems. It's difficult to help someone like me who has so many children. They help me with my emotional strength. They support me when necessary.

It's a difficult life here. I tried to start a business selling Sudanese food and tea, but I became ill, a problem with my kidneys, and now working that hard is impossible. I'm trying to get the medicine I need. Perhaps if I get that medicine I'll feel stronger. If I do, I will resume work.

I hope my children have an easier life than mine. I want peace for them, and opportunity. We will see.

GAZAFI ABDALLA

AGE: *33*
TRIBE: *Masalit (paternal), Bargu (maternal)*
BIRTHPLACE: *Geneina, Darfur*
INTERVIEWED IN: *Cairo, Egypt*

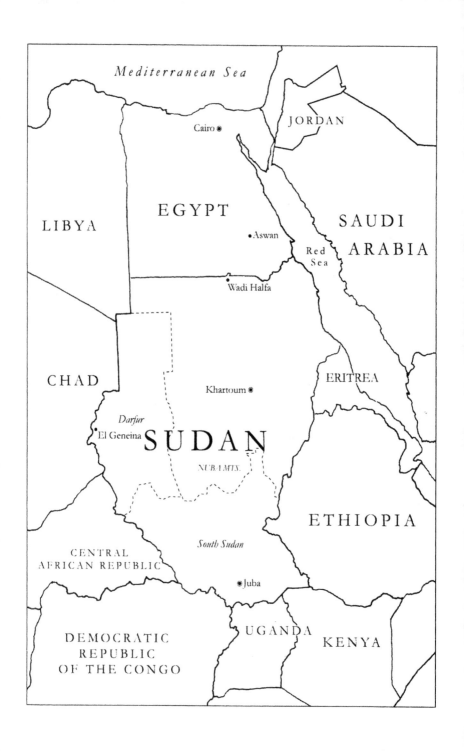

NOW I HATE SOMETHING
CALLED SUDAN

Gazafi lives in an apartment on the outskirts of Cairo. Chickens and goats wandered around the courtyard outside his window. He spoke in quiet Arabic and his sentences were short, but he was willing to answer every question asked. He smiled when his daughter came to show her progress on a school assignment. She is learning the English alphabet, and she is determined to teach her father the ABCs as well.

I was born in Geneina, a large town in the west of Darfur. I am of the Masalit. It's a famous tribe. But my mother is from a different tribe. My mother is not Masalit, but Bargu. Geneina town is like a kingdom of the Masalit. My father is Masalit, and he told us many times about the king of Masalit and so on. Actually, I can't describe a unique thing about the Masalit. For me, regardless of tribe or things like this, I am more concerned that we are Sudanese and we are human beings. It's better to look at people from this angle. I have no specific opinion about the opinions of others. In my vision, I treat people in this way.

We left Geneina when I was young. My parents brought us to

Khartoum. Seven brothers and three sisters. I'm the oldest son, but there is an older sister named Maria. Now the youngest is about nineteen, eighteen. A brother lives in Kassala, in eastern Sudan, but the rest are in Khartoum.

In Khartoum, my family worked as traders. It was my father's job. We had a clothes store and also a transportation office for shipping. The offices were in Omdurman, in Souk Libya, the large Libyan market, full of shops and offices, and people hawking goods on the streets. You can buy or sell or trade anything there. It's loud and dirty, with lots of life. People of all different ethnicities are there. I am Masalit, but I was treated normally, like all others. My friends were people I knew from the market and some people who used to live next to me, in the neighborhood. I played football with the local club.

It was a very happy childhood in Khartoum. I finished primary school. I started working with my father, helping him in the store. We would bring the goods from other cities and distribute them to the other markets. Sometimes I used to measure the weight of the furniture to send it to western Sudan. This was the nature of our work, and I enjoyed it. The business was successful. I took responsibility for many things. My father took the business seriously, and he found that I took it seriously. He was always very serious in his job. He encouraged all the family to follow the mandate and to be accurate. He always told me, "As my son, you should be serious at your work, at your study, at everything. You should take life seriously.' And I did, and I still do. I respected my job, and I ran the business in a good way.

When we weren't working, we would all sit together as a family, have a nice discussion with each other. Social chats. Talk about the general life. We were happy.

I never served in the army. I had no desire to work in the army. The general environment at the time was not good, with the war in the South. It's a war between Sudanese, a war without morality. Everyone fought in order to gain the power—always to gain the power—on both sides. It was a bad war, of course. I'm a simple man, with no power or ability to change anything. I'm not thinking about it too much. Yes, they called me to do military service, and I paid someone a bribe to avoid it. It's common. You pay someone and he makes a fake medical report for you, and suddenly you are not able to do military service due to your physical condition.

I have been married since 1999. My wife's name is Halima Alissa. She is of the Barno tribe. Her brother was my colleague in the market, and he would come and visit me, and I used to visit him also. I used to visit him at home, and he visited me at my home. I saw her. I discussed the issue with my friend. I told him, "I want to know your sister." I sat with her to know her more. We sat outside and we went to parks. I understand her and she understands me. We are Muslims. This is the way. After that, we wore the rings. And after that, I married her. She seemed happy.

WE THOUGHT, IT'S A SIMPLE THING, AND IT'S FINISHED

And then problems took hold in Darfur.

In the beginning of 2004, the security men came to search our store and the transportation office. My father was standing in the store. As they came and they showed us their identities, he didn't try to stop them; he let them do what they wanted. They searched all the documents. They searched and searched, and they found nothing. They never told us what they were searching for. They just came to the office and started searching, and I thought, They must think that we have prohibited stuff inside. They came and searched and found nothing. They accused us of helping someone in Darfur. They told us, "You are Darfurian, and the government suspects that you might support someone in Darfur." We said nothing. After they finished searching they got out; they just left.

I was scared but thought that they were finished, because they didn't find anything they wanted—no charts, no receipts, nothing. And they had just left. My father was very upset. He said, "It's discrimination because they just choose my store and search it, and no one else's! No one else's store has been searched!"

We didn't connect it to the troubles in Darfur. We thought it was a simple thing, and it was finished. We'd heard from the news that there are warring troubles inside Darfur, that some towns have been attacked and some bodies have been buried. That was what we knew. We had no contact with my family in Darfur at this time.

We found out that someone with a store next to us had been arrested. We asked if he was from Darfur also. They said, "Yes, he's Darfurian." He died in detention.

Our friends who were not Darfurian felt sorry for us. But they couldn't do anything; they couldn't help us at all. This is the government. You can't do anything.

THEY HAD WEAPONS,
AND THEY DIDN'T ASK QUESTIONS

In April 2004, they took my father to the detention center. They came to our transportation office. I was not there. They closed the office and they took my father. I heard the news. I went to the office and saw that it was closed. We started searching for my father in the police station and all over. We didn't know where to find him. Nobody said anything for days.

A client of our business used to work as a nurse at the military hospital. He came one day to inform us that my father was in the hospital and in serious condition. I asked him if he could take me with him to go and see my father. He took the family. When we saw my father, he had deteriorated. He said nothing. I don't know what they did to him. He couldn't speak. He stayed in the hospital for three days and died. My father died in 2004.

Nobody explained anything. The hospital didn't even allow us to take the body to our house to wash it and prepare it for burial. They just did everything themselves and handed us the body. A security officer followed us when we went to bury my father.

After that I, too, had an experience with detention. Security men wearing civilian clothes came to my house at night. They knocked on the door. My wife opened the door. I was tired, lying down in the bed. They just asked me, "Are you Gazafi?"

"Yes I'm Gazafi," I said.

"Come with us." It was obvious they were security men, because they had weapons and they didn't ask any questions. They came directly toward me, and they attacked me in my home. They beat me and beat me—they just kept beating. They took me with them to the detention center.

The first day at the detention center, no one spoke with me at all. They just kept beating me. They kept on top of me: "You are betraying Sudan, and you are spying." They kept me in a cell. The next morning, someone started asking me questions. He told me, "You used to send goods to the west of Sudan. Who works with you in this? And who do you send this stuff for? Who do you send this stuff to in the west of Sudan?"

I only asked, "Send what?"

I denied all his accusations. He didn't believe me. He told me, "It's better to cooperate and tell me why you are saying this stuff and who cooperates with you." He asked me about my family, and about my family's friends. He wanted to know who receives these goods in the west, and who carries them to my office in Khartoum.

I explained to him that it's just a general trade transportation office. "I have no idea what you're talking about."

OUT OF EXILE

I was telling him the truth. He didn't believe me. They had all
my records from the shop. He still didn't believe me, and he asked
the security men to start beating me again. Hard. After this hard
beating, I lost consciousness.

Eventually I found myself at the hospital. I stayed four days at
the hospital. I got better, and they sent me back again to the same
place. The same person started asking me the same questions. I told
him, "I have no idea what you are talking about." I kept trying:
"I have nothing to tell you."

I never learned the man's name. There was no relationship between us. He would just ask questions I should answer. When I first
arrived, he offered a cigarette to me. I took it. That was the only
cigarette.

I was very scared. I thought that if this man keeps accusing me
like this, I will face the same end as my father. And I had a daughter
at this time. Maria. I thought of her.

The detention lasted eight days. They let me go, with some conditions: I had to cooperate with them. I had to give them information about the people who worked with my father, and the people
in Geneina. Every Saturday and Tuesday, I would have to come to
report to their office. I must not speak with anyone about what happened to me, about my experience in detention. If I wanted to go
anyplace, I would have to get permission from security. I must cease
any activities against the government. I said okay. After that they
released me.

When I got out, I feared for my life. They released me on the
condition that I would give them information about the people who
used to work with my father, but I didn't know what they wanted,
I didn't know what the people did. I was only a transporter. I had
no idea how to answer what the security would ask about. If I said,
"I don't know anything," they would not believe me.

I did not go home. Secretly, I went to my uncle's house.

I stayed with my uncle in his house, and he helped me get a passport. He had some connections. He also used to work as a trader, so he knew officers and people like this. Three or four days after I was released, my passport and visa were ready. I could not leave yet, though. People said that security is around, and it's not safe for me to leave. The visa expired. My uncle renewed the visa again. And the same thing happened, the same talk of the tight situation, the same advice that I couldn't leave peacefully.

I became scared and worried. I had to stay in one place, inside my uncle's house, the whole time. I couldn't move. I couldn't see my family, my wife, my child, my mother. Even my uncle didn't tell them that I was with him at his house. My uncle told me, "If they—your wife or your mother—know you are here, and the security men come and press them, they might confess under the force; they might give them information about where you are." He told me, "Just keep it between me and you, and don't worry."

Once more, my uncle got the same visa for me. I insisted on going this time. I told him that I would try, and hopefully I would leave.

My uncle came with the car, and we drove to Wadi Halfa, the Sudanese port to the north. From Halfa, I took a ferry to Aswan, to Egypt. At the border my uncle did everything for me—he used to know some people in Halfa. It was quiet. It was all quiet. I had no chance to say goodbye to my family.

I STAY. I JUST STAY

In Egypt, I still faced troubles.

I used a microbus to get to Cairo. Aswan to Cairo is about fifteen hours. It's a very hard trip through the desert. All of us on the bus were Sudanese. We talked: "Have you been to Cairo before? Is this your first time?" They were all escaping in the same way as me.

I came to Cairo. I stayed in a hotel the first night. I knew nobody.

A man in the bus from Aswan told me that one of his relatives was staying in Cairo. I explained that I didn't know anyone there, and I had no idea about the city. He told me we should live together, and he called his brother. On the second day in Cairo, his brother came to us at the hotel. We went to his house and I stayed with them. The brother advised us to go to the UNHCR office. I went to UNHCR to tell them my problem.

The first day, UNHCR didn't allow us to submit our testimony, because they mentioned that we had arrived too late that day. This same thing happened all the first week: we would come every day and they would tell us, "We have already taken the number of cases we can take today, you must come back tomorrow." We would come the next day and it was the same thing. We were back and forth between home and UNHCR for a week. After this week, they allowed us to enter the office. They gave us a paper, asked us to write down our problem. They took a photocopy of my passport and they gave me this yellow card. I thought that if I faced any problem or anyone harassing me, I thought this yellow card could protect me. Soon I found out it's not useful at all, because I faced many troubles. I reported them to UNHCR, I reported them to the police, and that doesn't make any difference.

I came to Cairo seeking peace and security. Just that. They gave me this yellow card, a temporary protection card. Since that time I stay. I just stay.

I found a way to work as a vendor on the street, selling wallets, pencils, socks, and stuff like this. I buy things from stores that sell cheap, and then I sell it on the street. Walking the streets all day. Somehow it's enough and at the same time it's not quite enough. In a day, sometimes, it's twenty pounds or twenty-five. Sometimes it's fifteen.

I was living in the neighborhood of Ardeliwa, sharing an apartment with a group of Sudanese. I was not speaking to my family. I wrote a letter to my uncle in Sudan, and I gave him my contact number. My uncle used to call me from Sudan and give me the news. He gave my contacts to my mother, to my brothers, and to my family. And then they called me. I told my uncle to send my wife and my children to me.

My wife came to Cairo on May 26, 2005. She came the same way as I did—my uncle facilitated the procedure, and my wife went with my children to Aswan. Yes, children! When I left Sudan, my wife was pregnant, and she had delivered a baby boy named Abdullah. She came to Cairo with Abdullah and Maria. I met my son for the first time here in Cairo. I had not known he had been born. I was very surprised. You can imagine.

Now with the family, twenty, twenty-five pounds in a day is not enough. Sometimes my family sends us money from Sudan. We survive.

NO ONE CAN DO ANYTHING TO THEM

I had a security problem with the Sudanese embassy. It started on May 25, 2005, just when my wife was set to arrive.

The Sudanese security came to my apartment at Ardeliwa. They asked me to go with them to the embassy for some paperwork procedure. I left Sudan because of a problem just like this—how could I go to the embassy now? It wasn't reasonable, so I refused to go.

I reported that to the Egyptian police, and I moved from Ardeliwa to 6 October City, on the edge of Cairo. It's called 6 October in honor of the Egyptian war with Israel.[1] Everywhere in Cairo you

[1] On October 6, 1973, Egypt and Syria invaded Israel, marking the first day of the Yom Kippur War.

have 6 October: 6 October City, 6 October Bridge, 6 October Street. It's their proudest day. I moved on May 26, 2005, the day after the Sudanese embassy security came. I went to the police station and asked the police to make an agreement with the Sudanese embassy to stop following me. The police informed me that they have no ability to do that. Something about the embassy rules. I didn't understand.

I went to UNHCR for help, to try to find a solution with the police or do anything to stop the security of the Sudanese embassy from following me. They sent my case to AMERA, the Africa and Middle East Refugee Assistance organization. At AMERA, a legal advisor named Mohammed informed me that he couldn't do anything, because the problem belongs to the Ministry of Foreign Affairs. He said the embassy has immunity. No one can do anything to them. They told me the best way to stay safe is to move from my home to another place. I told my lawyer that I'd already moved from my place to 6 October City. That was all I could do, and that was all they did for me.

THEY HAVE DEMANDS,
AND I HAVE DEMANDS ALSO

Months passed, and I did not feel safe at all. Eventually I decided to complain to UNHCR and to tell them about all my problems. When I went to the UNHCR's office, I found some Sudanese people protesting outside the office. A big number. At that time about fifty or sixty. I asked, "What's going on?" and other refugees told me that all these people had troubles and had complaints, and they were staying. They had demands. I had demands also. I felt safe in this place among the Sudanese refugees. I stayed with them. I stayed with the Sudanese outside of Mustafa Mahmoud Park, in front of UNHCR. We built shelters there—tents of sticks and rugs and plastic. We lived in the park outside the UNHCR office. It was October 2005.

Soon there were fifteen hundred of us, maybe two thousand! I stayed until the end.

After that first day, I went home and took my family to join the protest. All of us were there. We brought our clothes and things. We stayed three months, day and night. It was very hard, it was very cold, and the people slept down on the ground. People even died during those months of the protest. A woman delivered a baby inside the park. And it was very hard to find food—just a sandwich sometimes.

Disagreements took place inside the park. By December—the last days of the demonstration—the park was divided in two groups. One group wanted to accept the offer of the UNHCR: to meet with groups of twenty refugees at a time and to reassess each case. UNHCR would pay us some money for rent and then we would have to leave the park. I was with the UNHCR on this. I agreed when the UNHCR offered to assist my case, to give me an interview, and then pay for my rent. I was ready to leave the park.

Unfortunately, most of the people—especially from South Sudan—refused this offer. Officially, there was peace in South Sudan, you know. It makes it a tough case for them. They asked the people to stay, because they disagreed with UNHCR's offer. So everybody stayed.

THEY HAD A PLAN FOR US

In late December, after months of all this, the policemen came and told us, "The Muslim Brotherhood wants to make a demonstration in the park, and we want to protect you from the Muslim Brotherhood."[2] This was a reason, or an excuse, to make us leave. At the same time, they already had a plan. They surrounded the place. They had a plan for us.

---

[2] A powerful international Islamist organization with a strong following in Egypt.

They yelled at us with loudspeakers in the cold night: "You should leave this place! You should get inside the bus!" They had buses waiting for us. When we refused to get in, they started scaring us by making sounds and doing all this military behavior. Stomping, marching, yelling. And still all the people refused to get out of the park.

After that, they opened the water cannons. They sprayed us; it was so cold. We held up plastic sheets to try and protect ourselves. It seems that they sprayed us by water, but there was something that made me feel like I lost consciousness somewhat. Like I was numb. It was like the water was mixed with some chemical. They told us to leave again, and our people insisted on staying. After that, they surrounded the park from all directions, came at us, and started beating us. My wife lay down on the ground and started screaming. At that time, I was holding my daughter in my left arm and holding Abdullah in my right arm, carrying him, carrying both of them.

When the policemen got inside the park, they beat us with sticks. One of them beat my son in the neck. They broke his neck, and I just fell down on the ground and I lost my daughter. I fell down on the ground, and I lost both of my children. Two policemen came and dragged me along the ground, and I saw my daughter fall down. I tried to grab her, to pick her up and take her with me, but one of the policemen beat me with the stick again. They dragged me inside the bus, and they sent all of us in the bus to Toura prison. And it was over.

I expected that they would try to scare us, to break the demonstration in a different way. No one expected this end.

Many buses arrived at Toura prison where I was, and after some time I saw my wife come in one of these buses. People were calling on their mobiles between the two prisons, and they told me that my daughter was in the other prison.

One of the people who was protesting with us, he had found my son in the park. He took my son's body with him. I found him in the prison. By that time, my son was already dead. I asked the police to send away the body of my son, and to send me with my son, so I could bury him. I was very, very angry and very upset, and I insisted on going with the body to the morgue. The officer told me, "Okay, go. Get your wife and go." They let me leave the room and go find my wife where the women were. When I brought my wife back, I found that the car had already taken my son to the morgue. They didn't wait for me.

Even then, the way that the police treated us was not humane at all. They promised to send us to the morgue. Me and my wife, and others with dead relatives—I think it was nine people all together.[3] They just drove us to a parking lot somewhere near the morgue and asked us to wait for an official, someone meant to come help us. The police car drove away. Soon, security men came and asked us, "What are you doing here?" They just kicked us out, told us to leave.

My wife was completely, completely traumatized. Everyone who saw it was shocked and traumatized. Afterward, I can only tell you this: no one could say anything.

After three days, they released my daughter. It took three months to get back my son's body and bury it. Three months. We are still in pain. Our psychological state is very bad, but we try to go forward. We try, and life goes on. We have a new child now, born on April 26, 2006. Thanks be to God.

BLUE CARD OR YELLOW CARD, THE SECURITY DOESN'T NOTICE

To this day, I continue to have trouble with Sudanese security in Cairo. They approach me in my neighborhood. They tell me to go

---

[3] The number of fatalities is unclear. Reports range between twenty and fifty dead, with many others injured, and at least a thousand people detained.

888

9

back to Sudan. They threaten me and my family. They say that worse things are coming if I do not report to the embassy.

On April 2, 2007, my family visited the UNHCR to report the security problems I was still having in Cairo. I don't know what I was hoping for, just protection, just anything. I'd made an appointment the previous Wednesday, and on this Monday morning I wanted to meet with a protection officer.

I approached the garden outside of the UNHCR office, the place where the officers meet the refugees. Suddenly several Egyptian security officers approached, took hold of me and said they were taking us to prison. I asked, "Why, why?" The officers who arrested me did not tell me why. My wife, my four-year-old daughter, and my one-year-old son were also arrested with me. We were taken to the Dokki police station.[4]

I was separated from my wife and my children at the police station, and I was placed in a room with nine other refugees who had been arrested at the same time as us. A police officer beat us with a stick. I was hit repeatedly in the middle of my back, over my kidney. After some hours, they told me my wife and children had been released.

In the evening, I was transferred to the prosecutor's office. The prosecutor wrote reports about why I was arrested, but he appeared to be making up his own information for the report. After the prosecutor wrote the report, I met with a lawyer. My lawyer requested to see the report and the prosecutor refused. My lawyer requested that I be examined by a doctor after this beating, but the officers refused again.

The prosecutor then sent me to the detention center in Giza. I was put in a crowded room with forty other people. There were criminals and gang members in the room, and they asked for money and belong-

---

[4] Dokki is a district in the greater Cairo metropolitan area.

ings from me. When I told them I did not have anything, they told me to go sleep standing up in the toilet area. I was in this room for four days, during which I did not receive any food from the officers. The only food I received was the remains of food that other detainees' relatives brought. The only water I had was water from the toilet, and the water from the toilet ran dry at times and flooded at other times. I drank from the toilet of an Egyptian prison for four days.

While I was at the detention center, inspectors would come into the room every night. The inspector would insert his hands inside my pants, beat me in my chest, and yell at me to go back to Darfur. I could not go, though. I was still held in prison.

After four days of detention, I appeared in front of a judge. The judge asked where I was from in Sudan and extended my period of detention to an additional fifteen days. I spent the next fifteen days back in the detention center. I then went in front of the judge again. The judge commented that I looked like I had gained weight in detention, though I had certainly not. I was then sent back for another week at the detention center. After the week, I went before the judge again. He asked me to make a deal.

The judge told me that he would release me if I promised never to approach UNHCR again. He told me that if I did approach UNHCR again, I would be sentenced to six years in jail. Without waiting for a response, the judge said he released me. He told me that if I did not know his reputation, I should ask other people to find out. He assured me he is a very tough judge. Even after the judge told me I was released, I was forced to spend five more days in the detention center.

After those final five days, I was taken to a security center. In the car on the way to the center, I was blindfolded. I was taken from the car inside a building. I could hear stretchers moving around me, and I was very frightened. I heard my name called, and I was asked why I was there. They asked me where I was from in Sudan, and why

I was at the security center. I was told to go outside and stand with a group. I was then taken to the car. After sitting in the car for one or two hours, I was taken back inside. I was taken into a room, and the blindfold was removed. A security officer told me to write a statement saying I would never approach the UNHCR again. I was told that if I repeated this behavior again, it would be a violation of Egyptian law and I would be deported. After I wrote what he wanted, I was blindfolded again. I was put in a car and taken back to the detention center in Giza. I spent the night there and was then taken to the Mogamma, the huge interior ministry building in downtown Cairo. At the Mogamma, the employees researched my criminal background. They found nothing, of course, and then released me.

On May 7, 2007, three officers in civilian clothes broke into my house in 6 October City and took me in their car. The officers took me, and I was blindfolded in the car and taken to an unknown place. They interrogated me about the group of people arrested on April 2, the group of us that was taken from outside the UNHCR office. They asked me about where I was from in Sudan, and about why I was in Cairo. I explained to them the problem that brought me here from Sudan. They advised me to go back to Sudan and threatened that if I did not, they would fabricate a crime and throw me in jail. They took my UN card and released me the next day at around five p.m.

I am frightened and believe that the police could come back at anytime to fabricate a story to have me thrown in jail or be deported. Sometimes I'm so afraid that I move away from my family for days or weeks at a time, staying in friends' houses, locked inside. For weeks after the detention incident, I did not have my UNHCR card. The lawyers at the AMERA organization helped me get a blue card after some weeks. A blue card is supposed to be less temporary, is supposed to be a stronger protection for official refugees, but I don't know. Blue card or yellow card, same for me. The Sudanese security doesn't care about a blue card or a yellow card.

IT MAKES ME HATE EVERYTHING

If you ask me what has changed, I say there is nothing new to mention. We do not feel comfortable, we are not relaxed. And for the future, I'm not sure about anything. Many Sudanese have a blue card, and they don't find an opportunity for resettlement. I would go anywhere that I can live in peace, anywhere. But I might be killed if I return to Sudan. And now, psychologically, I hate something called Sudan. They killed my father there, and what I have seen there is horrific. I think about the treatments that I faced in Sudan, and it makes me hate everything.

I don't know if I will ever again see my family that is still in Sudan. Maybe if someday I live anyplace else, I can invite them to visit me. I do not think I will ever see my home in Sudan again.

My children, thank God, they are okay. My boy is a smart one, and my daughter, too, she's very smart. She goes to the nursery school with Egyptian children. I have no Egyptian friends, but she does.

The Egyptian society is difficult, because when I walk down the street I hear words that are completely inhumane. *Abeed, hunga bunga, chokolata.* I worry for my daughter, even though she does well now. When she grows, she will hear the same as me. She has my same color, so she will be seen the same. Even in fifteen years, it's difficult to think, but we will probably still be here, and she will probably hear the same words.

AFTERWORD

by Emmanuel Jal

Emmanuel Jal was born in the village of Tonj, in South Sudan. At the age of about seven, he fled from war and walked, with thousands of others, to seek refuge in Ethiopia. From there, he was soon recruited by the Sudan People's Liberation Army; he became a child soldier in the rebel forces for several years. After escaping the army and finding refuge with British aid workers, Emmanuel was resettled in Kenya, where he began his career as a hip-hop artist. His third album, Warchild, *was released in May 2008. On June 27, 2008, he performed at Nelson Mandela's ninetieth birthday concert in Hyde Park, London.*

I saw my village in South Sudan burned to ashes, and all that we had owned we lost. I lost my mother, which cut me deeply.

Life as a refugee is very tormenting. You run away from your home, and all that you had is lost. You feel you have no reason to live.

When I was in a refugee camp in Ethiopia, I cried many times because I missed my parents, my brothers, and sisters. We were thousands of kids in an empty space. Imagine it: even though we were given food, hundreds starved, because we did not know how to cook.

What sticks in my mind still to this day is the sight of children burying the dead. Many children went crazy. They would rub themselves with feces, running around screaming and beating up people, laughing for no reason. Many committed suicide.

The Sudan People's Liberation Army, the army of South Sudan, came to the camps and recruited us, the children, to fight. They did not have to convince us much. I and many others wanted to pay back the people who had turned our lives into such turmoil. My training began when I was about eight years old and my desire was to kill as many Arabs and Muslims as possible. I was unaware of the politics of the war and only wanted to avenge the deaths of my family and of my people.

In a place called Wa'at, I was disarmed and rescued by a British aid worker.

In the years since my time as a child soldier, I have learned the art of forgiveness.

Now I am a musician. I see my music as a method of therapy to help push past each day as it comes, to keep my dreams alive, and to keep the past from haunting me. It is part of my prayer that I shall make a difference in this world.

As I travel the world telling my story I am doing it for my people. They have been crying for help, yet every corner ignores them.

In this book, there are stories from the people of Sudan, the place of my birth. When reading them, I feel a personal connection and can relate to some of the things they go through. I see myself in the stories, I feel the pain as well as a sense of hope.

When I tell my own story it is very difficult and depressing. Sometimes I feel as though I lose a sense of pride by sharing my experiences. The war affected the core of my family and I lost my childhood. I remember feeling that life had no meaning, and I remember the many occasions when I contemplated suicide. It took me time to accept myself and my past, to allow myself to move on with what I have and to achieve something.

What keeps me going is the knowledge that my people are still starving and suffering, and that I may be in a position to help change that.

I have found a way of communicating easily without experiencing so much pain. I use artistic expression, putting my story into poems. When I started sharing my story to people through music, I found it therapeutic. I believe art is one of the most effective ways to help people overcome a horrific past. My music has the power to speak to your soul, mind, body, and spirit without your permission.

As you reflect on this book, I would advise each reader to put themselves into the shoes of a refugee. The effects of war are universal. I hope that this collection of experiences offers you a different perspective on life, and some things you take for granted will become more valuable.

I choose to tell my story to represent the pain of my people and to contribute to making this world a better place. The narrators you have met here will do the same. It is my hope that this will be a blessing to many.

APPENDIX A

SUDAN—HISTORY, LAND, WAR, AND PEACE

I. TIMELINE OF INDEPENDENT SUDAN

The following timeline lays out the most recent eras in Sudan's history, beginning with colonial occupation.

1821: Ottoman-supported Egyptian forces led by Mohammed Ali occupy Sudan and establish the Turkiyah regime. The new government enslaves tens of thousands of Sudanese, sending them back to Egypt for training as soldiers.

1860: European pressure leads Egypt to ban the slave trade in Sudan. However, lack of enforcement allows private Baggara Arab armies to continue to grow rich from capturing and selling slaves.

1863-1877: Under the reign of Ismail, Egypt works to organize the provinces of Sudan, and in 1874, annexes Darfur. Ismail takes steps to eliminate the northern slave trade, which upsets many Baggara Arabs.

1873: The British, seeking to defend their interest in the Suez Canal, take a larger role in Egyptian affairs, eventually forcing Ismail from power in 1877. Egyptian interests in Sudan suffer as a result of the power shift. Newly unemployed Sudanese soldiers harass the local population.

1880–1885: Mohammed Ahmad, a passionate religious zealot, rallies the support of discontented merchants and slave traders, and declares a *jihad* against the Turkiyah government. He stages a successful insurrection against Anglo-Egyptian rule. Declaring himself Al Mahdi al Muntazar ("the awaited guide in the right path"), Ahmad establishes the Mahdist regime—the first Sudanese nationalist government—and imposes traditional Islamic law.

1892–1899: Britain renews interest in Sudan, and Anglo-Egyptian forces retake the country from the Mahdi. Egypt and Britain sign a condominium agreement, whereby the two countries would share control of Sudan.

1922–1925: After some dispute, Britain establishes sovereignty over Sudan, following Egypt's declaration of independence in 1922.

1920–1946: Britain's policy in Sudan is one of indirect rule. To varying degrees, they allow traditional leaders to administer local government. Throughout the colonial era, Britain seeks to isolate Southern Sudan, preparing it for eventual integration with other British east African colonies. They bar access to the region, and seek to sever its ties with Arab traditions.

1946: Concern over Southern Sudan's viability as an independent state leads Britain to reverse its policies and unite the country. The British abruptly decide to abolish trade restrictions, admit northerners to southern administrative posts, and establish Arabic as the official administration language in the South. Some British colonial officers, as well as members of the southern population express concern that the South will be overrun by northern Arabs.

1956: On January 1, Sudan gains its independence from Britain without conflict. The newly independent nation is faced with numerous problems, including finalizing a constitution and stabilizing the South. Southerners, upset by the replacement of British administrators with northerners, threaten rebellion.

FIRST CIVIL WAR, 1955–1972

1955: Four months before Sudan gains independence, southern troops mutiny in Torit to protest their transfer to stations under the command of northern officers. The rebels kill hundreds, and Khartoum responds by executing seventy southerners for sedition.

1958: The situation in the South contributes to discontent with the new independent government. In November, General Ibrahim Abbud leads a military coup and dissolves civilian-run government. The resulting Abbud regime finds modest success in economic matters, but adopts harsh policies of assimilation in the South.

1963: The Abbud government's policies of suppression and Arabization in the South sparks southern leaders to intensify the armed conflict that began in 1955. The rebellion is conducted by guerrilla forces known as the Anya Nya.

1964–1969: Popular discontent with Abbud's inability to quell the southern insurrection leads to violent riots in October. Abbud dissolves the military government and transitions rule to civilian hands. Partisan politics hinder the country for the next five years, as the southern conflict remains unresolved.

1969: In May, Colonel Jaafar an Nimeiri stages a military coup and establishes the ten-member Revolutionary Command Council. Nimeiri is committed to establishing a socialist Sudanese state, and a plebiscite elects Nimeiri to a six-year presidential term.

1971: By the late 1960s, approximately 500,000 people have died as a result of violence between north and south. Both sides of the conflict have grown increasingly well-equipped, thanks in large part to foreign powers. In 1971, Joseph Lagu, leader of the southern opposition, founds the Southern Sudan Liberation Movement (SSLM), uniting Anya Nya leaders and southern politicians. Nimeiri's government establishes contact with the SSLM in October.

A FRAGILE PEACE, 1972-1983

1972: Nimeiri and Lagu sign the Addis Ababa Agreement on March 27, despite protests from both leaders' constituencies. The accords grant considerable autonomy to the South.

1974: Conservative Muslim opposition to Nimeiri's policies, especially his perceived surrender to the South, lead to the formation of the National Front, which eventually attempts an unsuccessful coup in 1976.

1977–1978: In spite of political unrest, Nimeiri is elected to a second six-year term. Meanwhile, Sudan's increasing international debt; the discovery of oil deposits in the South; unresolved border disputes; and the proposed Jonglei Canal, which would funnel water out of the South, contribute to growing dissatisfaction with the terms of the Addis Ababa Agreement on both sides of the border.

1978: Chevron discovers oil reserves in the Upper Nile region of South Sudan.

1980: Nimeiri and the National Assembly attempt to redraw the boundaries of Southern Sudan, transferring possession of oil fields to the North. The ensuing protests and strong opposition from southern members of the National Assembly force Nimeiri to abandon this plan.

SECOND CIVIL WAR, 1983–2005

1983 (May): Nimeiri divides the South into three traditional regions and revokes southern autonomy. The 105th Battalion of the Sudanese army, stationed at Bor and composed mostly of ex–Anya Nya troops, mutinies and flees to Ethiopia. Colonel John Garang is sent to quell the insurrection, but instead joins them. The Bor mutiny is one of several that occur around the country.

1983 (July): The newly formed Sudanese People's Liberation Movement/Army (SPLM/A), led by John Garang, issues a manifesto stating its aims and grievances with the Addis Ababa accords.

1983 (September): Nimeiri issues a set of decrees, known as the September Laws, imposing *sharia* law throughout the country.

1983: As armed conflicts intensify, the Sudanese government enlists militias of Baggara Arabs *(murahaleen)* to terrorize and displace Dinka and Nuer people.

1985: The deteriorating situation in the south leads to Nimeiri's downfall. On April 6, a military coup led by Lieutenant General Abdulrahman Suwar al-Dahab overthrows the Nimeiri government. A transitional military government takes power, promising to resolve the conflict with the South and return power to a civilian government in twelve months.

1986: The International Monetary Fund declares Sudan bankrupt. The Dahab-led military council cannot resolve the conflict in the south, or prevent famine from claiming hundreds of thousands of lives. In April, Sadiq Al-Mahdi is elected president in a general election.

1988: Scorched-earth tactics employed by *murahaleen* militias contribute to a famine that causes an estimated 250,000 deaths, many of them in Bahr al-Ghazal. Relief attempts are thwarted as both sides attempt to control the supply rails.

1989 (June): After years of inability to unify Sudan's political parties in a stable coalition government, Al-Mahdi is overthrown in a coup led by Brigadier General Omar al-Bashir and supported by the fundamentalist National Islamic Front (NIF) and Islamist leader Hassan al-Turabi. The new government bans opposition parties, revokes the constitution, and increases efforts to Islamicize the country. The war escalates in the South.

1989 (October): Northern and southern opposition forces unite under the banner of the National Democratic Alliance.

1991: The overthrow of Ethiopian dictator Mengitsu Haile Mariam leads to the loss of major SPLA supply lines in Ethiopia. Large numbers of Sudanese refugees fleeing Ethiopia are targeted by government air strikes. Meanwhile, ethnic conflict within the SPLM/A leads to a split into two groups: the Mainstream party led by John Garang, and the SPLA-Nasir led by Riek Machar. Khartoum exploits this infighting by supplying arms to the Machar faction.

1991 (December): The regional government of Kordofan declares a *jihad* against Nuba dissidents.

1992 (May): Peace talks commence between the SPLM/A factions and the Khartoum government in Abuja, Nigeria. The two sides fail to reach an agreement.

1992 (July): The United Nations High Commissioner for Refugees (UNHCR) establishes Kakuma Refugee Camp in Kenya in response to the entry of some 23,000 refugees from Sudan (13,000 of which are unaccompanied boys).

1992 (December): In the wake of government-sponsored massacres of Toposa and Nuba people, the UN General Assembly adopts a resolution expressing "deep concern at the serious human rights violations in the Sudan, including summary executions, detentions without due process, forced displacement of persons, and torture."

1993 (March): Members of John Garang's SPLM/A join SPLM/A-Nasir to form SPLM/A-United.

1993 (September): After a second round of peace talks break down in Abuja, the African-based Intergovernmental Authority on Drought and Development (IGADD) hosts further peace talks in Addis Ababa. A four-nation mediation committee forms comprising leaders from Ethiopia, Uganda, Eritrea, and Kenya.

1994 (May): The IGADD committee produces the Declaration of Principles (DOP), listing the elements needed for a successful peace agreement. The DOP establishes self-determination as an inalienable right, but also gives priority to national unity.

1994 (September): Bashir refuses to acknowledge the South's right to self-determination and secularism, ending the fourth round of IGADD talks. Diplomatic relations begin to break down between Khartoum and the leaders of Ethiopia, Eritrea, and Uganda.

1994 (September): SPLM/A-United is renamed the South Sudan Independence Movement/Army (SSIM/A).

1995: As Bashir's government grows more resistant to international diplomacy, the United States initiates the Frontline States strategy. The U.S. provides aid to the SPLA-NDA through Sudan's neighbors, and isolates the Bashir regime.

1996: Machar's SSIM signs a peace charter with Khartoum, foregoing their demands for an autonomous southern state.

1997 (January): The NDA and SPLA, with the assistance of the Ethiopian army, make significant military advances.

1997 (April): Six rebel factions and the Sudanese government sign the Khartoum Peace Agreement, which does not address self-determination for the South. Former rebel leaders, including Riek Machar assume marginalized government positions. The SPLM/A does not sign the agreement.

1997 (December): The governor of Darfur complains of deteriorating security conditions.

1998 (March): A major famine strikes the Bahr al-Ghazal region. The World Food Programme estimates that 350,000 people are in urgent need of food. Khartoum limits relief flights into SPLA territory.

1998 (December): Numerous villages are destroyed in western Darfur as intertribal conflicts over water and grazing rights intensify.

1999 (January): After a protracted power struggle with parliamentary leader Hassan al-Turabi, President Bashir dissolves parliament to make way for new elections. The National Congress (formerly the National Islamic Front) is the only registered party. Riek Machar's United Democratic Salvation Front agrees to register as a party, but it is bound by law to support national unity and *sharia* law. In Darfur, Masalit tribesmen claim that four hundred of their people have been killed by paramilitary Arab horsemen.

1999 (July): The United States announces that it will resettle more than three thousand Sudanese refugees from Kakuma, members of the so-called "Lost Boys" group.

1999 (December): Bashir dissolves parliament again, heading off debates that would potentially limit his power.

2000 (January): Khartoum announces a new government with the National Congress in control. Riek Machar resigns from government.

2000 (December): Bashir is re-elected to a five-year presidential term in an election that was boycotted by opposition groups.

2001 (January): The Sudanese government begins a new offensive, employing both regular army forces and *murahaleen* militia.

2001 (June): Egypt and Libya present a nine-point peace plan, calling for immediate cessation of violence, and the formation of an interim unity government. The plan ignores the issues of self-determination outlined in past IGAD discussions. Khartoum accepts the plan unequivocally, while the SPLM/A agrees in principle, with reservations.

2001 (September): Following the September 11 attacks, Khartoum begins cooperating with the U.S. in tracking down terrorism suspects. The U.S. abstains from a vote lifting diplomatic sanctions on Sudan.

2002 (January): Machar and Garang sign the Nairobi Declaration, joining their two factions under the banner of the SPLM/A.

2002 (February): Following a helicopter gunship attack on a UN aid center at Bieh by Sudanese forces, the U.S. suspends participation in the peace process.

2002 (July): The government and SPLM/A sign the Machakos Protocol, establishing a framework for final peace talks. Khartoum agrees to a referendum on secession for Southern Sudan after a six-and-a-half-year period, while the SPLM/A agree to *sharia* law in the north.

2002 (September): Khartoum withdraws from peace talks after the SPLA retakes Torit.

THE PEACE PROCESS AND DARFUR, 2003-2008

2003 (February): Two groups emerge at the forefront of a new rebel movement in Darfur: The Sudan Liberation Movement/Army (formerly Darfur Liberation Front) and the Justice and Equality movement. The SLM/A shares many ideological similarities with the SPLM/A.

2003 (April): The SLA and JEM stage an attack on government forces at al-Fasher airport, damaging several Sudanese air force planes. Fighting escalates between the rebels and government forces.

2003 (September): As hundreds of thousands of refugees pour into his country, Chadian president Idriss Deby initiates peace negotiations between the Sudanese government and the SLM/A. Airstrikes and *janjaweed*-led attacks ravage Darfur as both sides fail to secure a lasting ceasefire.

2004 (February): An estimated 750,000 people have been displaced by the conflict in Darfur.

2004 (May): The government and SPLM/A agree to a power-sharing protocol and commit themselves to working toward a permanent peace agreement.

2004 (August): The African Union organizes peace talks between the SLM/A and Khartoum in Abuja, Nigeria, but these collapse within a month. The UN Security Council passes a resolution demanding that the Sudanese government disarm the *janjaweed* and end the violence against civilians in Darfur. This proves ineffective.

2004 (September): Estimates surface that the number of internally displaced people has reached 1.45 million as a result of violence in Darfur.

2004 (November): Under pressure from the UN, the SPLM/A and Khartoum pledge to reach a final peace settlement by the end of the year.

2005 (January): On January 9, Khartoum and the SPLM/A sign the Comprehensive Peace Agreement (CPA) in Nairobi. The CPA is based on the protocols established by the Machakos agreement, laying down arrangements for wealth sharing, a government of national unity, a 2011 referendum on southern autonomy, and a permanent ceasefire. Some contentious issues remain unresolved, including whether or not the oil-rich border territory of Abyei will become part of the North or South.

2005 (June): The UN Mission in Sudan (UNMIS) is established, comprising up to 10,000 military personnel and 715 police officers, intended to support the AU Mission in Sudan (AMIS) in establishing peace in Darfur and enforcing the terms of the CPA.

2005 (July): John Garang is sworn in as First Vice President of Sudan, but dies in a helicopter crash three weeks later. A rash of violence ensues.

2005 (August): Salva Kiir Mayardit assumes leadership of the SPLM/A and is sworn in as the First Vice President of Sudan. In Darfur, internal strife within the rebel groups slows peace talks in Abuja.

2005 (September): Between 2,500 and 3,000 Sudanese refugees in Cairo begin a sit-in protest in Mostafa Mahmoud Park outside the office of the UN High Commissioner for Refugees (UNHCR). Protesters complain of unfair treatment and neglect by the UNHCR.

2005 (December): On December 30, Egyptian police storm the Mostafa Mahmoud protest, killing at least twenty, and detaining many others. In Darfur, the UN accuses the SLM of complicity in hundreds of civilian deaths, banditry, and impeding humanitarian efforts. Meanwhile, Chad declares that it is in a state of war with Sudan along the Darfur border, accusing Khartoum of sponsoring rebels intent on overthrowing the Chadian government.

2006 (April): Chad severs diplomatic relations with Sudan as violence continues to spread across the border. President Deby threatens to expel two hundred thousand Sudanese refugees living in Chad.

2006 (May): One of three rebel factions (Minni Minnawi's arm of the SLM/A) signs the Darfur Peace Agreement (DPA), calling for a comprehensive ceasefire, the disarmament of the *janjaweed,* and self-determination for Darfur.

2006 (September): Khartoum rejects a UN resolution calling for the deployment of up to 22,500 troops to Darfur to aid the AMIS.

2006 (October): As violence continues in spite of the DPA, the Sudanese government expels the UN's top official in the country, Jan Pronk, for describing Sudanese military setbacks in his personal blog.

2006 (November): Heavy fighting between Sudanese armed forces and the SPLA occurs in the town of Malakal, breaching the CPA ceasefire.

2007 (July): As plans circulate for a joint AU/UN taskforce, U.S. special envoy to Sudan, Andrew Natsios, reports that Khartoum has resumed aerial bombing in Darfur. On July 31, UN resolution 1769 creates the United Nations

African Union Mission in Darfur (UNAMID), an ambitious peacekeeping force of 26,000 soldiers and civilian officers. Though UNAMID has the support of the Sudanese government, it is limited in its scope.

2007 (July): Severe floods displace tens of thousands throughout Sudan.

2007 (September): As the UN and AU prepare for peace talks in Libya, the town of Haskanita in Darfur is attacked and razed, killing ten AU peacekeepers. The Sudanese government and rebel factions both blame each other for the attack, which displaced an estimated 7,000 residents.

2007 (October): Much-anticipated peace talks falter when various rebel factions boycott the discussions. UNAMID operations begin in al-Fasher.

2008 (March): Violent clashes occur between former southern rebels and armed tribesmen in the still-disputed territory of Abyei.

2008 (May): Two rounds of fighting between the SPLA and the Sudanese army effectively level the main town in Abyei, and threaten to upend the terms set in the CPA. An estimated 90,000 people are displaced by the violence.

2008 (June): President Bashir and First Vice President Kiir sign an agreement to end the conflict in Abyei, pending the 2011 referendum on whether Abyei will become part of the North or South. Meanwhile, due to opposition from the Sudanese government, and a lack of international support, only 9,000 of the 26,000 uniformed personnel expected to make up the UNAMID taskforce have been deployed. Violence continues in Darfur between various factions of the SLM and Sudanese armed forces. An estimated 200,000 people have died as a result of the Darfur conflict, and an additional 2.5 million have been displaced.

2008 (July): Luis Moreno-Ocampo, prosecutor at the International Criminal Court, requests an arrest warrant for President Bashir, on charges of genocide, war crimes, and crimes against humanity. It is the first time such action is taken by the court against a sitting head of state.

2009 (March): The International Criminal Court charges Bashir with five counts of crimes against humanity, marking the first time the Court has ever sought to detain a sitting head of state. In response, Bashir accuses thirteen aid organizations of providing false evidence to the Court, and orders that they stop all aid operations.

II. THE NORTH-SOUTH CIVIL WARS

Sudan has been engaged in civil conflict for longer than it has existed as an independent nation. Land disputes and religious conflict have driven a wedge between North and South Sudan culminating in the eruption of civil war in 1955. Since then, there has been no lasting peace between North and South. The Comprehensive Peace Agreement, signed in 2005, is the latest attempt at reconciliation and a tenuous ceasefire. For more on the efficacy of the CPA, see page 392.

WAR

The first civil war between North and South began approximately one year before Sudan gained independence from British rule in 1956. There were several factors that led to the first series of conflicts, including disputes over political power, natural resources, and the role of religion and language within Sudanese society. As a result, the Sudanese government was engaged in a guerilla-style war for seventeen years, primarily with members of the southern rebel group Anya Nya.

The signing of the Addis Ababa Accords in 1972 produced ten years of reduced violence, and granted considerable autonomy to the South. But conflict began again when President Jaafar Nimeiri, frustrated by the discovery of oil fields in the South, revoked southern autonomy. Nimeiri declared a "state of emergency" and implemented various Islamicization laws aimed at imposing Islamic *sharia* law and diluting the political power of South Sudan. In 1983, Colonel John Garang was sent to quell a group of Army officers in rebellion, but instead joined them and formed the Sudan People's Liberation Movement/Army (SPLM/A).

The second phase of the Sudanese civil war lasted for twenty-two years, and was marked by the Sudanese government's employment of Baggara militias known as *murahaleen*, who terrorized and displaced thousands of civilians throughout the country. Among this group of refugees was the so-called "lost boys," who trekked across Sudan in search of safety in the Kakuma refugee camp. While little statistical data is available, some estimate that the Sudanese civil war resulted in over two million deaths, and displaced twice as many.

TENTATIVE RECONCILIATION

The heads of the member states of the Intergovernmental Authority on Drought and Development (IGADD) became involved in an initiative to bring together the government of Sudan and the SPLM/A in 1993. Over the course of the next twelve years, the peace process progressed slowly in the form of numerous IGADD-sponsored talks. Finally, in 2005, John Garang and Sudanese President Omar al-

Bashir signed the Comprehensive Peace Agreement (CPA). The CPA is built on the framework of six accords signed in Machakos and Naivasha, Kenya from 2002 to 2004. The CPA established a national government of unity (and the structure of that body), and provides for a referendum on southern autonomy in 2011. John Garang was sworn in as First Vice President of Sudan in July of 2005.

The CPA also includes provisions for security arrangements, and wealth sharing. However, it leaves a considerable question in whether the oil-rich border territory of Abyei will become part of the North or South. That issue came to a head in early 2008 as the SPLA and Sudanese army renewed their conflict with heavy fighting that resulted in the near destruction of Abyei's main town.

THE FUTURE

As of early 2008, the overall effectiveness of the Comprehensive Peace Agreement (CPA) remains questionable. The death of John Garang shortly after his appointment to the vice presidency led to riots throughout the country. Since then, President Bashir has ignored numerous protocols of the CPA, with little response from the international community. The National Islamic Front is still in control of a vast majority of the nation's resources, and its monopoly over Sudan's oil revenues has provided them with a substantially larger portion of the profits gained from Sudanese oil production. This not only violates the Comprehensive Peace Agreement protocol of power sharing, but the protocol of wealth sharing as well. By increasing and maintaining its stronghold on Sudan's natural resources, northern Sudan is not only monopolizing political and economic power, but is choking off the resources of Southern Sudan. Additionally, the National Islamic Front-led northern Sudanese government is continuing its harassment of humanitarian and development operations in Southern Sudan and Darfur. They have made it increasingly difficult for aid to enter the southern region of Sudan through various bureaucratic obstructions.

III. LOOKING FORWARD
DEMOCRACY: A KEY TO PEACE IN SUDAN

The following briefing was written by Sudan experts John Prendergast and Roger Winter for the ENOUGH Project, a joint venture of the International Crisis Group and the Center for American Progress. For more information, visit enoughproject.org.

The establishment of strong democratic institutions and processes in Sudan will be a key prerequisite for peace in Darfur and the South. By setting forth a timetable for elections, the 2005 Comprehensive Peace Agreement seeks to give Sudanese citizens significantly more control in how their country is governed. However, the CPA election clock is ticking and neither the institutional foundations nor the requisite electoral processes are in place. These electoral processes in the context of the implementation of the CPA provide Sudan's best hope for peace—a political transformation through democracy.

There are three major electoral milestones critical to the implementation of the CPA over the next three years: 1) the population census in April 2008; 2) the national elections by July 2009; and 3) a self-determination referendum for Southern Sudan by March 2011.[1]

Sudan has been torn apart by internal conflict for most of its independence, in part because of the lack of democratic processes or institutions. Resolving Sudan's ongoing conflicts and preventing future violence means seizing the opportunity provided by the CPA to start building these foundations. The international community must demand full and timely implementation of the CPA—particularly these electoral provisions—and deploy additional personnel and resources *now* to ensure that this historic opportunity is not missed. As well, donors must provide significant support to civil society organizations in the North and South and to Southern Sudanese government institutions to strengthen the forces promoting democracy in Sudan.

There should be penalties for non-compliance with the CPA timetable. The U.N. Security Council endorsed the CPA and key Security Council members helped negotiate it. But much more could be done to ensure that the CPA's provisions have not been violated repeatedly by the National Congress Party (NCP). The Security Council should consider targeted sanctions against those officials who are most responsible for obstructing the implementation of the CPA. If the Council will not act, the United States and the European Union should consider appropriate, coordinated responses, and encourage the African Union and Arab League to join in demanding implementation of this critical peace deal.

MILESTONE #1: THE 2008 CENSUS

A new, national census is directly linked to the 2009 elections in two key ways. First, the CPA states that representation of the North and South at the national level will be based on the population ratio. The power sharing percentages currently stipulated by the CPA shall be "confirmed or adjusted on the basis of the census results."[2] Currently, the ruling NCP has 52 percent of the seats in the National Assembly, the Sudan People's Liberation Movement (SPLM) 28 percent, and other political parties 20 percent. The NCP and the SPLM negotiated these percentages during the drafting of the CPA, but without new, valid census data, it is not possible to confirm that these percentages accurately reflect Sudan's current demography. The census results will also provide the basis for determining constituencies and for voter registration.

The ruling NCP has a keen understanding of the critical relationship between the census and the fairness of the 2009 elections, and has attempted to derail the census. The CPA mandated that the census be undertaken by July 2007 in order to allow sufficient time to collect, process, and analyze the data before the election. Because of funding delays by the NCP, however, the census date slipped from July 2007 to November 2007, then to February 2008, and has most recently been rescheduled for April 2008. If the date slips yet again, the rainy season will prevent the census team from gaining full access to Southern Sudan and tip the balance toward the North.

The NCP tried to make unilateral changes to the census questionnaire that would have thwarted the ability to count the Southerners who live in Northern Sudan. This was important because the war was waged in the South and the majority of Sudan's displaced citizens are Southerners, and between two and four million now reside in the North. The South/SPLM had to push hard to ensure that the census questionnaire would accurately determine the number of Northerners and Southerners throughout the entire country. This will ensure that there is a way to determine the precise number of Southerners who reside in the North and the precise number of Northerners who reside in the South.

The international community can help to ensure that the census—now scheduled from April 15-30, 2008—is successful first and foremost by providing sufficient numbers of qualified international observers of the census.

MILESTONE #2: THE 2009 ELECTION

The election has the potential to reshape the distribution of political power at all levels of governance in Sudan. Elections are mandated to take place at six levels of government: the Presidency of the Government of National Unity, the Presidency of the Government of Southern Sudan, the National Assembly in Khartoum, the Southern Sudan Legislative Assembly in Juba, 25 State Legislatures, and 25 State Governors.

The immediate requirement for a sound election is for the National Assembly to pass an election law that meets international standards. Without the passage of a new law, the National Electoral Commission cannot be established and extensive preparations needed for elections cannot begin. These preparations include: selection and training of election commission staff; voter registration; construction of electoral commission buildings in the South and identification of buildings in the North (one in each state capital); procurement and distribution of ballots (the number will depend on the type of electoral system), ballot boxes, voters rolls, and vehicles; training and recruitment of domestic and international election observers[3] and polling agents; and massive voter education campaigns.

Sudan's Election Bill was scheduled to be passed by the National Assembly by December 2007, but the Assembly failed to do so. Even the best case scenario presents major challenges. If the law is passed in January 2008, the electoral commission established in February, and the election scheduled between March 2009 and July 2009, the commission will only have one year to accomplish the myriad tasks listed above.

There are two further practical issues: dates and costs. Although the CPA allows for elections to take place as late as July 9, 2009, it is critical that elections be held before the onset of the rainy season in order to ensure that all Sudanese are able to vote. Conducting a complex election in Africa's largest country with one of the most underdeveloped infrastructure systems on the continent will pose a massive and expensive logistical challenge. Assuming that half of the estimated 38 million Sudanese will be of voting age in 2009, the United Nations estimates that the election will cost between $400 and $500 million. The 2006 elections in the Democratic Republic of Congo demonstrate that, with requisite resources and will, large underdeveloped countries can hold successful elections.

MILESTONE #3: THE 2011 SELF-DETERMINATION REFERENDUM

The premise of the CPA is that during the six years between the signing of the agreement in 2005 and the self-determination referendum in 2011, the NCP, SPLM, and the agreement's international guarantors and supporters work to "make unity attractive," thereby increasing the likelihood that Southerners would vote for unity. However, given that the war was fought principally in the South and Southerners were the primary victims of a conflict that killed 2 million people, the burden to make unity attractive rests overwhelmingly with the NCP in Khartoum.

The NCP could take any number of steps to make unity more attractive:

- genuine power sharing in the Government of National Unity

- a real resolution of the Darfur crisis

- free and fair elections whose results represent the will of the people

- a clear demonstration that all Sudanese citizens are equal, and that the

interim period is not just about the North "granting" the South some
scraps of political or economic benefits

- a tangible peace dividend that demonstrates that critical resources like oil
  will yield equitable gains for the whole of Sudan, including the South

- faithful implementation of the CPA

The clock is ticking, and the NCP must soon demonstrate a real commitment
to unity. At this juncture, the chances for a vote for unity are remote. First,
throughout the war, the desire for independence grew in direct proportion to the
amount of force used against the South – and the war was sufficiently violent,
and government forces were sufficiently unrelenting, so a significant portion of
the Southern Sudanese people decided that independence was the only option.
Second, John Garang—who had the credibility to champion the cause of unity
in the South because he had the power to press unity upon the North – is no
longer on the scene. And third, Khartoum has not only failed to make unity
appear attractive, it has taken steps that signal genuine unity is impossible –
by thwarting the implementation of the CPA, by its actions in Darfur, by its
handling of oil resources, by its rejection of the Abyei Boundaries Commission's
findings, etc.

The National Democratic Institute has conducted a series of focus group
surveys in Southern Sudan, the first conducted just before the CPA was signed
and the most recent in May 2007. A report released in April 2006 concluded
the following:

> Nothing appears to shake Southerners from the conviction that separa-
> tion is their best, and perhaps only, choice. Participants in the study
> were presented with several scenarios designed to make unity a more
> attractive option and were then asked if any of these could possibly
> alter their opinion about how they would vote in the 2011 self-deter-
> mination referendum. For most, neither direction from the leadership,
> the promise of more development, nor the possibility of re-igniting the
> conflict is enough to deter them from the belief that—come 2011—
> they will be voting for separation.[4]

KEEPING THE DEMOCRATIC TRANSFORMATION ON TRACK

Looking at other post-conflict or post-dictatorship situations, not only in Africa
but also in Latin America and even in Iraq, the credibility of peace and democracy derives from two things. First, credible institutions that work; i.e., that
enable people to resolve their differences and determine their political futures.

And second, tangible economic dividends; i.e., real change in the standard of living, in wealth distribution, etc.

Those economic dividends will result from the degree to which the NCP shares the wealth of the country and the commitment of the Government of Southern Sudan to transparent governance. And the credibility of the census, the election, and the referendum -- if carried out openly, transparently, and honestly—will demonstrate whether the NCP is committed to a truly united Sudan based on equality and respect. Thus far, the NCP has not demonstrated that commitment.

It will be up to the citizens of Southern Sudan to cast their vote in the referendum on whether unity has been made attractive. Those votes will create a new Sudan—in either one or two parts—that will be born of the people, by the people, and for the people.

Therein lies the power—and the promise—of the CPA. *Whether this promise is realized depends in large part on the international community's support for the census, the election, and the self-determination referendum.*

[1] Abyei will have a separate self-determination referendum at the same time the South has its referendum. The ENOUGH Project will discuss the Abyei issue in a forthcoming report.

[2] To read the full text of the Comprehensive Peace Agreement go to, http://www.unmis.org/English/documents/cpa-en.pdf.

[3] The CPA mandates international observation of the election, and citizens both North and South are aware of this provision and embrace it.

[4] Traci Cook, "Searching for a Path to Peace," National Democratic Institute for International Affairs, April 12, 2006. Available at http://www.accessdemocracy.org/library/2034_su_report_041206.pdf.

IV. MURAHALEEN AND JANJAWEED

Sudan's civil wars have been exceedingly violent affairs. A major driving force behind this violence is the government's strategy of using tribal militias as proxy paramilitary forces. When rebel groups form and take action against the state, the government responds by channeling weapons, money, and supplies to local tribal groups, encouraging them to kill and displace civilians in the contested areas.

Two main tribal militias have been utilized by the Sudanese government in recent history: the *murahaleen,* used to fight Sudan's civil war in the South, and the *janjaweed*, used against the rebel factions in Darfur. These two groups are responsible for innumerable atrocities: unchecked killing, scorched-earth tactics, pillage and rape, massacre, the abduction of women and children, the looting of cattle and other livestock, the burning of houses, and destruction of grain supplies.

MURAHALEEN

In the mid-1980s, when Sudan's armed forces were losing ground to the Sudan People's Liberation Army (SPLA), the government began giving arms, ammunition, and military training to tribal Arab militias in southern Kordofan and other regions along the border of Southern Sudan. Baggara Arab tribes (Rizeigat, Miseriya, and others) were economically marginalized due to drought and the recent mechanization of agriculture in the region, and harbored historic enmity against the non-Muslim southern tribes (Dinka, but also Nuer). The cattle-herding Muslim Arabs, who had been competing with the southern tribes for ages over pasture lands—and abducting southerners as slaves—were easy conscripts for the *jihad* against the South. In arming these ethnic minority groups and sending them to fight a holy war, the Sudanese government played on deep-seeded values of race, religion, and cultural animosities.

The *murahaleen* used brutal force against Southern Sudanese, specifically the Dinka tribes of northern Bahr al-Ghazal and South Kordofan states. While usually operating independently of the armed forces, the *murahaleen* sometimes fought alongside the regular army. Large raiding parties of five hundred to a thousand men on horseback would descend on civilian villages, fanning out from a train railway that ran through the region. Their methods have been well-documented: After burning the village, killing the men, abducting the women and children, stealing cattle and other loot, the militias would finally burn grain supplies and harvests, pollute water wells, and destroy any other food sources. They would load their spoils onto trains for transport to points north. Abducted women and children would be traded or kept in slavery.

Murahaleen raids occurred from the mid- to late-1980s and throughout the 1990s, but they were at their peak in 1986 and 1987. One of the worst massacres occurred at ad-Da'ein in 1987, when more than one thousand unarmed Dinka were killed—many of them burned to death—in retaliation for SPLA military advances. Throughout the course of the war, raiding resulted in the deaths of hundreds of thousands of Southern Sudanese.

The militias targeted civilian communities, purportedly to undermine the SPLA's recruitment base. But such large-scale attacks on the civilian population resembled ethnic cleansing: the systematic elimination of the Dinka people through killing and displacement. Many victims died from starvation after the raids, as the government's "scorched earth" policy contributed to famines in the region.

The actions of the *murahaleen* were made possible and tacitly encouraged by the government of Sudan. In 1989, the tribal militias were centralized and given government legitimacy, under the name "Popular Defense Forces" (PDF).

The decision was sponsored by Brigadier General Omar al-Bashir, who went on to topple President Sadiq al-Mahdi in a military coup.

While the civil war officially ended in 2005 with the signing of the Comprehensive Peace Agreement, the *murahaleen* militias are still active in disputes with the SPLA, mostly as part of the PDF, and reportedly maintain a strong presence in some areas.

JANJAWEED

The *murahaleen*'s legacy is clear in the raiding militias of today's Darfur conflict: the *janjaweed*, fearsome Arab militias mounted on camels and horses, armed with government-supplied automatic weapons.

When the Darfur conflict began—sparked by the actions of two non-Arab armed movements called the Sudan Liberation Army (SLA) and the Justice and Equality Movement (JEM)—Khartoum responded by mobilizing, arming, and directing the Arab-supremacist *janjaweed* militias. The counterinsurgency strategy was familiar: scorched earth, massacre, rape, abduction, and starvation. The *janjaweed*'s actions have contributed to what the UN calls "the world's worst humanitarian crisis."

Janjaweed differ from the *murahaleen* in several ways: in the South, the Muslim militias fought non-Muslim Christians, while in Darfur almost the entire population follows Islam. The conflict is rooted in economic and ethnic inequalities, and has pitted the nomadic Arab-identifying Muslims against the sedentary non-Arab Muslims of the region. The SLA and JEM rebel groups are mainly drawn from three major ethnic groups in the province: the Fur, the Masalit, and the Zaghawa. The *janjaweed* militias are composed of members of the Rizeigat, Miseriya, and Beni Hussein tribes—cattle-herders, who are notorious for their Arab supremacism and racism.

The *janjaweed* first received arms and military purpose in the 1980s, when Colonel Muammar al-Gaddafi of Libya attempted to invade Chad, using North Darfur as a launching pad. He failed, but the legacy of arms, militia organization, and the Arab supremacist agenda lived on. After Libya's defeat by Chadian President Hissène Habré, the Arabist forces retreated to Um Jalul in Darfur, where they aligned with Sheikh Musa Hilal—a founder of the *janjaweed*. The militia first organized in the early 1990s, and has been at odds with Darfur's sedentary population at numerous times since then.

In February 2003, when SLA and JEM forces rebelled, the Sudanese government employed the *janjaweed* as its main counter-insurgency force in Darfur. Khartoum supplied the militias with unprecedented amounts of firearms, vehicles, uniforms, and logistical support—including aerial bombings of villages.

Janjaweed attacks followed a similar pattern of destruction to *murahaleen* raids in the South. Mounted *janjaweed* commandoes burn villages; they kill and mutilate the inhabitants, often raping the women; they steal livestock and torch fields; wells, schools, clinics, and mosques are methodically destroyed.

The *janjaweed* have the benefit of aerial support, artillery, military advisors, thousands of newly-recruited tribal fighters, and camps established throughout Darfur—some shared with government forces, and include helicopter pads, satellite phones, and government vehicles. They were allowed to act with impunity by the Sudanese government, and often attacked following aerial bombardment by the Sudanese Air Force.

Janjaweed raids have displaced millions of Darfuris, and the militiamen are actively involved in obstructing humanitarian aid. *Janjaweed* raids have even been known to occur within the boundaries of refugee and IDP camps. All told, an estimated 400,000 Darfuris have been killed during the conflict, largely from *janjaweed*-related violence.

V. SLAVERY IN SUDAN

Slavery as a practice has been endemic to Sudan and the surrounding area for many hundreds of years. Under the Turko-Egyptian and Mahdist rule of the 19th century, slavery was a lucrative enterprise, with non-Muslim inhabitants of Southern Sudan being targets for slave raids by Turko-Egyptian and northern Sudanese raiders, who would either hold export them to Egypt and other Arab states by the thousands. Slavery was officially abolished in 1924 by a series of laws put in place by the Anglo-Egyptian Condominium, yet the practice persisted. While small-scale intertribal abduction (in response to local conflicts) remained common, Sudan's second civil war, which began in 1983, brought with it the resurgence of organized kidnapping and human trafficking.

The slave trade during the North-South conflict was a byproduct of the Sudanese government's militia-based military strategy. As an incentive for their military service, *murahaleen* were allowed to take women and children as spoils of their raids on southern villages. The trade played off of ethnic tensions that had existed for centuries. Many northerners referred to South Sudanese as *abeed* (slaves) and historical ideologies of dominance were used in order to portray the South as a resource for the North. Many of the raiders came from the Rizeigat and Miseriya people, both groups belonging to the larger Baggara population, a cattle-herding Arabic-speaking population found in the Kordofan and Darfur regions.

Under the banner of the government-sponsored Popular Defense Force, paramilitary *murahaleen* killed, raped, and abducted women and children throughout the Bahr al-Ghazal region. Abductees were sent North as spoils of war along with other stolen goods and cattle.

In 1996, while continuing to deny the existence of slavery, Khartoum set up an investigation into the allegations, the results of which blamed abductions on "tribal conflicts." In 1999, Khartoum admitted that "abductions" had taken place during the civil war, eschewing the term "slavery," which the UN considers a crime against humanity.

The number of slaves taken has proven impossible to ascertain due to population migration, and the lack of systematic field-based research. While some villages kept records of those killed or abducted, the constant state of conflict has made estimating on a national level difficult. Several reports offer varying sketches of slavery's scope. Experts John Ryle and Jok Madut Jok documented over 11,000 abductions from 1983–2002. Meanwhile, the Dinka Chiefs Committee (DCC) estimated that 14,000 people had been abducted; UNICEF said between 10,000 and 17,000; and the Christian Solidarity International estimated the number to be over 100,000.

What is known is that the primary targets of slave raids have been Dinka, but Nuer and Nuba populations of Bahr al-Ghazal have been targeted as well. Abductees are used as cooks, maids, concubines, forced wives, and farm laborers. There have even been reports of abductees being branded with the names of their owners. Young boys have been forcibly recruited into militias, where they are sometimes forced to fight against their own people. Teenage males have been forcibly castrated and a number of females, sexually mutilated.

While the rampant abductions of the '90s have abated, human trafficking continues to be a prominent issue within Sudan. Much of the focus has shifted toward finding, transferring, and integrating abductees back to the South. Initially, retrieval and release of abducted people was accomplished informally through payments by the family, but in the 1990s, a variety of organizations began addressing the issue. In 2002, Christian Solidarity International claimed to have bought 65,000–70,000 people their freedom back. Yet buy-backs remain controversial. There is also the risk of creating a monetary incentive for slave traders, and of fraudulent slave sales. Some families have even complained that outside interference drives up the cost of buy-backs. Overall, buying back captured people funnels money back into the militias, making it a short-term solution at best.

VI. SEXUAL VIOLENCE

The Sudanese government has been known to encourage militia forces to rape and impregnate women in conflict areas—particularly in Darfur, the Nuba Mountains, and South-

ern Sudan. Rape is accepted as one of the spoils of war for soldiers, and violence against women is considered a weapon of war. Rape has wide-ranging consequences. It accelerates social breakdown through displacement and the weakening of ethnic lines.

The International Commission of Inquiry on Darfur—established in 2004 by UN Secretary-General Kofi Annan in part to investigate human rights abuses in Darfur—revealed that government-sponsored forces have used sexual violence as a "deliberate strategy with a view to achieve certain objectives, including terrorizing the population, ensuring control over the movement of the IDP population, and perpetuating its displacement."

Organizations such as Human Rights Watch and Médecins sans Frontieres have documented numerous instances of rape involving women and young girls, perpetrated by government soldiers and *janjaweed* militia. While a large number of these assaults occur during attacks on villages, women residing in internally displaced persons camps in Sudan and other areas affected by war continue to live with the constant threat of sexual violence.

RAPE AND SEXUAL VIOLENCE IN THE CAMPS

Numerous women and girls residing in displacement camps have been victims of rape and sexual violence. A majority of reported attacks occur when women leave the camp to collect firewood or water, or make trips to the market. These tasks are traditionally the responsibility of women, and thus it often falls upon them to travel along dangerous rural roads to neighboring towns. The risk is compounded in camps where women outnumber men, thus increasing the responsibility placed upon them to provide for their families.

Even in Chadian refugee camps, women and girls have reported assaults by both civilians and militia members from across the border. As a result, many refugees have been moved to camps farther from the border. Still, instances of rape persist. Women have been detained by Chadian officials for collecting wood outside of the camps, only to be raped by other inmates.

On both sides of the border, women inside of the camps may also find themselves coerced into sexual service in exchange for the protection of male officers. Finally, evidence suggests that rape and sexual violence—including domestic violence—is dramatically underreported, and may even be on the rise.

OTHER ISSUES

Punishing the men who commit violence against women, specifically rape, is difficult for a number of reasons. First, because a woman who has been raped is usually perceived as being unpure, or "damaged," there is a stigma against discussing rape, and a good chance that the woman's family will not be support-ive. Being raped can be grounds for terminating a marriage engagement, which may result in a woman living alone and thus being at greater risk of further violence. In cases where a woman does come forward, authorities have a his-tory of denying the allegations and intimidating the victims and witnesses into withdrawing the charges. Further, under Islamic law, rape has become virtually impossible for a woman to prove. In most cases, guilt can only be proven by a male witness. Moreover, if a woman is pregnant and cannot prove that she was raped, she can be punished by *sharia* law for having sexual intercourse outside of marriage.

The violence is not limited to the government and militia side, however. In a phenomenon Sudan scholar Jok Madut Jok calls, "nationalization of the womb," SPLA officers and rebel supporters encourage women to make them-selves more sexually available in order to support the war in a reproductive role. In practice, this gives men sexual rights to women, and often results in rape.

VII. FUELING THE WAR MACHINE

The government in Khartoum maintains its decades-long campaigns in Darfur and South Sudan by maneuvering carefully through the international community. Using oil and in-telligence about terrorist figures as leverage, it is able to fund its wars and leverage inter-national authorities into staying out of the way.

OIL

Throughout the relatively peaceful 1970s, Sudan attempted to cultivate its oil business interests with the United States. Chevron was first granted access to Sudan in 1974, and by 1978 had discovered reserves in Southern Sudan, a region declared autonomous under the Addis Ababa Agreement six years earlier. When Sudan tumbled back into civil turmoil and U.S. companies sold their Sudanese oil rights in 1992, other Western oil interests took up where they left off. In the 1990s, Canadian Arakis Energy Corporation began operations in Sudan's oil fields, but the company was eventually acquired by Talisman Energy, Inc.

In 1998, oil revenues made up none of Sudan's total annual revenue. By 2001, they accounted for nearly 42 percent, 60 percent of which was then fun-neled into the purchasing of military equipment. That year, Talisman Energy Inc. was paying nearly $1 million per day to the Sudanese government in royal-ties, roughly the same amount that the Washington Office on Africa estimated

Khartoum spent on military systems. A 2000 report by Canadian advisor John Harker, which concluded that oil operations were funding and prolonging the Sudanese conflict, along with pressure from religious and human rights organizations, led the company to abandon its projects in 2003.

India's national oil company bought the stake in the Greater Nile Oil Petroleum Operating Company (an international joint venture dominating Sudan's oil production) that Talisman Energy had left behind. In 2002, Russia signed a $200 million deal to develop new Sudanese oil fields, part of a larger agreement that grants oil concessions in exchange for the right to manufacture Russian military equipment for Sudanese use. Yet no emerging economy plays a greater role in modern Sudan than China.

China's industrial growth has led them to look for sources of energy in countries where wary Western companies play smaller roles. China National Petroleum Corporation now owns the largest single share in the Greater Nile Oil Petroleum Operating Company (40 percent), and has invested extensively in Sudan's petroleum infrastructure, building a 1,500-km pipeline to the Red Sea, where Chinese tankers await in the Port of Sudan. As much as eighty percent of Sudan's oil production is purchased by China. In exchange, China is Sudan's largest supplier of arms, arming them with tanks, fighter planes, rocket-propelled grenades, bombers, and small arms.

Foreign relations built on the oil trade mean that multilateral international pressure on Khartoum is difficult to accomplish. In recent years, western powers have been increasingly vocal in their condemnation of regional conflicts. Efforts to send UN peacekeeping forces, however, have been repeatedly hindered by Khartoum. Meanwhile, Chinese President Hu Jintao has declared that, "Any solution [in Darfur] needs to respect the sovereignty of Sudan and be based on dialogue." China has also threatened to use its veto power in the UN Security Council to block economic sanctions supported by the United States and other Western states.

THE WAR ON TERROR

Relations between the U.S. and the Sudanese government deteriorated in the 1990s, with Washington removing its staff from its embassy in Khartoum. In 1992, the U.S. declaring Sudan to be a state sponsor of terrorism, and barred further economic activity between the two countries. In 1999, U.S. Secretary of State Madeleine Albright met with rebel leader John Garang in order to discuss humanitarian aid for the SPLA.

However, after the September 11 attacks of 2001, relations entered a new and controversial chapter in which Khartoum and Washington cooperated and coordinated intelligence in the ongoing "War on Terrorism." The Bush administration approached the Sudanese government in hopes of improving relations as early as July 2001, and later arranged secret meetings in England and Kenya to discuss intelligence cooperation. By November, the CIA was actively participating in Khartoum, running surveillance, with the assistance of Mukhabarat, the Sudanese equivalent to the CIA. Sudan had access to information regarding Osama bin Laden's five years of residency in Sudan and shared them with the U.S. intelligence. Working with Mukhabarat gave the U.S. access to organizations in the region that they had been previously unable to penetrate. Cooperation through the sharing of intelligence was also considered to be a practical means of keeping relations afloat when political dialogue was all but non-existent.

Yet Khartoum's record makes it a tenuous ally. Aside from their involvement in atrocities currently taking place within Sudan, a good deal of their intelligence stems from the fact that officials currently heading the government were heavily involved with terrorist organizations throughout the '90s. Involvement in organizations ranging from the Lord's Resistance Army, to Hamas, to the Eritrean Islamic Jihad, to al Qaeda indicate that many of Khartoum's officials have supported destabilizing agents in and outside of the region. Furthermore, the U.S. government has repeatedly acknowledged that Sudan's policies and involvement in international terrorism constituted "an extraordinary threat to the national security and foreign policy" of the United States.

In return for its cooperation, Sudan has requested it be removed from the list of states sponsoring terrorism, and a lifting of economic sanctions. Both governments find themselves straddling a fine line. A number of organizations have characterized the Bush administration's reaction to the Darfur situation as a study in prolonged foot-dragging and wonder if the conflict of political and humanitarian interests has not stalled progress in applying pressure. On the other side, Bashir's government has been accused by hardliners of peddling to Western forces. In October 2007, bin Laden called for a *jihad* against Darfur peacekeepers along with the country that granted them access.

VIII. POLICE AND SECURITY FORCES IN SUDAN AND EGYPT

Khartoum has long used police and secret service forces to retain power and exert force over oppositional regions and populations within Sudan. Refugees settling in Egypt have found treatment by that country's security forces to be hauntingly familiar.

IN KHARTOUM

In Sudan's capital, police are used to intimidate religious organizations, and suppress political expression. Censorship, harassment, torture, and detention are not uncommon. For example, in 2001, police tear-gassed students and forced their way into All Saints' Episcopal Church, where a protest was being held in response to the arrest of Christian demonstrators the day before. Three people were seriously injured and fifty-seven detained and held a one-hour trial the next day, with no legal representation for the defendants. Several boys and girls were flogged and the rest of the male detainees received a sentence of twenty days in jail.

Then there is the systematic destruction and relocation of internally displaced persons living in camps around the city. For years, Khartoum has bulldozed thousands of homes in IDP camps and carted people to destinations far from the city center, sometimes resulting in violent clashes between police and residents.

IN DARFUR

In 2004, one year after a sharp increase of violence in Darfur, the government of Sudan sent over a contingent of 10,000 police officers in order to establish security in the region. In August of that year, a UN humanitarian situation report noted a growing problems of sexual abuse and exploitation of women by the officers. Women were especially vulnerable while venturing outside of the IDP camps to gather firewood and other supplies.

In the four years since, conditions have failed to improve. The poorly equipped officers, along with joint African Union and United Nations forces, have been able to exert some control over the region. Yet, this has not necessarily meant protection or safety for the communities under their supervision. Reports have also surfaced of brutality perpetrated against humanitarian aid workers by police officers. After repeated incidents of abuse by officers at Kalma, the largest refugee camp in southern Darfur, local police officers were restricted from accessing the compound but have been supplanted by other violent groups. In other cases, some officers who choose not to participate in criminal activity still turn a blind eye, to *janjaweed* raids.

IN EGYPT

Sudanese refugees who have fled to Egypt may have escaped their conflicts with Khartoum, but still face the terrors of police brutality. When current president Hosni Mubarak came to power in 1981, following the assassination of President Anwar el-Sadat, he enacted a series of emergency powers allowing the use of police to arrest and detain suspects for indefinite periods of time without charge. Government supporters claim that these privileges are instrumental to protecting the government and controlling the Muslim Brotherhood (a large opposition group accused of involvement in Sadat's assassination) but observers note that these measures are also used as a means of repression and stifling political dialogue.

Poverty and the lack of repercussions fuel crimes perpetrated by police against the citizenry. Egyptian police officers earn $41 per month—half the average Egyptian wage—and can be found in Egypt's tourist areas begging for money, demanding bribes, and taking food. Officers are rarely held accountable for misdeeds and victims who choose to file complaints often find themselves and their families harassed and threatened. Brutal tactics are used on Sudanese refugees, whose protection from the law is minimal. The most famous incident of brutality occurred in 2005 when Egyptian police descended upon protesters outside of UNHCR offices, killing dozens, and detaining hundreds more. For more on these protests and the refugee situation in Cairo, please see page 424.

IX. HUMANITARIANISM

Darfur hosts the world's largest humanitarian relief operation. Meanwhile UNAMID, the ambitious AU/UN hybrid peacekeeping force announced in 2007 remains stalled by a lack of resources.

DARFUR

The humanitarian aid operation in Darfur encompasses approximately 17,100 aid workers from an estimated eighty non-governmental organizations (NGOs) and fourteen UN agencies. In order to address severe access limitations, organizations employ Sudanese nationals, which now account for 95 percent of all aid workers in the region. These workers are attempting to support 2.45 million IDPs and another 1.8 million in need of humanitarian aid, while facing bureaucratic obstacles and being denied access to affected areas. In May 2007, the UN estimated that 566,000 of those affected by the conflict in Darfur were beyond the reach of humanitarian assistance. In early 2008, the UN reported that aid efforts were being severely hampered by increased violence directed at humanitarian agencies, "including hijacking of cars and abduction of personnel, physical violence... road ambushes, destruction of NGO assets and armed break-ins in humanitarian compounds/centres."

UNITED NATIONS/AFRICAN UNION MISSION IN DARFUR (UNAMID)

The international community's major plan for Sudan is the United Nations/ African Union Mission in Darfur, a hybrid operation that began deploying in October 2007 to protect the people of Darfur and enforce the terms of the CPA. However, as of mid-2008, only 9,213 total uniformed personnel of an expected 26,000 have deployed to the region. The force also lacks the necessary equipment to carry out its mandate.

SOUTHERN SUDAN

Aid efforts in Southern Sudan are now more focused on education, infrastructure development, public service, and economic rehabilitation. As refugees from Southern Sudan return to their homes, there is a pronounced need to address the abject poverty that plagues some remote communities. The difficulty lies in the lack of humanitarian presence now in the region. World Emergency Relief has reported a marked decrease in the availability of aid since the signing of the CPA and outbreak of the crisis in Darfur.

CRITIQUES

According to Dr. Barbara Harrell-Bond, author of Imposing Aid, "the objective of any assistance programme is to make refugees 'independent', 'independence' being minimally defined as independent of relief food." By this assessment, the massive aid effort in Western Sudan is so far failing, with up to 4 million refugees in the area still entirely dependent on food aid. Harrell-Bond goes on to assert the need for medical analysis of the aid recipients as an indicator of the success of the effort. In the case of Darfur, such an analysis is difficult as a result of ongoing violence.

Harrell-Bond's remarks carry resonance, particularly in the wake of other similar crises, such as the Rwandan genocide that is still impacting refugees nine years later. She writes, "Imposing aid can never be successful. And if this course is pursued further, humanitarians will only continue to contribute to the breakdown of societies which in turn will call for greater and more terrifying methods of controlling them." For those who grow dependent on aid infrastructure and medical and food support, beginning a life literally from the ground up in the event of a ceasefire is a daunting, if not impossible task. The argument for more sustainable aid that fosters production and development for the displaced cannot be overlooked where such massive numbers are concerned.

APPENDIX B
DISPLACEMENT AND REFUGEEISM

I. DISPLACEMENT IN GLOBAL CONTEXT

At the end of 2007, there were approximately 31.7 million refugees, internally displaced persons (IDPs), asylum-seekers, returnees, and stateless persons under the responsibility of the UN High Commissioner for Refugees (UNHCR). Combined with estimates of persons not under the responsibility of the UNHCR, the worldwide number of refugees and IDPs alone is 67 million.

REFUGEES

The UNHCR abides by the 1951 UN Convention Relating to the Status of Refugees, which defines refugees as: People outside the country of their nationality and who are unable to avail themselves of the protections of that country, owing to fear of persecution for reasons of race, religion, nationality, or membership to a particular political group. The UNHCR is careful to distinguish between refugees, asylum-seekers, and economic migrants. Migrants choose to leave their country of origin in search of better lives. An asylum-seeker claims to be a refugee, but has not had his or her claim evaluated.

UNHCR estimates that the global refugee population under their responsibility was 11.4 million in 2007. Afghan refugees make up the largest portion of that population at 27 percent. Following a repatriation campaign in 2006, the number of Sudanese refugees decreased from 635,000 to 523,000 in 2007. However, this remains the fourth largest refugee population in the world.

FIGURE 1. LARGEST NUMBER OF REFUGEES BY
COUNTRY OF ORIGIN, 2007

Country of Origin	*Number of Refugees and people in refugee-like situations*
Afghanistan	3,057,661
Iraq	2,309,247
Colombia	551,744
Sudan	523,032
Somalia	457,357
Burundi	375,727
Democratic Republic of Congo	370,374

Source: UNHCR 2007 Statistical Yearbook

FIGURE 2. ASYLUM COUNTRIES HOSTING THE MOST REFUGEES, 2007

Country of Asylum	Number of Refugees
Pakistan	2,035,023
Syrian Arabic Republic	1,503,769
Republic of Iran	963,546
Germany	578,879
Jordan	500,281

Source: UNHCR 2007 Statistical Yearbook

INTERNALLY DISPLACED PERSONS (IDPS)

IDPs are people who are forced to leave their homes as a result of violent conflict or violations of human rights, but have not crossed international borders. As a result many IDPs remain vulnerable to violence and severe lack of resources, as they are forced from their homes to more remote areas.

The global number of IDPs displaced by conflict was estimated at 26 million in 2007, according to the Internal Displacement Monitoring Centre. Until recently, no real protocol existed for the protection and aid of IDPs. In December 2005, the UNHCR joined an international "cluster approach," assuming joint responsibility with other international organizations for the support of IDPs. However, the UNHCR remains limited in its abilities, providing direct or indirect aid to approximately 13.8 million IDPs in 2007.

FIGURE 3. COUNTRIES WITH THE HIGHEST ESTIMATED
NUMBERS OF INTERNALLY DISPLACED PERSONS, 2007

Country	Number of IDPs
Sudan	5,800,000
Iraq	2,480,000
Colombia	2,390,000–4,000,000
Democratic Republic of the Congo	1,400,000
Uganda	1,300,000

Source: Internal Displacement Monitoring Center, 2007 Global Overview

II. THE UNHCR

Established in 1950, the office of the United Nations High Commissioner for Refugees (UNHCR) is charged with the worldwide protection of refugees' rights. It is also responsible for seeking one of three durable solutions for refugees: voluntary repatriation, integration into their asylum country, or resettlement into a new country.

HISTORY

The UNHCR began work in earnest on January 1, 1951. The organization's original mandate was for a three-year program with the goal of providing assistance to approximately one million civilians displaced by World War II. However, the refugee cause expanded as worldwide crises created millions of new refugees. A 1967 protocol expanded the scope of UNHCR's responsibilities to include displacement problems around the world. UNHCR has since become the world's largest organization charged with the protection of refugees.

As the refugee crisis grows more complex, the UNHCR has evolved to service a larger population, which includes refugees, internally displaced persons, and stateless persons. It now plays a major role in addressing the international IDP population, who lack an international support agency dedicated to their plight. In 2007, the UNHCR provided aid to 26 million people, in hundreds of refugee camps/centers, and urban locations.

LIMITATIONS

While the UNHCR was established as a neutral, non-political body, its task often makes this impossible. The organization must contend with asylum and origin countries, where refugees are viewed as both causes and products of domestic upheaval. This is especially important considering a prime facet of the UNHCR's limited authority: Governments ultimately remain responsible for the protection of refugees in their countries. The UNHCR can offer protection and services to refugees, but only when granted access by host states.

Resources also limit the UNHCR, especially as its role grows as a general international humanitarian organization. The more it is charged with duties outside of its original mandate, the further it must stretch financial and personnel resources. Moreover, the organization largely depends on donations from a handful of industrialized states. This often reflects an unwillingness on the part of host states to support the UNHCR's activities in their country.

CRITIQUES

The work of the UNHCR is often criticized by analysts and organizations that work with refugees. Gil Loescher, a senior fellow at the International Institute for Strategic Studies in London, points out that UNHCR has historically had a tendency to adopt narrow courses of action, and neglecting alternative solutions. Specifically, he refers to the organization's single-minded policy of repatriation in the 1980s, that resulted in a degradation of local integration and long-term refugee programs.

Dr. Barbara Harrell-Bond, an internationally recognized expert in the field of forced migration studies, criticizes the UNHCR's current system of protecting refugees and IDPs. She contends that the UNHCR is tremendously overextended, noting that their original mandate was to be a refugee protection agency but have now expanded their efforts to oversee IDPs. She questions their emphasis on repatriation, especially in countries still in the throes of violent conflict. Harrell-Bond explains that UNHCR's swelling international concerns creates "contradiction in roles and the temptation has been to become the largest welfare organisation in the world, not the protection agency."

III. THE DARFUR/CHAD CAMPS

As a result of five years of armed conflict between the government of Sudan and rebel groups, approximately 2.45 million people are living in IDP camps in Darfur, and another 240,000 have fled to neighboring Chad. In the first few months of 2008 alone, an estimated 60,000 more people were displaced from Darfur, with 13,500 fleeing to Chad.

DARFUR'S IDP CAMPS

There are at least a hundred IDP camps spread across Darfur, many of which lie along the violent Chad-Sudan border. In some instances, these camps sustain as many as 120,000 IDPs. Numerous camps are located in areas deemed outside the reach of humanitarian assistance, and many groups of IDPs are located far from any official camps. Moreover, IDPs in Darfur are especially vulnerable due to the ongoing conflict around them. Many find themselves consistently exposed to attacks, sexual violence, arbitrary arrests, forced military enrollment, and a lack of food, water, and shelter. Venturing outside of camps is an especially dangerous proposition, yet a lack of resources within camps forces many to seek food and firewood outside of camp boundaries. The Internal Displacement Monitoring Centre lists the Darfur region of Sudan as one of the worst displacement situations in the world.

EASTERN CHAD'S REFUGEE CAMPS

At least 240,000 Darfuris have fled to neighboring Chad, where the internal instability and an ongoing conflict with the government of Sudan produce an almost equally undesirable situation for refugees. Most refugees reside in one of twelve camps set up by UNHCR that house between 13,000 and 30,000 people. Meanwhile, outside of the camps, thousands of refugees are camping in the open near the Sudan-Chad border, awaiting openings in camps. Of the camp residents, UNICEF estimates that 60 percent are children. These factors combine to make for a substantial burden on Chad, which must also accommodate 185,000 IDPs of its own, and 46,000 additional refuges from the Central African Republic. For every 1,000 Chadians, there are 29 refugees, a considerable number considering Chad also possesses one of the lowest gross domestic product (GDPs) per refugee housed.

IV. REFUGEE STATUS DETERMINATION AND RESETTLEMENT

The process of obtaining refugee status can be long and arduous. However, for many it is the only viable option once they have fled their countries of origin. Refugee status is a pathway to more "durable solutions," including resettlement.

REFUGEE STATUS DETERMINATION

The international protections afforded to refugees are only available to those who have confirmed their status with the authorities of their host country. Among the crucial rights guaranteed by refugee status are:

1. *Non-refoulement* is the most basic of refugees' rights, protecting them from being returned to a country where they face the risk of persecution. International law also dictates that asylum-seekers not be *refouled* while awaiting their status determination.

2. Protection against physical violence, particularly due to racism or xenophobia.

3. Unhindered access to courts in the host country.

4. Guarantee of basic physical and material needs. The UNHCR recommends that states allow refugees free access to job markets in order to foster self-reliance.

5. Freedom of movement within the country.

6. Access to adequate education.

7. Reunification with other family members in the asylum country.

Furthermore, refugees are entitled to support in finding more permanent solutions to their situations, including voluntary repatriation, local integration, and resettlement in another country.

There is no standardized process for refugee status determination. UNHCR handles the job in some countries but state governments handle the majority of asylum applications worldwide. In 2007, of 647,200 asylum claims, UNHCR processed 79,800—19,000 of which were submitted at their Kenya offices.

Individual systems for determining refugee status vary from country to country, but it generally comes down to interviews between applicants and adjudicators. In most cases, asylum seekers cannot provide documentary proof of their risk of persecution, so it is between applicant and decision-maker to establish whether or not there is a well-founded fear of persecution. The UNHCR encourages decision-makers to consider inclusion before exclusion, as there can be grave consequences for asylum-seekers who are denied refugee protections.

PRIMA FACIE

In certain situations involving mass inflows of refugees—especially into undeveloped countries ill-equipped to handle large caseloads—the UNHCR or host governments can choose to immediately grant refugee status. This is known as *prima facie* determination. For example, in 2000, with the population of Kakuma refugee camp in Kenya swollen to 65,00 inhabitants, Kenya offered asylum to refugees on a *prima facie* basis.

RESETTLEMENT

A limited number of countries take part in UNHCR resettlement programs. Of the 75,300 refugees resettled in 2007, for example, 49,600 were resettled by UNHCR. Host countries arranged the remaining resettlements. The solution also remains available to an extremely small population. In 2007, less than 1 percent of refugees benefited from resettlement.

FIGURE 1. TOP FOUR COUNTRIES OF RESETTLEMENT FOR
RESETTLED REFUGEES, 2006

Country of Resettlement	*Number of Refugees*
United States of America	41,300

Australia	13,400
Canada	10,700
Sweden	2,400

Source: UNHCR 2006 Statistical Yearbook

FIGURE 2. TOP FOUR COUNTRIES OF ORIGIN FOR RESETTLED REFUGEES, 2006

Country of Origin	*Number of Refugees*
Somalia	11,100
Sudan	6,400
Russian Federation	6,200
Myanmar/Burma	6,000

Source: UNHCR 2006 Statistical Yearbook

FIGURE 3. TOP FOUR COUNTRIES OF RESETTLEMENT FOR REFUGEES ORIGINATING FROM SUDAN, 2006

Country of Resettlement	*Number of Refugees*
Australia	3,663
United States of America	1,848
Canada	692
United Kingdom	63

Source: UNHCR 2006 Statistical Handbook

V. RESETTLEMENT IN THE UNITED STATES

Below are excerpts from a publication released by the United States Committee for Refugees and Immigrants (USCRI), titled "How Refugees Come to America."

II. SEEKING ADMISSION TO THE U.S. RESETTLEMENT PROGRAM

Referral to the U.S. Program

Only refugees who have been referred by the UNHCR or by the U.S. embassy in the country of asylum are eligible for the U.S. Refugee Resettlement Program. Usually refugees with families are referred together as a single group.

Adjudication

Refugees who meet the criteria for application to the U.S. program are interviewed by an INS officer who travels to the country of asylum.

A refugee may receive assistance in preparing his or her resettlement application from a resettlement organization or non-governmental organization contracted by the Department of State for this purpose. The application typically consists of INS form I-590, family tree and biographical information.

The INS officer decides whether the applicant is a refugee as defined under U.S. law. An individual designation as a refugee by UNHCR is not guaranteed admission to the U.S. Refugees must also pass an INS interview.

Approval

If the INS officer approves the refugee's application for U.S. resettlement, he or she will be matched with an American resettlement organization. Most of these nonprofit organizations rely on professional and volunteer staff to assist refugees in the resettlement process.

If rejected, the applicant has thirty days to file a motion to reconsider the denial with the nearest INS district office. Generally, a motion is considered only if it contains new information not available at the original interview.

III. REFUGEE RESETTLEMENT IN THE U.S.

Being Matched with an American Resettlement Organization

Detailed information on all refugees approved for U.S. resettlement is sent to the Refugee Data Center (RDC) in New York. RDC matches refugees with one of ten voluntary agencies that provide reception and placement services for refugees coming to the U.S.

Pre-Travel Activities

In order to insure that a refugee understands that everyone living in America is expected to be self-sufficient and that no refugee should be an undue burden to American society, he or she must complete several additional steps before traveling to the U.S. These activities are undertaken concurrently and can take from 2 months to 2 years to complete.

• Assurance Process

The American resettlement organization must "assure" the Department of State that it is prepared to receive each matched refugee. This "assurance" is a written guarantee that various basic services will be provided to the refugee and any accompanying family members in the initial resettlement phase.

At this time the resettlement organization determines where in the U.S.

the refugee will be resettled. The availability of housing, employment, needed services, readiness of host community and a variety of other factors determine exact placement. However, if a refugee has a relative in the U.S., every effort is made to resettle the refugee near that relative.

Refugees do not have to have U.S. sponsors to be resettled in the U.S.

• Security Clearance

All refugees must undergo a security clearance procedure prior to coming to the U.S. The level of clearance needed depends on the refugee's country of origin. Most refugees submit to a "name check" process whereby the refugee's name is checked against the FBI's database of known terrorists and undesirables and the State Department's database of people who have been denied visas to enter the U.S. in the past.

• Cultural Orientation

All refugees receive some American culture orientation prior to coming to the U.S. Most programs emphasize the importance of self-sufficiency in American culture as well as what to expect in the initial resettlement phase. Most refugees attend classes ranging in length from 3 hours to several days.

First Steps in U.S. Resettlement

The resettlement organization that assured a refugee's case is responsible for assisting the refugee in the initial resettlement phase. Each resettlement organization provides a variety of services to promote early self-sufficiency and cultural adjustment. The following activities take place within the first thirty days of arrival.

• Application for Social Security Number

Most newly arrived refugees desperately want a permanent home. Resettlement organizations work hard to find housing for refugees that is safe, sanitary, of a sufficient size, affordable, and accessible to public transportation. Some U.S. cities and towns offer more housing options than others. Refugees need social security numbers in order to seek employment or enroll in school. All refugees register with the Social Security Administration as soon as possible.

• School Registration

All refugee children are enrolled in school upon arrival in the U.S.

• English Language Training

Refugees often do not speak any English when they arrive. Learning English is an essential step to becoming self-sufficient. Voluntary agencies often provide English as a Second Language (ESL) classes or help refugees find classes offered in their community.

IV. BECOMING A FULL MEMBER OF THE COMMUNITY

Finding Employment
Refugees enter the U.S. with authorization to work. The U.S. government expects a working-age refugee to find a job within six months of arrival. Resettlement organizations often have employment specialists who help refugees with their job search. Many states have a designated agency that receives state funds to help refugees find work. This function is usually coordinated by the State Refugee Coordinator.

Gaining Permanent Residency
Refugees can apply for Permanent Resident Alien (PRA) status—a green card—after they have been in the U.S. for one year.

Becoming a Citizen
Refugees can apply for U.S. citizenship after residing in the U.S. for five years. Many resettlement organizations have citizenship programs that assist and encourage refugees as they go through the naturalization process.

Building a New Life
Refugees spend many years overcoming past trauma, locating family members, adjusting to American culture, building careers, raising families, finding their first dream home, and creating a new life for themselves in the U.S.

VI. WAREHOUSING

Refugees caught in protracted situations—the middle ground between escaping the conflict at home and finding a safe and permanent settlement elsewhere—often fall through the cracks of an international aid system that focuses on emergencies. These refugees can be the hardest to reach through traditional aid efforts: from 1993-2004, while the number of refugees worldwide dropped from 16.3 to 9.2 million, the percentage of refugees in protracted situations rose from 48 to 61 percent. The worst cases, where host states confine refugees in camps, characterized by forced idleness, restricted mobility, and dependency, are known as "warehousing."

While a camp stay is meant to be temporary, settlements built quickly are often ill-equipped to become communities for their inhabitants. If temporary stays become lengthy, as they often do, camps designed with transitory migrants in mind prevent refugees from establishing stable lives in a new country. Due to the laws and security concerns of the host country, some "warehoused" inhabitants may be prevented from traveling or working; the food and health care supply in the camps is often insufficient to combat hunger or disease; overcrowding, despondency, and violence set in. Some families have stayed in camps for generations.

For obvious reasons, politicians and lawmakers do not defend prolonged encampment, but very few have made explicit efforts to end or improve it. Prolonged refugee situations are usually approached with a focus on one of three "durable" solutions: voluntary repatriation, resettlement, or permanent local integration. What occurs before these solutions can be achieved, but after the refugee population is no longer in an immediate emergency, is often neglected. As pointed out succinctly in the U.S. Committee for Refugees 2004 *World Refugee Survey*, "the key feature of warehousing is not so much the passage of time as the denial of rights." The 1951 UN Refugee Convention, which codified the term "refugee" and enumerated refugees' legal rights, listed freedom of movement, freedom to wage-earning employment, rights to travel documents and public education, alongside others that remain absent in today's camps. Even the most fundamental refugee right, *non-refoulement*—the protection against forcible expulsion to lands where one would face danger or persecution—has been threatened indirectly by camp restrictions on refugee economic activity and violence, which encourage some refugees to attempt a dangerous return to their home countries.

Warehouse camps are often cut off not only geographically, but from the legal and judicial systems of their host countries as well. Sudanese women in Uganda's Achol-Pii camp have reported that rape by Ugandan soldiers, rebels, locals, and other refugees is common; domestic violence is worse in the camps in Kakuma, Kenya than in the regions of Southern Sudan from where most of the camp's refugees originate. Camps have served as safe havens for rebels, and some become points of contact for gun and drug smuggling, human trafficking, and illegal logging.

Additionally, there is often an economic incentive for host countries to create warehousing camps and keep them running. The interests of governments of host nations as well as international aid groups are met by confining the refugee population. Host populations are often threatened by the UN Refugee Convention's approach favoring refugee integration into local communities, and so attempt to obstruct the implementation of aid packages that give refugees the ability to compete in local economies. Meanwhile, international aid models popular in the 1980s and 1990s viewed the undeveloped world as passive aid recipients ripe for modernization. Host governments received aid funding to improve local and national infrastructure (bridges, dams, roads, etc) in exchange for the creation of asylum settlements. The World Bank, UN Development Programme, and other development agencies agreed to segregate these refugee settlements in order to implement their own development plans without opposition from local governments and unrest on the ground. Often, the existence of camps has been maintained by government ministries and offices created with the specific purpose of attracting funds earmarked for refugee relief—requiring, of course, large numbers of refugees with a need for aid.

VII. POST-TRAUMATIC STRESS DISORDER

The populations of war-torn southern Sudan and Darfur are especially vulnerable to post-traumatic stress disorder. PTSD can exhibit itself through reclusive behavior and crippling recollections of traumatic events.

PTSD IN REFUGEE COMMUNITIES

Post-traumatic stress disorder is an anxiety disorder that results from exposure to violent or distressing events. Witnesses to violent conflicts, sexual abuse, combat, or natural disasters can exhibit symptoms ranging from social anxiety and hyperarousal, to crippling recollections of traumatizing events.

While many refugees fleeing conflict-plagued areas adjust well to their surroundings, a significant portion remain crippled by exposure to violence perpetrated against themselves or family members in their home countries. Furthermore, those who arrive as refugees without having witnessed traumatic incidents are not in the clear. Refugee populations are vulnerable to violent acts, even within the boundaries of their camps. Moreover, the stresses of exile—from the journey, to the difficulties associated with resettlement—can be equally psychologically damaging.

Experts disagree on the accuracy of studies on the occurrence of PTSD in refugee settlements. Varying methodologies make it difficult to draw quantitative conclusions. Bearing that in mind, a 2004 study published in the journal *African Health Sciences* reported the population prevalence of PTSD among Sudanese refugees in Uganda at 46 percent, while 48 percent of Sudanese nationals living in conflict areas exhibited PTSD symptoms.

OBSTACLES TO TREATMENT

The rapid growth of the refugee population in recent decades has posed a challenge for the study and treatment of psychological problems among this community. Relief workers and doctors disagree on the best method of treatment for mental health issues among refugee communities. Traditional treatments often revolve around therapeutic discussion, which can be hindered by language barriers. Champions of preventative or protective measures argue that surrounding refugees with family, educational opportunities, and nurturing environments can reduce the incidence of PTSD. Most importantly, measures must be taken to improve security in refugee camps and reduce the populations' vulnerability to violent acts.

VIII. THE KHARTOUM CAMPS

There are more than six million internally displaced persons (IDPs) in Sudan; approximately two million live in or around the capital of Khartoum. The area surrounding Khartoum is dotted with four IDP camps, and numerous peripheral statements. Exact camp populations are difficult to determine, but some estimates range between 100,000 and 200,000 at the major camps (Omdurman El Salaam, Wad El Bashir, Mayo Farm, Jebel Aulia).

LIVING CONDITIONS

Since the signing of the Comprehensive Peace Agreement in 2005, various community-based organizations have reported a decrease in the number of NGOs aiding IDPs in and around Khartoum, as well as in the availability of health and aid services. Further exacerbating the situation is Khartoum's restriction of humanitarian access to IDP camps.

As a result, basic needs are not being met. Sanitation is an issue, as is the lack of access to healthcare and job opportunities. IDPs living in squatter camps far from the city center find it impossible to commute to jobs. The number of children suffering from malnutrition in one camp was eleven times higher than the average malnutrition rate in Khartoum in 2006. Moreover, the main causes of death in the camps are preventable and treatable ailments, including malaria, diarrheal diseases, and pneumonia.

Some estimates of the size of Khartoum's IDP population have decreased as a result of surveys that suggest that a large number of camp residents have effectively become permanent residents of the city. However, many of those people are still living as displaced persons, enduring joblessness and struggling to survive. In other words, the situation for IDPs living in and around Khartoum remains dire.

DESTRUCTION OF IDP CAMPS

One of the most devastating Khartoum's IDPs has been the government's destruction of squatter camps. As part of a campaign to both discourage squatters and reclaim land for the city, city agencies have forcefully relocated hundreds of thousands of IDPs to desert camps far from the city. This practice has been in place since Khartoum began absorbing large numbers of IDPs in the 1980s. "Re-planning" efforts entail the unannounced demolition of thousands of homes and aid facilities, and the allocation of new government-assigned plots. However, Khartoum's government routinely underestimates the number of IDPs living in camps, as well as the effect that demolitions will have. Squatters are forced to choose between finding another place to squat, attempt to rebuild their home, or purchase a government-designated "plot" at an alternative site.

A particularly jarring example of forced relocation occurred in May, 2005, when a group of soldiers and police arrived at Soba Aradi squatter camp to relocate residents. An argument ensued and escalated into violence, resulting in the death of at least eighteen inhabitants, and fourteen police officers.

IX. INTERVIEW EXCERPT: OWNING A PIECE OF LAND

As the oil economy has led to a booming expansion of the capital city of Khartoum, the Government of Sudan has forcibly displaced hundreds of thousands of citizens from settlements throughout the city. The evictees are not compensated for their loss. Below is an edited excerpt from an interview conducted with a Southern Sudanese woman named Jacquline, whose house was destroyed in one of these incidents, in a neighborhood called Jahiz. She was removed to Al-Fatah III camp, an internally displaced persons (IDP) camp in the desert northwest of Khartoum. She now resides there along with tens of thousands of others. The interview was conducted through a translator in Khartoum in August 2007.

When I moved to Jahiz in 2003 there was no one there. Everybody just came there and took a place. Most were from South Sudan and from Darfur. Some of us lived there for years. Then there was a private developer, one of the richest people in Sudan, who bought the land from the government.

One morning in 2006 they came in with bulldozers. They surrounded the area, and they told everyone to get out. They told us, "We want to break down this area, and you people should go." They told us, "This place does not belong to you, and you must leave." Some people refused to leave their houses, and the bulldozers would just come and break everything inside the house. Crush everything. Some people started fighting the soldiers, and that's how they got killed. About thirteen people died, and some of them were children. The children's parents were fighting with the soldiers, and so the soldiers just sprayed them all with bullets. I saw this but I couldn't do anything. I couldn't even hide.

They broke down houses and left, but people built on top of the rubble.

They started making tents around the camp. So the soldiers brought cars in, and they would forcefully go into someone's house, start taking all the dishes and put them in a truck. Then they would say, "Look, if you want your stuff, you have to come with us, because we're going to move you to Fatah Camp."

For about a week or so they kept moving people by truck. I started taking apart my house, keeping the sheets of plastic and strong sticks. We were driven to Fatah outside of the city. We were in a big truck crowded with everything, even goats. It was just in a big desert. It's the middle of nowhere. People were hungry.

The first thing I did was just look for a piece of land that we could build on. Just a couple days after I got there it started raining. We had no place to go, so I just covered myself with plastic.

Finally, I paid some workers and we started to make a mud brick house for me. I am still in Fatah. The difference is I now have an official piece of paper that says I own this land.

X. CAIRO, REFUGEE CAPITAL

Located at the geographic nexus of three continents, Egypt is a transit country for hundreds of thousands of refugees and forced migrants fleeing persecution, war, and disaster in their home countries. The destination is usually Cairo, which plays host to refugees from more than thirty countries. The majority are from Sudan, Palestine, and, most recently, Iraq, but there are also large numbers of refugees from Somalia, Ethiopia, Eritrea, Sierra Leone, Rwanda, and other areas of North, Central, and West Africa.

Since the late 1990s the number of refugees in Egypt has grown considerably, as the displaced victims of Africa's conflicts arrive by foot, ferry, plane, truck, train, camel, and horseback. The border is open and entry is relatively easy; however, Egyptian hospitality toward refugees ends there. The life of a refugee or asylum-seeker in Egypt is anything but easy. There are no refugee camps, Egyptian culture is often hostile and racist toward the displaced foreigners, and there is little support or assistance for them in vast urban areas like Cairo, where it is difficult for aid organizations to identify and help refugees. Most refugees are unable to work legally and face unbearable living conditions. They live in constant fear of identity checks, arbitrary detention, and deportation, as well as brutal violence by police and civilians, and sexual harassment of women.

The question of who is responsible for the welfare of Cairo's refugees has always been a murky issue. The Egyptian government ultimately has the legal responsibility: Egypt is party to the 1951 Refugee Convention guaranteeing refugees' rights to asylum, work, personal status, and access to public services. But instead of implementing these mandates with legislation, the Egyptian government generally ignores refugees. They have handed over most refugee responsibilities to the United Nations High Commissioner for Refugees (UNHCR).

The actual number of refugees in Cairo is unknown. An accurate figure is impossible, since a huge portion of Cairo's displaced people are unregistered, undocumented, or not officially recognized as refugees. Officially, there are more than 30,000 Sudanese, 70,000 Palestinian, and 150,000 Iraqi refugees in and around the city. However, high-end estimates of the unregistered Sudanese refugee population in Egypt number in the hundreds of thousands, and some claim the number is over one million.

Obtaining the much-sought-after UNHCR "blue card" of official refugee status is incredibly slow and difficult. In a process called refugee status determination, asylum seekers are interviewed to assess whether the violence they suffered in their home countries constitutes a "fear of persecution" extreme enough to make return too dangerous.

Refugee status determination is administered—slowly and without much success—by the UNHCR. Cairo's displaced people wait daily at UNHCR's offices, filing form after form in the hope that they will someday be granted an actual interview, but many wait months or years. During the interviews, UNHCR listens for any sign of inconsistency or falsehood in a refugee's story of the violence and persecution they endured. A refugee can be denied status on any grounds, but the UNHCR does not provide reasons for rejection beyond the tag LOC, Lack of Credibility. Negative decisions can be appealed, but there is no independent body for review other than the UNHCR. A "closed file" indicates the unfortunate conclusion to this process, when a refugee has not only been denied status, but has been informed that any further appeal will be rejected. These unregistered refugees are trapped in Cairo—they receive no protection or human rights, and yet are often unable to leave, for many practical reasons and for their own valid fears of persecution upon return to their home country.

In 2004 the issue became more dire for Cairo's Sudanese refugees. In May, the UNHCR suspended refugee status determination procedures. Until then, recognized refugees from Sudan could hope to be resettled by UNHCR to countries where their rights would be respected. But with this change in policy, Sudanese were only granted the temporary protection of "yellow cards," indicating they were asylum-seekers and not candidates for resettlement. The decision was based on the improving situation in South Sudan, which signed a Comprehensive Peace Agreement with the central government of Sudan in 2005. For unregistered and unrecognized Sudanese refugees in Cairo, this decision meant that they would be forced to either repatriate to Sudan, trusting this untested new truce, or continue their difficult limbo existence in Egypt.

The result of these circumstances is that the majority of Cairo's refugees face unbearable living conditions. They squat in derelict shantytowns with little access to clean water, electricity, or sanitation. Diseases are endemic, and children often suffer from open sores and scabies. Work permits are nearly impossible to obtain, even for registered refugees, due to more labyrinthine process requirements put in place by the Egyptian government. Most are therefore pushed to find work on the black market. Refugees are given no rights to public education or access to health services. Most rely on humanitarian aid for basic health, education, and welfare stipends.

MUSTAFA MAHMOUD PROTESTS

Facing these serious difficulties and left with few alternatives, in September 2005, Sudanese refugees in Cairo began a peaceful sit-in to protest the unfair treatment they were receiving. The protest began with several dozen participants outside Mustafa Mahmoud Park, across from the UNHCR's offices. That number grew quickly, and throughout the protest, an average of approximately 1,500–2,000 protesters were present. Some estimate that as many as 4,000 people were in the park at the end of December. Most had heard of the protest by word of mouth and arrived spontaneously.

Throughout October, November, and December, Egyptian authorities and UNHCR officials met with protest representatives to attempt peaceable resolution. An agreement was purportedly reached between the UNHCR and the demonstration leaders on December 17, yet most people refused to leave the park until refugee status determinations were resumed and completed.

Late in the evening of December 29, 2005, police began gathering around the park, telling protesters that they were there to protect them from members of the Muslim Brotherhood. Shortly after one a.m., 4,000 Egyptian security forces gathered around the park and announced that they would be bringing protesters to safe camps and forceably removing those who resisted. An hour later, after blasting park residents with water cannons, police entered the park from all sides and began indiscriminately beating and detaining protesters.

Estimates of the number of casualties vary between twenty and fifty dead. Thousands more were removed or detained, and for the next month, rumors of deportations persisted. Neither UNHCR nor the Egyptian government claimed responsibility for the events of December 30, and many report that conditions have not improved for refugees and asylum-seekers in Cairo since the protest and the ensuing disaster.

XI. THE GANGS OF CAIRO: RULE MAKING AND RULE BREAKING IN FRAGMENTED SOCIETIES

The following was written by Jacob Rothing, a researcher at the American University in Cairo.

> "No, I was not part of the violence; I only used to enjoy the Gang Rebel. It is a style; many enjoy the Gang Rebel, even ladies. It is a way of enjoying life with ladies. You look for a group and you dress up with nice clothes, like the American people are wearing. You want to be good, so people can see you in the street and say ... hey, nice!"

There are many Sudanese groups who "enjoy the Gang Rebel" in Cairo: Black Boy Brothers, KK, Cashmoney, P2K, Big Twelve, Junit, All Stars, Jewnet, and Steel Dog are only some of them. They are comprised of young men who shared a neighborhood in Khartoum or met each other at work or school in Cairo. The boys try to protect each other from Egyptian or Sudanese harassment and share economic burdens, substituting for the extended family of their past. They love western rap artists: the way they walk, the way they talk. But perhaps more than anything, they love to hang out together, "dance dirty" with the girls and party.

There are hundreds of all-male refugee households and dozens of groups, but only two have developed into gangs which are associated with violence: the Lost Boys and the Outlaws.

LIVING A HEALTHY LIFE?

The Lost Boys and the Outlaws have evolved into the largest youth gangs in Cairo with a capacity to persist independently of their leaders. Most of the members are 18–22 years old, but children as young as twelve who mimic gang elders have been targeted and injured on several occasions, perhaps because they do not take part in the elders' early warning mechanisms. Men in their late 20s are also active in the groups, and they look after the gang "children" like a father looks after his son.

There are no economic incentives for joining the Outlaws or the Lost Boys. Contrary to what many believe, the members become poorer when they join the gang, mostly because they have new expenses like bribes and hospital bills. They also lose income: it is difficult to hold on to a job when living the gang lifestyle. The absence of economic incentives is a decisive factor in how gang dynamics gets distorted and helps indicate how an intervention aiming to minimize group violence can be designed.

> "*The purpose of forming the group is to keep the youth together, to help each other, to give each other support so they do not drift away in this harsh environment. We formed the group to live our lives as young people, and not make trouble (...) So far I would say that the program is going well; they are still united. The purpose of the Outlaws is to make the youth think about their future; live a healthy life while they are in Egypt. {And} the activities are still going on. We still organize picnics, Nile cruises.*"

The Outlaws have an ambitious agenda that involves more than just fighting. They organize activities and have a formal structure with clear expectations for both leaders and other members. Among the key positions are the president, vice president, area managers, and those responsible for finance, logistics (i.e., purchase and storage of knives and sticks) and public relations. Rappers, DJs and comedians also have a high status. Despite their pretentious discourse, Outlaws' actions demonstrate a level of self-denial. The increased militarization has brought the fighters to the forefront of the group, meaning that the Outlaws is not a social organization anymore.

The Lost Boys does not exist as a group beyond collective violence, and they do not have formal rules or a formal structure governing in-group relations. Many youth prefer the looseness of the Lost Boys' organization, which enables them to recruit emerging party-elites, church leaders and drunken troublemakers alike.

Both groups represent a social organization encompassing many tribes and reflect innovation. The hip-hop image is the most visible component of this innovation but it is better seen as a reaction to failing traditional structures amongst diasporas in an urban setting.

While integration poses great challenges both for refugees and host communities, one segment is particularly visible: groups of young men associated with violent behavior. The big question thus becomes why these two gangs are trapped in cycles of violence. Why do they fight?

THE MAN WHO LOVED A GIRL FROM JUBA

Dispute resolution, which is managed by the extended family or tribe, is more difficult in a refugee setting. Families are fragmented. Nonetheless, the tribes live together in the city. They share urban space and a need to obey common rules in order to manage erupting conflicts. This is not the case among Southern Sudanese in Cairo, where tribes and parties are split and rivalries flourish. Settling disputes related to money lending, pregnancies and marriages is instead partially outsourced to youth groups like the Lost Boys and the Outlaws. But the youth are not ready for it.

"There are three distinct provinces in southern Sudan which have been up-graded to states: Wau, Malakal and Juba. Seliim is from the Wau province, the Balanda people. He started the problem when he loved a girl from Juba. She is from the Baria tribe. A person from Juba cannot marry a person from Wau, at least not without the consent of her family. But the girl became pregnant, and without her family's consent. This is when it all began, when she got pregnant. He broke the law. In the Wau tradition, when you get a girl pregnant, it means that you are fighting her family."

The role of pregnancies cannot be overstated when it comes to how tribal and gang–issues get intertwined. Some of the boys violate the code and others try to uphold it by forcing the man to either pay compensation or marry the girl. According to the code, the extended family has the right to use force to achieve this, and the person who caused the pregnancy has no right to retaliate. In other words, the wrong-doer cannot retaliate against the law-abiding party.

But when enforcement is outsourced to multi-tribal gangs without legitimacy in the eyes of the attacked party, that party will retaliate and violence can escalate. Seliim, who is referred to in the quote above, could not tolerate being beaten by Kerim, the girl's self-appointed protector, and decided to round up his allies and seek vengeance.

This type of family or local conflict, which was once managed, has a lot to do with why the Lost Boys and the Outlaws, who were once friends, today kill each other.

WHEN THE UMPIRE BREAKS THE RULES

"We decided that we had to arrest Tango ourselves. We agreed through a lawyer called Hesham with State Security. We knew the lawyer through William's father who works at the {Sudanese} embassy (...) {So} we waited for them at the Wekalat Al Balah market when Lost Boys came back from church. A big fight broke out, but then the Egyptian traders and thugs got involved and started to fight with Sudanese, including Maher (a fourteen-year-old who had nothing to do with the groups). When the police came, they broke up the fight and took Belingo, Tango and Maher first to the hospital and then to the police station. William and four more Outlaws were also detained."

This case is typical of the relationship between the gangs and the police. Tango, a Lost Boys leader, was suspected of a murder, and the police did little or nothing to arrest him and put him on trial. So Outlaws decided to arrest him and hand him over to the Egyptian authorities. However, during their "arrest operation," they were surprised by the Egyptian traders, who got invovlved and injured a young Sudanese boy. When the police finally intervened, they arrested and later deported those Outlaws members who had made a pact with State Security. Furthermore, they arrested and deported Tango, the presumed murderer, not for murder but for injuring the Sudanese boy, Mahem, a crime which was in fact committed by someone else.

The Cairene police, in their arbitrariness, fail to provide clear rules for Sudanese boys in Cairo. Fighting is not necessarily punished, and obedient, lawful behavior is not necessarily rewarded. Apart from exceptional cases, the police do not act against an aggressor unless someone pays them to do so. Instead, they arrest people arbitrarily and take bribes to release them. If we look at the mass arrests of Sudanese carried out by the police in two Cairo neighborhoods in early October 2006, only two out of more than 160 detainees were gang members. This is despite the fact that the problems began with gang violence.

LOYALTY—FOR GOOD AND FOR BAD

Outlaws and Lost Boys live by one essential rule: You lose the protection of other group members if you do not participate in a raid in which you are expected to take part. This rule has strong implications: Given that the Outlaws and the Lost Boys have each grown to between 120–180 members, and each member has to respond to provocations, it is difficult to know how different events are related. The number of disputes is too difficult to track, even for trained statisticians.

While in-group loyalties are common in gangs elsewhere, Sudanese refugee gangs are also defined by their relationship to other groups (e.g. territorial, ethnic, familial), each with their own codes. These relationships, which often evolve into strategic and opportunistic alliances, can influence and determine violent developments.

> *"One of the SPLM members got a phone call about the Lost Boys attacking one Nuer person in the Abassia area on Tuesday and information that 400 Nuers were gathering to retaliate. On Sunday morning we were surprised to see security forces at the Sakakini church gate, and when we asked what it was all about they told us that they had gotten a tip that the church was going to be attacked."*

The Nuers had evidently plotted retaliation against both the attack on one of their members and what they believed was a generalized campaign of discrimination against them by the Dinka-dominated church and SPLM. However, some of this was manipulated. The Outlaws were deliberately orchestrating attacks by the Dinka-dominated Lost Boys to make them appear as if they were part of a violent campaign against the Nuers in general, rather than just against the Outlaws. And since the Lost Boys hang out near the Sakakini church and that church is almost exclusively visited by Dinkas, the church was chosen as a symbol of Dinka oppression. The pastor of the Sakakini church was thus shocked when he witnessed four armored vehicles and truckloads of soldiers surrounding his church to protect it from imminent attack.

This is an example of how threats against an individual can be seen as a generalized threat against the group and thus challenges the social order. In this case, the Outlaws were right. The Lost Boys did indeed have Dinka support and benefitted from it. It was not before a meeting between Dinka leaders on the 4th of July, called in response to a murder committed by Lost Boys, that the Dinkas decided to stop supporting the gang. This meeting marked the end of the golden era of the Lost Boys and the beginning of Outlaw rule, and is evidence of the decisive nature of alliances in local warfare.

THE IMPRECISE ART OF TARGETING

The logic of violence can lead to escalation if conflicts are not managed adequately. The harming of innocents is an inevitable aspect of collective violence. Although Cairo gangs generally target either rival gang leaders or the people directly responsible for attacks, they rarely find their targets. A hitman knows how to hide; an innocent is exposed. And since retaliation requires an immediate response, innocent persons who happen to be nearby or share a social network with the intended targets are often harmed instead.

But this is not the only reason why innocents are harmed. Gang members in Cairo try not to clash with armed enemies, especially if those enemies are numerous. Instead a little brother or neighbor or unarmed friend is struck, involving each one of them and their immediate social circle in the cycle of violence.

How then can the violence among refugee youth be understood? We know that refugees experience accelerated social change and adaptation. Refugee gangs will engage in violence if the larger refugee community from which they come lacks shared norms and mechanisms for managing conflicts. Where, as in Egypt, the host society does not help in building common social norms that can govern refugee groups, disputes among refugees are also more likely to escalate.

Youth violence is made worse by several factors. Loyalty to perceived members of one's group can lead to conflicts multiplying and the persistence of violence associated with gangs. Moreover, the existence of external alliances can cause violence to escalate and change. In Cairo, violence has gone through different phases, depending on strategic and transitory alliances. When political parties and ethnic groups refuse to ally with gangs, violent acts, such as attacking a neighbor or cousin, are unlikely to unleash new waves of violence.

XIV. SUDANESE INTO ISRAEL

Nomadic Bedouin tribes have raised and traded livestock in the Sinai and Negev deserts for centuries. In recent decades, they have also served as runners on Israel's "sin alley," smuggling drugs and prostitutes across the border from Egypt into Israel. Now, for about US$400, Bedouins will smuggle Sudanese through checkpoints on the Sinai Peninsula and drop off their customers close to the Egyptian-Israeli border fence.

The hardship of life in Egypt has fueled many Sudanese refugees to smuggle themselves across the borders of Israel and ask for protection and immunity from extradition back to Egypt or, worse yet, back to Sudan. A Sudanese decree passed in 1993 authorizes detention of people who have been away for over twelve months, and authorizes "investigations" and "necessary security measures" as remedies. Under Sudanese law, a citizen who has been to Israel could be subject to charges of spying or treason upon return to Sudan. A death sentence could be the penalty.

The problem is that under Israeli Law, Sudanese citizens are considered "enemy nationals." According to the Enemy Infiltration Law, Israel cannot offer asylum to anyone from a country that does not recognize the Jewish state. Sudan is one of those countries. While Israel is a signatory to the 1951 Geneva Convention Protocol, which commits the country to accepting refugees whose life or freedom are threatened, refugees have been incarcerated by Israeli guards and have been denied the right to appeal against their detention.

Like Bob, who tells his story in this book, many of the first Sudanese refugees to come to Israel were sent back to Egypt. Israeli human rights groups were outraged. Israel's Interior Minister, Meir Sheetrit stated, "Israel, with its history, must offer assistance. It can't stand by and shut its eyes."

By 2005, Sudanese asylum-seekers were being held in detention but not returned to Egypt. News began to spread that some refugees were being offered temporary accommodations and work permits in kibbutz communities and tourist resorts. When word of these developments spread, hundreds more refugees attempted to sneak across the border.

In June of 2007 Prime Minister Ehud Olmert reportedly made informal agreements with Egyptian President Mubarak that Egypt would accept and return two thousand migrants that had tried to enter Israel from Egypt. Israel reasserted that because Sudanese refugees are from an "enemy state" they would not admit them into the country.

Israeli policy toward the refugees continued in an ad hoc fashion. Some refugees remained in various jails for lack of other facilities in which to house them. Others were taken in by various kibbutz communities and families. At the same time, Israeli officials indicated they would start pursuing a policy of "hot return," in which Israel's border guards would force asylum-seekers back into Egyptian territory.

A new wave of criticism came in August 2007 when forty-eight refugees were sent back to Egypt, five of whom were then reportedly deported to Sudan. In the same month, allegations arose that Egyptian border guards killed three migrants trying to cross the border. In September 2007, Israel promised to grant residency to five hundred Darfurian refugees.

It is uncertain what Israel's policy will be for the migrants in the future. Three reports from January 2008 illuminate the complexity of the situation. First, Israel began to issue residency permits to Darfurians, as promised months earlier. In that same week the Hotline for Migrant Workers, an Israeli NGO, filed a petition to the Israeli high court demanding that the state immediately close the "tent camp" at Ketziot prison, near Beersheba, where one thousand Sudanese asylum-seekers—over two hundred of them women and children—were being held in what the petition called "harsh conditions." At the same time, Ketziot prison states that it has resorted to turning away Sudanese who come to its gates asking to be detained and registered. Prison officials say their facility is filled to capacity. Refugees are being told to leave the prison grounds and continue walking.

XV. LIFE IN KAKUMA

The following is an edited excerpt from an interview with a twenty-year-old Southern Sudanese man living in Kakuma Refugee Camp, in Kenya. The interviewee wishes to remain anonymous. Here, he describes various aspects of day-to-day life in the refugee camp there. He has lived in Kakuma for over ten years.

NO BREAKFAST, NO PROBLEM

We made it to Kenya, and, well, it was a very nice place.

We arrived in 1994 in the town of Lokichoggio, in northwest Kenya. We had to stay there first for two weeks for a period of adjustment. UNHCR has a branch office there that is the transitional center, where people are brought into life as refugees. I showed them my traveling documents, showing how I left Sudan. They assign you to a zone in the camp, based on your needs. They interview you and give you letters that you then take to Kakuma, which is maybe one hundred kilometers away. I came to Kakuma camp on May 30, 1994.

I was really impressed by the kind of life people were leading in Kakuma. I saw young people going to school and that made me happy. We were encouraged to play sports. They gave us shirts and trousers for school uniforms. I was really happy, except I also kept thinking about how to get my parents to join me here.

I could write letters to them from my camp to their camp. They always said that life wasn't bad for them. I asked them to come to Kakuma and get their refugee status, but they said no. They asked me, "Could we get jobs in Kakuma?" I said no. So they said, "Why should we go and stay there?" They preferred still being in Sudan.

I arrived here in Kakuma thirteen years ago. I learned my English in Kakuma. I know Dinka; I know a bit of Arabic, but just the spoken version. English is what I learned best. I finished high school in 2005, at the age of twenty-five.

Since I arrived in Kakuma, there have been many good changes. Communication is better. We have phones and even email. I see people acquiring education, and the education is much better than we would have gotten if we had stayed in Sudan. You can see that people around here have gotten to know the importance of education, and that transforms their lives.

The physical camp has undergone some good development. When I first arrived, it was not as green as it is now. But you can see now that people have started planting trees. They ensure that they conserve soil so things can grow. Some people are even growing food in their yards.

The camp has grown so much. Initially, we had only Kakuma 1, with all its zones. Now we have Kakuma 2, Kakuma 3, and Kakuma 4, plus the reception area. The buildings have changed too. Initially people made their homes with thatch and mud, but they collapsed quickly from the extreme heat and wind. When it rains, they just fell. Now we have stronger iron sheeting on some houses. This is a good change.

The big markets started in, I don't know, 1998. Hong Kong Market is one of the oldest, and maybe it existed even before then. Initially it had no light, no electricity. Now you can go there and of course there's light from generators. There are even satellite televisions. You can go into the bars and find direct satellite television with many channels. The economy really has grown. At first, people had no knowledge of business, but they have come to learn how to make their work prosper. You can get microloans from the International Rescue Committee or from the Don Bosco church. People learn about business here, because they have to work within the limits of Kenyan standards. They have to keep prices the same and fair so they are within the rules. Some have even started businesses just teaching others how to run a business!

When you come to this place, you see an old fence. It is fenced for security purposes. Some armed men have come into the place and disrupted life. Sometimes they even shoot people, killing people. I haven't had trouble myself. I've met the Kenyans here, and I do have Kenyan friends. I speak Swahili, so I have good relations with the Kenyan people. But sometimes you hear people have been shot. The Kenyan people who have been in schools, who are in the working class—you find that they have a good relationship with the camp. But those from the interior, who don't know about the refugees, or about other ways of life, they think that the only thing is to fight. So they just interrupt people.

Some people may find that it is not really good living in the camp because they are so lonely, lacking family or their people. If they're lonely they get stressed, and that stress may lead to depression. We have counselors now who can try to help calm them. I can remember in 1994—people used to fight. Rumbling fights just within the camp. But now it is a rare case. Before, people were arriving here from different social, political, and economic backgrounds, and there was a mutual distrust. But we find that nowadays people have changed. People understand each others' lives, because they have been to school together and have shared common ground in school. And each and every person has an aim to do something. That's why you find that there's a change. A good change.

There are some gender violence issues as well. But nowadays there are some centers established—we have the Jesuit Refugee Service, and they want to prevent what we call sexual exploitation and abuse. These people ensure that whoever has a problem can come to the center to be counseled, rehabilitated, and to become better people.

In my life as a refugee, I have come to socialize with people of different cultures, understand them, and appreciate them. And then also I have come to know different political ideas. When I came to Kenya as a refugee, I could look back at my own country and criticize the things going on there, which are not good. For example, we should not detain people when they have not had a chance for justice. Here in Kenya, if you are detained, you have a chance to justify and defend yourself. But in Sudan, it is very hard to get that. You can only depend on yourself. When I learn new things and see that things are done differently in different places, I realize that I have to criticize my own country, and say, "This is not good, and this is why." Remember the military mind that many are still using in Sudan—it does not criticize. But now refugees have identified our rights. I don't want to be detained, and I don't want you to be detained. I want freedom and peace.

INTERVIEW CREDITS

ABUK BAK MACHAM
Interviews conducted by Craig Walzer and Rebecca Hansen
Edited by Craig Walzer and Rebecca Hansen

PANTHER ALIER
Interview conducted by Rebecca Hansen
Edited by Craig Walzer and Rebecca Hansen

Interviews conducted and edited by Craig Walzer:

MATHOK AGUEK	MUBTAGA MOHAMMED ALI MOHAMMED
MOTUZ SALAH AL-DEEN (AL-LIMBI)	GAZAFI ABDALLA
NADIA EL-KAREEM	MARCY NAREM
ROSE KOI	TARIG OMER
ALWEEL KOL	AHMED ISHAG (BOB)
BENJAMIN BOL MANYOK	MARGARET IBADYO BAGET YON
JOHN MAYIK	

Interviews conducted and edited by Dave Eggers and Valentino Achak Deng:

ACHOL MAYUOL	APOBO KALIFA

The editors wish to thank the following people and organizations for logistical support in Sudan, Kenya, and Egypt: Sudan Social Development Organization, Sudan Environmentalist Association, Valentino Achak Deng and his foundation, SCASO Association, Dr. Barbara Harrell-Bond, Peter Mabior Riinj, Martin Yai, and Shane Bauer.

Craig Walzer wishes to thank: His hostesses, Juschi (Aufkirchen) and Pauline (Paris), His host, etc. Chris Bloomfield, Rebecca Hansen, VII Photo Agency, Omar Fekeiki, William Brady, Lisa Basten, Dr. Barbara Harrell-Bond (again), Yaser and Akram, Mom, Dad, AJ, and Karen, and of course Franziska. Vielen Herzlichen Dank.

Most of all, thank you to every interviewee who participated in this project. Thank you for your energy, your bravery, your grace, and your kindness in telling your stories so others may know.

ABOUT THE EDITOR

CRAIG WALZER has traveled extensively in Sudan, Kenya, and Egypt. He is currently working toward graduate degrees from Harvard Law School and the Kennedy School of Government.

ABOUT THE CONTRIBUTING WRITERS

As a leader of the Sudanese diaspora, VALENTINO ACHAK DENG advocates for the universal right to education and the freedom of his people in Sudan. He is the founder of the Valentino Achak Deng Foundation, the recipient of all author proceeds from *What Is the What*. The Foundation's goal is to increase access to educational opportunities for those affected by the conflicts in Sudan. In early 2008, Deng returned to Marial Bai to construct an educational center comprising a twelve-classroom secondary school, a teacher-training college, a women's educational and vocational resource center, athletic facilities, and a public library. After graduating from college in the United States, Deng plans to continue the work of the Foundation by constructing similar centers throughout South Sudan and by aiding the educational pursuits of Sudanese students throughout the world.

EMMANUEL JAL was born in the village of Tonj, in South Sudan. At the age of about seven, he fled from war and walked, with thousands of others, to seek refuge in Ethiopia. From there, he was soon recruited by the Sudan People's Liberation Army and became a child soldier in the rebel forces for several years. After escaping the army and finding refuge with British aid workers, Emmanuel was resettled in Kenya, where he began his career as a hip-hop artist. His third album, *Warchild*, was released in May, 2008. On June 27, 2008, he performed at Nelson Mandela's ninetieth birthday concert in Hyde Park, London.

ABOUT VOICE OF WITNESS

Voice of Witness (VOW) is an award-winning nonprofit that advances human rights by amplifying the voices of people impacted by—and fighting against—injustice. VOW's work is driven by the transformative power of the story, and by a strong belief that an understanding of systemic injustice is incomplete without deep listening and learning from people with firsthand experience. Through two key programs—our oral history book series and education program—we amplify these voices, teach ethics-driven storytelling, and partner with advocates to:

- support and build agency within marginalized communities;
- raise awareness and foster thoughtful, empathy-based critical inquiry and understanding of injustices;
- and inform long-term efforts to protect and advance human rights.

THE VOICE OF WITNESS BOOK SERIES

The VOW Book Series depicts human rights issues through the edited oral histories of people—VOW narrators—who are most deeply impacted and at the heart of solutions to address injustice. The VOW Education Program connects over 20,000 educators, students, and advocates each year with these stories and issues through oral history–based curricula, trainings, and holistic educational support. Other titles include:

MI MARÍA
Surviving the Storm: Stories from Puerto Rico
Edited by Ricia Chansky and Marci Denesiuk
"Moving, unsettling, and eye-opening." —Yarimar Bonilla

HOW WE GO HOME
Voices of Indigenous North America
Edited by Sara Sinclair
"A chorus of love and belonging alongside the heat of resistance." —Leanne Betamosake Simpson

SOLITO, SOLITA
Crossing Borders with Youth Refugees from Central America
Edited by Steven Mayers and Jonathan Freedman
"Intense testimonies that leave one . . . astonished at the bravery of the human spirit." —Sandra Cisnero

SAY IT FORWARD
A Guide to Social Justice Storytelling
Edited by Cliff Mayotte and Claire Kiefer
"Reminds us the process through which we document a story is as important and powerful as the story itself." —Lauren Markham

SIX BY TEN
Stories from Solitary
Edited by Mateo Hoke and Taylor Pendergrass
"Deeply moving and profoundly unsettling." —Heather Ann Thompson

CHASING THE HARVEST
Migrant Workers in California Agriculture
Edited by Gabriel Thompson
"The voices are defiant and nuanced, aware of the human complexities that spill across bureaucratic categories and arbitrary borders." —*The Baffler*

LAVIL
Life, Love, and Death in Port-Au-Prince
Edited by Peter Orner and Evan Lyon
Foreword by Edwidge Danticat
"*Lavil* is a powerful collection of testimonies, which include tales of violence, poverty, and instability but also joy, hustle, and the indomitable will to survive."
—*Vice*

THE POWER OF THE STORY
The Voice of Witness Teacher's Guide to Oral History
Compiled and edited by Cliff Mayotte
Foreword by William Ayers and Richard Ayers
"A rich source of provocations to engage with human dramas throughout the world." —*Rethinking Schools Magazine*

THE VOICE OF WITNESS READER
Ten Years of Amplifying Unheard Voices
Edited and with an introduction by Dave Eggers

PALESTINE SPEAKS
Narratives of Life under Occupation
Compiled and edited by Cate Malek and Mateo Hoke
"Heartrending stories." —*New York Review of Books*

INVISIBLE HANDS
Voices from the Global Economy
Compiled and edited by Corinne Goria
Foreword by Kalpona Akter
"Powerful and revealing testimony." —*Kirkus*

HIGH RISE STORIES
Voices from Chicago Public Housing
Compiled and edited by Audrey Petty
Foreword by Alex Kotlowitz
"Gripping, and nuanced and unexpectedly moving." —Roxane Gay

REFUGEE HOTEL
Photographed by Gabriele Stabile and edited by Juliet Linderman
"There is no other book like *Refugee Hotel* on your shelf." —*SF Weekly*

THROWING STONES AT THE MOON
Narratives from Colombians Displaced by Violence
Compiled and edited by Sibylla Brodzinsky and Max Schoening
Foreword by Íngrid Betancourt
"Both sad and inspiring." —*Publishers Weekly*

INSIDE THIS PLACE, NOT OF IT
Narratives from Women's Prisons
Compiled and edited by Ayelet Waldman and Robin Levi
Foreword by Michelle Alexander
"Essential reading." —Piper Kerman

PATRIOT ACTS
Narratives of Post-9/11 Injustice
Compiled and edited by Alia Malek
Foreword by Karen Korematsu
"Important and timely." —Reza Aslan

OUT OF EXILE
Narratives from the Abducted and Displaced People of Sudan
Compiled and edited by Craig Walzer
Additional interviews and an introduction by Dave Eggers and Valentino Achak Deng
"Riveting." —*School Library Journal*

NOWHERE TO BE HOME
Narratives from Survivors of Burma's Military Regime
Compiled and edited by Maggie Lemere and Zoë West
Foreword by Mary Robinson
"Extraordinary." —Asia Society

UNDERGROUND AMERICA
Narratives of Undocumented Lives
Compiled and edited by Peter Orner
Foreword by Luis Alberto Urrea
"No less than revelatory." —*Publishers Weekly*

VOICES FROM THE STORM
The People of New Orleans on Hurricane Katrina and Its Aftermath
Compiled and edited by Chris Ying and Lola Vollen
"*Voices from the Storm* uses oral history to let those who survived the hurricane
tell their (sometimes surprising) stories." —*Independent* UK

SURVIVING JUSTICE
America's Wrongfully Convicted and Exonerated
Compiled and edited by Lola Vollen and Dave Eggers
Foreword by Scott Turow
"Real, raw, terrifying tales of 'justice.'" —*Star Tribune*

ABOUT HAYMARKET BOOKS

Haymarket Books is a radical, independent, nonprofit book publisher based in Chicago.

Our mission is to publish books that contribute to struggles for social and economic justice. We strive to make our books a vibrant and organic part of social movements and the education and development of a critical, engaged, international left.

We take inspiration and courage from our namesakes, the Haymarket martyrs, who gave their lives fighting for a better world. Their 1886 struggle for the eight-hour day—which gave us May Day, the international workers' holiday—reminds workers around the world that ordinary people can organize and struggle for their own liberation. These struggles continue today across the globe—struggles against oppression, exploitation, poverty, and war.

Since our founding in 2001, Haymarket Books has published more than five hundred titles. Radically independent, we seek to drive a wedge into the risk-averse world of corporate book publishing. Our authors include Noam Chomsky, Arundhati Roy, Rebecca Solnit, Angela Y. Davis, Howard Zinn, Amy Goodman, Wallace Shawn, Mike Davis, Winona LaDuke, Ilan Pappé, Richard Wolff, Dave Zirin, Keeanga-Yamahtta Taylor, Nick Turse, Dahr Jamail, David Barsamian, Elizabeth Laird, Amira Hass, Mark Steel, Avi Lewis, Naomi Klein, and Neil Davidson. We are also the trade publishers of the acclaimed Historical Materialism Book Series, of Dispatch Books, and of the Voice of Witness Book Series.